EUROPEAN

SPACE AGENCY AND PROGRAMS HANDBOOK

STRATEGIC INFORMATION AND CONTACTS

International Business Publications, USA
Washington DC, USA - Belgium

EUROPEAN
SPACE AGENCY AND PROGRAMS HANDBOOK:
STRATEGIC INFORMATION AND CONTACTS

UPDATED ANNUALLY

Cover Design: **International Business Publications, USA**

We express our sincere appreciation to all government agencies and international organizations which provided information and other materials for this handbook

THIS HANDBOOK IS BASED ON OFFICIAL MATERIALS OF THE EUROPEAN UNION AND THE EUROPEAN SPACE AGENCY

2016 Updated Reprint International Business Publications, USA
ISBN 1-4387-1665-6

This handbook provides basic information for starting or/and conducting business in the country. The extraordinary volume of materials covering the topic, prevents us from placing all these materials in this handbook. For more detailed information on issues related to any specific investment and business activity in the country, please contact Global Investment Center, USA
Please acquire the list of our business intelligence and marketing reports and other business publications. We constantly update and expand our business intelligence and marketing materials. Please contact the center for the updated list of reports on over 250 countries.

in the USA: **Global Investment Center, USA.**
P.O.Box 15343, Washington, DC 20003
Phone: (202) 546-2103, Fax: (202) 546-3275, E-mail: rusric@erols.com

For additional analytical, marketing and other information please contact
Global Investment Center, USA

Printed in the USA

EUROPEAN
SPACE AGENCY AND PROGRAMS HANDBOOK
STRATEGIC INFORMATION AND CONTACTS

TABLE OF CONTENTS

EUROPEAN SPACE POLICY - IMPORTANT DEVELOPMENTS 9

COMPONENTS OF THE POLICY 9
Satellites *9*
Launch systems *9*
ISS *10*
Science and technology *10*
EUROPEAN INTEGRATION IN SPACE 10
Funding *11*
Roles and Responsibilities *11*
EUROPEAN STRATEGY FOR SPACE 13
Three lines of action *13*
Three co-ordinated activities *13*
Access to space *13*
Space flights and exploration *14*
New markets *15*
Three main areas *15*
Two initiatives *15*
A new operational relationship *16*

EUROPEAN SPACE AGENCY: STRATEGIC INFORMATION 17

IMPORTANT FACTS AND DEVELOPMENTS 17
The European Space Research Organisation (ESRO *18*
The European Preparatory Commission for Space Research *19*
Space race *20*
MISSION STATEMENT 20
BASIC RULES AND REGULATIONS 21
ESA Procurement Regulations and related Implementing Instructions *21*
General Clauses and Conditions for ESA Contracts *21*
Security Regulations *21*
Rules on Information, Data and Intellectual Property *21*
ESA Financial Regulations *22*
Additional Rules on Arbitration *22*
ESA Staff Regulations *22*
MEMBER COUNTRIES AND BUDGET 23
Membership and contribution to ESA *23*
Associate members *25*
Budget appropriation and allocation *25*
Enlargement *26*
Associate Members *27*

Enlargement ... 27
Budget appropriation and allocation ... 28
LAUNCH VEHICLE FLEET ... 29
Ariane 5 ... 29
Soyuz ... 30
Vega ... 30
HUMAN SPACE FLIGHT ... 30
Astronaut Corps ... 31
Manned launch vehicles ... 31
COOPERATION WITH OTHER COUNTRIES AND ORGANISATIONS ... 32
European Union ... 32
National space organisations of member countries ... 33
NASA ... 33
Cooperation with other space agencies ... 33
International Space Station ... 34
Languages ... 34
Facilities ... 34

EUROPEAN SPACE AGENCY: BASIC INFORMATION ... 35

PARTICIPATING STATES ... 35
Membership ... 35
Associate members ... 36
Enlargement ... 37
Completed enlargements ... 37
Current progress ... 38
Possible future cooperation ... 39
ESA FACTS AND FIGURES ... 39
ESA's address ... 39
BASIC INFORMATION ... 39
SA headquarters ... 40
The ESA Council ... 41
International cooperation ... 41
Planning for the future ... 42
Communications ... 42
Administration ... 42
Launchers ... 43
THE EUROPEAN ASTRONAUT CORPS ... 43
Charta of the European Astronaut Corps ... 44
Charta of the European Astronaut Corps ... 44
European astronauts in space ... 45
European astronauts in new functions ... 48
Training programme ... 50
Training development ... 51
Training facilities ... 53
RELATED ORGANIZATIONS ... 54
European Space Research and Technology Centre (ESTEC) ... 54
EUROPEAN SPACE OPERATION CENTER ... 55
ESRIN - the ESA Centre for Earth Observation ... 56
European Astronaut Centre ... 57
Ground stations ... 58
ESOC: Focal point for ESA space debris activities ... 61
EUROPEAN ASTRONAUT CORPS ... 63
Current members ... 63

Selection of new astronauts ... *64*
After the ISS ... *64*
Non ESA European Astronauts ... *64*
Shuttle missions ... *65*
Missions on space stations ... *65*
Missions ... *66*
The European Space Research Organisation (ESRO) ... *66*
The founding of ESRO ... *67*
The European Preparatory Commission for Space Research ... *67*
The Blue Book ... *67*
Organisation and functioning ... *68*
European Space Research and Technology Centre ... *69*
ESLAB ... *69*
ESRANGE ... *70*
ESTRACK and ESDAC ... *70*
ESLAR ... *70*
ESRO headquarters ... *70*
Scientific activities ... *71*
Sounding rockets ... *71*
Original satellite programme ... *71*
LAS ... *72*
Second generation satellites ... *72*
The first package deal ... *72*
The second package deal ... *73*
Telecommunications Satellite Programme ... *73*

EUROPEAN SPACE AGENCY PROGRAMS ... **74**

AURORA EXPLORATION PROGRAM ... 74
Aurora's origins ... *74*
Exploring space ... *74*
Advanced technology ... *74*
International cooperation ... *75*
Step-by-step approach ... *75*
Exploration Programme Advisory Committee ... *75*
Aurora Board of Participants ... *75*
Industry ... *75*
THE GALILEO PROGRAMME ... 75
The transition with European Geostationary Navigation Overlay Service (EGNOS) ... *77*
INTERNATIONAL SPACE STATION ... 78
COLUMBUS: EUROPEAN LABORATORY ... 80
AUTOMATED TRANSFER VEHICLE (ATV) ... 83
ERA: EUROPEAN ROBOTIC ARM ... 86
DMS-R: ESA'S DATA MANAGEMENT SYSTEM FOR THE RUSSIAN SEGMENT OF THE ISS ... 88
NODE 2: CONNECTING MODULE ... 89
NODE 3: CONNECTING MODULE ... 91
CUPOLA ... 94
TELEMEDICINE ALLIANCE ... 97

DOING BUSINESS WITH ESA ... **98**

FREQUENTLY ASKED QUESTIONS ... 98
The weightlessness environment: what are the advantages? ... *100*
THE COOPERATION AGREEMENT PARTNERS ... 101
ESA COMMERCIAL PROMOTION OFFICE ... 102

Technology demonstration ... 104
Sponsorship ... 104
Broadcasting ... 104
The full experience ... 104
Education and educational sponsorship ... 105
Commercial infrastructures and services ... 105
COMMERCIAL AGENT NETWORK ... 105
ESA'S ISS FACILITIES, RESOURCES AND SERVICES ... 105
Facilities ... 106
Payload ... 106
Crew time ... 106
Payload qualification and safety ... 107
Data services ... 107
ISS BUSINESS GLOSSARY ... 107
SELECTED SPACE RESEARCH PROGRAMS ... 111
Galileo - The European programme for Global Navigation Services ... 119
IMPORTANT OFFICIAL MATERIALS ... 121
FRAMEWORK AGREEMENT BETWEEN THE EUROPEAN COMMUNITY AND THE EUROPEAN SPACE AGENCY THE EUROPEAN COMMUNITY, AND THE EUROPEAN SPACE AGENCY ... 121
ARTICLE 1 Purpose of the Cooperation ... 121
ARTICLE 2 Principles of Cooperation ... 122
ARTICLE 3 Fields of Cooperation ... 122
ARTICLE 4 Implementation ... 123
ARTICLE 5 Joint initiatives ... 123
ARTICLE 6 Consultation and information ... 124
ARTICLE 7 External dimension of the cooperation ... 124
ARTICLE 8 Coordination and facilitation of cooperative activities ... 124
ARTICLE 9 Exchange of personnel ... 125
ARTICLE 10 Public relations ... 125
ARTICLE 11 Settlement of disputes ... 125
ARTICLE 12 Entry into force, duration, amendments and termination ... 126
ARTICLE 13 Signature and authenticity ... 126
EURPEAN SPACE POLICY ... 126
The international dimension ... 126
THE AMBITIONS OF EUROPE IN SPACE ... 129
CONVENTION FOR THE ESTABLISHMENT OF A EUROPEAN SPACE AGENCY ... 132
INTRODUCTORY NOTE ... 132
Article I ESTABLISHMENT OF THE AGENCY ... 133
Article II PURPOSE ... 133
Article III INFORMATION AND DATA ... 133
Article IV EXCHANGE OF PERSONS ... 134
Article V ACTIVITIES AND PROGRAMMES ... 134
Article VI FACILITIES AND SERVICES ... 135
Article VII INDUSTRIAL POLICY ... 135
Article VIII LAUNCHERS AND OTHER SPACE TRANSPORT SYSTEMS ... 135
Article IX USE OF FACILITIES, ASSISTANCE TO MEMBER STATES, AND SUPPLY OF PRODUCTS ... 136
Article X ORGANS ... 136
Article XI THE COUNCIL ... 136
Article XII DIRECTOR GENERAL AND STAFF ... 139
Article XIII FINANCIAL CONTRIBUTIONS ... 139

Article XIV COOPERATION ... 140
Article XV LEGAL STATUS, PRIVILEGES AND IMMUNITIES ... 141
Article XVI AMENDMENTS ... 141
Article XVII DISPUTES ... 141
Article XVIII NON-FULFILMENT OF OBLIGATIONS ... 142
Article XIX CONTINUITY OF RIGHTS AND OBLIGATIONS ... 142
Article XX SIGNATURE AND RATIFICATION ... 142
Article XXI ENTRY INTO FORCE ... 142
Article XXII ACCESSION ... 143
Article XXIII NOTIFICATIONS ... 143
Article XXIV DENUNCIATION ... 143
Article XXV DISSOLUTION ... 144
Article XXVI REGISTRATION ... 144
EUROPEAN SPACE POLICY: "ESDP AND SPACE" ... 144
THE ADDED VALUE OF SPACE FOR CFSP/ESDP ... 145
IMPROVING EU CAPABILITIES ... 147
A GLOBAL EU SPACE POLICY ... 148
CONCLUSION AND WAY AHEAD ... 150
THE INTERNATIONAL SPACE STATION AND THE SPACE SHUTTLE ... 151
Most Recent Developments ... 152
The International Space Station (ISS) ... 152
ISS Design, Cost, Schedule, and Lifetime ... 153
The Space Shuttle ... 156
Issues for Congress ... 157
THE EUROPEAN SPACE POLICY ... 158
I A vision for Europe in space ... 159
II Current Priorities ... 160
New priorities within the European Space Policy ... 163
EUROPEAN SPACE PROGRAM - PRELIMINARY ELEMENTS ... 166
1. INTRODUCTION: RATIONALE OF THE EUROPEAN SPACE PROGRAMME ... 166
2. DRAFT PROGRAMMATIC OBJECTIVES ... 167
EUROPEAN PARLIAMENT RESOLUTION OF 10 JULY 2008 ON SPACE AND SECURITY ... 174
4TH SPACE COUNCIL RESOLUTION ON THE EUROPEAN SPACE POLICY ... 180
I Vision for Europe and General Strategy ... 181
II Further Steps – Programmes and Implementation ... 183
"SPACE COUNCIL" ORIENTATIONS/ COUNCIL RESOLUTION ... 187
EUROPEAN SPACE POLICY PROGRESS ... 191
1. INTRODUCTION ... 191
2. SPACE APPLICATIONS ... 191
3. SPACE FOUNDATIONS ... 195
4. A COMPETITIVE EUROPEAN SPACE INDUSTRY ... 197
5. GOVERNANCE ... 198
6. EMERGING ISSUES ... 200
Elements for a European Strategy for International Relations in Space ... 200
REPORT OF THE PANEL OF EXPERTS ON SPACE AND SECURITY ... 204
1. The SPASEC Panel of Experts ... 205
2. The New Security Environment ... 206
3. Sources of threat ... 207
4. Diverse communities, common objectives ... 208
5. Trends and tactics ... 213
6. User needs ... 216
7. Cross Cutting issues ... 223
8. Capabilities and capability gaps ... 225
9. Programme options ... 233

10. Financial planning ... *237*
11. Conclusions and recommendations ... *237*
Appendix A: SPACE SYSTEM NEEDS AND SCENARIOS MATRIX ... *241*
Appendix B: SCOPE OF TECHNOLOGY, INTEROPERABILITY AND OPERATIONAL SYSTEMS TASKS ... *246*
Appendix C: COSTS ESTIMATES OF EUROPEAN SPACE SYSTEM FOR ESDP ... *248*

IMPORTANT PROGRAMS AND PROJECTS ... **253**

AEROFAST ... 253
Space Research and Development ... *254*
GEOLAND ... 256
MYOCEAN ... 258
SPACE WEATHER FORECAST ... 261
POWER AMPLIFICATION IN A SPACECRAFT ... 263
COSMOS ... 265
MACC ... 268
SAFER ... 269
STAVE ... 271
ULISSE ... 273

SUPPLEMENTS ... **275**

SPACE AGENCIES ... 275
Space agencies with launch capability ... *275*
Space agencies with manned spaceflight capability ... *276*
achievements of space agencies with lunar landing capability ... *276*
Expected future space agencies ... *276*
BUDGETS ... 277
Budgets of different space agencies. ... *277*
BUDGETS BY COUNTRY ... *278*
FUNDED RESEARCH PROJECTS - SPACE ... 278
2013 - Projects under negotiation ... *278*
2012 ... *279*
2011 ... *279*
2010 ... *279*
2009 ... *280*
BASIC TITLES ON EUROPEAN UNION (EU) ... 281

EUROPEAN SPACE POLICY - IMPORTANT DEVELOPMENTS

A formal **European Space Policy** was established on 22 May 2007 when a joint and concomitant meeting at ministerial level of the Council of the European Union and the Council of the European Space Agency adopted a *Resolution on the European Space Policy*. The policy had been jointly drafted by the European Commission and the Director General of the European Space Agency.

Currently each member state pursues their own national space policy, though often co-ordinating through the independent European Space Agency (ESA). Enterprise and Industry Commissioner Günter Verheugen has stated that even though the EU is "a world leader in the technology, it is being put on the defensive by the US and Russia and that it only has about a 10 year technological advantage on China and India, which are racing to catch up."

A communication outlining the policy was released on 26 April 2007 which set out orientations for

- Coordinating more effective civil space programmes between ESA, EU and their respective Member States to ensure value for money and eliminate unnecessary duplication, thus meeting shared European needs.
- Developing and exploiting European space applications such as GALILEO and GMES (Global Monitoring for the Environment and Security) and satellite communication applications.
- Preserving EU autonomous access to space.
- Increasing synergy between defence and civil space programmes and technologies and pursue, in particular, interoperability of civil/military systems.
- Ensuring that space policy is coherent with, and supports the EU's external relationships.

COMPONENTS OF THE POLICY

SATELLITES

The policy expresses support for an operational and autonomous Global Monitoring for Environment and Security (GMES) satellite capability before the end of 2008, and for a global navigation satellite system under European civil control, i.e. the Galileo positioning system.

GALILEO

The European Union has already started work on a project to create the **Galileo positioning system**, to break dependence on the United States GPS system. This is in cooperation with ESA as well as other countries.

COPERNICUS PROGRAMME

Copernicus is a European system for monitoring the Earth and consists of earth observation satellites and in situ sensors. The program provides services in the thematic areas land, marine, atmosphere, climate change, emergency management and security.

LAUNCH SYSTEMS

The policy emphasises the importance for Europe to maintain independent, reliable and cost-effective access to space through European launch systems, without mentioning any specifically by name. The policy statement affirms support for the "EC-ESA Framework Agreement" and the resolution on the evolution of the European launcher sector adopted in 2005.

ISS

The policy reaffirms a continuing European commitment to the International Space Station (ISS), and describes ESA participation in future international exploration programmes as being important.

SCIENCE AND TECHNOLOGY

The policy includes the goal of maintaining programmes that give Europe a leading role in selected areas of science. It also calls for development of technologies that allow European industry to avoid dependency on international suppliers

EUROPEAN INTEGRATION IN SPACE

On 22 May 2007, the member states of the European Union have agreed to create a common political framework for space activities in Europe by unifying the approach of the **European Space Agency** (ESA) with those of the individual European Union member states

However, ESA is an intergovernmental organisation with no formal organic link to the EU, indeed the two institutions have different Member States and are governed by different rules and procedures. ESA was created in 1975 by merging ELDO with ESRO. The 10 founding members were Belgium, Denmark, France, Germany, Italy, The Netherlands, Spain, Sweden, Switzerland and the United Kingdom. The Republic of Ireland joined on 31 December 1975. In 1987, Austria and Norway became member states. Finland joined in 1995, Portugal in 2000, Greece and Luxembourg in 2005, and the Czech Republic in 2008. Thus, currently, it has 18 member states: all the EU member states before 2004, plus Czech Republic, Norway and Switzerland. Further, Canada has had the special status of a Cooperating State under a cooperation agreement since 1979.

ESA is likely to expand in the coming years with the countries which joined the EU in both 2004 and 2007. Thus, Estonia, Hungary, Poland and Romania have already signed a European Cooperating State (ECS) Agreement; Cyprus, Latvia, Slovakia and Slovenia have signed Cooperation Agreements with ESA; and finally, Lithuania and Malta have also announced its aim to join ESA.

Space activities are strategic for their contribution to the construction of Europe. Space is a tool to serve the interests of the Union, its Member States and its citizens: strategic influence, scientific progress, economic growth in the knowledge economy and security.

The EU is increasingly a global actor. After enlargements, the EU's strategic influence has increased. This requires reflection, adaptation and creation of the necessary instruments, including space policy.

Space is a strategic industrial sector for growth and employment, and thus part of the Growth and Employment strategy. Space applications underpin economic activity and crucial government services, taking their significance beyond the research environment. Their effectiveness depends on integration with terrestrial systems, to exploit the comparative advantage of each. Their benefits are spread across Europe. New applications markets will be driven by innovation, in particular through SMEs.

Space-based science and applications play an important role in strengthening the competitiveness of the knowledge-based society in Europe. Major successful space research missions under European leadership have placed ESA and its Member States, the European science community and both manufacturing and services industries at the forefront. Scientific and industrial space research is a strong driving force for new technology developments with many subsequent applications of benefit to society and the environment. Space is an asset of European integration, not only through its technical capacities but also through the global adventure and challenge it represents for Europe.

European security policy is developing rapidly. Space based situation awareness and reaction capability will play a substantial role in this policy. The differentiation between defence infrastructure and internal security infrastructure and systems is becoming blurred and common use needs to be clarified. The Council of the EU has recognised that space assets could contribute both to making the EU more capable in the field of crisis management and to fighting other security threats. It has therefore approved the idea that identified and agreed upon ESDP requirements should be reflected in the global EU space policy and European space programme.

Today, European companies are key actors in the world-wide commercial market of satellite manufacturing, launch services and satellite operators; Europe has a sound technology base; and scientific excellence has been established. All this has been achieved with public expenditure in space representing six times less than that of the US. The European space sector needs to maintain excellence at an affordable cost.

Member States expressed their wish to see an increased EU dimension in space policy at the first 'Space Council' in November 2004. They recognised the possibilities for space activities to contribute to European policy objectives in a number of areas, while the implementation should draw on the existing European capabilities, notably the European and National Space Agencies.

FUNDING

Bringing about the full potential of scientific, technological, industrial as well as economic and strategic benefits of space will require sustained funding commitments. In addition to existing ESA and national funding lines, EU funding will prove crucial. Given the relatively limited volume of public funding available for space-related activities when compare to e.g. the US, it is essential to make the most efficient use possible of resources and achieve value for money.

The EU must take into account that a large part of the infrastructure which Europe comes to rely on is owned by its Member States and not necessarily shared on an EU-level, particularly in defence-related systems, that there are gaps which will not be met by current plans and that, even for existing and planned satellites, data interfaces are not always harmonised. Galileo and Global Monitoring for Environment and Security (GMES) are the currently most advanced applications projects. Space is increasingly a key element for key EU policies, including transport, agriculture, environment, security and information society, integrated with terrestrial components in monitoring and communications networks and services.

ROLES AND RESPONSIBILITIES

Role of the EU:

- define the priorities and requirements for space based systems at the service of the EU's main objectives and policies and citizens' needs;

- aggregate the political will and user demand in support of these;
- ensure the availability and continuity of services supporting EU policies by funding relevant up-stream research activities; purchasing services or securing the deployment and operational phases of space systems, as appropriate; and in due course stimulating user funding;
- ensure integration of space-based systems with related ground and in-situ systems in promoting the development of user-driven application services supporting EU policies;
- create an optimum regulatory environment to facilitate innovation;
- promote coordination of the European position in international cooperation. EU space activities will be implemented through existing European capabilities, notably through the European, National Space Agencies, industry, etc. The EU also stimulates the development of innovative services to exploit space systems which bring benefits across Europe, to industry and citizens.

Role of ESA:

- support the technical specification of the space segment of space application programmes, taking particular account of EU requirements;
- develop and implement space technologies, in particular in access to space, science and exploration;
- pursue excellence in scientific research in, of and from space;
- advise the EU on space segment requirements to support availability and continuity of services;
- implement international cooperation within the ambit of ESA-led programmes.

Member States:

The Member States will identify in the European Space Policy the rationale for programmes conducted nationally, taking into account the principle of subsidiarity, and propose the part these should play in the overall European Space Programme, where they contribute to its objectives. Most Member States of the EU and of ESA are already investing in operational meteorological, climate and environmental monitoring satellites through their membership of EUMETSAT and could consider with other EUMETSAT members their role in relation to operational GMES services.

In addition, the European Space Programme will take account of private sector stakeholders. Programme management will maximise the development of products and services to be supplied by the private sector to governmental and commercial customers. In particular, risksharing public private partnerships will be explored wherever possible. All stakeholders will be consulted during the setting up and periodic review of the programme.

EUROPEAN STRATEGY FOR SPACE

The joint European Commission (EC) and European Space Agency (ESA) Communication Europe and space: turning to a new chapter, issued on 27 September 2000, has been a major step in establishing a coherent approach - including the political dimension - for space in Europe.

The aim is to mobilise Member States and private actors to invest in research and development of European space capabilities and associated services.

THREE LINES OF ACTION

The European approach is built around three pillars:

- **Strengthening the foundation for space activities** . This allows Europe to preserve an independent and affordable access to space (launchers) and ensures a broad technology base with the industrial capability for designing, manufacturing, and operating satellite systems and the associated ground infrastructure.

Strengthening the foundation of space activities: Space technology

Europe has to maintain a broad technological base in order to develop new space-based services and preserve the competitiveness of its space industry. But a strong and innovative approach must be adopted in order to compensate for the investment gap between the European space sector and its competitors in space systems and terrestrial solutions (1).

This can only be achieved through a fruitful dialogue between technology providers, users and operators, for instance those involved in the information society.

Furthermore, all efforts to coordinate research and technology development programmes at European Space Agency, EU and national level should be encouraged.

THREE CO-ORDINATED ACTIVITIES

The plan is to continue the technology development process through three different but co-ordinated activities:

- development of basic technologies, to be pursued essentially with public support;
- early demonstration of developed technologies through pilot projects and validation activities, in which the public sector and commercial operators jointly participate;
- development of applications and services, to be driven by market considerations and user demand.

(1) In particular, the contract volume from the US Department of Defense in space research is three times higher than the total public spending in Europe, and the total US public spending is more than five times higher.

ACCESS TO SPACE

Europe has to secure independent access to space in order to undertake its projects and develop its space-based services. Therefore public support is needed for the development of innovative technologies, new vehicles and stages, and associated ground infrastructure.

- European launchers must maintain a competitive position in the world market for launch services, which is constantly and rapidly evolving.
- Inextricably linked with this is the need to maintain the European spaceport in Kourou at an appropriately high standard.

However, access to space must also remain affordable.

The condition of affordability for Europe requires the search for complementary private investment whenever a return on investment can be expected within a reasonable time frame. **Enhancing scientific knowledge** for a better understanding of our planet and its atmosphere, the solar system and the Universe.
Enhancing scientific knowledge

Space systems provide a unique means to explore the solar system and the Universe, provide a constant flow of readily comparable global data for the understanding of our planet and its atmosphere, and give us access to microgravity.

It is therefore important for Europe to pursue cutting-edge themes of space science, and space-based contributions to the understanding of the climate and our planet, such as:

- the behaviour of our Sun and its influence on Earth;
- the origins of the solar system and the evolution of its planets, including our own;
- the origin and evolution of stars, planetary systems and Earth-like planets - including the possibility of discovering life on them;
- the structure, evolution and destiny of the Universe, and the fundamental laws that govern it;
- the investigation of the phenomena of global change and all major Earth-science themes, such as the Earth's interior, its physical climate, its geosphere/biosphere, the atmosphere and the marine environment and their impact on mankind.

SPACE FLIGHTS AND EXPLORATION

Europe has acquired competence in all areas of space technology, including human space flight.

It is a full partner in the International Space Station (ISS), as a sensible alternative to developing its own complete space and ground infrastructure for human space flight.

The European Union should now concentrate on optimising use of the ISS as a European research infrastructure for all space science disciplines, especially in life and physical sciences, applied research, technology development and validation.

The ISS should also become a powerful educational tool and a test bed for the 'next step' in human space exploration: the exploration of the solar system.

Visit ESA's Web Site on space flights and the ISS (http://www.spaceflight.esa.int/index.cfm)

- **Exploiting the benefits of space-based** tools for markets and society through a demand-driven exploitation of their capabilities, notably for telecommunication, navigation or environmental purposes

Markets and Society: Space is coming down to earth

The exploitation of up-to-date space technologies in order to seize market opportunities and meet the new demands of our society is key to European Union strategy.

- Parts of our society have become critically dependent on the use of satellites and space-based technologies, particularly with the advent of a 'knowledge based economy'.

- Space tools are also a major asset for the policy-maker when defining, implementing and monitoring EU policies in areas such as agriculture, environment, transport, telecommunication, security and defence, etc.

NEW MARKETS

New markets are emerging for satellites, downstream services and user equipment. They are expected to rely on an optimal combination of space-based systems and conventional terrestrial infrastructure and also on the integration of future space-based information and communication systems and services.

This will open up new opportunities to generate revenue from satellites and launch services.

THREE MAIN AREAS

- Communications satellite systems. Relaying, broadcasting and generating signals from space is the main commercial activity in space.
  While national borders may block terrestrial communication links, satellite systems provide a means of transferring information across frontiers.
  They can therefore deliver pan-European and even global information services; this makes it possible to co-operate effectively for the development of societies in and outside Europe.

- Navigation and positioning satellite systems provide highly accurate and reliable time signals, which will become a global reference for synchronising networks for telecommunications, energy, transport, financial transactions etc.

- Observation satellite systems use optical, infrared and radar sensors to deliver a continuous flow of near-real-time data on any part of the planet.

- This is of vital importance for meteorology and global change studies, treaty verification, identifying environmental problems at regional and global levels, agricultural monitoring, resource management and urban planning, for early warning of crises and for arms control.

TWO INITIATIVES

The user-oriented and policy-driven approach to space is set out clearly in two EU initiatives:

- development of a civil **satellite navigation and positioning system** (Galileo); and

- building up coherent capacity in Europe for **global monitoring for environment and security** (GMES).

Research will also focus on the integration of the space segment (satellites) and terrestrial networks in the telecommunication sector.

A NEW OPERATIONAL RELATIONSHIP

Following the go-ahead given by EU Research ministers on 16 November 2000, the EC and the ESA executive entered into a new operational relationship, making the most of their respective competencies.

A Joint Task Force was set up to facilitate this working relationship, and to develop the space strategy for monitoring its implementation, as well as issuing joint annual reports on space. It is also involved in drawing up proposals for framework arrangements to manage joint projects such as Galileo, GMES or advanced telecommunication services.

The role of the European Commisssion

- To establish the right political and regulatory conditions for space activities.
- To catalyse joint R&D efforts in line with the objectives of a European Research Area.
- To bring together all actors around common political objectives in projects of Europe-wide interest.

EUROPEAN SPACE AGENCY: STRATEGIC INFORMATION

IMPORTANT FACTS AND DEVELOPMENTS

Acronym	ESA
Owner	20 European states
Established	1975
Headquarters	Paris, France
Primary spaceport	Guiana Space Centre
Administrator	Jean-Jacques Dordain
Budget	▲€3.339.3 billion
Official language(s)	English, French, and German
Website	www.esa.int

The **European Space Agency** (**ESA**) (French: **Agence spatiale européenne** - **ASE**; German: **Europäische Weltraumorganisation**) is an intergovernmental organisation dedicated to the exploration of space, with 20 member states. Established in 1975 and headquartered in Paris, France, ESA has a staff of more than 2,000 with an annual budget of about €4.28 billion / US$5.51 billion (2013).

ESA's space flight programme includes human spaceflight, mainly through the participation in the International Space Station programme, the launch and operations of unmanned exploration missions to other planets and the Moon, Earth observation, science, telecommunication as well as maintaining a major spaceport, the Guiana Space Centre at Kourou, French Guiana, and designing launch vehicles. The main European launch vehicle Ariane 5 is operated through Arianespace with ESA sharing in the costs of launching and further developing this launch vehicle.

ESA science missions are based at ESTEC in Noordwijk, Netherlands, Earth Observation missions at ESRIN in Frascati, Italy, ESA Mission Control (ESOC) is in Darmstadt, Germany, the European Astronaut Centre (EAC) that trains astronauts for future missions is situated in Cologne, Germany, and the European Space Astronomy Centre is located in Villanueva de la Cañada, Spain.

The **European Space Agency** (**ESA**), established in 1975, is an intergovernmental organisation dedicated to the exploration of space, currently with 18 member states. Headquartered in Paris, ESA has a staff of more than 2,000 with an annual budget of about €3.6 billion in 2009.

ESA's space flight program includes human spaceflight, mainly through the participation in the International Space Station program, the launch and operations of unmanned exploration missions to other planets and the Moon, Earth observations, science, telecommunication as well as maintaining a major spaceport, the Guiana Space Centre at Kourou, French Guiana and designing launch vehicles. The main European launch vehicle Ariane 5 is operated through Arianespace with ESA sharing in the costs of launching and further developing this launch vehicle.

ESA science missions are based at ESTEC in Noordwijk, Netherlands, Earth Observation missions at ESRIN in Frascati, Italy, ESA Mission Control (ESOC) is in Darmstadt, Germany, the European Astronaut Centre (EAC) that trains astronauts for future missions is situated in Cologne, Germany and the European Space Astronomy Centre is located in Villanueva de la Cañada, Spain

The European Union (EU) and ESA share a common aim: to strengthen Europe and benefit its citizens. While they are separate organisations, they are increasingly working together towards common objectives. Some 20 per cent of the funds managed by ESA now originate from the EU budget.

ESA is an intergovernmental organisation, whereas the EU is supranational. The two institutions have indeed different ranges of competences, different Member States and are governed by different rules and procedures.

However, in recent years the ties between the two institutions have been reinforced by the increasing role that space plays in supporting Europe's social, political and economic policies.

The legal basis for the EU/ESA cooperation is provided by a Framework Agreement which entered into force in May 2004. Under this agreement the European Commission and ESA coordinate their actions through the Joint Secretariat, a small team of EC's administrators and ESA executive. The Member States of the two organisations meet at ministerial level in the Space Council, which is a concomitant meeting of the EU and ESA Councils, prepared by Member States representatives in the High-level Space Policy Group (HSPG).

ESA maintains a liaison office in Brussels to facilitate relations with the European institutions.

European dimension

Guaranteeing European access to space

In May 2007, the 29 European countries expressed their support for the European Space Policy in a resolution of the Space Council, unifying the approach of ESA with those of the European Union and their member states.

Prepared jointly by the European Commission and ESA's Director General, the European Space Policy sets out a basic vision and strategy for the space sector and addresses issues such as security and defence, access to space and exploration.

Through this resolution, the EU, ESA and their Member States all commit to increasing coordination of their activities and programmes and their respective roles relating to space.

THE EUROPEAN SPACE RESEARCH ORGANISATION (ESRO

The **European Space Research Organisation** (**ESRO**) was an international organisation founded by 10 European nations with the intention of jointly pursuing scientific research in space. It was founded in 1964. As an organisation ESRO was based on a previously existing international scientific institution, CERN. The ESRO convention, the organisations founding document outlines it as an entity exclusively devoted to scientific pursuits. This was the case for most of its lifetime but in the final years before the formation of the European Space Agency (ESA), ESRO began a programme in the field of telecommunications. Consequently, ESA is not a mainly pure science focused entity but concentrates on telecommunications, earth observation and other application motivated activities. ESRO was merged with ELDO in 1975 to form the European Space Agency

After World War II, many European scientists left Western Europe in order to work either in the United States or the Soviet Union. Although the 1950s boom made it possible for Western European countries to invest in research and specifically in space related activities, Western European scientists realised solely national projects would not be able to compete with the two main superpowers. In 1958, only months after the Sputnik shock, Edoardo Amaldi and Pierre Auger, two prominent members of the western European scientific community at that time, met to discuss the foundation of a common western European space agency. The meeting was attended by scientific representatives from eight countries, including Harrie Massey (UK).

The origins of a joint European space effort are generally traced back to a number of initiatives taken in 1959 and 1960 by a small group of scientists and science administrators, catalysed by two friends, physicists and scientific statesmen, the Italian Edoardo Amaldi and the Frenchman Pierre Victor Auger. Neither Amaldi nor Auger was a stranger to the cause of scientific collaboration on a European scale. Indeed it was they who, in the early 1950s, were key actors in the process which led to the setting up of CERN, the European Organisation for Nuclear Research. Now, as the decade drew to a close, they turned their attention to space. Success was rapid. Within a year of the first formal discussions being held amongst scientists, European governments had set up a European Preparatory Commission for Space Research (COPERS) to explore the possibilities for a joint space research effort.

THE EUROPEAN PREPARATORY COMMISSION FOR SPACE RESEARCH

The COPERS held its first session in Paris on 13 and 14 March 1961. Its first task was to create the organs needed to define the scientific programme and the necessary infrastructure of the envisaged organisation, to draw up its budget, and to prepare a Convention for signature by those member state governments who wished to join it. To this end the meeting first elected its "bureau": chairman Harrie Massey, vice-chairmen, Luigi Broglio and Hendrik van de Hulst, and executive secretary Pierre Auger, all men who had played an important role in the debates in 1960 and, Auger apart, still active and eminent European space scientists. It then established two working groups. The first was the Interim Scientific and Technical Working Group (STWG).

Its task was to prepare the scientific programme for the future space organisation, paying particular attention to the technical and financial implications of its proposals. Lamek Hulthén, from the Royal Institute of Technology in Stockholm, was nominated chairman of this group; Reimar Lüst from the Max-Planck-Institut für Physik und Astrophysik in Garching, near Munich was appointed its coordinating secretary. The second was the Legal, Administrative and Financial Working Group (LAFWG). Its chairman was initially left open, though it was recommended that he be someone from the German Federal Republic. Alexander Hocker, a senior bureaucrat from Bad-Godesberg who was the chairman of the CERN Finance Committee at the time, took on this task. All Member States were to be represented on both working groups, which were empowered to set up subgroups to facilitate their work.

The Western European nations decided to have two different agencies, one concerned with developing a launch system ELDO (European Launch Development Organisation) and the precursor of the European Space Agency, ESRO (European Space Research Organisation). The latter was established on 20 March 1964 by an agreement signed on 14 June 1962. From 1968 to 1972, ESRO carried out numerous successful projects. Seven research satellites were brought into orbit, all by US launch systems. Ariane didn't exist at that time.

ESA in its current form was founded in 1975, when ESRO was merged with ELDO. ESA had 10 founding members: Belgium, Denmark, France, Germany, Italy, the Netherlands, Spain, Sweden, Switzerland and the United Kingdom. ESA launched its first major scientific mission in 1975, Cos-B, a space probe monitoring gamma-ray emissions in the universe first worked on by ESRO.

SPACE RACE

Beginning in the 1970s, when the space race between the US and the Soviet Union had cooled down and space budgets were cut dramatically in both superpowers, ESA established itself as a forerunner in space exploration. ESA joined NASA in the IUE, the world's first high-orbit telescope, which was launched in 1978 and operated very successfully for 18 years. A number of successful Earth-orbit projects followed, and in 1986 ESA began Giotto, its first deep-space mission, to study the Comets Halley and Grigg-Skjellerup. Hipparcos, a star-mapping mission, was launched in 1989 and in the 1990s SOHO, Ulysses and the Hubble Space Telescope were all jointly carried out with NASA. Recent scientific missions in cooperation with NASA include the Cassini-Huygens space probe, to which ESA contributed by building the Titan landing module Huygens.

As the successor of ELDO, ESA has also constructed rockets for unmanned scientific and commercial payloads. Ariane 1, launched in 1979, brought mostly commercial payloads into orbit from 1984 onward. The next two developments of the Ariane rocket were intermediate stages in the development of a more advanced launch system, the Ariane 4, which operated between 1988 and 2003 and established ESA as the world leader in commercial space launches in the 1990s. Although the succeeding Ariane 5 experienced a failure on its first flight, it has since firmly established itself within the heavily competitive commercial space launch market with 40 successful launches as of 2009. The successor launch vehicle of Ariane 5, the Ariane 6 is already in the definition stage and is envisioned to enter service in the 2020s.

The beginning of the new millennium saw ESA become, along with agencies like NASA, JAXA, and Roscosmos, one of the major participants in scientific space research. While ESA had relied on cooperation with NASA in previous decades, especially the 1990s, changed circumstances (such as tough legal restrictions on information sharing by the United States military) led to decisions to rely more on itself and on cooperation with Russia.

> “ Russia is ESA's first partner in its efforts to ensure long-term access to space. There is a framework agreement between ESA and the government of the Russian Federation on cooperation and partnership in the exploration and use of outer space for peaceful purposes, and cooperation is already under way in two different areas of launcher activity that will bring benefits to both partners. ”

Most notable for its new self-confidence are ESA's own recent successful missions SMART-1, a probe testing cutting-edge new space propulsion technology, the Mars Express and Venus Express missions as well as the development of the Ariane 5 rocket and its role in the ISS partnership. ESA maintains its scientific and research projects mainly for astronomy-space missions such as Corot, launched on 27 December 2006, a milestone in the search for extrasolar planets.

MISSION STATEMENT

Since the Cold War ended with the fall of the Soviet Union's "iron curtain," space agencies around the world had to refocus and revise their visions and goals. In an interview with JAXA, the Japanese national space agency, Jean-Jacques Dordain ESA's Director General (since 2003) outlined briefly the European Space Agency's mission:

> “ Today space activities are pursued for the benefit of citizens, and citizens are asking for a better quality of life on earth. They want greater security and economic wealth, but they also want to pursue their dreams, to increase their knowledge, and they want younger people to be attracted to the pursuit of science and technology. ”

I think that space can do all of this: it can produce a higher quality of life, better security, more economic wealth, and also fulfil our citizens' dreams and thirst for knowledge, and attract the young generation. This is the reason space exploration is an integral part of overall space activities. It has always been so, and it will be even more important in the future.

Article II, Purpose, Convention of establishment of a European Space Agency, SP-1271(E) from 2003 also defines ESA's mission statement:

" ESA's purpose shall be to provide for, and to promote, for exclusively peaceful purposes, cooperation among European States in space research and technology and their space applications, with a view to their being used for scientific purposes and for operational space applications systems:

- by elaborating and implementing a long-term European space policy, by recommending space objectives to the Member States, and by concerting the policies of the Member States with respect to other national and international organisations and institutions;
- by elaborating and implementing activities and programmes in the space field;
- by coordinating the European space programme and national programmes, and by integrating the latter progressively and as completely as possible into the European space programme, in particular as regards the development of applications satellites;
- by elaborating and implementing the industrial policy appropriate to its programme and by recommending a coherent industrial policy to the Member States. "

BASIC RULES AND REGULATIONS

The following regulations have been adopted by ESA.

ESA PROCUREMENT REGULATIONS AND RELATED IMPLEMENTING INSTRUCTIONS

The purpose of ESA Procurement Regulations and their annexes is to regulate the procurement for the execution of the Agency's activities and programmes, in accordance with the ESA industrial policy objectives set out in Article VII of its Convention and Annex V thereto.

GENERAL CLAUSES AND CONDITIONS FOR ESA CONTRACTS

The General Clauses and Conditions (GCC) of the European Space Agency (ESA) apply to contracts placed by ESA.

SECURITY REGULATIONS

The attached Security Regulations of the European Space Agency apply to the Agency, its Member States, its staff and, under certain conditions, to its contracting personnel and to its contractors.

RULES ON INFORMATION, DATA AND INTELLECTUAL PROPERTY

These Rules are designed to promote access to Information and Data and use of Intellectual Property resulting from Agency activities, while fully taking into account the provisions of the Convention and the interests of the Member States and of Persons and Bodies under their Jurisdiction.

ESA FINANCIAL REGULATIONS

The Financial Regulations constitute together with Annex II to the Convention the basic legal instrument for the Agency's financial framework, including planning and funding financial control, treasury and cost management, accounting, controlling and internal and external auditing.

ADDITIONAL RULES ON ARBITRATION

The arbitration procedure provided for by Article XVII of the Convention shall be carried out in accordance with this Article and with the provisions of the Additional Rules on Arbitration.

ESA STAFF REGULATIONS

The Staff Regulations apply to staff appointed pursuant to Article XII.3 of the Convention for the establishment of the European Space Agency. They do not apply to personnel governed by local labour legislation or to experts and consultants except in so far as may be provided for in the rules applicable to them or in the terms of their employment.

MEMBER COUNTRIES AND BUDGET

MEMBERSHIP AND CONTRIBUTION TO ESA

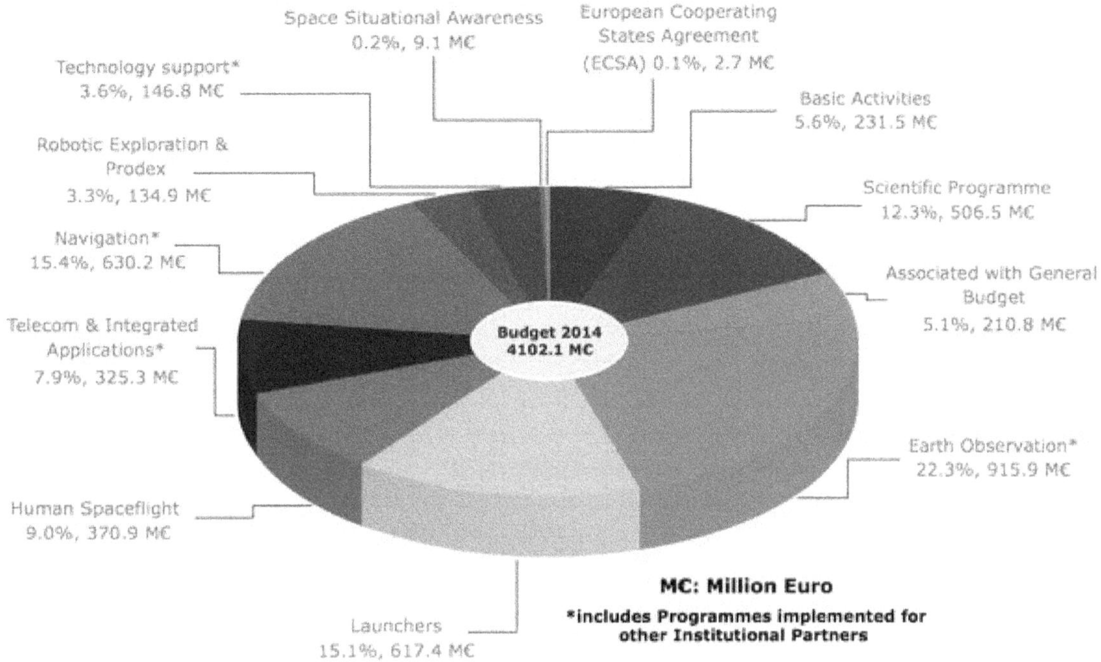

ESA is an intergovernmental organisation of 20 member states. Member states participate to varying degrees in the mandatory (25% of total expenditures in 2008) and optional space programmes (75% of total expenditures in 2008). The 2008 budget amounted to €3.0 billion the 2009 budget to €3.6 billion. The total budget amounted to about €3.7 billion in 2010, €3.99 billion in 2011 and €4.02 billion in 2012.

The following table lists all the member states and adjunct members, their ESA convention ratification dates, and their contributions in 2013:

Member state	ESA Convention	National Programme	Contr. (mill. €)	Contr. (%)
Austria	30 December 1986	FFG	50.1	1.6%
Belgium	3 October 1978	BELSPO	187.7	6.0%
Czech Republic	12 November 2008	CCMTSA	13.7	0.4%
Denmark	15 September 1977	DTU Space	25.7	0.8%
Finland	1 January 1995	TEKES	19.5	0.6%

Member state	ESA Convention	National Programme	Contr. (mill. €)	Contr. (%)
France	30 October 1980	CNES	747.5	24.0%
Germany	26 July 1977	DLR	772.7	24.8%
Greece	9 March 2005	ISARS	15.1	0.5%
Ireland	10 December 1980	EI	17.3	0.4%
Italy	20 February 1978	ASI	400.0	12.9%
Luxembourg	30 June 2005	Luxinnovation	15.0	0.5%
Netherlands	6 February 1979	NSO	79.5	2.6%
Norway	30 December 1986	NSC	56.3	1.8%
Poland	19 November 2012	CBK PAN	28.9	0.9%
Portugal	14 November 2000	FCT	16.1	0.5%
Romania	22 December 2011	ROSA	16.0	0.5%
Spain	7 February 1979	INTA	149.6	4.8%
Sweden	6 April 1976	SNSB	75.0	2.4%
Switzerland	19 November 1976	SSO	108.3	3.5%
United Kingdom	28 March 1978	UKSA	300.0	9.6%
Associate Members				
Canada	1 January 1979	CSA	15.5	0.5%
Total Members and Associates			2,900.1	72.1%
European Union	28 May 2004	ESP	911.1	21.3%
ECS states	various	various	4.6	0.1%
Other income	—	—	256.8	6.0%

Member state	ESA Convention	National Programme	Contr. (mill. €)	Contr. (%)
Total ESA			4,282.1	100.0%

ASSOCIATE MEMBERS

Currently the only associated member of ESA is Canada. Previously associated members were Austria, Norway and Finland, all of which later joined ESA as full members.

CANADA

Since 1 January 1979, Canada has had the special status of a Cooperating State within ESA. By virtue of this accord, the Canadian Space Agency takes part in ESA's deliberative bodies and decision-making and also in ESA's programmes and activities. Canadian firms can bid for and receive contracts to work on programmes. The accord has a provision ensuring a fair industrial return to Canada.

BUDGET APPROPRIATION AND ALLOCATION

ESA budget chart by programme for 2011

Earth Observation: 843.9 M€ (21.1%)

Navigation: 665.7 M€ (16.7%)

Launchers: 612.5 M€ (15.3%)

Science: 464.8 M€ (11.6%)

Human Spaceflight: 410.9 M€ (10.3%)

Telecommunications: 341.3 M€ (8.5%)

Basic Activities: 216.7 M€ (5.4%)

General Budget: 179.9 M€ (4.5%)

Robotic Exploration: 129.4 M€ (3.2%)

Technology: 105.1 M€ (2.5%)

Other (3.4%)

The budget of ESA was €2.977 billion in 2005, €2.904 billion in 2006 and grew to €3.018 billion in 2008, €3.600 billion in 2009, €3.745 billion in 2010, €3.994 billion in 2011 and €4.020 billion in 2012.

Every 3–4 years, ESA member states agree on a budget plan for several years at an ESA member states conference. This plan can be amended in future years, however provides the major guideline for ESA for several years. The last major conference was held at the end of 2008, setting the budget for the years to 2012.

The 2011 funding allocations for major areas of ESA activity are shown on the pie-chart on the right. The section called 'Other' includes Technology Development, Space Situational Awareness and spending related to European Cooperating States.

Countries typically have their own space programmes that differ in how they operate organisationally and financially with ESA. For example, the French space agency CNES has a total budget of €2015 million, of which €755 million is paid as direct financial contribution to ESA. Several space-related projects are joint projects between national space agencies and ESA (e.g.COROT). Also, ESA is not the only European space organisation (for example European Union Satellite Centre).

ENLARGEMENT

After the decision of the ESA Council of 21/22 March 2001, the procedure for accession of the European states was detailed as described here. Nations who want to become a full member of ESA do so in 3 stages. First a Cooperation Agreement is signed between the country and ESA. In this stage, the country has very limited financial responsibilities. If a country wants to cooperate more fully with ESA, it signs a European Cooperating State (ECS) Agreement.

The ECS Agreement makes companies based in the country eligible for participation in ESA procurements. The country can also participate in all ESA programmes, except for the Basic Technology Research Programme. While the financial contribution of the country concerned increases, it is still much lower than that of a full member state. The agreement is normally followed by a Plan For European Cooperating State (or PECS Charter). This is a 5-year programme of basic research and development activities aimed at improving the nation's space industry capacity. At the end of the 5-year period, the country can either begin negotiations to become a full member state or an associated state or sign a new PECS Charter. ESA is likely to expand quite rapidly in the coming years. Many countries, most of which joined the EU in both 2004 and 2007, have started to cooperate with ESA on various levels:

Applicant state	Cooperation Agreement	ECS Agreement	PECS Charter(s)	ESA Convention	National Programme
Hungary	April 1991	7 April 2003	1st: 5 November 2003 2nd: 26 September 2008	2013 or later	HSO
Turkey	15 July 2004				TÜBİTAK
Estonia	26 June 2007	10 November 2009	22 September 2010		through MoEC
Ukraine	25 January 2008				SSAU
Slovenia	28 May 2008	22 January 2010	30 November 2010		through MoHEST
Latvia	23 July 2009	19 March 2013			through MoES
Cyprus	27 August 2009				through MoCW
Slovakia	28 April 2010				through MoE
Lithuania	7 October 2010				through MoE

Applicant state	Cooperation Agreement	ECS Agreement	PECS Charter(s)	ESA Convention	National Programme
Israel	30 January 2011				ISA
Malta	20 February 2012				throughMCfST.

ASSOCIATE MEMBERS

Currently the only associated member of ESA is Canada. Previously associated members were Austria, Norway and Finland, all of which later joined ESA as full members.

CANADA

Since 1 January 1979, Canada has had the special status of a Cooperating State within ESA. By virtue of this accord, the Canadian Space Agency takes part in ESA's deliberative bodies and decision-making and also in ESA's programmes and activities. Canadian firms can bid for and receive contracts to work on programmes. The accord has a provision ensuring a fair industrial return to Canada.

ENLARGEMENT

After the decision of the ESA Council of 21/22 March 2001 the procedure for accession of the European states was detailed as described here. Nations who want to become a full member of ESA do so in 3 stages. First a Cooperation Agreement is signed between the country and ESA. In this stage, the country has very limited financial responsibilities. If a country wants to cooperate more fully with ESA, it signs a European Cooperating State (ECS) Agreement. The ECS agreement makes companies based in the country eligible for participation in ESA procurements.

The country can also participate in all ESA programmes, except for the Basic Technology Research Programme. While the financial contribution of the country concerned increases, it is still much lower that that of a full member state. The agreement is normally followed by a Plan For European Cooperating States (or PECS Charter). This is a 5 year programme of basic research and development activities aimed at improving the nation's space industry capacity. At the end of the 5 year period, the country can either begin negotiations to become a full member state or an associated state or sign a new PECS Charter. ESA is likely to expand quite rapidly in the coming years. Many countries, most of which joined the EU in both 2004 and 2007, have started to cooperate with ESA on various levels:

Applicant state	**Cooperation agreement**	**ECS agreement**	**PECS charters**	**National program**
Hungary	1991	7 April 2003	1st: 5 November 2003 2nd: 26 September 2008	HSO
Romania	1992	17 February 2006	1st: 16 February 2007	ROSA
Poland	January 1994	27 April 2007	1st: 28 April 2008	CBK-PAN
Turkey	July 2004			TÜBİTAK
Estonia	June 2007	10 November 2009		

Ukraine	January 2008			NSAU
Slovenia	May 2008			
Latvia	23 July 2009			
Cyprus	27 August 2009			

- Lithuania has also announced their intention to participate in the activities of ESA.
- Malta has also announced their intention to participate in the activities of ESA
- Slovakia has also announced their intention to participate in the activities of ESA

BUDGET APPROPRIATION AND ALLOCATION

ESA's activities fall into two categories – 'mandatory' and 'optional'. Programmes carried out under the General Budget and the Science Programme budget are 'mandatory'; they include the agency's basic activities (studies on future projects, technology research, shared technical investments, information systems and training programmes).

All Member States contribute to these programmes on a scale based on their Gross Domestic Product (GDP). The other programmes, known as 'optional', are only of interest to some Member States, who are free to decide on their level of involvement.

Optional programmes cover areas such as Earth observation, telecommunications, satellite navigation and space transportation. Similarly, the International Space Station and microgravity research are financed by optional contributions.

ESA budget chart by programme for 2011

Earth Observation: 843.9 M€ (21.1%)
Navigation: 665.7 M€ (16.7%)
Launchers: 612.5 M€ (15.3%)
Science: 464.8 M€ (11.6%)
Human Spaceflight: 410.9 M€ (10.3%)
Telecommunications: 341.3 M€ (8.5%)
Basic Activities: 216.7 M€ (5.4%)
General Budget: 179.9 M€ (4.5%)
Robotic Exploration: 129.4 M€ (3.2%)
Technology: 105.1 M€ (2.5%)
Other (3.4%)

The budget of ESA was €2.977 billion in 2005, €2.904 billion in 2006 and grew to €3.018 billion in 2008 and €3.600 billion in 2009. Every 3–4 years, ESA memberstates agree on a budget plan for several years at an ESA memberstates conference. This plan can be amended in future years, however provides the major guideline for ESA for several years. The last major conference was held at the end of 2008, setting the budget for the years to 2012.

ESA's budget in 2009 attributes about 18% or €660 million to launchers development and operations (Ariane 5), 16% or €586 million to Earth observation research, 12.1% or €434 million to space-related science, about 11% or €385 million each to Human Spaceflight and to Space-based Earth navigation systems (e.g. Galileo positioning system) and 9% or €320 million to telecommunications. The rest of the budget consists of funds for microgravity research, technology development, robotic exploration (e.g. Mars Express) and general budget items and administration.

Countries typically have their own space programmes that differ in how they operate organisationally and financially with ESA. For example, the French space agency CNES has a budget double the amount it contributes to ESA. Several space-related projects are joint projects between national space agencies and ESA (e.g. COROT). Also, ESA is not the only European space organisation (for example European Union Satellite Centre).

LAUNCH VEHICLE FLEET

ESA has made great progress towards its goal of having a complete fleet of launch vehicles in service, competing in all sectors of the launch market. ESA's fleet will soon consist of three major rocket designs, Ariane 5, Soyuz-2 and Vega. Rocket launches are carried out by Arianespace, which has 23 shareholders representing the industry that manufactures the Ariane 5 as well as CNES, at the spaceport in French Guiana. Because many communication satellites have equatorial orbits, launches from French Guiana are able to take larger payloads into space than from other northern spaceports. In addition, equatorial launches give spacecraft an extra 'push' of nearly 500 m/s due to the higher rotation velocity of someone standing on the equator than near the Earth's axis where rotation velocity approaches nil.

ARIANE 5

An Ariane 5

The Ariane 5 rocket is the primary launcher of ESA. Its maximum estimated payload is 6–10 tons to GTO and up to 21 tons to LEO. The launch craft has been in service since 1997 and replaced Ariane 4. The Ariane rocket exists in several specifications, the heaviest being Ariane 5 ECA, which failed during its first test flight in 2002, but has since made fifteen consecutive successful flights.

ESA's Ariane 1, 2, 3 and 4 launchers (the latter of which was ESA's long-time workhorse) have been retired.

SOYUZ

Soyuz-2 (also called the Soyuz-ST) is a Russian medium payload (ca. 3 metric tons to GTO) launcher to be brought into ESA service in April 2010.

ESA has entered into a €340 million joint venture with the Russian Federal Space Agency over the use of the Soyuz launcher. Under the agreement, the Russian agency manufactures Soyuz rocket parts for ESA, which are then shipped to French Guiana for assembly. ESA benefits because it gains a medium payloads launcher, complementing its fleet while saving on development costs. In addition, the Soyuz rocket—which has been the Russian's space launch workhorse for some 40 years—is proven technology with a good safety record, which ESA might eventually even use for launching humans into space. Russia also benefits in that it gets access to the Kourou launch site. Launching from Kourou rather than Baikonur will allow the Russians to almost double the Soyuz payload (3.0 tonnes vs. 1.7 tonnes to GTO), because of Kourou's closer proximity to the equator. Both agencies benefit from the long term strategic cooperation, which is also intended to enable future joint technology developments.

VEGA

Vega is ESA's small payload (ca. 1.5 metric tons to 700 km orbit) launcher; its first launch is planned for 2010. The leading ESA member state for the *Vega* Programme is Italy, contributing 65% of the costs. *Vega* itself has been designed to be a body launcher with three solid propulsion stages and an additional liquid propulsion upper module to place the cargo into the exact orbit intended. For a small-cargo rocket it is remarkable that *Vega* will be able to place multiple payloads into orbit.
Vega's first and main stage (P80) is a direct modification of the Ariane 5 EAP (solid boosters) developed by CNES, the French space agency.

HUMAN SPACE FLIGHT

At the time ESA was formed, its main goals did not encompass human space flight, rather it considered itself to be primarily a scientific research organisation for unmanned space exploration in contrast to its American and Soviet counterparts. It is therefore not surprising that the first non-Soviet European in space was not an ESA astronaut on a European space craft: It was Czechoslovak Vladimir Remek who in 1978 became the first non-Soviet European in space (the first European in space being Yuri Gagarin of the Soviet Union) — on a Soviet Soyuz spacecraft, followed by the Pole Mirosław Hermaszewski and East German Sigmund Jähn in the same year. This Soviet cooperation programme, known as Intercosmos, primarily involved the participation of Eastern bloc countries, however in 1982, Jean-Loup Chrétien became the first western European on a flight to the Soviet Salyut 7 space station.

Because Chrétien did not officially fly into space as an ESA astronaut, but rather as a member of the French CNES astronaut corps, the German Ulf Merbold is considered the first ESA astronaut to fly into space. He participated in the STS-9 Space Shuttle mission that included the first use of the European built Spacelab in 1983. STS-9 marked the beginning of an extensive ESA/NASA joint partnership that included dozens of space flights of ESA astronauts in the following years. Beside paying for seats on the Space Shuttle, ESA continued its human space flight cooperation with the Soviet Union and later Russia, including numerous visits to Mir.

During the latter half of the 1980s, European human space flights changed from being the exception to routine and therefore, in 1990, the European Astronaut Centre in Cologne, Germany was established. It selects and trains prospective astronauts and is responsible for the coordination with international partners especially with regards to the International Space Station. As of 2006, the ESA astronaut corps officially includes 12 members, including nationals from all the large Western European countries except the United Kingdom.

In the summer of 2008 ESA started to recruit new astronauts so that final selection would be due spring 2009. Almost 10,000 people registered as astronaut candidates till the registration ended in June 2008. 8,413 fulfilled the initial application criteria. Of the applicants 918 were chosen to take part in the first stage of psychological testing which narrowed down the field to 192. After two stage psychological tests and medical evaluation in early 2009 as well as formal interviews, 6 new members of the European Astronaut Corps were selected, 5 men and one woman.

ASTRONAUT CORPS

The astronauts of the European Space Agency are:

• Jean-François Clervoy	• Christer Fuglesang	• Thomas Pesquet
• Samantha Cristoforetti	• André Kuipers	• Thomas Reiter
• Frank De Winne	• Andreas Mogensen	• Hans Schlegel
• Pedro Duque	• Paolo Nespoli	• Gerhard Thiele
• Reinhold Ewald	• Claude Nicollier	• Michel Tognini
• Léopold Eyharts	• Luca Parmitano	• Roberto Vittori
• Alexander Gerst	• Timothy Peake	
• Umberto Guidoni	• Philippe Perrin	

1. have visited Mir
2. 2009 selection
3. have visited the International Space Station
4. retired now

MANNED LAUNCH VEHICLES

In the 1980s France pressed for an independent European manned launch vehicle. Around 1978 it was decided to pursue a reusable spacecraft model and starting in November 1987 a project to create a mini-shuttle by the name of Hermes was introduced. The craft itself was modelled comparable to the first proposals of the Space Shuttle and consisted of a small reusable spaceship that would carry 3 to 5 astronauts and 3 to 4 metric tons of payload for scientific experiments. With a total maximum weight of 21 metric tons it would have been launched on the Ariane 5 rocket, which was being developed at that time. It was planned solely for use in Low-Earth orbit space flights. The planning and pre-development phase concluded in 1991; however, the production phase was never fully implemented because at that time the political landscape had changed significantly. With the fall of the Soviet Union ESA looked forward to cooperation with Russia to build a next-generation human space vehicle. Thus the Hermes program was cancelled in 1995 after about 3 billion dollars had been spent.

In the 21st century ESA started new programs in order to create its own manned spacecraft, most notable among its various projects and proposals is Hopper, whose prototype by EADS, called Phoenix, has already been tested. While projects such as Hopper are neither concrete nor to be realised within the next decade, other possibilities for human spaceflight in cooperation with the Russian Space Agency have emerged. Following talks with the Russian Space Agency in 2004 and June 2005, a cooperation between ESA and the Russian Space Agency was announced to jointly work on the Russian-designed Kliper, a reusable spacecraft that would be available for space travel beyond LEO (e.g. the moon or even Mars). It was speculated that Europe would finance part of it. However, a €50 million participation study for Kliper, which was expected to be approved in December 2005, was finally not approved by the ESA member states. The Russian state tender for the Kliper project was subsequently cancelled in the summer of 2006.

In June 2006 ESA member states granted 15 million to the Crew Space Transportation System (CSTS) study, a two-year study to design a spacecraft capable of going beyond Low-Earth orbit based on the current Soyuz design. This project is pursued with Roskosmos instead of the previously cancelled Kliper proposal. A decision on the actual implementation and construction of the CSTS spacecraft is contemplated for 2008, with the major design decisions being made before the summer of 2007.
In the 47th press release of ESA in Autumn 2008 no plans to persuade an upgraded manned version of the ATV spacecraft had been mentioned. If and when exactly ESA will launch their own manned spacecrafts into space are therefor unclear.

COOPERATION WITH OTHER COUNTRIES AND ORGANISATIONS

ESA has signed cooperation agreements with the following states that currently neither plan to integrate as tightly with ESA institutions as Canada, nor envision future membership of ESA: Argentina, Brazil, China, India (for the Chandrayan mission), and Russia.

Additionally, ESA has joint projects with the European Union, NASA of the United States and is participating in the International Space Station together with the United States (NASA), Russia and Japan (JAXA).

EUROPEAN UNION

ESA is not an agency or body of the European Union (EU), and has non-EU countries such as Switzerland and Norway as members. There are however ties between the two, with various agreements in place and being worked on, to define the legal status of ESA with regard to the EU. There are common goals between ESA and the EU, and ESA has an EU liaison office in Brussels. On certain projects, the EU and ESA cooperate, such as the upcoming Galileo satellite navigation system. Space policy has since December 2009 been an area for voting in the European Council. Under the European Space Policy of 2007, the EU, ESA and its Member States committed themselves to increasing coordination of their activities and programmes and to organising their respective roles relating to space.

Former Italian astronaut Umberto Guidoni, during his tenure as a Member of the European Parliament from 2004 to 2009, stressed the importance of the European Union as a driving force for space exploration, "since other players are coming up such as India and China it is becoming ever more important that Europeans can have an independent access to space. We have to invest more into space research and technology in order to have an industry capable of competing with other international players."

An independent report on the future of ESA, requested by its director-general, recommends further integration of ESA into the structures of the EU. Space policy would be decided by the European Council and ESA would be the *de facto* space agency of the European Union, not excluding the possibility of making it a formal EU agency. This would also help with co-operation between space policy and environmental or security policy, Galileo itself has a security dimension.

The first EU-ESA International Conference on Human Space Exploration took place in Prague on 22 and 23 October. A road map which would lead to a common vision and strategic planning in the area of space exploration was discussed. Ministers from all 29 EU and ESA members as well as members of parliament were in attendance. If a roadmap is accepted at the November 2010

Brussels conference as planned, it is estimated that an additional €3 billion annually would be made available for European space exploration activities by the European Commission.

NATIONAL SPACE ORGANISATIONS OF MEMBER COUNTRIES

- The *Centre National d'Études Spatiales* (CNES) (National Centre for Space Study) is the French government space agency (administratively, a "public establishment of industrial and commercial character"). Its headquarters are in central Paris. CNES is the main participant on the Ariane project. Indeed CNES designed and tested all Ariane family rockets (mainly from its centre in Evry near Paris)

- The British National Space Centre (BNSC) is a partnership of the UK government departments which are active in space. Through the BNSC the partners provide delegates to represent the UK on the various ESA governing bodies. Each partner funds its own programme.

- The Italian Space Agency (*Agenzia Spaziale Italiana* or ASI) was founded in 1988 to promote, coordinate and conduct space activities in Italy. Operating under the Ministry of the Universities and of Scientific and Technological Research, the agency cooperates with numerous entities active in space technology and with the president of the Council of Ministers. Internationally, the ASI provides Italy's delegation to the Council of the European Space Agency and to its subordinate bodies.

- The German Aerospace Center (DLR) (German: *Deutsches Zentrum für Luft- und Raumfahrt e. V.*) is the national research centre for aviation and space flight of the Federal Republic of Germany and of other member states in the Helmholtz Association. Its extensive research and development projects are included in national and international cooperative programmes. In addition to its research projects, the centre is the assigned space agency of Germany bestowing headquarters of German space flight activities and its associates.

- The Instituto Nacional de Técnica Aeroespacial (INTA) (Spanish:National Technical Institute for Aerospace) is the spacial agency for Spain.

NASA

ESA has a long history of collaboration with NASA. Since ESA's astronaut corps was formed, the Space Shuttle has been the primary launch vehicle used by ESA's astronauts to get into space through partnership programs with NASA. In the 1980s and 1990s, the Spacelab program was an ESA-NASA joint research program that had ESA develop and manufacture orbital labs for the Space Shuttle for several flights on which ESA participate with astronauts in experiments.

In robotic science mission and exploration missions, NASA has been ESA's main partner. Cassini-Huygens was a joint NASA-ESA mission, the Infrared Space Observatory, INTEGRAL, SOHO, and others. Also, the Hubble space telescope is a joint project of NASA and ESA. Future unmanned projects that are in development right now and are ESA-NASA joint projects include the James Webb Space Telescope or the Laser Interferometer Space Antenna. NASA and ESA will also likely join together for a Mars Sample Return Mission.

COOPERATION WITH OTHER SPACE AGENCIES

Since China has started to invest more money into space activities, the Chinese Space Agency has sought international partnerships. ESA is, beside the Russian Space Agency, one of its most important partners. Recently the two space agencies cooperated in the development of the Double Star Mission.

ESA entered into a major joint venture with Russia in the form of the CSTS, the preparation of French Guyana spaceport for launches of Soyuz rockets and other projects. With India ESA agreed to send instruments into space aboard the ISRO's Chandrayaan in 2008. ESA is also cooperating with Japan, the most notable current project in collaboration with JAXA is the BepiColombo mission to Mercury.

INTERNATIONAL SPACE STATION

With regard to the International Space Station (ISS) ESA is not represented by all of its member states: 10 of the 18 ESA member countries currently participate in the project.

ESA is taking part in the construction and operation of the ISS with contributions such as Columbus, a science laboratory module that was brought into orbit by NASA's STS-122 Space Shuttle mission and the Cupola observatory module that was completed in July 2005 by Alenia Spazio for ESA. The current estimates for the ISS are approaching €100 billion in total (development, construction and 10 years of maintaining the station) of which ESA has committed to paying €8 billion. About 90% of the costs of ESA's ISS share will be contributed by Germany (41%), France (28%) and Italy (20%). German ESA astronaut Thomas Reiter was the first long-term ISS crew member.

As of 2008, the spacecraft establishing supply links to the ISS are the Progress, Soyuz and Space Shuttle. ESA has developed the Automated Transfer Vehicle (ATV) for ISS resupply. Each ATV has a cargo capacity of 7,667 kilograms (16,900 lb). The first ATV, *Jules Verne*, was launched on 9 March 2008 and on 3 April 2008 successfully docked with the ISS. This manoeuvre, considered a major technical feat, involved using automated systems to allow the ATV to track the ISS, moving at 27,000 km/h, and attach itself with an accuracy of 2 cm. No other spacefaring nations or space agency currently possess this level of autonomy in rendezvous and docking activities, considered key to future space exploration. With the Space Shuttle reaching its retirement age in 2010, until NASA has a replacement for it such as COTS the ATV together with Progress, Soyuz and the Japanese transporter HTV will be the only links between Earth and the ISS.

LANGUAGES

According to Annex 1, Resolution No. 8 of the *Convention for the establishment of a European Space Agency*, English, French and German may be used in all meetings of the Agency, with interpretation provided into these three languages. All official documents are available in English and French with all documents concerning the ESA Council being available in German as well.

FACILITIES

- Headquarters of ESA, Paris, France
- European Space Operations Centre (ESOC), Darmstadt, Germany
- Centre Spatial Guyanais, Kourou, French Guiana
- European Space Research and Technology Centre (ESTEC), Noordwijk, The Netherlands
- ESA Centre for Earth Observation (ESRIN), Frascati, Italy
- European Astronaut Centre (EAC), Cologne, Germany
- European Space Astronomy Centre (ESAC), Madrid, Spain
- ESTRACK European Space Tracking Network
- European Robotics and Climate Change Centre, Harwell Science and Innovation Campus, United Kingdom

EUROPEAN SPACE AGENCY: BASIC INFORMATION

PARTICIPATING STATES

Europe, through ESA, is one of the five partners (NASA, Russian Federal Space Agency, ESA, JAXA, CSA) contributing to the development of the ISS.

The European Space Agency (ESA) in its current form was founded in 1975 when the European Space Research Organisation (ESRO) merged with the European Launcher Development Organisation (ELDO). The ESA Convention was signed by the ESRO and ELDO members on 30 May 1975 and by Ireland on 31 December 1975. Canada signed the ESA Convention as an associate member on 9 December 1978. The Convention entered into force on 30 October 1980 after the ratification procedures in the 10 ESRO/ELDO members were finalised

Organization	Belgium	France	Germany	Italy	Netherlands	United Kingdom	Spain	Switzerland
ESRO	member	member	member	member	member	member	member	member
ELDO	member	member	member	member	member	member		
ESA in 1980	member	member	member	member	member	member	member	member

Organization	Sweden	Denmark	Australia	Ireland	Austria	Canada
ESRO	member	member				
ELDO			associate member			
ESA in 1980	member	member		member	associate member	associate member

MEMBERSHIP

The current membership of the European Space Agency includes 20 member states and one associate member as follows:

ESA Founding members	Signature	Ratification	National Program
Sweden	30 May 1975	6 April 1976	SNSB
Switzerland	30 May 1975	19 November 1976	SSO
Germany	30 May 1975	26 July 1977	DLR
Denmark	30 May 1975	15 September 1977	DNSC
Italy	30 May 1975	20 February 1978	ASI

ESA Founding members	Signature	Ratification	National Program
United Kingdom	30 May 1975	28 March 1978	BNSC
Belgium	30 May 1975	3 October 1978	BIRA
Netherlands	30 May 1975	6 February 1979	SRON
Spain	30 May 1975	7 February 1979	INTA
France	30 May 1975	30 October 1980	CNES
Ireland	31 December 1975	10 December 1980	SI
Associate members	Signature	Entry into force	National Program
Canada	9 December 1978	1 January 1979	CSA
ESA Convention entry into force: 30 October 1980			
Acceded members	Cooperation Agreement	ESA membership	National Program
Austria	1979 for associate membership	30 December 1986	ASA
Norway	1981 for associate membership	30 December 1986	NSC
Finland	1987 for associate membership	1 January 1995	TEKES
Portugal	1996	14 November 2000	CEP
Greece	January 2001	9 March 2005	ISARS
Luxembourg	September 2000	30 June 2005	through MoHER
Czech Republic	1996	8 July 2008	CSO
Romania	December 1992	23 December 2011	ROSA
Poland	28 January 1994	19 November 2012	CBK-PAN

ASSOCIATE MEMBERS

The ESA Convention does not require acquisition of the associate membership status in order for a state to become full member. The association status is envisaged to allow associate member states to take part in ESA's deliberative bodies and decision-making and also in ESA's programmes and activities. Associate member state firms can bid for and receive contracts to work on programmes. The accord has a provision ensuring a fair industrial return to the associate members.

Previously, associate members were Austria, Norway and Finland (through its Ministry of Trade and Industry all of which later joined ESA as full members.Portugal, Greece and Luxembourg skipped associate membership and moved from Cooperation Agreements to full ESA membership. The Czech Republic also skipped associate membership, but it went through the new enlargement process via Cooperation Agreement, ECS Agreement and PECS Charter implementation.

Currently the only associate member of ESA is Canada.

Despite that the provisions in the ESA Convention do not show restrictions that only European states can join, the ESA Council implements such rule de factoand that is why Canada has only the status of associate member. However, it is as tightly integrated with the ESA institutions as possible for a non-member state.

The ELDO associate member Australia (CSIRO) decided not to continue as an associate member of ESA. Nevertheless, on 5 March 2003 the first of ESA's deep space ground stations in the world opened in western Australia in an inauguration ceremony.

ENLARGEMENT

ESA member countries

2nd stage: ECS states

1st stage: signed Cooperation Agreement

Observer state negotiating cooperation agreement

ESA associate members

After the decision of the ESA Council of 21/22 March 2001 the procedure for accession of the European stateswas detailed as described here. Nations who want to become a full member of ESA do so in 3 stages. First a Cooperation Agreement is signed between the country and ESA. In this stage the country has very limited financial responsibilities. If a country wants to cooperate more fully with ESA it signs a European Cooperating State (ECS) agreement.

The ECS Agreement makes companies based in the country eligible for participation in ESA procurements. The country can also participate in all ESA programmes, except for the Basic Technology Research Programme. While the financial contribution of the country concerned increases, it is still much lower than that of a full member state. The agreement is normally followed by a Plan for European Cooperating State (or PECS Charter).

This is a 5-year program of basic research and development activities aimed at improving the nations' space industry capacity. At the end of the 5-year period, the country can either begin negotiations to become a full member state or an associated state or sign a new PECS Charter. ESA is likely to expand quite rapidly in the coming years. Many countries, most of which joined the EU in both 2004 and 2007, have started to cooperate with ESA on various levels.

COMPLETED ENLARGEMENTS

Applicant state	Cooperation Agreement	ECS Agreement	PECS Charter	ESA Convention signature	Full Membership	National Program
Austria	1979 for associate membership				30 December 1986	ASA
Norway	1981 for associate membership				30 December 1986	NSC
Finland	1987 for associate membership				1 January 1995	TEKES
Portugal	1996	NA	NA		14 November 2000	CEP
Greece	January 2001	NA	NA		9 March 2005	ISARS
Luxembourg	September 2000	NA	NA		30 June 2005	through MoHER
Czech Republic	1996	24 November 2003	24 November 2004		8 July 2008	CSO
Romania	December 1992	17 February 2006	16 February 2007	20 January 2011	23 December 2011	ROSA
Poland	28 January 1994	27 April 2007	28 April 2008	13 September 2012	19 November 2012	CBK-PAN

CURRENT PROGRESS

Applicant state	Cooperation Agreement	ECS Agreement	PECS Charter(s)	ESA Convention signature	National Program
Hungary	April 1991	7 April 2003	1st: 5 November 2003 2nd: 26 September 2008	not until 2013 or later	HSO
Turkey	15 July 2004				TÜBİTAK
Estonia	26 June 2007	10 November 2009	22 September 2010		through MoEC
Ukraine	25 January 2008				SSAU
Slovenia	28 May 2008	22 January 2010	30 November 2010		through MoHEST
Latvia	23 July 2009	19 March 2013			through MoES
Cyprus	27 August 2009				through MoCW
Slovakia	28 April 2010				through

Applicant state	Cooperation Agreement	ECS Agreement	PECS Charter(s)	ESA Convention signature	National Program
					MoE
Lithuania	7 October 2010				through MoE
Israel	30 January 2011				ISA
Malta	20 February 2012				through MCfST.

POSSIBLE FUTURE COOPERATION

The political perspective of the European Union (EU) is to make ESA an agency of the EU by 2014, although this date may not be met. The EU is already the largest single donor to ESA's budget and non-ESA EU states are observers at ESA.

The only EU member states that have not signed an ESA Cooperation Agreement are Bulgaria and Croatia. Bulgaria however, has announced its intention to participate in the activities of ESA and is in the process of negotiations.

- Bulgaria on 9 April 2009 announced their intention to participate in the activities of ESA through IKI-BAN. Bulgaria along with the other EU members that are not ESA members have started to participate as observers since 12 October 2011.

Besides EU countries, some members of ESA are also EEA and EFTA members, namely Norway and Switzerland. The remaining EEA/EFTA members, Icelandand Liechtenstein nor any of the EU candidates not listed above have yet to publicly express their intention for participating in the European Space Agency activities.

ESA FACTS AND FIGURES

ESA'S ADDRESS

European Space Agency
8-10 rue Mario Nikis
75738 Paris Cedex 15
France
Communication Department
Tel: + 33 1 5369 7155
Fax: + 33 1 5369 7690

BASIC INFORMATION

The European Space Agency is Europe's gateway to space. Its mission is to shape the development of Europe's space capability and ensure that investment in space continues to deliver benefits to the citizens of Europe.

ESA has 17 Member States. By coordinating the financial and intellectual resources of its members, it can undertake programmes and activities far beyond the scope of any single European country.

ESA's job is to draw up the European space programme and carry it through. The Agency's projects are designed to find out more about the Earth, its immediate space environment, the solar system and the Universe, as well as to develop satellite-based technologies and services, and to promote European industries. ESA also works closely with space organisations outside Europe.

ESA's headquarters are in Paris which is where policies and programmes are decided upon. ESA also has centres in a number of European countries, each of which has different responsibilities.

- ESTEC, the European Space Research and Technology Centre, is the design hub for most ESA spacecraft and technology development, and is situated in Noordwijk, the Netherlands
- ESOC, the European Space Operations Centre, is responsible for controlling ESA satellites in orbit and is situated in Darmstadt, Germany
- EAC, the European Astronauts Centre, trains astronauts for future missions and is situated in Cologne, Germany
- ESRIN, the ESA Centre for Earth Observation, is based in Frascati, near Rome in Italy. Its responsibilities include collecting, storing and distributing Earth Observation satellite data to ESA's partners, and acting as the Agency's information technology centre

In addition, ESA has liaison offices in Belgium, the United States and Russia; a launch base in French Guiana; and ground and tracking stations in various areas of the world.

In February 2005 the total number of staff working for ESA numbered approximately 1907. These highly qualified people come from all the Member States and include scientists, engineers, information technology specialists and administrative personnel.

ESA's mandatory activities (space science programmes and the general budget) are funded by a financial contribution from all the Agency's Member States, calculated in accordance with each country's gross national product. In addition, ESA conducts a number of optional programmes. Each Member State decides in which optional programme they wish to participate and the amount they wish to contribute.

ESA's budget for 2014 is an estimated €3,339.3 million. The agency operates on the basis of geographical return, i.e. it invests in each Member State, through industrial contracts for space programmes, an amount more or less equivalent to each country's contribution.

European per capita investment in space is very little. On average, every citizen of an ESA Member State pays, in taxes for expenditure on space, about the same as the price of a cinema ticket. In the United States, investment in civilian space activities is almost four times as much.

The ESA Council is the Agency's governing body and provides the basic policy guidelines within which the Agency develops the European space programme. Each Member State is represented on the Council and has one vote, regardless of its size or financial contribution.

The Agency is headed by a Director General who is elected by the Council every four years. Each individual research sector has its own Directorate and reports directly to the Director General. The present Director General of ESA is Jean-Jacques Dordain.

SA HEADQUARTERS

ESA has its headquarters in Paris. Here the Director General and the majority of the Programme Directors have their offices, and the decisions that shape ESA's present and future activities are made.

ESA Paris is also the administrative centre and contains the main offices for staffing, legal affairs, finance, budget, internal audit, strategy, international relations and communications. Each ESA Centre also has offices for personnel, finance and communications that report to ESA headquarters in Paris.

To facilitate its international relations, ESA has liaison offices in Brussels, Moscow and Washington together with an office in Houston, USA to support International Space Station activities and one in Kourou, French Guiana, for Europe's Spaceport.

THE ESA COUNCIL

ESA's governing body is the Council. This is composed of high-level representatives of ESA Member States and is responsible for drawing up the European Space Plan and ensuring the long-term funding of the Agency's activities. Each ESA Member State has one vote and is represented by a Council delegate from the ministry responsible for space activities in each Member State.

In general, Council meetings are held every three months at delegate level and every two to three years at ministerial level. Meetings at delegate level usually take place at ESA's headquarters.

Council is responsible for:

- drawing up the European Space Plan
- ensuring that it is being followed
- approving both ongoing and future Programmes
- deciding on the level of resources to be made available to ESA

ESA's activities are divided into nine Directorates, each headed by a Director who reports directly to the Director General. These are:

- Earth Observation Programmes
- Technical and Quality Management
- Launcher Programmes
- Human Spaceflight, Microgravity and Exploration Programmes
- Resources Management
- External Relations
- Science Programmes
- EU and Industrial Programmes
- Operations and Infrastructure

INTERNATIONAL COOPERATION

To ensure that ESA remains at the forefront of space research and exploration, ESA frequently joins in cooperative ventures with other spacefaring nations such as the United States, Russia, Canada and Japan. Negotiations with countries wishing to join ESA also take place in Paris.

International collaboration also includes assisting developing countries. ESA manages a worldwide network of ground-receiving stations to collect remote sensing data and has set up a network to transmit weather and environmental data to African countries.
ESA's Office for International Relations interacts with international organisations such as the United Nations World Meteorological Office, the United Nations Environment Programme and the United Nations Food and Agriculture Organization. The ESA headquarters in Paris also hosts the International Astronautical Federation (IAF).

PLANNING FOR THE FUTURE

A General Studies Programme has been set up in Paris to assist the ESA Council in selecting future programmes. This Programme selects innovative ideas for future activities by drawing upon ESA's technical experts, as well as institutions and industries in Member States.
Not all proposals materialise into funded programmes. Upon closer examination activities may prove to be too expensive, less interesting than expected or unrealistic with the foreseeable technology. Early feedback of this kind prevents ESA and European industry from making costly mistakes.

COMMUNICATIONS

Europe's citizens fund ESA, therefore, it is important to ensure that they are aware of ESA's achievements and of how public money is being spent.

ESA's Communication Office is responsible for keeping the world's media, decision makers and the public up to date with what is happening at ESA and providing news on all its latest activities. One of the main activities of ESA's Communication Office is to organise large media events and press conferences, and prepare written and audiovisual material for target groups. Communications policy is set up and coordinated by Paris but is delegated to the Agency's establishments for specific activities at regional level.

ESA takes part in all the major conferences, symposia and space-related events. These act as a forum for the exchange of ideas and help to increase public awareness of ESA. The Communication Office in Paris also organises exhibits, and maintains the main photo and video archives.

ADMINISTRATION

Even the most innovative space research can not be put into operation unless ESA has highly qualified staff capable of putting good ideas into effect. It is also important that ESA's activities are carried out efficiently and cost-effectively in order to ensure that the contributions of Member States are used wisely.

Staffing

To carry out its programmes ESA needs to recruit experts in many different fields from all ESA's Member States. ESA's recruitment policy is decided and administered at its Paris headquarters. Each ESA Centre also has an office for human resources that reports directly to the head office in Paris.

Finance

Careful controls are in place to ensure that ESA and its Centres work within their budgets. In addition, the Office of Internal Audit ensures transparency in all ESA's dealings.

Legal affairs
ESA's Legal Office is responsible for all legal matters concerned with ESA and space. Paris also hosts the European Centre for Space Law (ECSL). This organisation aims to improve research in space law within Europe as well as its practice.

LAUNCHERS

Although most of the programme activities of the ESA Directorates are handled by the ESA Centres within Europe, one Directorate - Launchers – is mainly based in Paris.

Without launchers space exploration would be impossible. ESA's Launchers Programme is responsible for researching and developing ideas for new launchers. It also oversees the launch and production facilities at Europe's Spaceport in Kourou, French Guiana.
ESA's Launchers Programme is responsible for developing the Ariane launchers that have proved so successful. Recent activities include further enhancements to the Ariane-5 launcher and the development of Vega, a new small launcher scheduled to make its first flight in 2007. Other ideas being studied for the not too distant future include plans for a reusable launcher. This development will greatly reduce the cost of launching satellites and spacecraft.

THE EUROPEAN ASTRONAUT CORPS

The European Space Agency began its manned flight programme with Spacelab, providing the opportunity for the selection of the first ESA astronauts in 1978. The three first astronauts selected were the German Ulf Merbold, the Dutch Wubbo Ockels and the Swiss Claude Nicollier.

Ulf Merbold was the first to fly in 1983 with STS-9 and Wubbo Ockels flew two years later. Claude Nicollier, who had to wait 14 years to experience his first flight with STS-46 in 1992, now leads the pack with four space flights.

The second ESA astronaut selection was in 1992 in the framework of two major ESA programmes: HERMES (today cancelled) and COLUMBUS. The larger number of astronauts selected and the variety of European nations represented reflected the increased public interest in Europe for manned flight in this period. More than 22 000 Europeans expressed interest in becoming astronauts, including 5500 serious candidates.

Six candidates were finally selected, including only one previously selected national astronaut: Jean-Francois Clervoy, the first French member of the Corps. Also selected were the second German astronaut, Thomas Reiter, Maurizio Cheli from Italy (resigned in 1996), Pedro Duque from Spain, Christer Fuglesang from Sweden and the first woman, Marianne Merchez from Belgium who has since resigned and did not fly.

On 25 March 1998, the ESA Council decided to build up the single European Astronaut Corps. The objective was to improve the management of the organisation in the framework of the International Space Station programme in which ESA plays a major role. France and Germany, who were the only European countries with a national Astronaut Corps, promoted the idea that the fusion was a good and necessary decision to optimise the astronaut resources.

The details of the Council resolution included the decision of the constitution of a corps of 16 Astronauts (four for Germany, France and Italy and four for all the other Member States). The integration process would culminate with the dissolution of the national Astronaut Corps at the end of June 2000. This agreement does not exclude the possibility of a Member State using an astronaut of the European Astronaut Corps for a space mission organised at the national level.

The first group of seven astronauts joined the Corps in 1998:

- Gerhard Thiele and Hans Schlegel from Germany
- Umberto Guidoni, Paolo Nespoli and Roberto Vittori from Italy
- Léopold Eyharts and Jean-Pierre Haigneré from France

Jean-Pierre Haignere left the Corps in November 1999, after his second flight, to become Head of the Astronaut Division. He is currently senior advisor to the ESA Director of Launchers, in charge of studying all aspects for a Soyuz human spaceflight programme from Europe's spaceport in French Guiana.
A second group of four astronauts joined in 1999 and included Reinhold Ewald from Germany, André Kuipers from the Netherlands and Claudie Haigneré (formerly André-Deshays) and Michel Tognini from France. Frank De Winne from Belgium joined the Corps at the beginning of 2000.

In June 2002 Claudie Haigneré took up the post of Minister for Research and New Technologies in the French government.

In May 2003, Michel Tognini left the European Astronaut Corps to follow-up Jean-Pierre Haigneré as Head of the Astronaut Division at EAC in Cologne, Germany.
Philippe Perrin from France, who joined the Corps in December 2002, left in May 2004 to become Experimental Test Pilot with Airbus Industrie in Toulouse.
Umberto Guidoni left the Corps in June 2004.

CHARTA OF THE EUROPEAN ASTRONAUT CORPS

The decision in 1998 to form one single European Astronaut Corps was a milestone for Human Spaceflight within ESA and for Europe. It was clear to all of us that a new era of human spaceflight in Europe had just begun and we were a part of it. We realised that it was our task to shape this new era in a truly European spirit and share it with the people of Europe.

This is no minor undertaking. We come from different countries and bring a variety of backgrounds into the European Astronaut Corps, educated as engineers, scientists, medical doctors, or test pilots. We acknowledged that our diversity was a strength in the pursuit of our common goal: peaceful human space exploration for the benefit of humankind at large and for the European people in particular.

Although we cherish our origin and our diverse cultural and national backgrounds, we like to see ourselves as true Europeans, who share common European values. And we know that we will be successful only if we work together as a team, a group of people inspired by the same dream about peaceful human exploration of space.

We want to share this dream and our experiences with the people of Europe.

This is why we decided to write a Charta of the European Astronaut Corps: to express and share our vision, our mission and our values with you!

The European Astronaut Corps

The text of the Charta is as follows:

CHARTA OF THE EUROPEAN ASTRONAUT CORPS

Our Vision Shaping and Sharing Human Space Exploration Through Unity in Diversity

Our Mission

We Shape Space by bringing our European values to the preparation, support, and operation of the space flights that advance peaceful human exploration.

We Share Space with the people of Europe by communicating our vision, goals, experiences, and the results of our missions.

Our Values

Sapientia: We believe that Human Space Exploration is a wise choice by and for humankind. Sapientia reflects our commitment to pursue our goals for the advancement of humanity.

Populus: We put people first, in two ways: First, the purpose of our mission is to contribute to a better future for people on Earth. Second: Populus serves as a reflection of our repect for the people with whom we work: that we value their opinions, praise their work and compliment them for their support.

Audacia: We acknowledge that Spaceflight is a dangerous endeavour. While accepting the risks inherently involved in space travel we work to minimise these risks whenever we can. Audacia reminds us that the rewards will be unparalleled if we succeed.

Cultura: We continue the exploration started by our ancestors. Conscious of our history and traditions, we expand exploration into space, passing on our cultural heritage to future generations.

Exploratio: We value exploration as an opportunity to discover, to learn and, ultimately, to grow. We are convinced that humankind must embrace the challenge of peaceful human space exploration. We, the European Astronauts, are willing to take the next step.

Cologne, this fifteenth day of August twothousandone anno domini

EUROPEAN ASTRONAUTS IN SPACE

Name	Participating organisation	Mission / payload	Space vehicle(s)	Date
S. Jähn (D)	Germany, former GDR	Interkosmos	Soyuz 31 Salut-6 Soyuz 29	26/08/78 - 03/09/78
J.-L. Chrétien (F)	CNES	Premier Vol Habité	Soyuz T 6 Salyut-7	24/06/82 - 02/07/82
U. Merbold (D)	ESA	Spacelab 1	STS-9	28/11/83 - 08/12/83
P. Baudry (F)	CNES	Spartan-1	STS-51 G	17/06/85 - 24/06/85
R. Furrer (D), E. Messerschmid (D), W. Ockels (NL)	DFVLR, ESA	Spacelab D-1	STS-61 A	30/10/85 - 06/11/85
J.-L. Chrétien (F)	CNES	Aragatz	TM 7	26/11/88 -

			MIR Soyuz TM 6	21/12/88
H. Sharman (GB)	Private financing	Juno	TM 12 MIR Soyuz TM 11	18/05/91 - 26/05/91
F. Viehböck (A)	Austrian Space Agency	Austromir	TM 13 MIR Soyuz TM 12	02/10/91 - 10/10/91
U. Merbold (D)	ESA	Spacelab International Microgravity Lab IML-1	STS-42	22/01/92 - 30/01/92
K.-D. Flade (D)	DARA/DLR	MIR'92	TM 14 MIR Soyuz TM 13	17/03/92 - 25/03/92
D. Frimout (B)	Belgian (bilateral)	ATLAS-1	STS-45	24/03/92 - 02/04/92
M. Tognini (F)	CNES	Antares	TM 15 MIR Soyuz TM 14	27/07/92 - 10/08/92
F. Malerba (I), C. Nicollier (CH)	ASI, ESA	EURECA-1, Tethered Satellite System	STS-46	31/07/92 - 08/08/92
H. Schlegel (D) U. Walter (D)	DLR	Spacelab D-2	STS-55	26/04/93 - 06/05/93
J.-P. Haigneré (F)	CNES	Altaïr	Soyuz TM 17 MIR Soyuz TM 16	01/07/93 - 22/07/93
C. Nicollier (CH)	ESA	Hubble Space Telescope 1st Servicing Mission	STS-61	02/12/93 - 13/12/93
U. Merbold (D)	ESA	EUROMIR 94	Soyuz TM 20 MIR Soyuz TM 19	03/10/94 - 04/11/94
J.-F. Clervoy (F)	ESA	ATLAS-3; CRISTA SPAS 1	STS-66	03/11/94 - 14/11/94
T. Reiter (D)	ESA	EUROMIR 95	Soyuz TM 22 MIR	03/09/95 - 29/02/96
C. Nicollier (CH)	ESA, ASI	Tethered Satellite	STS-75	22/02/96 -

M. Cheli (I) U. Guidoni (I)		System-1 Reflight USMP-3		09/03/96
J.-J. Favier (F)	CNES	Spacelab LMS-1	STS-78	20/06/96 - 07/07/96
C. André-Deshays (F)	CNES	Cassiopée	Soyuz TM 24 MIR Soyuz TM 23	17/08/96 - 02/09/96
R. Ewald (D)	DARA/DLR	MIR'97	Soyuz TM 25 MIR Soyuz TM 24	10/02/97 - 02/03/97
J.-F. Clervoy (F)	ESA	6th Shuttle flight to MIR	STS-84	15/05/97 - 24/05/97
J.-L. Chrétien (F)	CNES	7th Shuttle flight to MIR	STS-86	25/09/97 - 06/10/97
L. Eyharts (F)	CNES	Pégase	Soyuz TM 27 MIR Soyuz TM 26	29/01/98 - 19/02/98
P. Duque (E)	ESA	SpaceHab	STS-95	29/10/98 - 07/11/98
J.-P. Haigneré (F)	CNES, ESA	Perseus	Soyuz TM 29 MIR	20/02/99 - 28/08/99
M. Tognini (F)	CNES	Chandra X-Ray Observatory	STS-93	22/07/99 - 27/07/99
C. Nicollier (CH) J.-F. Clervoy (F)	ESA	Hubble Space Telescope 3rd Servicing Mission	STS-103	19/12/99 - 27/12/99
G. Thiele (D)	DLR, ESA	Shuttle Radar Topography Mission	STS-99	11/02/00 - 22/02/00
U. Guidoni (I)	ESA	9th ISS flight (6A) Raffaello MPLM	STS-100/ISS	19/04/01 - 01/05/01
C. Haigneré (F)	ESA, CNES	Andromède	Soyuz/ISS	21/10/01 - 31/10/01
R. Vittori (I)	ESA, ASI	Marco Polo	Soyuz/ISS	25/04/02 - 05/05/02
Perrin (F)	NASA/ESA	ISS assembly flight UF-2	STS-111/ISS	05/06/02 - 19/06/02
F. De Winne (B)	ESA	Odissea	Soyuz/ISS	30/10/02 -

				10/11/02
P. Duque (E)	ESA	Cervantes	Soyuz/ISS	18/10/03 - 28/10/03
A. Kuipers (NL)	ESA	DELTA Mission	8S/ISS	19/04/04 - 30/04/04
R. Vittori (I)	ESA	ENEIDE	10S/ISS	15/04/05 - 25/04/05

Mission assignments

Name	Participating organisation	Mission / payload	Space vehicle(s)	Date
T. Reiter (D)	NASA/ESA	Astrolab/ ISS crew	STS-121/ISS	July 2006
C. Fuglesang (S)	NASA/ESA	ISS assembly flight and crew exchange	STS-116/ISS	TBD

EUROPEAN ASTRONAUTS IN NEW FUNCTIONS

Maurizio Cheli

Maurizio Cheli, a former Lieutenant Colonel in the Italian Air Force, was selected in 1992 by the European Space Agency as an astronaut and started the Mission Specialist Training at Houston/Texas in August 1992. From 22 February 1996 until 9 March 1996 he flew on Shuttle Mission STS-75 together with the European astronaut Claude Nicollier and the Italian astronaut Umberto Guidoni.

The principle payloads on STS-75 were the reflight of the Tethered Satellite System (TSS) and the third flight of the United States Microgravity Payload (USMP-3). The TSS experiment produced a wealth of new information on the electrodynamics of tethers and plasma physics and before it broke at 19.7 km, just short of the 20.7 km goal distance from the Shuttle orbiter, it successfully demonstrated the ability of tethers to produce electricity. Maurizio Cheli left the Agency on 30 June 1996.

Dirk Frimout

Dirk Frimout, former ESA staff member at ESTEC, was proposed by the Investigator Working Group for the Shuttle STS-45 (Atlantis) mission as payload specialist. The STS-45 mission marked the first flight of the Atmospheric Laboratory for Applications and Science-1 (ATLAS-1), mounted on non-deployable Spacelab pallets in the orbiter cargo bay. The United States, France, Germany, Belgium, United Kingdom, Switzerland, the Netherlands and Japan provided 12 instruments designed to perform 14 investigations in four fields: atmospheric science instruments/investigations, solar science, space plasma physics and ultraviolet astronomy. EAC participated in the mission and supported Dirk Frimout who flew as Belgian payload specialist on the ATLAS-1 mission from 24 March 1992 until 2 April 1992.

Umberto Guidoni

From 22 February – 9 March 1996, Umberto Guidoni flew as a Payload Specialist on the 16-day STS-75 mission. In April 2001, Umberto Guidoni participated in the Space Shuttle's STS-100 mission, during which he became the first European on board the International Space Station. In July 2004 Guidoni left the European Astronaut Corps to become a Member of the European Parliament.

Claudie Haigneré

Claudie Haigneré is a rheumatologist with a doctorate in science, majoring neurosciences.

In 1985, the French Space Agency, CNES, selected her as an astronaut. In August 1996, she participated in the French-Russian Cassiopée mission to the Mir station. She took up training as back-up for Jean-Pierre Haigneré on the French-Russian Perseus mission in May 1998, and in July 1999 she became the first woman to qualify as a Soyuz Return Commander. In November 1999, Claudie Haigneré joined the Astronaut Corps of the European Space Agency ESA. From 21-31 October 2001, Claudie Haigneré participated in a "taxi flight" to the International Space Station as Soyuz Flight Engineer.

In June 2002, Claudie Haigneré was appointed to the post of Minister for Research and New Technologies by the French Prime Minister.

Jean-Pierre Haigneré

Jean-Pierre Haigneré started his astronaut career when he was selected to be a CNES astronaut in 1985. Before that he served as Chief Test Pilot at the French Bretigny-sur-Orge Flight Test Centre. His first spaceflight was to the Russian Mir Space Station during the 21-day French Altaïr mission in 1993. In June 1998 Jean Pierre Haigneré joined ESA's European Astronaut Corps.

His second spaceflight took him as an ESA astronaut on a long-duration flight on board the Mir space station during the French-sponsored Perseus mission from 20 February to 28 August 1999 (189 days).

Haignere left the corps in November 1999 after his second flight to become Head of the Astronaut Division.

Jean-Pierre Haigneré is currently senior advisor to the ESA Director of Launchers, in charge of studying all aspects for a Soyuz human spaceflight programme from Europe's spaceport in French Guiana.

Ulf Merbold

Ulf Merbold was the first ESA astronaut to fly in space and the first non-American to fly on the Space Shuttle. He became an ESA astronaut in 1978 and was assigned to fly on the first Spacelab mission STS-9 (FSLP) on board Columbia, from 28 November to 8 December 1983. During his second flight he flew as Payload Specialist on Space Shuttle Discovery, STS-42 (IML-1) between 22-31 January 1992. His third spaceflight, Euromir'94, took him on a 32-day mission to the Russian Space Station Mir from 3 October to 4 November 1994, making him the first ESA astronaut to fly to the Mir space station. From the end of 1999 until 2004, Ulf Merbold was responsible for the Utilization Promotion Management in the Microgravity Promotion Division of the ESA Directorate of Manned Spaceflight and Microgravity, at ESTEC, Noordwijk, the Netherlands.

Ernst Messerschmid

Ernst Messerschmid flew the German Spacelab Mission D1 on board of Challenger (STS-61A) between 30 October - 6 November 1985. In 1986 he became Professor of the University of Stuttgart and Director of the Space Systems Institute. From 1989 to 1993 he became Deputy and Dean of the Aerospace Faculty, then Vice President for Research and Technology. From 2000 to 2004 he was Head of the European Astronaut Centre, in Cologne, Germany.

Wubbo Ockels

Wubbo Ockels was selected by the European Space Agency to be in the first group of three ESA astronauts to be trained for the Spacelab-1 mission. During the mission he served as ground-communicator and liaison-scientist for the crew on board STS-9 (1st Spacelab mission). Wubbo

Ockels flew as payload specialist during STS-61-A (STS-22), on board Challenger (Spacelab D-1) from 30 October to 6 November 1985.

From 1986, Wubbo Ockels was stationed at ESA's research and technology centre, ESTEC, in Noordwijk, the Netherlands, where he supported activities for future human spaceflights. He became Head of ESA's Education and Outreach Office. During this time he also held a part-time professorship in Aerospace at the Delft University of Technology.

From September 2003, in close coordination with ESA, Wubbo Ockels became full-time professor of Aerospace for Sustainable Engineering and Technology at the Delft University of Technology, the Netherlands.

Philippe Perrin

Philippe Perrin served as a mission specialist (MS1) on STS-111 (June 5-19, 2002) onboard Space Shuttle Endeavour. The STS-111 mission delivered a new ISS resident crew and a Canadian-built mobile base for the orbiting outpost's robotic arm.

In May 2004, he became Experimental Test Pilot with Airbus Industrie in Toulouse.

Gerhard Thiele

From 11-22 February 2000, Thiele participated as mission specialist in the STS-99 Mission. The Shuttle Radar Topography Mission (SRTM) was dedicated to the first, three-dimensional, digital mapping of the Earth surface on a nearly global scale.

In August 2005, Gerhard Thiele was assigned as the Head of the Astronaut Division of the European Astronaut Centre (EAC).

Michel Tognini

Between May 2003 – December 2004, Tognini was Head of the Astronaut Division at the European Astronaut Centre (EAC), in Cologne, Germany. Since January 2005, Tognini is Head of the European Astronaut Centre.

TRAINING PROGRAMME

The objective of the Station training programme is to provide astronauts and ground personnel with the appropriate knowledge, skills and attitude required for Station operations, safety and mission success.

The training programme sequence is based on three training phases with specific objectives, characteristics, contents and certification:

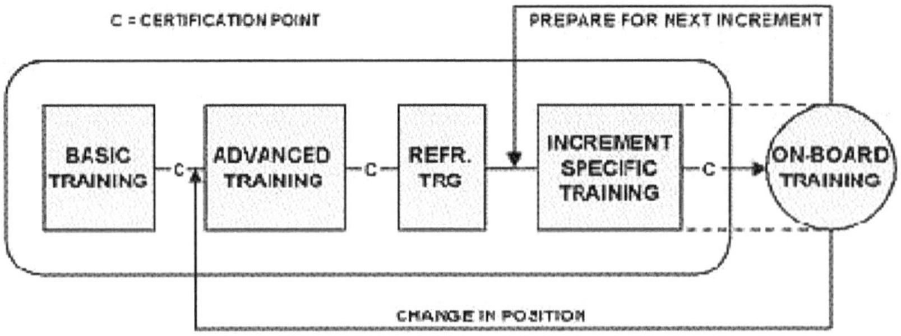

Basic training

Basic training provides candidate astronauts with basic knowledge on space technology and science, basic medical skills and basic skills related to their future operational tasks, including those related to the Station systems and operations. It also includes training for special capabilities, e.g. scuba diving.

This training phase is a candidacy period and upon completion, successful candidates are certified as being career astronauts. Basic training has a duration of up to one year and follows the basic training core curriculum.

Advanced training

Advanced training provides Station astronauts with the knowledge and skills related to the operation of the Station space elements, payloads, transport vehicles and related interaction with the ground. It builds upon the basic training and is still independent of a specific increment. Upon successful completion of advanced training an astronaut is eligible for assignment to a mission. The duration of advanced training is approximately one year.

Increment specific training

Increment specific training provides a Station international crew (and a backup crew if applicable), assigned to an increment, the knowledge and skills required to perform the onboard tasks for this increment. To enable good crew integration, the crew is trained together as far as possible. The duration of increment specific training is approximately one and a half years.

Increment specific training is comprised of the following:

- Job oriented training: mainly in the L-18 to L-12 month timeframe, however it may occur up to launch.

- Partner element training: mainly in the L-12 to L-3 timeframe, uses team-oriented training involving tasks and systems knowledge, and concentrating on multiple crew member training on multiple jobs.

- Multi-segment training: in the last six months of training the crew participates in multi-segment training (MST) putting together payload and systems operations for the entire Station. The crew works as a team, sometimes with ground controllers via integrated simulations.

- On-board training: This is considered to be part of increment specific training and is used by the crews to retain proficiency in skills and knowledge gained in ground training. On-board trining (OBT) will limit the need for extensive training on all aspects of a particular job and make the training period shorter and more effective, e.g. specific maintenance actions. In general the training will cover medical, core drills and servicing, and robot operations specific skills. OBT may require special on-board simulators.

  Each astronaut receives basic and advanced training once and specific courses as refresher training as required.

The limited time available for training, extended periods between training on specific systems and payloads, and actual on-board operations due to the distributed training system will require on-board training in particular as refresher training.

TRAINING DEVELOPMENT

The Instructional Development Process

The development of astronaut training follows the Instructional Development Process (IDP), a system used to plan, design, develop and evaluate training. It is a system-engineering approach to training development which is systematic, objective-oriented and incorporates validation and feedback. The information in the following pages is based on the NASA Instructional Development Process.

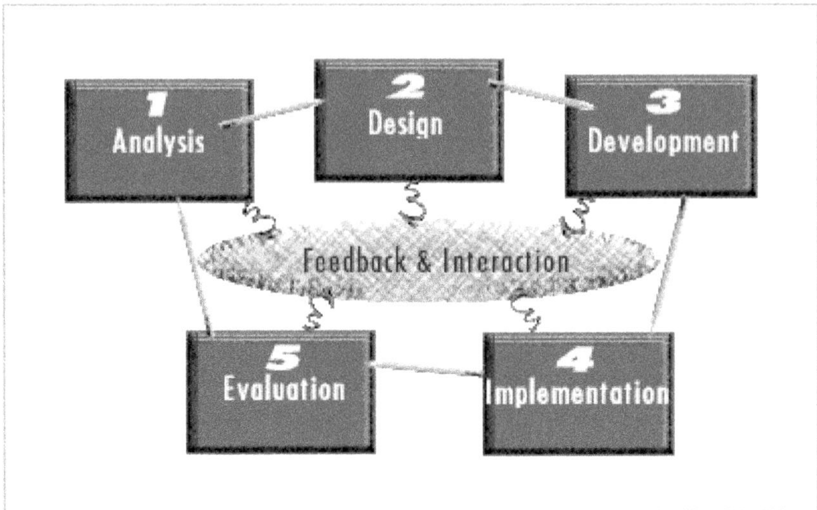

Training Development

	Phase	Tasks	Tools
1	**Training Analysis**	- Identification of tasks that need to be performed and of skills, knowledge and attitudes (SKAs) associated with each task - Identification of knowledge, skills and attitudes already possessed by the learner -Training Requirements Ready	Curriculum Development Assistant - ATD Training Document Templates Training Library - ATD
2	**Training Design**	- Development of training objectives from the training requirements - Definition of evaluation techniques - Grouping of objectives into courses, blocks and lessons - Definition of lesson flows - Selection of instructional methods and media - Development of training curricula (training catalogues) - Flight element curriculum broken down into courses, blocks and lessons	Curriculum Development Assistant - ATD Catalogue editor/browser - ATD Training Document Templates Training Library - ATD

3	**Training Development**	- Development of lesson plans - Validation of training objectives and media selection - Development of courseware - Training readiness reviews - Lesson plans and courseware ready and validated	Catalogue editor/browser - ATD Lesson Development Support Tool - ATD Training Document Templates CBT and WBT templates Training Library - ATD Review Item Discrepancy System (RID)
4	**Training Implementation**	- Planning and conduct of training activities - Generation of training reports - Record keeping (student records) - Maintenance of courseware and facilities - Training conducted and training material distributed	Catalogue browser - ATD Training Library - ATD Session Editor/Manager - ATD Timeline Manager - ATD Training Reports Editor/Browser - ATD Review Item Discrepancy System (RID)
5	**Training Evaluation**	- Analysis of student feedback - Assesment of student knowledge, skills and attitudes - Feedback on training effectiveness and change/update requirements	Training Reports Editor/Browser - ATD

TRAINING FACILITIES

The ESA training facilities provide training opportunities for Station astronauts for all ESA systems, subsystems and payloads for nominal, off-nominal, repair and maintenance operations in stand-alone, combined and integrated training. The training facilities must support Station-system interface training and stand-alone, integrated and joint-integrated operations simulations.

Training in Europe is based primarily at the European Astronaut Centre (EAC) with support from the Control Centres and various industrial sites and user centres in Europe. The training facilities described below are located in Europe unless specifically stated.

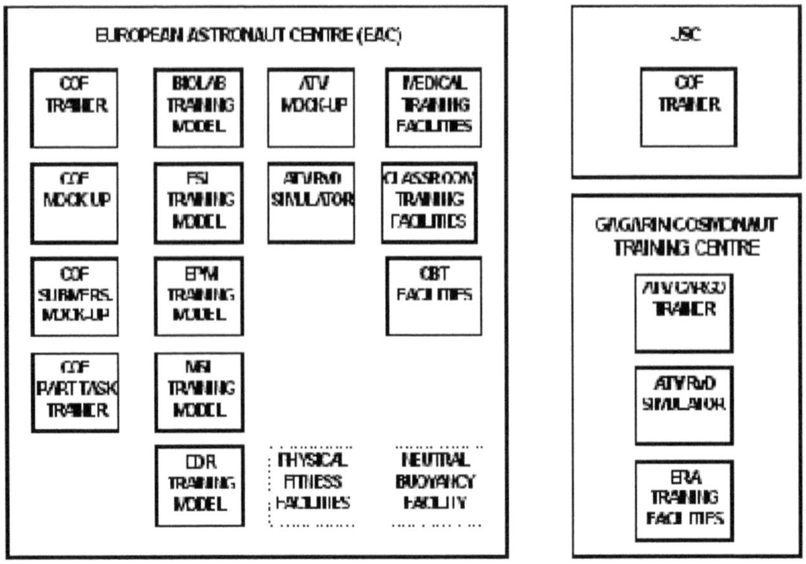

RELATED ORGANIZATIONS

EUROPEAN SPACE RESEARCH AND TECHNOLOGY CENTRE (ESTEC)

The European Space Agency (ESA) and its 17 Member States work together to pursue a wide range of ambitious and exciting goals in space. Together, they create fascinating projects that would not be feasible for the individual Member States. These projects generate new scientific knowledge and new practical applications in space exploration, and contribute to a vigorous European aerospace industry

ESA has sites in several European countries. The European Space Research and Technology Centre (ESTEC), the largest site and the technical heart of ESA—the incubator of the European space effort—is in Noordwijk, in the Netherlands. Most ESA projects are born here, and this is where they are guided through the various phases of development. More than 2000 specialists work here on dozens of space projects.

Except for launchers, nearly all ESA projects are managed from ESTEC. In Noordwijk, people work on science missions, on human spaceflight, telecom, satellite navigation, and Earth observation. ESTEC also houses a large pool of people with highly specialised technical knowledge, who are assigned to space projects when their expertise is needed for missions. If you want to know more about ESTEC, please have a look at the ESTEC Tour!

Contact information
ESTEC is located in Noordwijk, The Netherlands. Our postal address is:

European Space Research & Technology Centre
Keplerlaan 1
Postbus 299
2200 AG Noordwijk (The Netherlands)

If you want to get in touch with ESTEC via ESA, please send your question to contact@esa.int

Telephone:

General number	+31 (0)71 565 6565
Communications Office	+31 (0)71 565 3006
Hotel desk	+31 (0)71 565 5858
Travel desk	+31 (0)71 565 8030
Conference bureau	+31 (0)71 565 5056

EUROPEAN SPACE OPERATION CENTER

Address:

ESA/ESOC
Robert-Bosch-Str. 5
64293 Darmstadt
Germany

ESOC switchboard:
+49 6151 90 0

Public Relations:
+49 6151 90 2516

Personnel:
+49 6151 90 2394

External Services:
+49 6151 90 2502

ESOC Travel Office:
Tel: +49 6151 90 2885
Fax: +49 6151 90 495

Critical mission phases

As soon as the first data is acquired, the complex operations of the Launch and Early Orbit Phase (LEOP) begin. LEOP includes the solar array deployment, which consists of the transfer of the spacecraft to its final orbit and the gradual switch-on of the payload. Once the proper functions of the satellite are confirmed, staff at ESOC monitor the routine operations of the craft to ensure that the spacecraft conveys its products and meets mission objectives.

Since its creation in 1967, the European Space Operations Centre (ESOC) has planned missions, operated more than 50 satellites and ensured that spacecraft meet their mission objectives. The mandate of ESOC is to conduct mission operations for ESA satellites and to establish, operate and maintain the necessary ground segment infrastructure.

Detailed mission preparations

ESOC's involvement in a new mission normally begins with the analysis of possible operational orbits or trajectories and the calculation of the corresponding launch windows—selected to make sure that the conditions encountered in this early phase remain within the spacecraft capabilities. The selection of the operational orbit is a complex task with many trade-offs involving the scientific objectives of the mission, the launch vehicle, the spacecraft and the ground stations. Once the final orbit has been selected, the ground stations, which are used to communicate with the satellite, are selected according to the mission phase and what has to be done.

The variety of orbits and conditions require that ESOC engineers and maintains a versatile global network of ground stations in correlation with the supporting communication systems, known as the Ground Stations Segment. Very often missions have special requirements, which cannot be covered by the Ground Segment services; thus, significant integration and development of operating stations provide a smooth environment for operating spacecraft. Thanks to this versatile network of ground stations, ESOC is capable of supporting almost any type of mission, from Low-Earth Orbit to interplanetary.

Worldwide network of ground stations

Over the past few years, ESOC's mandate has evolved to allow the extension of availability of operational infrastructure and expertise to the general competitive industry. The term operational infrastructure includes ESOC ground segment elements and related facilities, which are established for use during several projects. The infrastructure consists of laboratories, environmental test facilities, ground stations, operational control centres, communication networks, information systems, information technology infrastructure as well as buildings and associated facilities.

Working with Industry

ESOC, and ESA in general, works closely with European industry to advance the state of European technology in the areas of spacecraft operation and communications. This is done by placing research and development contracts and studies, and by transferring the knowledge and experience during the execution of these contracts. ESOC has a substantial base of strategic assets and depth of expertise that have benefited many of its international partners.

ESRIN - THE ESA CENTRE FOR EARTH OBSERVATION

ESRIN, known as the ESA Centre for Earth Observation, is one of the five ESA specialised centres situated in Europe. Located in Frascati, a small town 20 km south of Rome in Italy, ESRIN was established in 1966 and first began acquiring data from environmental satellites in the 1970s.

Earth observation

Earth Observation data has grown in importance as more and more international and national agencies recognise the many uses to which it can be put. Satellites for Earth observation keep a constant watch over the Earth and the data they provide help to safeguard the planet in which we live.

Since 2004, ESRIN has been the headquarters for ESA's Earth Observation activities. Dr Liebig, the Head of ESRIN, is also the Director of Earth Observation.

A multi-faceted centre

A number of other activities are also carried out at ESRIN, each of which is making an important contribution to ESA's work.

- *Vega Programme:* the management team for Europe's new small-scale launcher
- *Information systems:* the design, development, provision and maintenance of the information systems and software used by the Agency
- *Telecom lab:* providing European industry and institutions with easier access to space telecom infrastructure
- *European Centre for Space Records:* appraising and preserving the valuable technical records of completed ESA projects
- *ESA Web Portal:* keeping the public informed about ESA's many activities

- *Virtual Reality Theatre:* visual presentations of complex Earth Observation and geographic data for both specialists and students

How ESRIN works

ESRIN acts as an interface between ESA and those who use its services. The centre has close links with European industry, the European Union and the civil protection, agriculture and environment ministries within ESA Member States. ESRIN also cooperates with international organisations including UN agencies and the European Commission, and plays an important role in many international projects. These include the Geosphere/Biosphere Programme, the Committee for Earth Observation Systems and the International Charter on Space and Major Disasters.

In all its activities ESRIN pursues ESA's objective of increasing interaction with users in order to develop new products and services, and support the competitiveness of the European space industry. ESRIN is helping to bring about a fertile mix between the two worlds of science and space applications for the benefit of all Europeans.

EUROPEAN ASTRONAUT CENTRE

For enquiries about the European Astronaut Centre and its activities, contact EAC Public Relations: Jean.Coisne@esa.int

If you want to organise a conference or interview an astronaut please fill in our request form which can be found at http://www.eac.esa.int/paros/external/prf.htm

Address

ESA/EAC, Linder Hoehe, 51147 Cologne, GERMANY

The European Astronaut Centre of the European Space Agency is situated in Cologne, Germany. It was established in 1990 as a result of Europe's commitment to human space programmes and is the home base of the 13 European astronauts who are members of the European Astronaut Corps.

The role of the EAC is to prepare and implement astronaut training programmes for a variety of missions, including those for the International Space Station. It also coordinates astronaut training between ESA and its International Space Station Programme partners.

EAC is responsible for the preparation, planning and scheduling of the European astronauts' tasks and flight assignments as well as coordinating astronaut activities with other countries. The EAC provides support ranging from public relations assistance to medical monitoring. This support, which includes support to the families of astronauts both at home or abroad, is especially important during extended stays by astronauts on space flight missions and at ESA's partner training centres.

Finally, EAC supports ESA's astronaut candidate selections.

AC - Organisation and structure

The European Astronaut Centre is organised into four groups: the Astronaut Division, the Astronaut Training Division, the Medical Crew Support Office, and Management and Support.

The personnel of the European Astronaut Centre is composed of:

- the astronauts constituting the European Astronaut Corps

- ESA staff covering functions which are either closely related to the astronauts or to the functioning of EAC as an ESA centre
- experts of other organisations who have proven experience in astronaut matters

The EAC - Mission participation and support

With its foundation in 1990, the EAC formed the home base for three astronauts. They had originally been selected for the First Spacelab Mission, in which the German astronaut Ulf Merbold participated in 1983. The Dutch astronaut Wubbo Ockels flew with Spacelab D1 in 1985 and Claude Nicollier - of Swiss nationality - was at the time in training at NASA.

Since then, the list of missions flown by European astronauts, most of them supported by the EAC, has lengthened substantially.

The participation of EAC staff in these missions has resulted in the accumulation of substantial human, technical, operational and scientific expertise in manned space flight activities. The EAC provides not only substantial parts of the training and operational support during missions, but also medical support to the astronauts and their families at their duty stations in the USA and Russia.

Today an impressive number of 38 space missions have been performed by 31 astronauts from ESA and its Member States, providing the EAC with much accumulated experience on manned space activities.

GROUND STATIONS

Ground stations provide the link between the satellite in orbit and the operations control centre on the ground. ESOC has established a network of ground stations around the world to support ESA missions, and those of industrial customers. This network of ESA tracking stations is known as the ESTRACK network.

Cebreros (Spain)

ESA's newest deep space tracking station is located in Cebreros, Spain, and was inaugurated in September 2005. The station features a new, highly accurate pointing control system and a 35-metre antenna with transmission and reception in X-band and reception in Ka-band, significantly boosting ESA's deep-space communication capability. Cebreros will provide daily support to Venus Express for routine operations, back-up support to Mars Express and Rosetta and, in the future, will support Herschel/Planck, Lisa-Pathfinder, Gaia and BepiColombo.

New Norcia (Australia)
Engineers designed the New Norcia ground station for deep-space satellite missions. It provides support to missions such as Rosetta, Mars Express, and Venus Express. These satellites reach areas in space far beyond those of other ESA satellites that have been controlled from the existing ESTRACK network.

Maspalomas (Spain)
The Maspalomas S-band and X-band ground station is located in the southern part of the Canary Island, at Montaña Blanca, municipal district of San Bartolomé de Tirajana. The site is about 1.6 kilometres from the main road which goes from Las Palmas city to Mogán and 1750 metres from the coast. The station is operated by INTA, and is used for the Japanese ETS7 satellite, and also general support for satellites' LEOPs.

Perth (Australia)

The Perth S-band and X-band station is located about 20 kilometres north of the city of Perth, on the western coast of Australia. The station is situated in the Perth International Telecommunications Centre complex, which is operated by Xantic. Engineers will use the Perth station for the XMM-Newton mission during its routine phase, and for other satellite's LEOPs.

Kourou (French Guiana)
The Kourou Diane S-band and X-band station, also known as KOUROU 93, is located on a site about 27 kilometres from the town of Kourou, and 90 kilometres from Cayenne, the capital of French Guiana, in the north-east of South America. The station site is 19 kilometres from the Centre Spatiale Guyanais (CSG). The Kourou station will be used for the XMM-Newton mission during its routine phase, and for other satellites' Launch and Early Orbit Phases (LEOP).

Kiruna (Sweden)
The Kiruna S-band and X-band station primarily supports the European Remote Sensing satellites, Envisat and ERS-2. It is equipped for tracking, telemetry, and command operations as well as for reception, recording, processing, and dissemination of data from the sensor instruments on board the two satellites.

Redu (Belgium)
The Redu site, which hosts multiple ground terminals, is located in the Ardennes region of Belgium, about 1 km from the village of Redu which is in the Belgian province of Luxembourg. The terminals provide tracking capabilities in VHF, C-band, L-band, S-band, Ku-band and Ka-band, and provide in-orbit tests (IOT) of telecommunication satellites. The S-band station is presently used for Integral. The station reference point co-ordinates are 5.146231°E longitude, 50.002685°N latitude. This reference point is 378.3 m above sea level. The geostationary visibility above 10° elevation, is between 54.9°W and 65.1°E.

Villafranca (Spain)
The Villafranca del Castillo site, which hosts multiple ground stations, is located about 31 kilometres west of Madrid, Spain. The stations are flexible and can be configured to support missions of different nature and operating in a very wide range of frequencies. The S-band station VIL-1 is mainly used to support the ESA Science mission, Cluster. The S-band station VIL-2, provides satellites' LEOPs, as well as support to missions like XMM-Newton, Cluster, Envisat and Integral.

ESOC has procured a transportable S-band ground station, for deployment by road, sea, or rail to locations anywhere in the world under a wide range of climatic conditions. The station is designed to support S-band spacecraft operations (tracking, telemetry, and command) for spacecraft in LEOP or near-Earth orbit. The station is presently located on the Villafranca site, and is used as backup station for missions such as ERS-2, Envisat and MSG1.

Cooperative ESTRACK stations

In addition to the ESA owned stations, ESOC has cooperative agreements with other organisations for the use of ground station services, including the installation of ESA equipment on them if necessary. The most important ones are:

- Malindi (MAL), located in Kenya, used in cooperation with the University of Rome (Italy)
- Santiago (AGO), located in Chili, used in cooperation with Centre for Space Studies of the University of Chili
- Svalbard (SVA), located in Norway, used in cooperation with Konsberg Spacetec

The ground station system provides the link between the satellite in orbit and the Operations Control Centre (OCC) on the ground. ESOC has established a network of ground stations around the world, which is called ESTRACK. The stations include:

Kiruna, Sweden

ESA Satellite Station
P.O. Box 815
SE-981 28 Kiruna
Sweden

Telephone: +46 980 760 00
Fax: +46 980 171 21

Kourou, French Guiana

ESA Station Diane
Boite Postal No. 27
97311 Kourou Cedex
Guyane Francaise

Telephone: +594 33 6338
Fax: +594 33 6336

New Norcia, Australia
Xantic BV
Perth International Telecommunications Centre
P.O. Box 1115
Wangara
W.A. 6065
Australia

Telephone: +61 9 3022000
Fax: +61 9 3432671

Perth, Australia
Xantic BV
Perth International Telecommunications Centre
P.O. Box 1115
Wangara
W.A. 6065
Australia

Telephone: +61 9 3022000
Fax: +61 9 3432671

Redu, Belgium
Agence Spatiale Europeenne
Station de Redu
B-6890 Redu
Belgium

Telephone: +32 61229 511
Fax: +32 61229 544

Villafranca, Spain
European Space Agency
Villafranca del Castillo Satellite Tracking Station
P.O. Box 50727
E-28080 Madrid
Spain

Cebreros, Spain
European Space Agency (ESA)/Agencia Europea del Espacio
Cebreros Satellite Tracking Station
P.O. Box - Apartado 50727
E- 28080 MADRID (Spain)

Cebreros Satellite Tracking Station
Road/Carretera AV-562 , Km 10
E-05260 CEBREROS (Avila, Spain)

Tel: +34 91 896 38 00
Fax: +34 91 896 38 13

Ma
lindi, Kenya

Operated in cooperation with the University of Rome (Italy)

Maspalomas, Spain
In cooperation with INTA

INTA Estacion Espacial de Maspalomas
Apartado 29
35100 Maspalomas
Gran Canaria
Canary Islands, Spain

Telephone: +34 928 727100
Fax: +34 928 727124

ESOC: FOCAL POINT FOR ESA SPACE DEBRIS ACTIVITIES

Since the launch of Sputnik on 4 October 1957, more than 4,200 launches have placed some 5500 satellites into orbit. Currently about 700 satellites are used operationally for science and other applications. Space debris comprise the ever-increasing amount of inactive space hardware in orbit around the Earth as well as fragments of spacecraft that have broken up, exploded or otherwise become abandoned.

The debris field comprises burnt-out launch vehicle upper stages, dead or inactive spacecraft and other objects ranging in size from as big as an automobile to microscopic dust. To avoid damage to operational satellites, ESA uses the DISCOS database to track all space debris.

In 1986, the Director General of ESA created a Space Debris Working Group with the mandate to assess the various issues of space debris. The findings and conclusions are contained in ESA's Report on Space Debris, issued in 1988.

In 1989, the ESA Council passed a resolution on space debris where the Agency's objectives were formulated as:

- minimise the creation of space debris
- reduce the risk for manned space flight
- reduce the risk on ground due to reentry of space objects
- reduce the risk for geostationary satellites
- examine the legal aspects of space debris
- acquire, through own facilities and in cooperation with other space agencies, the data on space debris necessary to assess the extent of the problem and its consequences

The Inter-Agency Space Debris Coordination Committee

Te Inter-Agency Space Debris Coordination Committee (IADC) is one of the world's leading technical organisations with space debris is. ESA is a founding member of IADC, together with NASA, the Russian Aviation and Space Agency, ROSA VIAKOSMOS, and Japan. Subsequent members include ASI (Italy), BNSC (UK), CNES (France), the Chinese National Space Administration (CNSA), DLR (Germany), ISRO (India) and the National Space Agency of the Ukraine (NSAU).
IADC's primary purpose is to exchange information on space debris research activities, to facilitate opportunities for cooperation in space debris research, to review the progress of ongoing cooperative activities and to identify debris mitigation options.
The IADC comprises a Steering Group and four spezialized Working Groups:

- **WG 1 Measurements**
- **WG 2 Environment and database**
- **WG 3 Protection**
- **WG 4 Mitigation**

European Conference on Space Debris

ESA organizes workshops, tutorials and conferences on space debris. Foremost among these is the European Conference on Space Debris, held every four years. The next one is due in April 2005.

Summary

Space debris have been recognized as a potential problem. Even though the current space debris population may not represent an immediate and excessive danger, the risk of collision with debris is continuously growing. Now is the time to take action to preserve the commercially valuable space environment for future space users.

Current growth reduction measures will lead at best to a stabilization in the growth of the debris population. More efficient measures will be needed including selective deorbiting of spacecraft and rocket stages at completion of their mission.

External services

The framework of ESOC's third party activities is the 1998 Council Resolution authorising the Director General to offer ESA's Flight Operations spare capacity to commercial and institutional customers. Services offered by ESOC refer to the utilisation of Flight Operations facilities and/or personnel.

Their main objective is to add value in supporting and responding to requests from Industry, often in cooperation with National Space Agencies such as CNES, DLR or ASI. Although ESOC offers, in principle, spare capacity in providing these services, any additional facilities required for a particular service can be funded by the customer or procured via cooperative agreements.

EUROPEAN ASTRONAUT CORPS

The **European Astronaut Corps** is the group of astronauts of European Space Agency. There are currently eight active members of the Corps, all men. The European Astronaut Corps is based at the European Astronaut Centre in Cologne, Germany. They can be assigned to various projects both in Europe (at ESTEC, for instance) or elsewhere in the world, at NASA Johnson Space Center or Star City.

CURRENT MEMBERS

There are 15n astronauts in the corps.

1. Jean-François Clervoy
2. Samantha Cristoforetti
3. Pedro Duque
4. Frank De Winne
5. Léopold Eyharts
6. Christer Fuglesang
7. Alexander Gerst
8. André Kuipers
9. Andreas Mogensen
10. Paolo Nespoli
11. Luca Parmitano
12. Timothy Peake
13. Thomas Pesquet
14. Hans Schlegel
15. Roberto Vittori

Eight of the members of the corps have flown in space. All experienced members, except Jean-François Clervoy, have visited the ISS.

De Winne is the member of the Corps who has spent the most time in space, more than 198 days, the European record belonging to former German astronaut Thomas Reiter with 350 days.

The youngest member of the corps is Thomas Pesquet, born in 1978, while the oldest is Hans Schlegel, born in 1951. The Corps currently includes one woman. Only two women have previously been members of the corps. Marianne Merchez who never flew, and Claudie Haigneré who resigned after two flights to start a political career in France. The only minority participation is that Léopold Eyharts belongs to the Basque ethnic group in France.

SELECTION OF NEW ASTRONAUTS

According to French weekly *Air & Cosmos*, only six astronauts (Fuglesang, Schlegel, Nespoli, Eyharts, De Winne and Kuipers) remain available for immediate flight. Vittori and Clervoy are on temporary leave or assigned to other duties. The head of human spaceflight at ESA recommended that at least four more astronauts (plus four other in reserve) should be added after the launch of Columbus in February 2008.
On April 3, 2008, ESA director general Jean-Jacques Dordain announced that recruiting for a new class of European astronauts will start in the near future.. The selection program for 4 new astonauts was launched on May 19, 2008 with applications due by 16 June 2008 so that final selection would be due spring 2009. Almost 10 000 people registered as astronaut candidates 2008-06-18. 8413 fulfilled the initial application criteria. From these 918 were chosen to take part in the first stage of psychological testing which lead to 192 candidates in 2008-09-24. After two stage psychological tests 80 candidates will continue to medical evaluation in January/February 2009. 40 or so candidates will head to a formal interviews to select the four new members to European Astronaut Corps.

AFTER THE ISS

The funding by NASA of the International Space Station is scheduled to end in 2015. The role and activities of European astronauts beyond this date, and in particular their involvement in the Vision for Space Exploration, including missions to the Lunar outpost, is unclear.

NON ESA EUROPEAN ASTRONAUTS

WARSAW PACT COSMONAUTS

- Aleksandar Panayotov Aleksandrov
- Georgi Ivanov
- Mirosław Hermaszewski
- Sigmund Jähn
- Vladimír Remek
- Anatoly Solovyev
- Bertalan Farkas
- Dumitru Prunariu
    - Excluding Soviet cosmonauts from European Russia.

WESTERN EUROPE ASTRONAUTS

- Klaus-Dietrich Flade

- Reinhard Furrer
- Ernst Messerschmid
- Ulrich Walter
- Patrick Baudry
- Jean-Loup Chrétien
- Jean-Jacques Favier
- Franco Malerba
- Dirk Frimout
- Franz Viehböck
- Ivan Bella
- Helen Sharman

SHUTTLE MISSIONS

Astronauts from the European Astronaut Corps have participated to various missions before the ISS era, in particular in the frame of Spacelab, as Payload Specialists.

PAYLOAD SPECIALISTS

- Ulf Merbold - STS-9 / Spacelab, STS-42 / Spacelab
- Wubbo Ockels - STS-61-A / Spacelab

AS MISSION SPECIALISTS

- Claude Nicollier - STS-46, STS-61, STS-75, STS-103
- Maurizio Cheli - STS-75
- Jean-François Clervoy - STS-66, STS-84, STS-103
- Gerhard Thiele - STS-99
- Pedro Duque - STS-95

MISSIONS ON SPACE STATIONS

MIR VISITS

Astronauts from the European astronaut Corps have also flown to Mir both on board Soyuz vehicles or on board the Space Shuttle.

- Ulf Merbold - Euromir 94 - Soyuz TM-20 - 03.10. - 04.11.1994

- Thomas Reiter - Euromir 95 - Soyuz TM-22 - 03.09.1995 - 29.02.1996
- Jean-François Clervoy - STS-84

ISS VISITS

ESA astronauts to have visited the ISS are:

- Guidoni, ESA, 9th ISS flight (6A) MPLM Raffaello, STS-100/ISS
- Vittori, ASI Eneide, Soyuz/ISS
- Vittori, ASI Marco Polo, Soyuz/ISS
- Claudie Haigneré, CNES Andromède, Soyuz/ISS
- Perrin , NASA/CNES, ISS assembly flight UF-2, STS-111/ISS
- De Winne, ESA, Odissea, Soyuz/ISS
- Duque, ESA, Cervantes, Soyuz/ISS
- Kuipers, ESA, DELTA Mission, 8S/ISS
- Reiter, ESA Astrolab, ISS assembly flight ULF 1.1, STS-121/ISS, Expedition 13
- Fuglesang, ESA Celsius, ISS assembly flight 12A.1, STS-116/ISS
- Nespoli, ESA Esperia, ISS assembly flight 10A, STS-120/ISS
- Schlegel, ISS assembly flight 1E, STS-122/ISS
- Eyharts, STS-122/ISS, Expedition 16
- Fuglesang, ESA Alisse, ISS assembly flight 17A, STS-128
- De Winne, Expedition 20 and ISS Commander of Expedition 21

MISSIONS

CREW MEMBERS

- Roberto Vittori - STS-134
- Paolo Nespoli - Expedition 26 and Expedition 27
- Andre Kuipers - Expedition 30 and Expedition 31

BACK-UP CREW MEMBERS

- Paolo Nespoli - Expedition 24 and Expedition 25

THE EUROPEAN SPACE RESEARCH ORGANISATION (ESRO)

The **European Space Research Organisation (ESRO)** was an international organisation founded by 10 European nations with the intention of jointly pursuing scientific research in space. It was founded in 1964. As an organisation ESRO was based on a previously existing international scientific institution, CERN. The ESRO convention, the organisations founding document outlines it as an entity exclusively devoted to scientific pursuits. This was the case for most of its lifetime but in the final years before the formation of the European Space Agency (ESA), ESRO began a programme in the field of telecommunications. Consequently, ESA is not a mainly science focused entity but concentrates on telecommunications, earth observation and other application motivated activities. ESRO was merged with ELDO in 1975 to form the European Space Agency

THE FOUNDING OF ESRO

The origins of a joint European space effort are generally traced back to a number of initiatives taken in 1959 and 1960 by a small group of scientists and science administrators, catalysed by two friends, physicists and scientific statesmen, the Italian Edoardo Amaldi and the Frenchman Pierre Victor Auger. Neither Amaldi nor Auger was a stranger to the cause of scientific collaboration on a European scale. Indeed it was they who, in the early 1950s, were key actors in the process which led to the setting up of CERN, the European Organisation for Nuclear Research. Now, as the decade drew to a close, they turned their attention to space. Success was rapid. Within a year of the first formal discussions being held amongst scientists, European governments had set up a European Preparatory Commission for Space Research (COPERS) to explore the possibilities for a joint space research effort.

THE EUROPEAN PREPARATORY COMMISSION FOR SPACE RESEARCH

The COPERS held its first session in Paris on 13 and 14 March 1961. Its first task was to create the organs needed to define the scientific programme and the necessary infrastructure of the envisaged organisation, to draw up its budget, and to prepare a Convention for signature by those member state governments who wished to join it. To this end the meeting first elected its "bureau": chairman Harrie Massey, vice-chairmen, Luigi Broglio and Hendrik van de Hulst, and executive secretary Pierre Auger, all men who had played an important role in the debates in 1960 and, Auger apart, still active and eminent European space scientists. It then established two working groups. The first was the Interim Scientific and Technical Working Group (STWG). Its task was to prepare the scientific programme for the future space organisation, paying particular attention to the technical and financial implications of its proposals. Lamek Hulthén, from the Royal Institute of Technology in Stockholm, was nominated chairman of this group; Reimar Lüst from the Max-Planck-Institut für Physik und Astrophysik in Garching, near Munich was appointed its coordinating secretary. The second was the Legal, Administrative and Financial Working Group (LAFWG). Its chairman was initially left open, though it was recommended that he be someone from the German Federal Republic. Alexander Hocker, a senior bureaucrat from Bad-Godesberg who was the chairman of the CERN Finance Committee at the time, took on this task. All Member States were to be represented on both working groups, which were empowered to set up subgroups to facilitate their work.

THE BLUE BOOK

By the third meeting of COPERS on 24 and 25 October 1961 in Munich, the STWG had prepared a 77 page document outlining the future European Space Research Organisation. The so called Blue Book was divided into 5 parts, each devoted to one of the following subjects:

- a general outline of ESRO
- ESRO's scientific programme
- its technology centre

- data handling
- ranges and vehicles

The Blue Book foresaw the firing of some 435 sounding rockets and the successful development and launching of 17 satellites in the 8 years covered by the ESRO Convention, namely 11 small satellites, 4 space probes, and 2 large satellites. It was assumed that 2 launchings would be required to orbit one successful spacecraft, so the number of satellite and space probes launchings budgeted for was doubled. The total cost of the satellite programme was estimated at 733.5 MFF, of which 450 MFF was for launchers and launch operations and 283.5 MFF for spacecraft development.
It should be noted that the Blue Book was more a manifesto of interests and expectations than a concrete working hypothesis. It only reflected the intentions and hopes of important sectors of the European scientific community while ignoring their lack of capacity to fulfill these intentions. The fact that transforming the manifesto into a true operational programme would be a long and laborious process and the results sometimes disappointing.

ORGANISATION AND FUNCTIONING

THE *AUGER YEARS* (1964-67)

The ESRO Convention entered into force on 20 March 1964. The ten founding states were Belgium, Denmark, France, (Federal Republic of) Germany, Italy, Netherlands, Spain, Sweden, Switzerland and the United Kingdom. Two other countries which had participated in the early COPERS activities, Austria and Norway, decided not to join the new organisation but retained an observer status. The first meeting of the Council opened in Paris three days later with Harrie Massey in the Chair. Pierre Auger was appointed ESRO's first Director General.

THE LEGISLATIVE ARM

At the decision making level (the "Legislative" in the ESRO jargon), the supreme governing body was the Council, made of delegations from its Member States. Each member state had one vote in the Council, where it could be represented by not more than two delegates, one of whom was generally a scientist, the other an important national science administrator. One or more advisers were usually included national delegations. The main tasks of the Council were to determine the Organisation's scientific, technical and administrative policy; to approve its programme and annual work plans; and to determine its level of resources both annually, and every third year for the subsequent three-year period. The Council was advised by two subordinate bodies, the Administrative and Finance Committee (AFC) and the Scientific and Technical Committee (STC).

THE EXECUTIVE ARM

At the executive level, ESRO was managed by a Directorate based in Paris, including the Director General assisted by a Scientific Director, a Technical Director and a Head of Administration . The directors of ESRIN, ESDAC and ESLAB reported to the Scientific Director; the director of ESTEC, who had also responsibility for ESRANGE and ESTRACK, reported to the Technical Director. The "Executive", as it was eventually called, was responsible for the implementation of approved programmes within the established financial envelope and under general control from the Scientific and Technical Committee. It was also called to perform feasibility studies of space missions proposals coming from the scientific community and recommended by the STC, in view of their eventual adoption in the programme.

THE *BANNIER REPORT* AND ITS CONSEQUENCES

Only two years after the formation of ESRO, problems with its structure became painfully obvious. By mid-1966 it had climbed to 50%, placing enormous pressure on the operational programme.

For this reason the Council set up a group of experts led by J.H. Bannier to investigate and solve the problem. Bannier quickly relieved the pressure on the AFC by raising the limit below which the Executive could award contracts without having to seek committee approval. He further increased the role of the Executive by transferring certain competencies from the Legislative to the Directorate. But this was only a stop-gap measure.

Bannier realised that the entire structure of ESOC had to be changed. Firstly, they were emphatic that the executive function of the organisation should be clearly separated from the policy and the planning function. Secondly, as far as the scientific programme was concerned, they recommended that there be a clear institutional distinction drawn between spacecraft development and spacecraft operation after launch. To achieve these objectives, the Bannier group suggested that ESRO's top management structure be completely changed. The dichotomy between scientific and technical directorates was, in Bannier's view, wrong in principle for an organisation like ESRO. To overcome it, he suggested that the two posts be abolished. In its stead a new structure was proposed. It comprised the Director General (DG) plus four directors, two of whom were essentially responsible for policy-making and two for policy execution. A new post was to be created in the first category, a so-called Director of Programmes and Planning (DPP), whose task it would be to prepare draft programmes of the Organisation, based on the scientific, technical, financialand time implications of the different proposals. The second member of the directorate concerned with forward planning would be the Director of Administration (DA) whose task it would be to prepare policy on the future needs of personnel, finance and contracts, and to organise and implement the necessary procedures to maintain an a posteriori control over the Organisation's functioning. The two posts in the Directorate having executive authority would be filled by the director of ESTEC and of ESDAC, which was to be renamed ESOC, the European Space Operations Centre. As for ESRIN, the Bannier group judged its research to be marginal to the major activities of the Organisation. Its director, they felt, should not be a member of the directorate but should rather report directly to the DG.

EUROPEAN SPACE RESEARCH AND TECHNOLOGY CENTRE

The European Space Research and Technology Centre (ESTEC) was to be a facility at the very core of ESRO. Its responsibilities included the engineering and testing of satellites and their payloads, the integration of scientific instruments in these payloads, and making arrangements for their launch. In some cases member states were to produce the scientific instruments for ESRO or produce them as part of their own national effort and compensate ESTEC for its service. In practise, national organisations simply used ESTEC as a service organisation and left it to pay for their efforts from the ESRO budget. After the Bannier Report the facility gained overall executive authority for spacecraft development and was merged with ESLAB. The satellite control centre was also moved to ESOC. ESTEC was originally to be located in Delft (Holland) but because of unforeseen difficulties, Noordwijk was chosen instead.

ESLAB

The situation with ESRO's laboratory, ESLAB was similar. It lacked the staff to function as an independent organisation. But this wasn't surprising since the ESRO Convention describes ESLAB's role in the following manner:

> ...to undertake joint research programmes on the minimum scale deemed necessary by the Council [...] to complete or complement the scientific studies carried out in Member States.
>
> – ESRO Convention

This meant that ESLAB was little more than a venue for visiting scientists. ESLAB's role was later expanded. It acted as the interface between national scientific groups and ESTEC engineering groups as well as conducted its own research within the scope of the large astronomical satellite project. After the Bannier Report ESLAB was merged with ESTEC.

ESRANGE

In 1964 ESRANGE was established as an ESRO sounding rocket launching range located in Kiruna (Sweden). This location was chosen because it was important to carry out a sounding rocket programme in the auroral zone, and essential that ESRO equip itself with a suitable range in the northern latitudes. Access to Kiruna was good by air, road and rail, and the launching range was relatively close to the town of Kiruna. Finally and perhaps decisively, ESRANGE could be located near Kiruna Geophysical Observatory (subsequently renamed the Swedish Institute of Space Physics). In 1972 ownership and operations of the range was transferred to the Swedish Space Corporation.

ESTRACK AND ESDAC

Space science data handling has two aspects. Firstly, it requires the setting up of a network of tracking and telemetry stations which can receive signals from spacecraft (ESTRACK). This network comprised four stations situated in the following locations:

- Redu (Belgiam)
- Fairbanks (Alaska)
- Spitsbergen (Norway)
- Falkland Islands

Secondly, it requires a central facility which edits and processes the information from the tracking network. The facilities at the centre, initially labelled ESDAC (European Space Data Acquisition Centre), were essentially a large mainframe computer or computers, which wAS made available both to its in-house staff and to visiting scientists and fellows who wished to use them to analyse and study the recovered data. ESDAC was later renamed ESOC, the European Space Operations Centre. ESOC is located in Darmstadt (Germany). After the Bannier Report it gained overall executive authority for spacecraft operation. ESOC's director also became responsible for ESRANGE and for ESTRACK.

ESLAR

ESLAR, a laboratory for advanced research was created in 1966 mainly to break the political deadlock over the location of ESLAB. Later renamed ESRIN, and acronym for European Space Research Institute, ESLAR was based in Frascati (Italy). The ESRO Convention describes ESRINs' role in the following manner:

> ...to undertake laboratory and theoretical research in the basic physics and chemistry necessary to the understanding of past and the planning of future experiments in space.
>
> – ESRO Convention

The facility began acquiring data from environmental satellites in the 1970s.

ESRO HEADQUARTERS

ESRO headquarters was home to the Executive arm of ESRO. After the Bannier Report it became responsible for policy, planning and *a posteriori* control.

SCIENTIFIC ACTIVITIES

The ESRO convention outlined the organisation as one which would be solely devoted to space science. As a consequence, scientific work was the main area of ESROs early operations. As the organisation and its capabilities matured it shifted from a strictly scientific programme to one where applicational activities played a more dominant role.

SOUNDING ROCKETS

The fact that sounding rockets are relatively inexpensive, have a short lead time, provide a test bed for more ambitious project and have a low risk of failure made them an ideal first project for the newly formed European Space Research Organisation.
The first two ESRO sounding rockets were launches from the Salto di Quirra range in Sardinia on 6 and 8 July 1964. They released a payload of barium and ammonia into the ionosphere. The first launch from ESRANGE was made in November 1966. From this point onward the frequency of sounding rocket launches increased dramatically. The Norwegian base in Andøya was also used as a launch site.

The British Skylark (83) and French Centaure (64) were the main rockets utilised for the programme. The American Arcas (14), French Bélier (4) and Dragon (2), British Petrel (1) and German/Swiss Zenit (1) were also used. In total, the program oversaw the launch of 168 sounding rockets with an average success rate of 75%. During the course of the programme, the size and payload of the sounding rockets used by ESRO increased from 2.7 to 5.55 m (in length) and from 140 to 310 kg respectively.

About half of the 168 sounding rockets were dedicated to ionospheric and auroral studies, about a quarter to atmospheric physics and the rest to solar, stellar and gamma-ray studies. While the number of launched rockets was lower than foreseen, the project exceeded expectations due to higher than anticipated payload capacity and longer range of the rockets.

ORIGINAL SATELLITE PROGRAMME

The Blue Book foresaw the launching of 11 small satellites, 4 space probes, and 2 large satellites. These ambitions were never realized mainly due to financial troubles. The programme went through many revisions and in the end only a handful of projects produced concrete results. These were the two small, non-stabilised satellites ESRO I and ESRO II, launched in 1968 and renamed after launch Aurorae and Iris respectively; the two small highly eccentric orbit satellites HEOS-A and HEOS-A2, launched in 1968 and 1972 and then renamed HEOS-1 and HEOS-2; the medium size, stabilised satellite TD-1, launched in 1972; and the small satellite ESRO IV, also launched in 1972, which replaced the second satellite of the TD series (TD-2). All of these were multi-experiment satellites, i.e. the spacecraft carried a payload comprising several instruments provided by different research groups.

ESRO I AND ESRO II

These were small, non-stabilised spacecraft, carrying very simple experiments designed to measure the radiation environment around the spacecraft. They represented the direct satellite descendants of the experience gained with the sounding rocket experiments. ESRO I's origin in the sounding rocket programme was particularly obvious. It studied auroral phenomena and the polar ionosphere. ESRO II was dedicated to the fields of solar astronomy and cosmic rays. Sometimes the two satellites are also referred to as ESRO-1A or Aurora and ESRO-2B Iris respectively.

HEOS-A

Later renamed as HEOS-A, the first highly eccentric orbit satellite was designed to make measurements of plasma, magnetic field and cosmic ray particles. There were disagreements over the cost of this project. Since the existing ESTRACK grid had been designed with low orbit satellites in mind it would be insufficient for tracking and receiving data form a satellite in a highly eccentric (escape) orbit. A solution was found in the form of upgrading an ELDO facility in Australia and integrating it at a relatively low cost.

THE TD PROGRAMME

Named after the workhorse medium launch system used by ESRO at the time, the Thor Delta, the TD programme initially foresaw the launch of 3 satellites: TD-1, TD-2 and TD-3. TD-1 was devoted to stellar astronomy, TD-2 was to be devoted to solar astronomy while TD-3 was to study the ionosphere. Later TD-2 and 3 were merged to save funds. But subsequent financial difficulties and political disagreements led to the abandonment of the TD-2/TD-3 spacecraft. Later some of the experiments destined for launch aboard the TD-2/TD-3 ware flown on the ESRO IV satellite.

LAS

The Large Astronomical Satellite was to be an orbiting observatory with the mission of providing basic knowledge about celestial objects through the use of a high-resolution ultraviolet spectrometer. The project started in the late 1950s and was cancelled in 1968 because of the lack of financial support and political squabbles.

SECOND GENERATION SATELLITES

COS-B

COS-B was the first successful ESRO science satellite. The mission was first proposed by the scientific community in the mid 1960s, approved in 1969 and launched in 1975. It was shut off in 1982 after contributing a great deal of scientific data on cosmic gamma rays, which continues to be analised today. This was the first ESRO satellite which carried only one experiment.

GEOS

GEOS was a geostationary multi-experiment satellite dedicated to magnetospheric research. The instruments for this project were provided by multiple European institutions. When GEOS was launched in 1977, the launcher malfunctionned and the planned orbit was not achieved. A modified qualification model of the same payload was successfully launched in 1978 and remained in operation until 1982 when it was turned off.

THE FIRST PACKAGE DEAL

This was the name of a policy shift negotiated by ESRO members in 1971 which drastically reduced scientific funding in favor of application activities doubling the overall budget. This first lead to a change in the administrative structure and a 50% reduction of the scientific staff. Given the new budgetary environment, LPAC had to choose which two missions to fly among the five which had been planned thus far. It eventually chose HELOS, renamed Exosat, and the IMP-D, renamed ISEE-2, projects.

EXOSAT

Main article: EXOSAT

ISEE-2

This satellite was the second of 3 International Sun-Earth Explorer (ISEE) spacecraft. The project was a cooperative effort between NASA and ESRO (later ESA) designed to study the interaction between the Earth's magnetic field and the solar wind. The program used three spacecraft, a mother/daughter pair (ISEE-1 and ISEE-2) and a heliocentric spacecraft (ISEE-3, later renamed ICE). The instruments on board ISEE-2 were designed to measure electric and magnetic field properties.

THE SECOND PACKAGE DEAL

This new ESRO policy, negotiated in 1973, gave the organisation overall responsibility for the development of the European Ariane launcher. This task was entrusted to CNES. The second package deal enabled ESRO to enter into cooperation with NASA on the Spacelab project as well as manage the MAROTS maritime satellite navigation project. This agreement made funding easier and more flexible for the contributing nations which led to a doubling of the organisation's overall budget. ESRO also participated in the International Ultraviolet Explorer mission with NASA under these policy guidelines.

TELECOMMUNICATIONS SATELLITE PROGRAMME

The first step towards an telecommunications program within ESRO was made in the end of 1966 when the European Conference on Satellite Communications requested that the organisation examine the potential for a European telecom satellite project. Although studies were carried out at this early stage as well as during the subsequent 5 years the ESRO council would not approve research and development activities until 1971 when the first package deal took effect. The delay was due to ESROs rigid decision making structure and the unfavorable political situation which existed among ESRO members at the time. These problems were largely done away with as part of the 1971 policy change which, among other things, outlined a fully voluntary mechanism for application project financing. Under the first package deal ESRO pursued a project to establish a European satellite system by the early 1980s in partnership with the European Conference of Postal and Telecommunications Administrations and the European Broadcasting Union. ESRO merged with ELDO to form the European Space Agency in 1975 before the first satellite of the effort, the Orbital Test Satellite, would be successfully launched in 1978

EUROPEAN SPACE AGENCY PROGRAMS

AURORA EXPLORATION PROGRAM

AURORA'S ORIGINS

Aurora is part of Europe's strategy for space, endorsed by the European Union Council of Research and the ESA Council in 2001. This strategy calls for Europe to:

- explore the solar system and the Universe
- stimulate new technology
- inspire the young people of Europe to take a greater interest in science and technology

As a result of this challenge, in 2001 ESA set up the Aurora Programme. The primary objective of Aurora is to create, and then implement, a European long-term plan for the robotic and human exploration of the solar system, with Mars, the Moon and the asteroids as the most likely targets.

A second objective is to search for life beyond the Earth. Future missions under the programme will carry sophisticated exobiology payloads to investigate the possibility of life forms existing on other worlds within the solar system.
It is clear from these objectives that the interdependence of exploration and technology is the basis of the Aurora Programme. On the one hand the desire to explore provides the stimulus to develop new technology while on the other, it is the introduction of innovative technology that will make exploration possible.

EXPLORING SPACE

Curiosity about our world, and the Universe that surrounds us, has been the driving force behind human progress since prehistoric times. Today, the exploration of space remains one of the most stimulating and exciting areas of scientific research.

Many exciting and innovative ideas for future exploration have been proposed by industry and academia since the Aurora Programme began. In 2001 ESA received more than 300 replies when it asked the space community to put forward suggestions for future exploratory missions. This was followed in 2002 by another 'call for ideas' for the technology needed to make these missions possible. All proposals were accompanied by a preliminary time schedule and an assessment of feasibility and cost.
Suggestions received included an investigation of Pluto, the smallest and outermost planet in the solar system; establishing a launch site on the Moon; and the human exploration of Mars.
The Aurora Programme carefully assesses the feasibility - both technical and financial - of all the ideas received. European industry is then encouraged to develop the technology needed to bring these ideas to fruition.

ADVANCED TECHNOLOGY

Each phase of exploration on the way to the human exploration of Mars will require increasingly complex technology. In some cases existing technology can be further developed or adapted, but in many cases European industry will be asked to come up with new innovative technology to make future exploration missions possible.

The technological studies to be carried out under the Aurora Programme will enable Europe to select which of the many technologies on offer should be given priority for development within Europe, as well as the value of the technologies offered by possible partners. Among the technology needed to make a human mission to Mars possible are: aerobraking, precision navigation and landing, propulsion systems that offer cheaper, faster travel; and life-support systems to enable humans to live in hostile space environments.

INTERNATIONAL COOPERATION

Close cooperation within ESA, as well as collaboration with European and Canadian industry and academia, is a key aspect of Aurora.
Although Aurora is an ESA programme and will promote European industry, many missions will involve international cooperation. For instance Canada, which has a cooperation agreement with ESA, is already participating in the Aurora Progamme.
International cooperation is important because it reduces costs and allows the countries involved to gain from one another's expertise. The Aurora programme will ensure that ESA achieves the maximum benefits from joint enterprises with international partners.

STEP-BY-STEP APPROACH

Aurora's step-by-step approach means that missions will increase in complexity over time, culminating - if all goes well - in a human expedition to Mars by the year 2030. Steps on the way to Mars will probably include exploration of the Moon as well as:

- remote sensing of the Martian environment
- robotic exploration and surface analysis
- Mars sample return missions
- a robotic outpost

Not all these steps towards the ultimate goal of sending humans to Mars will necessarily be part of the Aurora Programme. As the result of international cooperation, various collaborating agencies will make a contribution to those missions that best meet their particular requirements and areas of expertise.

EXPLORATION PROGRAMME ADVISORY COMMITTEE

All ideas received are examined to assess their feasibility and to ensure that they are in line with Europe's space strategy. They are then sent to Aurora's Exploration Programme Advisory Committee (EPAC) for further discussion. This body includes European experts from technology and science as well as an ESA astronaut.

AURORA BOARD OF PARTICIPANTS

The Aurora Board of Participants (ABP) has the final decision on the choice of missions and technology. This Board is made up of representatives of all the ESA Member States that have joined the Aurora Programme, as well as Canada. At present it has 10 members.

INDUSTRY

Once an exploration mission and the associated technology have been approved, European and Canadian industry will be invited to tender for the work needed to bring the project to fruition. The Aurora Programme office will carefully follow each project at all stages to ensure that everything is proceeding to plan.
The ultimate challenge
ESA's Aurora Programme is one of the most exciting enterprises ever undertaken in Europe, an endeavour that will involve the best of European minds and industry.

THE GALILEO PROGRAMME

DIRECTORATE-GENERAL FOR ENERGY AND TRANSPORT

tren-galileo@cec.eu.int
European Commission
Directorate-General for Energy and Transport
Unit E.4
DM28, 1/68
B-1049 Brussels/Belgium

GALILEO JOINT UNDERTAKING

info@galileoju.com
GALILEO Joint Undertaking
Rue de Luxembourg 3
B-1000 Brussels/Belgium

Just like mobile telephony, the Galileo European satellite radionavigation programme will revolutionise many sectors of the economy - starting with transport. Initiated by the European Commission and the European Space Agency (ESA), this project is set to be the industrial and technological flagship of the joint space strategy by 2008.

WHAT IS RADIONAVIGATION?

Satellite radionavigation allows the possessor of a transmitter/receiver to determine and communicate his position very precisely in longitude, latitude and altitude at any moment, by picking up signals emitted by a number of satellites. This continuously available 'guardian angel' from space is revolutionising:

- air traffic control;
- the management of ship and lorry fleets;
- road and rail traffic monitoring;
- the mobilisation of emergency services;
- the tracking of goods carried by multimodal transport.

NEW APPLICATIONS IN SIGHT

It is not just in transport that radionavigation techniques are opening up new applications. Other possibilities are:

- tracking dangerous materials;
- locating oil and gas deposits;
- identifying fishing areas;
- locating the site of wrecks;
- guiding the visually impaired;
- facilitating the work of emergency aid teams or humanitarian operations.

Specific uses could also develop in other sectors such as medical (remote treatment of patients), justice (tracking of parole prisoners) or customs (investigations in the field).

WHY A EUROPEAN INITIATIVE?

Today's two principal satellite radionavigation systems, Global Positioning System (GPS) and Glonass, are both under military control, the former controlled by the US and the latter by Russia. Both are also open to civil applications in Europe and elsewhere.

They already enablet tracking on roads, at sea, in mountain or desert regions - but with no guarantee of precision or continuous service, particularly in urban areas and northern latitudes. Moreover, the military authorities in both countries are capable of stopping or downgrading the signal at any time for reasons of national security.

As Europe is in the process of developing an integrated transport system, it is vital to develop independent positioning and navigational systems which are precise and reliable.

Put simply, the European Union cannot afford to be absent or dependent on other countries when dealing with a technology whose potential market is estimated at 9 billion a year and which is likely to generate 140 000 jobs.

WHAT WILL GALILEO LOOK LIKE?

Managed and controlled by civil players, this future European satellite radionavigation system is set to be open, global and fully compatible with the GPS, while offering its users a precision in the range of 5m - to 10m compared to 25-30m for the GPS.

It will use a constellation of 30 **satellites in medium orbit** (23 000 km altitude) linked to a network of terrestrial command stations and centres required for the provision of services.

HOW WILL IT BE FINANCED?

The start-up costs through to 2008 for this system are estimated at 3.25 billion. Much of the financing will be raised through an open public-private partnership scheme.

- **Study phase**
  Almost 80 million from European funds have already been allocated for this study phase, now nearing completion.

- **Development phase (2001-2006)**
  A joint (Union/ESA) public funding of 1.1 billion is budgeted. On March 2001, a group of industrialists (service providers, operators, space system and parts manufacturers) agreed to set up a joint company with an investment of 200 million. They will play an active role in defining the services offered by Galileo.

- **Deployment phase (2006-2007)**
  The satellite deployment phase should be achieved with a financing of 2.1 billion, most of which will be raised by the private sector.

- **Operational phase (2008)**
  Maintenance costs are estimated at 220 million a year.

THE TRANSITION WITH EUROPEAN GEOSTATIONARY NAVIGATION OVERLAY SERVICE (EGNOS)

The European EGNOS initiative, launched by ESA, should make it possible in the meantime to improve the performance of GPS satellites by 2003.
The function of this transitional system, whose infrastructure will later be integrated into Galileo, is

to inform the user within a very short time of any malfunction likely to affect the quality of the signal transmitted by geostationary satellites.

This EGNOS quality control is essential for applications in the transport sector. If it is rapidly made commercially available, it will serve to open up the market and interest future private partners in Galileo.

INTERNATIONAL SPACE STATION

Versatile permanently inhabited research institute in Low Earth Orbit

The International Space Station is a versatile research institute and a large observation platform in outer space for scientific research and applications. It also serves as a test centre to facilitate introduction of new technologies. This permanently human occupied outpost in outer space should also serve as a stepping stone for further space exploration.

Dimensions and mass	
Width	108 m
Length	74 m (~88 m incl. ATV or Progress)
Height	45 m
Pressurized volume	1200 m^3
Total mass at completion	~450 000 kg

Propulsion	
	Monomethyl hydrazine fuel and Nitrogen tetroxide oxidizer for orbit raise and attitude control when
	Control Moment Gyros or Gyrodynes are not used or for unloading of them.
	To prevent wear out of the Stations rocket motors, attitude control and re-boost functions are also
	performed by visiting spacecraft like the European Automated Transfer Vehicle, the Soyuz, Progress
	and Space Shuttle.

Communications infrastructure	
TDRS	50 Mb/s Ku-band link (up-link and down link with the same bitrate)
	192 kb/s S-band down-link
	72 kb/s S-band up-link
ARTEMIS (planned)	20 Mb/s S-band
	3 x 150 Mb/s Ku-band

Environmental control	
Minimum crew	6 (after completion)

Internal pressure	958 - 1013 hPa
Internal temperature	18° - 27°C
	Temperature and humidity control
	Carbon dioxide removal
	Trace contaminants control
	Atmosphere components monitoring
	Oxygen production
	Waste water processing to potable water
	Pre-treated urine to urine distillate processing
	Crew urine and fecal collection and processing

Electrical power	
Maximum power output	110 kW (Provided by large solar arrays. Power is converted to 120 V DC by the station)

Configuration	
On launch	
	Launched in components on different launch vehicles
	Provided by 4 of the 5 participating partners and assembled in orbit.
1st launch	20 November 1998
Assembly complete	2006
On orbit	
	final assembled configuration as shown in drawings
Orbital altitude	370-460 km
Orbital inclination	51.6°
Orbital velocity	7.7-7.6 km/s (~27 500 km/h)
Attitude	Torque equilibrium attitude control and X-vector in velocity direction

Available launch vehicles	
	European Ariane-5 launcher
	Japanese H-IIA launcher
	Russian Proton launcher
	Russian Soyuz launcher
	United States Space Shuttle

Available transport vehicles for crew and/or supplies	

European Automated Transfer Vehicle (ATV)	Servicing and logistics vehicle
Japanese HII Transfer vehicle (HTV)	Servicing and logistics vehicle
Russian Soyuz spacecraft	Manned spacecraft that accommodates 3 cosmonauts
Russian Progress vehicle	Servicing and logistics vehicle
US-European Crew Return Vehicle (CRV)	Manned vehicle that evacuates the crew in case of an emergency
US Space Shuttle	Manned spacecraft for up to 7 astronauts
	Equipped with the Multi Purpose Logistics Module (MPLM), the Un-pressurized Logistics Carrier (ULC)
	or other space station structural parts in its cargo bay

Partners	
	Canada, Canadian Space Agency (CSA)
	Europe, European Space Agency (ESA) represented by 11 of the 17 Member States
	Japan, National Space Development Agency (NASDA)
	Russia, Russian Space Agency (RKA)
	USA, National Aeronautics and Space Administration (NASA)

Other participants	
	Brazil, Instituto Nacional de Pesquisas Espaciais (INPE)
	Italy, Agenzia Spaziale Italiana (ASI)

COLUMBUS: EUROPEAN LABORATORY

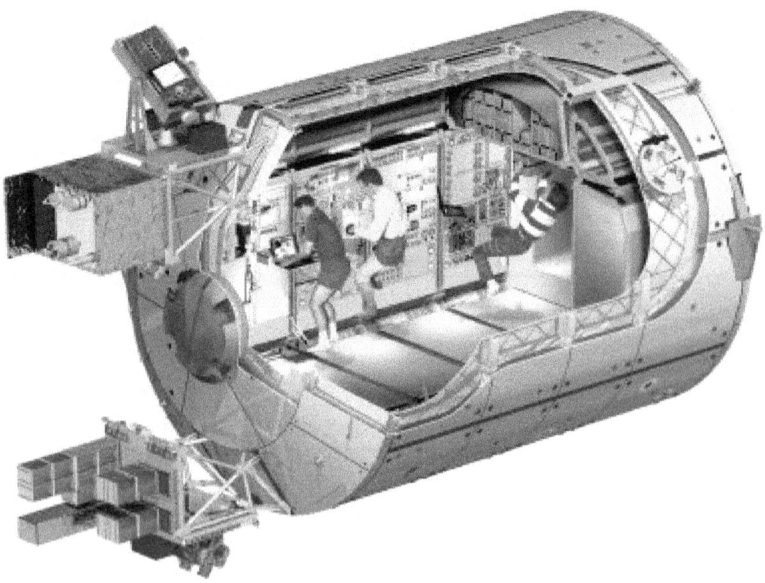

Cut-away view of the Columbus Laboratory

Research laboratory which is permanantly attached to the International Space Station and provides internal payload accommodation for experiments in the field of multidisciplinary research into material science, fluid physics and life science. In addition, an external payload facility hosts experiments and applications in the field of space science, Earth observation, technology and innovative sciences from space.

Launch configuration	
	Fluid Science Laboratory, European Physiology Module, Biolab, European Drawer Rack
	European Stowage Rack Remaining racks will be installed while on orbit.
Launch vehicle	Space Shuttle (flight 1E)
Launch site	Kennedy Space Center
Launch date	TBD

Flight Hardware	
	Biolab, Fluid Science Laboratory, European Physiology Module, European Drawer Rack
	European Stowage Rack (first 5 launched inside Columbus)
	Data and mission computers Command/Measurement Units, High rate multiplexer, Mass Memory Unit
	Video Camera (2), and Monitor Audio system, Master AlarmLight panel (2), Fire extinguisher (2)
	Portable Breathing Aperture (2), Inter Module Ventilation valves and fans
	Thermal Control System valves, Power Distribution Unit, Vital Telemetry Computer units
	Heat exchangers Circulation fan assy External payload facility (4)

On-orbit configuration	
Payload accommodation	Attached to Node 2 starboard docking port. 10 International Standard Payload Racks (ISPR)
	(maximum 1.5 m^3 or 700 kg each) 4 external payload facilities

Dimensions	
Total module length	6871 mm
Largest diameter	4477 mm
Total internal volume	75 m^3
Total volume of payload racks	25 m^{3}</SUP< font>

Mass budget	

Mass without payload	10 300 kg
Launch mass	12 800 kg (2500 kg payload)
Maximum payload mass	9000 kg (maximum)
Maximum on orbit mass	19 300 kg

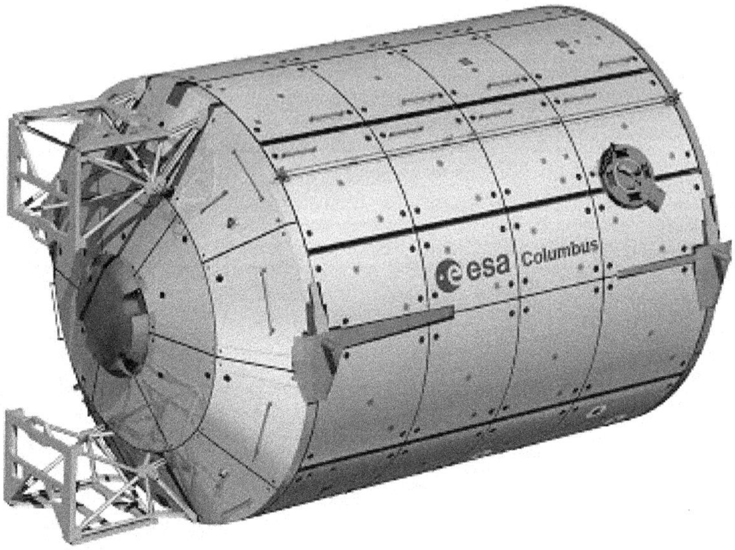

External view of the Columbus laboratory

Communications infrastructure	
Down-link via Artemis	50 Mb/s (Ka-band)
Down-link via TDRS	50 Mb/s (Ku-band) 50 192 kb/s (S-band)
Up-link via TDRS	72 kb/s (S-band)

Environmental control	
Supported crew	3
Cabin temperature	Between 16° and 30°C
Air pressure	Between 959 and 1013 hPa
Heat rejection	Up to 22 kW through moderate and low temperature cooling loops

Electrical power	
Total power	20 kW (120 V dc) provided by the station
Payload power	13.5 kW

Construction material	
Pressure shell	Aluminum 22 194 mm thick, increasing to 7 mm for the

	end-cones
Micrometeoroid and Debris Protection System	Aluminium bumper made of Al-6061-T6 for the primary barrier
	Kevlar/resin panels for secondary barrier
Thermal Protection Material	Goldised Kapton Multi Layer Insulation blanket
Internal secondary structure	Aluminum 7475 Aluminum 7075 Aluminum 2024
External payload facility	Aluminum 7075 Aluminum 7050
Payload Racks	Carbon fiber: NASA racks Aluminum 7075: ESA racks
Noise reduction	Heavy double acoustic barrier material: (multi layer cloth material)

Main contractor	
	Astrium GmbH (Bremen, Germany), leading a consortium of many sub-contractors

AUTOMATED TRANSFER VEHICLE (ATV)

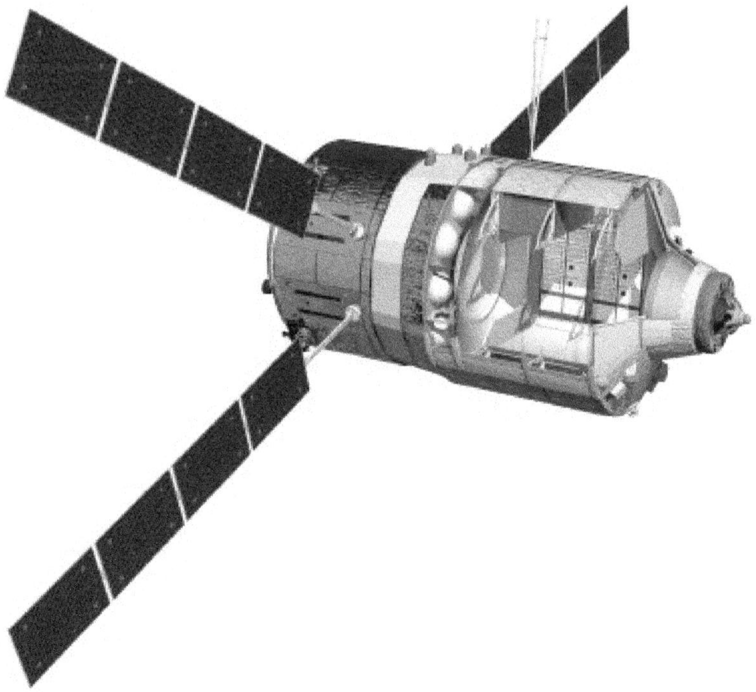

The Automated Transfer Vehicle (ATV)

European Servicing and Logistics vehicle

The Automated Transfer Vehicle is an unmanned vehicle which is put in orbit by the European Ariane 5 launcher. It provides the International Space Station with: pressurized cargo, water, air, Nitrogen, Oxygen and attitude control propellant. It also removes waste from the station and re-boosts the Station to a higher altitude to compensate for atmospheric drag.

Launch Configuration	
Payload envelope	2 x 0.314 m^3 and 2 x 0.414 m^3 for each of 8 racks
Cargo mass	Dry cargo: 1500-5500 kg
	Water: 0-840 kg
	Gas (Nitrogen, Oxygen, air, 2 gasses/flight): 0-100 kg
	ISS re-boost and attitude control propellant: 0-4700 kg
	Total cargo upload capacity: 7667 kg
Launch vehicle	Ariane 5 (260x260 km, 51.6° transfer path)
	ATV will be launched with its solar panels folded to the body of the spacecraft.
	Electrical power will be supplied by non rechargeable batteries.
Launch site	Kourou, French Guiana

On Orbit Configuration	
	Deployed solar arrays,with a total span of 22.3 m, that provide electrical power to recharchable
	batteries for eclipse periods.
	Automated flight towards the International Space Station.

Flight Hardware	
	Propulsion and re-boost system
	Avionics equipment
	Guidance Navigation and Control system
	Communications system
	Power generation and storage system
	Thermal Control System
	Russian docking and refuel system

Dimensions	
Length:	9794 mm
Largest diameter:	4480 mm
Solar arrays span:	22281 mm

Flight hardware	
Spacecraft dry mass:	5320 kg
Cargo carrier dry mass:	5150 kg
Total mass dry mass:	10470 kg
Air/Consumables:	2613 kg
Cargo upload capacity:	7667 kg
Mass at launch:	20750 kg
Waste download capacity:	6340 kg
	(5500 kg dry + 840 wet)

Propulsion	
Main propulsion system:	4 x 490 N thrusters
	(Pressure fed liquid bi-propellant system)
Attitude control system:	28 x 220 N thrusters
	(Pressure fed liquid bi-propellant system)
Propellant:	Monomethyl hydrazine fuel and Nitrogen tetroxide oxidizer
Pressurization:	Helium pressurant at 31.4 MPa
Communications infrastructure	
To ground:	S-band via TDRS satellite
ATV to ISS:	S-band antenna
Navigation:	GPS
Thermal/Environmental control	
Thermal Control:	Multi Layer Isolation material, active thermal control using Variable & Constant
	Conductive Heat Pipes and paints
Life support control:	Fire detection, air circulation, air temperature monitoring

Electrical power	
Ascent to ISS and de-orbit:	4 Solar panel wings of 4 panels each and 40 Ah rechargeable batteries
Number of arrays:	4
Number of panels/array:	4
Generated power:	3800 W after 6 months in orbit
Required power	<400 W Dormant mode

supplied by ISS:	<900 W Active mode
Main construction material	
Pressure shell	Al-2219
Micrometeoroid and Debris Protection System:	
Primary bumper:	Al-6061-T6
Secondary bumper:	Nextel/Kevlar blankets
Internal structure (racks):	Al-6061 T6
Thermal insulation:	Multi Layer Insulation blankets and aluminised betacloth
Solar arrays	Silicium Solar Cells on 4 Carbon Fibre Reinforced Plastic Sandwich panels
Main contractor	
	EADS Space Transportation, Leading a consortium of many sub-contractors

ERA: EUROPEAN ROBOTIC ARM

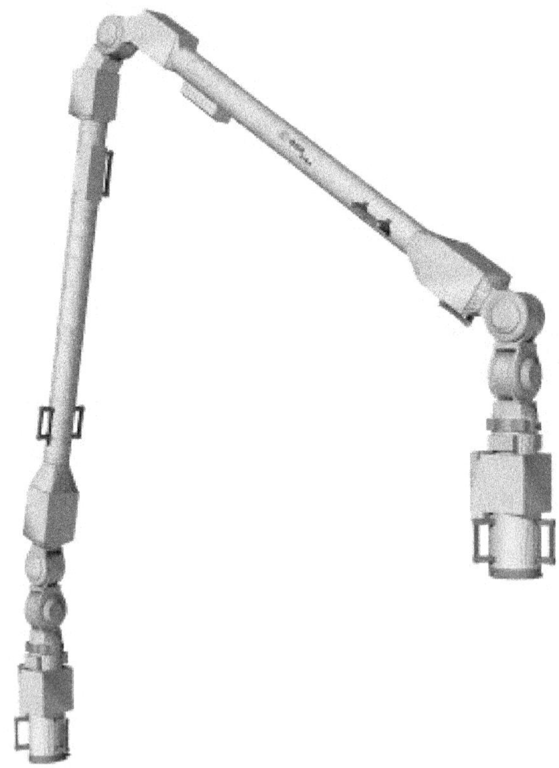

The European Robotic Arm (ERA)

Large re-locatable symmetrical robotic arm with 7 degrees of freedom

ERA acts as a tool for: Installation, deployment and replacement of Solar Array Drive and arrays of the Russian Science and Power Platform (SPP), Inspection of the Russian segment of the Space Station, support/transfer of EVA cosmonauts, transfer of Orbital Replacement Units and other assembly tasks. The arm consists of 2 End-Effectors, 2 Wrists, 2 Limbs and 1 Elbow joint together with electronics and cameras. Both ends act as either a "hand" for the robot or the base from which it can operate.

Utilisation relevant data	
Launch configuration	
	Launched in so called «Charlie Chaplin» configuration with power off
Launch vehicle:	Proton
Launch site:	
Launch date:	November 2007
On-orbit configuration	
	Attached to different locations on the Russian Multipurpose Laboratory Module

Flight hardware	
	End Effector with electronic box (2)
	Base Points (2 on launcher interface and multiple on ISS)
	Wrist (comprising roll,yaw and pitch joints) with electronics box (2)
	Camera and Lighting Units (4x) are provided for proximity control and over views
	Intra Vehicular Activity Man Machine Interface via a laptop computer
	Extra Vehicular Activity Man Machine Interface via a control panel

Control infrastructure	
From the inside of the station with the Intra Vehicular Activity Man Machine Interface:	via a laptop computer and the Control Post Computer
From the outside of the station with the Extra Vehicular Activity Man Machine Interface:	via a control panel and the Control Post Computer

Specifications	
Dimensions	
Total length:	11 300 mm
Reach:	9700 mm
Tip position accuracy:	3 mm
Maximum tip speed:	200 mm/s

Mass budget	
Launch mass:	630 kg
Mission handling capability:	8000 kg
Communications infrastructure	
	Power, data and video signals cabling and special fixtures on End Effector and Base point.
Electrical power	
Average operation power:	475 W (120 V dc)
Peak operation power:	800 W (120Vdc)
Main construction materials	
Limb:	Carbon fibre tube and Aluminum interfaces
Wrist, Elbow and End Effector:	Composed of many different materials
Thermal Protection:	Beta Cloth Blankets
Main contractor	
	Dutch Space (Leiden, the Netherlands), leading a consortium of many subcontractors

DMS-R: ESA'S DATA MANAGEMENT SYSTEM FOR THE RUSSIAN SEGMENT OF THE ISS

DMS-R: ESA's Data Management System for the Russian Segment of the ISS

The DMS-R, installed in the Russian Service Module 'Zvezda', is the set of on-board computers, their avionics and software that provide for the overall control, mission and failure management of the entire Russian segment of the ISS.

The DMS-R performs functions as:

- guidance, navigation and control for the entire ISS,
- on-board systems and subsystems control,
- mission management with supervisory control by the on-board and ground crews,
- failure management and recovery,
- time distribution, time tagging and synchronisation,
- data acquisition and control for on-board systems and experiments
- exchange of data and commands with the other parts of the ISS

The ESA-provided on board units are:

- 2 Fault Tolerant Computers: a Control Computer and a Terminal Computer
- 2 Control Posts for command and control by the crew, for commanding experiments and ERA

The DMS-R has been developed by ESA with an industrial team lead by ASTRIUM (Bremen, Germany).
The application software for the on-board computers has been developed by the Russian Zvesda contractor, RSC Energia, using an ESA-provided ground system - the hardware and software environment supporting software design, development, simulation, test and validation.
The Russian Service Module, with the ESA-developed D-MSR, was succesfully launched in July 2000, and is working nominally since then.

NODE 2: CONNECTING MODULE

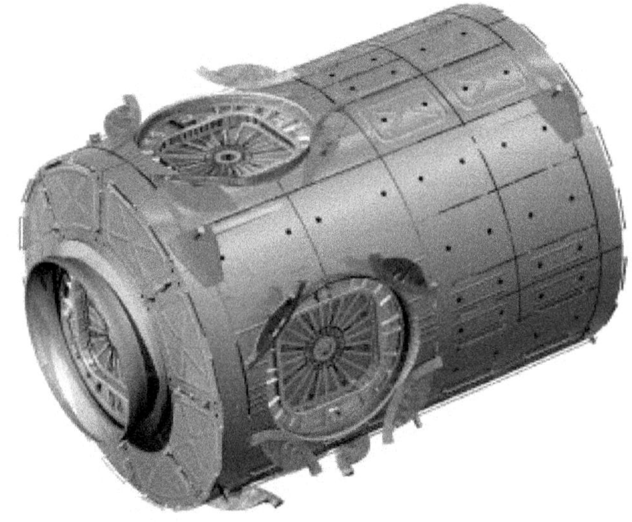

The Node 2 connecting module

Node 2 controls and distributes resources from the Truss structure and the US laboratory Destiny to the connected elements; European Columbus Laboratory, Centrifuge Accommodation Module, Japanese Experiment Module (Kibo), Multi-Purpose Logistics Module and H II Transfer Vehicle. It also provides a working base point for the Space Station Remote Manipulator System.

Specifications	
Dimensions	
Length	6706 mm
Diameter	4480 mm
Maximum envelope of MDPS	4519 mm
Mass Budget	
Launch Mass	14 500 kg
On orbit payload mass	15 300 kg

Communications and data infrastructure	
	Audio and video communications via optical fibers, analog lines and coax.
Data acquisition and processing to support	
	Power distribution, thermal control and environmental control inside the Node
	Data exchange between Node and attached elements including Space Station Remote Manipulator System

Environmental control	
	Cabin ventilation via Inter Module Ventilation Ducts
	Atmosphere sampling
	Temperature and humidity control
	Nominal and emergency illumination
	Smoke detectors

Electrical power	
	Regulation and distribution of electrical power to attached elements and internal Node loads
	Sized for 56 kW

Main construction material	
Pressure shell	Aluminum 2219 -T851
Micrometeoroid and orbital Debris Protection System	Aluminum Al-6061-T6, bumper for the primary barrier Kevlar/resin panels for the secondary barrier
Thermal control	Goldised Kapton Multi-Layer Insulation blanket

Ownership and development authority	
	Technical and programmatic responsibility delegated by ESA to ASI.
	Delivered to NASA (final owner) under a barter agreement for the launch of the
	European Columbus Laboratory by the US Space Shuttle
Main contractor	Alenia Spazio (Turin, Italy), leading a consortium of European sub-contractors

Configuration		
On launch		
	Launched with 4 racks installed, remaining racks	

	installed on orbit	
Launch vehicle	Space Shuttle (Flight 10 A)	
Launch site	Kennedy Space Center	
Launch date	November 2003 (Assembly sequence revision F)	
On orbit		
	Temporarily attached (until Space Shuttle departure) to Node 1 (Unity)	port-port Common Berthing Mechanism
	then relocated to US laboratory (Destiny)	forward Common Berthing Mechanism

Flight hardware	
	4 avionics racks
	4 rack locations utilized for stowage or crew quarters

Controls and distributes	
	Electrical power (56 kW, stabilized 120 V dc)
	Low and medium temperature water cooling
	Inter-module ventilation
	Atmosphere sampling
	Waste water and fuel cell water
	Oxygen and Nitrogen

External secondary structures	
	Meteoroids and debris protection panels
	(98 panels with different characteristics like single or double bumper, shapes and dimensions)
	Support restraints and mobility aids for EVA operations
	Power and Data Grapple Fixture which serves as a base point for the Space Station
	Remote Manipulator System
	Flight Releasable Grapple Fixture used for deployment from Space Shuttle cargo bay

NODE 3: CONNECTING MODULE

The Node 3 connecting module

Node 3 controls and distributes resources from Node 1 to the connected elements; Crew Return Vehicle, Cupola, Pressurised Mating Adapter 3 and Habitation Module. It also houses redundant key environmental control and Life Support systems for atmosphere revitalisation, oxygen generation, crew hygiene, waste management and water processing. It also accommodates equipment to support internal habitability and the distribution of avionics and fluid resources.

Specifications	
Dimensions	
Length	6706 mm
Diameter	4480 mm
Maximum envelope of MDPS	4519 mm
Mass Budget	
Launch Mass	15 500 kg
On orbit payload mass	19 000 kg

Communications and data infrastructure	
	Audio and video communications via optical fibers, analog lines and coax.
Data acquisition and processing to support	
	Power distribution, thermal control and environmental control inside the Node
	Data exchange between Node and attached elements

Environmental control	

Air Revitalization System rack	Carbon dioxide removal, trace contaminants control and atmosphere components monitoring
Oxygen Generation System rack	Oxygen production from water electrolysis (plus CO_2 reduction to water)
Waste Recovery System rack 1	Waste water processing to potable water
Waste Recovery System rack 2	Pre-treated urine to urine distillate processing
Waste & Hygiene Comptiment 1& 2	Crew urine and fecal collection and crew personal hygiene

Electrical power	
	Regulation and distribution of electrical power to attached elements and internal Node loads
	Sized for 23 kW

Main construction material	
Pressure shell	Aluminum 2219 -T851
Micrometeoroid and orbital Debris Protection System	Aluminum Al-6061-T6, bumper for the primary barrier Kevlar/resin panels for the secondary barrier
Thermal control	Goldised Kapton Multi-Layer Insulation blanket

Ownership and development authority	
	Technical and programmatic responsibility delegated by ESA to ASI.
	Delivered to NASA (final owner) under a barter agreement for the launch of the
	European Columbus Laboratory by the US Space Shuttle
Main contractor	Alenia Spazio (Turin, Italy), leading a consortium of European sub-contractors

Configuration	
On launch	
	Launched with 2 Avionics and 2 ECLSS racks
Launch vehicle	Space Shuttle (Flight 20 A)
Launch site	Kennedy Space Center
Launch date	July 2005 (Assembly sequence revision F)
On orbit	
	Attached to Node 1 (Unity) Nadir port
	Houses Crew Return Vehicle, Cupola, Habitation Module and Pressurised Mating Adapter 3

	1 Common Berthing Mechanism remains free

Flight hardware	
	6 Environmental Control and Life Support System racks
	2 Flight Crew System racks

External secondary structures	
	Meteoroids and debris protection panels
	(98 panels with different characteristics like single or double bumper, shapes and dimensions)
	Support restraints and mobility aids for EVA operations
2 Flight Releasable Grapple Fixtures used for	Deployment from Space Shuttle cargo bay
	Installation on Node 1

CUPOLA

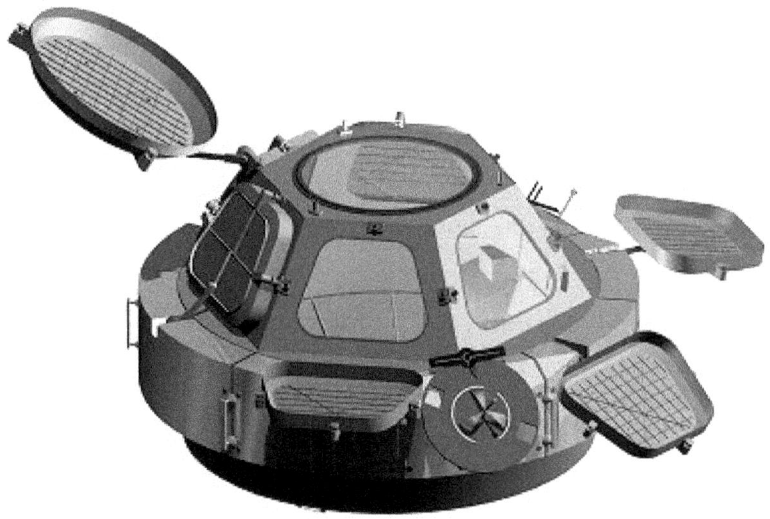

Observation module

Cupola provides a pressurised observation and work area for the Space Station crew giving visibility to support, the control of the space station remote manipulator system and general external viewing of the Earth, celestial objects and visiting vehicles.

Specifications	
Dimensions	
Overall height	1500 mm
Maximum diameter	2955 mm
	Including Micro-meteoroid and orbital Debris Protection System

	(MDPS) with shutters closed
	Including Flight Releasable Grapple Fixture
Mass Budget	
Launch Mass	1805 kg
On orbit mass	1880 kg

Communications and data infrastructure	
	Via Audio Terminal Unit that is connected to Node 3 and the rest of the station
	1553B buses via Utility Outlet Panel
	Dedicated discrete lines for Robotic Work Station

Environmental control	
	Environmental Control and Life Support air from Node Inter Module Ventilation
	With manual temperature adjustment

Electrical power	
Direct from the Node 120 V interface	Window heaters
Via the Utility Outlet Panel, 120 V interface	Robotic Workstation
	Portable Computer System
	Portable light system

Main construction material	
Dome	Forged Al 2219-T851
Skirt	Al 2219-T851
Thermal control	Goldised Kapton Multi-Layer Insulation blanket
Windows	Fused Silica and borosilicate glass
MDPS shutters	Al-6061-T6, AL 7075-T7352 and Kevlar/Nextel sheets

Ownership and development authority	
	The Cupola is provided by ESA to NASA in exchange for the transport of 5 external payloads
Prime contractor	
	Alenia Spazio (Turin, Italy), leading a consortium of

	European sub-contractors

Configuration	
On launch	
	Launched inside the Orbiter cargo bay, mounted on a Spacelab pallet via a Manual Berthing Mechanism
Launch vehicle	Space Shuttle (Flight 2J.A)
Launch site	Kennedy Space Center
Launch date	TBD
On orbit	
	Transferred from Orbiter cargo bay to the Node location by the Shuttle Remote Manipulator System
	and Station Remote Manipulator System interfacing with the Cupola
	Initially berthed to Node 1 Port-port, later relocated to Node 3 Forward-port.
	(Node 3 Aft-port for contingency)

Outfitting on-orbit	
Permanently	1 Audio Terminal Unit and 2 Utility Outlet Panels
Periodically	Robotic Work Station
	Portable Computer System
	Portable light system
	Foot restraint device to support crew operations

Flight hardware	
Primary	Forged/Machined Aluminium dome welded to skirt
	Window Assy, (6 side and 1 top), glass panes and window heaters and thermistors.
	Passive Common Berthing Mechanism bolted to the skirt.
	Micro-meteoroid and orbital Debris Protection
	System Aluminum bumper on the cylindrical portion
	2 Flight Releasable Grapple Fixture interfaceplates
Secondary	Internal closure panels equipment & harness support brackets
	Crew System Kit; seat tracks, handrails, handholds, tethers.
	Manually operated shutters for each window (also serves as MDPS).
	2 Window Change Out Covers to support on orbit window assy replacement.

	Thermal Control System; water supplied from Node High Temperature loop.
	Passive thermal control utilizes Multi-Layer Insulation and thermo optical properties.
	Environmental Control and Life Support air from Node Inter Module Ventilation.
	MIL-1553 Bus, Discrete I/O, Audio, Video

TELEMEDICINE ALLIANCE

Satellites, televisions, radios, mobile phone and computers are now being used to improve health services and to make the best use of valuable medical services.

ESA, WHO, ITU and the Information Society Technologies programme of the European Commission, are now working together within the Telemedicine Alliance to smooth the way for the expansion of telemedicine, and its benefits, to all of Europe's citizens.

Over the past two decades ESA has gained considerable experience in the development and use of telecommunications satellites, and in monitoring the health of Earth-orbiting space crews. ESA also has a wide experience of transmitting and receiving highly complex satellite data and implements state-of-the-art sensor technology. For these reasons two ESA departments are concerned with telemedicine: human spaceflight and telecommunications.

For more information see the Telemedicine Alliance website: http://www.esa.int/telemedicine-alliance.

DOING BUSINESS WITH ESA

FREQUENTLY ASKED QUESTIONS

1. What is ISS commercialisation?

ISS commercialisation is a new business opportunity in a unique environment: the International Space Station (ISS).

The research facilities on board the ISS, together with regular access and the possibility for continual use, offer an unprecedented opportunity for industry to carry out their own research in conditions of weightlessness.

Also, the ISS commercialisation programme offers companies the opportunity to test its innovations and technology in the harsh conditions of the space environment and use the ISS out-of-this-world-image for extraordinary marketing campaigns.

2. What are typical commercial activities?

Applied research and development, technology demonstration, sponsorship, broadcasting, full experience, education and educational sponsorship, commercial infrastructures and services are the typical commercial activities that can take place on the ISS.

However, there is no limit to the imagination. Through the proposals made to us by companies like yours, the Permanent Open Call mechanism has already shown us just how diversified the commercial opportunities around the ISS are. For example: the leasing of medical equipment on board the ISS, the adventure of space training at the European Astronaut Centre, and the testing of food preservation methods in space.

3. Is everybody eligible to participate in commercial activities on board the ISS?

Yes. In principle everybody can access the International Space Station. The ISS is open for business to natural and legal persons, like your company.

Any company from one of the ISS International Partners has the right to access the ISS. Others should request and obtain an ad-hoc authorisation from the ISS International Partners. The ESA Commercial Promotion Office will help you to obtain this authorisation.

Customers from one of the 15 ESA Member States (Austria, Belgium, Denmark, Finland, France, Germany, Ireland, Italy, Netherlands, Norway, Portugal, Spain, Sweden, Switzerland, United Kingdom) have the right to access the ISS and they do not require any ad-hoc authorisation.

4. Are there any constraints?

Yes. First of all, there are few basic ethical constraints. ESA cannot accept commercial proposals having any form of association with the following: alcohol, tobacco, religion, politics, intolerance, violence, firearms, pornography, obscenity, gambling and narcotic drugs.

Also, there are some technical aspects typical of and unique to the space environment, which need to be considered. If your commercial idea implies the space flight of one of your products, or of anything that is for us a payload, a number of safety and related issues will have to be considered.

5. How long does it takes to implement my project?

Commercial activities that take place 400 kilometres above our heads are by nature non-conventional and non-standardized.

The implementation of a project normally takes a few months, however the actual duration of the preparation can vary depending on the complexity of the project and a number of technical aspects that may be involved.

6. How much would my commercial activity cost?

Less than you think. You may be surprised to discover that there are less exclusive and probably non-unique ventures that you are already undertaking on Earth for a higher price.

The actual price depends upon the kind of commercial project you have in mind: for example the complexity and the duration of the project, the permanence of your payload on board the ISS, the level of astronauts involvement and the marketing rights you require will all effect the final price.

7. How does ESA help customers?

ESA is able to help customers in different ways, for example:

- Providing the services of the ESA Commercial Promotion Office, which coordinates all ESA's commercialisation efforts and is at your disposal for any questions
- Offering a wider range of services through the Co-operation Agreement Partners, which complement those directly offered by ESA
- Offering an opportunity to get your project partially financed

Would you like to enter into a fascinating and innovative commercial project, which may be financially important for your company? Then you might consider that under certain conditions you may be granted Promotion Support from ESA and/or its Co-operation Agreement Partners.

8. What about confidentiality and IPR?

ESA has recently defined a policy in relation to Intellectual Property Rights (IPR), which is formulated broadly to leave sufficient room for negotiation.
In this connection two key principles have been established:

- The customer paying the totality of the utilisation costs will have exclusive ownership, access and use of the Information, Data and Intellectual Property resulting from that utilisation
- When ESA partially funds the customer activities, or is otherwise involved in the customer activities, the access to and use of Information, Data and Intellectual Property to be reserved by ESA will be negotiated in accordance with the applicable policy, with a view to securing payment to ESA of royalties on the Information, Data and Intellectual Property exploitation or fees relating to the provision by ESA of services or financial support.

ESA ensures its customers a high-level of confidentiality starting from the very early days of a commercial project.

9. What do I need to do to get 'on board'?
You simply need to submit your commercial idea to the Commercial Promotion Office.
Read this website, get inspired, and then contact ESA's Commercial Promotion Office.
Remember, the only formal and effective response to the Open Call mechanism is to submit your Commercial Proposal to ESA.
A detailed Commercial Proposal, which is in line with the guidelines contained in this website, will save you a lot of time later on and will shorten the negotiation and implementation phases.

10. Who do I contact for questions about ISS commercialisation?
Contact ESA's Commercial Promotion Office.
We will be pleased to respond to your questions and to help you in developing your business idea, either by taking direct care of your project, or pointing you towards the most suitable Commercial Agent for your project.
For more information, please contact us at:
issbusiness@esa.int
Or phone us at: +31 71 565 5068
Or write to us at:

European Space Agency
ESTEC
ISS Commercial Promotion Office
Directorate of Human Spaceflight
Keplerlaan 1
NL – 2201 AZ Noordwijk
The Netherlands

THE WEIGHTLESSNESS ENVIRONMENT: WHAT ARE THE ADVANTAGES?

We take gravity for granted. We never think it odd that a plant should grow straight up. What happens if we take away that 'up'? Would a plant think 'up' is the opposite of where its roots are? Is it just growing towards the Sun? Will it grow towards any source of light? What about the human body in weightlessness? If you 'float' around all day without carrying your own weight, what will happen to your muscles and bones? And how will this affect the circulation of your blood?

The ISS environment allows physical phenomena to be observed without the 'distortion' generated by Earth's gravity. The ISS provides a unique environment, non-reproducible on Earth, that combines the absence of gravity effects, vacuum and specific radiation patterns due to the absence of atmosphere. In this environment, experiments continue to yield surprising effects for researchers.

In the area of cell biology for instance, evidence has emerged, especially as a result of the flights of the ESA Biorack, that some biological cells and unicellular organisms function differently in conditions of weightlessness than they do on Earth. This may help our understanding of how evolution works at the cellular level, since all life on Earth evolved in the presence of gravity.

Also, scientists are putting weightlessness to work, for example, to understand the growth of proteins as near-perfect crystals, allowing them to decode the protein's role in health or disease. Cells grown in space can also produce longer-lived cultures to help us understand the growth of tumours and perhaps give insight into how we might control this growth process.

Weightlessness also causes subtle changes in the structure and functions of the brain, nerves, muscles, bones, the immune system, and other parts of the body. Studying these may help us improve health care on Earth while protecting the lives of astronauts in space.

In tissue and cell engineering, the absence of gravity effects provides new ways of isolating the various mechanisms inherent in the evolution of tissue structure. This knowledge can then be used, for example, for the production on Earth of improved artificial organs for medical purposes and for the design of bioreactors recreating the normal conditions of growth of tissues and cells.

In fluid physics the absence of gravity effects allows the study of other important forces that on Earth are dominated or masked by gravity. In weightlessness, sedimentation and buoyancy-induced flows are virtually eliminated and the possibility of measuring thermo-physical properties of materials (e.g. metals, advanced foams, emulsions, high-quality crystals and high-performance alloys) under such conditions may lead to high accuracy, which is critical for developing new materials. Studies on combustion processes may lead to a reduction in fuel consumption and pollution.

Also, new technologies can be tested by making use of the crew and of the internal ISS environment or by using the external mounting points on the ISS to expose them to vacuum, radiation and micro-meteoroids.

THE COOPERATION AGREEMENT PARTNERS

In 2002, ESA concluded a Cooperation Agreement with a number of private industries, mainly active in the space industry, to jointly develop commercial use of the ISS.

These Cooperation Agreement Partners perform two types of activities:

- **'General promotion activities'**, to heighten the public awareness of the ISS in general (ISS image) and of the inherent benefits of the ISS in particular (as a microgravity R&D laboratory).
- **'Promotion support activities'**, to help customers make their project commercially feasible.

As part of their 'Promotion support activities', these companies provide a set of ground-based facilities, resources and services under promotional conditions to help the first customers of the ISS. These services are listed in the Promotion Support Catalogue, and are necessary to complement those offered by ESA itself - particularly the ESA pre-flight services which are needed for any project that requires flying a payload to the ISS. If you are unable to cover the full costs of your project, you may be eligible to access these services under promotional conditions. This has to be negotiated on a case-by-case basis with the Cooperation Agreement Partner.

The Commercial Promotion Office and the Commercial Agent Network both have a duty to help you get these facilities, resources and services from the Co-operation Agreement Partners, and to help you secure promotional conditions if appropriate.

The Cooperation Agreement Partners

Alenia Spazio

Website: http://www.aleniaspazio.it

Altec

Website: http://www.spacegate-altec.it

BEOS Space Operators

Website: http://www.beos-space.de

Bird & Bird

Website: http://www.twobirds.com

Bradford

Website: http://www.bradford-space.com

Contraves

Website: http://www.contravesspace.com

Dutch Space

Website: http://www.dutchspace.nl

EADS Space Transportation

Website: http://www.eads.net

Kayser Threde

Website: http://www.kayser-threde.de

Kesberg, Büttering & Partner

Website: http://www.kbp-bonn.de

OHB System

Website: http://www.ohb-system.de

ESA COMMERCIAL PROMOTION OFFICE

Commercial Promotion Office
Directorate of Human Spaceflight, Microgravity and Exploration
Keplerlaan 1
NL – 2201 AZ Noordwijk
The Netherlands

Tel: +31 71 565 5068
Fax: +31 71 565 5232

E-mail: issbusiness@esa.int

The Commercial Promotion Office coordinates ESA's commercialisation efforts for the ISS from its base at ESA's research and technology centre, ESTEC, in Noordwijk, the Netherlands.

The Commercial Promotion Office is your first point of contact with ESA. On behalf of ESA, the Commercial Promotion Office also deals with the Commercial Agent Network and the Co-operation Agreement Partners.

The Commercial Promotion Office is there to meet your needs. Contacts the office to discuss your ideas, to ask a specific question or just to get more information about commercialisation with ESA.

The Commercial Promotion Office will be pleased to respond to your questions and to help you develop your idea. We'll either take care of your needs directly, or refer you to the Commercial Agent best placed to help you.

What we do

We provide access to the International Space Station (ISS) for commercial customers, the only place where human beings live and work beyond Earth.

The ISS presents business with extraordinary new opportunities. It offers sophisticated research facilities, a crew of trained astronauts, regular access by both manned and unmanned spacecraft, continuous availability and an intellectual property regime tailored to your needs.

Thanks to ISS, you can finally carry out your own R&D in conditions of complete weightlessness. You can expose your innovations to the harsh conditions of outer space. And you can use the Station's out-of-this-world image to create extraordinary marketing campaigns for your products and services.

We, the European Space Agency's (ESA) Commercial Promotion Office, stand ready to help you make the most of this extraordinary asset.

Our ambition is to help you turn your dreams into reality. Our team stands ready to help, all the way from developing your vision to the successful conclusion of a complex project. We help you achieve your business goals by providing a comprehensive set of services - and attractive conditions.

Please take a minute to discover some of the projects that far-sighted clients are already pursuing on board the ISS. You may have a similar need. Or you may have thought of something totally new. If it can be done, we'll help you do it.

ESA. Your partner for the International Space Station.

Applied research and development

The ISS offers laboratories tailored to carry out cutting-edge research in biology, physiology, physics, material sciences and much more. Customers have already used the ISS for research in:

- **Biotechnology and biomedical research**
  e.g. tissue growth, protein crystallisation
- **Health**
  e.g. research into osteoporosis, crew health monitoring devices with applications to patient management on Earth

- **Food**
  e.g. production processes or new products for the food and nutrition industry

- **Environment**
  e.g. combustion processes for the energy and automotive industry

- **New materials products and processes**
  e.g. metallic foams

TECHNOLOGY DEMONSTRATION

Space is a unique environment for product testing. Lack of gravity, high vacuum, exposure to harsh radiations, large fluctuations in temperatures, and strict mass and safety constraints all encourage industries to continuously improve their technology - with direct benefits for customers on Earth.
Technology demonstration is ideal for clients that want to showcase the performance of their products aboard the ISS and use the resulting publicity to increase their market share on Earth.

SPONSORSHIP

The ISS is our only outpost beyond the final frontier. Across the world, people yearn for the day that they, too, will be able to leave the surly bonds of Earth behind.
To countless millions, astronauts embody the drive to explore that is embedded so deeply in our genes. They are inspirational heroes, noble and selfless, and the bearers of our hopes for the future.

Tomorrow, they may conquer the stars. Today, their home is the ISS. To give clients the opportunity to associate their brand with these extraordinary values, ESA offers a range of sponsorship packages, ranging from a global sponsorship of ESA's Human Spaceflight programme or of a specific manned or unmanned mission all the way to the support of a particular project. Different publicity and marketing rights packages are available to ensure that your brand reaps the benefits you seek from this association.

BROADCASTING

Just imagine broadcasting from the ISS... Through the porthole, the distant Earth appears, beautiful and fragile. Panning around, a uniquely advanced space habitat –and its inhabitants- is revealed. Objects slowly float past, seemingly suspended in mid-air. And beyond it all, countless stars light the sky, many more than can ever be seen through Earth's foggy atmosphere. It's not often that you encounter such a unique opportunity for broadcasting. It's the only choice available for realistic zero-gravity images.

THE FULL EXPERIENCE

Already, two private citizens, Dennis Tito and Mark Shuttleworth, have flown to the ISS. More will follow. But even those who cannot yet indulge in the ultimate flight experience can get a realistic taste of what it's like to live and work in space. ESA's European Astronaut Centre (EAC) is designed to prepare astronauts for missions to the ISS. Now, a very few ordinary citizens, too, can experience the ultimate in flight training: the EAC offers a rigorous 2-day training programme for those who want to check if they have the right stuff. Learn about working in weightlessness. Use real space tools to assemble elements of the International Space Station in the EAC's immersion tank. And later, find out what really goes on up there from those who know it from the inside – ESA's astronauts.

EDUCATION AND EDUCATIONAL SPONSORSHIP

Increasingly, Europe's economic success depends on a large, educated, scientifically literate workforce. Yet across Europe, enrolment in science courses is dropping.
The ISS lets you claim science back from the dry dust of formulas on a blackboard. Step into a classroom connected to the ISS and feel the wonder of young minds absorbing the majestic glory of science, broadcast from the place beyond the sky.
By its very nature, the ISS illustrates fundamental principles of physics, chemistry, biology and geography. It is science coming off its ivory tower and saying, *"Hi, I'm your friend, and I want to grow with you"*.

Educators and educational institutions are already working with the ISS to boost their pupil's scientific literacy. Join them to see what the ISS can do for your science programmes.

The educational potential of the ISS is also ideal for companies wishing to associate their brands with youth related initiatives. Design your own programme, or sponsor an existing one – and reap the reputational benefits.

COMMERCIAL INFRASTRUCTURES AND SERVICES

The ISS offers a range of dedicated internal laboratories and external mounting sites that can be used to add new infrastructures and services. Medical equipment, scientific instruments, and devices for environmental monitoring, meteorological observations or navigation services can all be added to the Station on a commercial basis – showcasing your most innovative products to your most discerning customers.

COMMERCIAL AGENT NETWORK

In order to support the commercialisation of the ISS and to provide a more effective end-to-end service to the customers, ESA decided to set up a network of Commercial Agents in selected market sectors throughout Europe.

From a customer point of view, the Commercial Agent offers the most important help in developing the initial business idea into a commercially feasible project. The Commercial Agent in charge of your project will help you in identifying the required end-to-end services and in negotiating these services with the Cooperation Agreement Partners at the best conditions for your company; also, the Commercial Agent will support you in the entire process that leads to the submission of your Commercial Proposal to ESA, including helping you in the drafting of the Commercial Proposal.

In order to reach customers more efficiently and effectively, there will be one network for each market sector and each Commercial Agent will be a specialist in that particular sector; the German company ISS ISS Lab Ruhr GmbH has been appointed by ESA as its first Commercial Agent for the biotechnology, health, food and nutrition market sector throughout Europe.

Through its management skills, as the exclusive Commercial Agent in the above-mentioned sectors, ISS LabRuhr GmbH also coordinates the European marketing and selling activities of its highly experienced and specialist partners, namely: Enterprise Management Technology Transfer GmbH (EMBL-EM), Germany - the commercial arm of the European Molecular Biology Laboratory (EMBL); the French Institute for Space Medicine and Physiology (MEDES), and the AGT Group, Italy.

ESA'S ISS FACILITIES, RESOURCES AND SERVICES

Orbiting at an altitude of about 400 kilometres, the International Space Station is the biggest man-made structure ever assembled in space. With its final weight of 460 tonnes and a pressurised volume equivalent to that of two 747 passenger jets, it is the result of a cooperative effort among five International Partners: the United States, Russia, Japan, Canada and Europe through the European Space Agency (ESA).

Since 1998, many massive elements developed by all five partners have been transported into space and assembled by astronauts on space walks with the support of a various robotic arm.

The ISS will guarantee at least 10 years of full utilisation. Although not yet completed, it is already operational. It has been permanently crewed since 2000, and scientific research and commercial activities have already begun.

ESA's facilities, resources and services on board the ISS provide for the accommodation and utilisation of customer's samples and products (so-called 'payloads'). Earthbound facilities and services allow the testing and qualification of payloads, monitor correct operation while aboard the ISS, and collect relevant data.

FACILITIES

ESA provides access to a constantly evolving variety of facilities on board the ISS. These can be as easy to use as a fully functioning existing laboratory element, or as adaptable to your exact requirements as an on-board drawer or locker offering room, a power supply and connectivity to your own equipment.

On the ground, ESA's facilities include design centres, testing facilities, laboratories, clean rooms, drop towers, the astronaut-training centre, and access to its highly trained specialists.

PAYLOAD

ESA will ship your payload to the Space Station on board one of the available launch vehicles. These include the Russian Soyuz and Proton rockets, the American Space Shuttle, and from 2005 onwards, the European Automated Transport Vehicle launched on an Ariane-5 rocket. ESA will also ensure the payload's return to Earth, if necessary.

The cost of shipping payloads depends on several variables. The most important is weight. (most transport costs are charged by kilogramme of mass). The second most important is whether the payload must be returned to Earth, or whether it can be abandoned after use to burn harmlessly in the Earth's atmosphere. The third most important is whether the payload must be carried inside a pressurized vehicle or not.

ESA can arrange for every aspect of your payload's transportation, from initial testing and certification, through the flight itself, to its return to Earth.

CREW TIME

Crew time is available for two kinds of activities: IVA or 'Intravehicular Activity'. This covers all activities carried out by astronauts operating within the Space Station.

EVA or 'Extravehicular Activity'. This is the famous space-walk. The term covers all activities carried out outside the Station by astronauts wearing spacesuits.

Both types of crew time can be arranged for commercial clients, but be forewarned: EVAs are complex, dangerous, and demand a lot of training and preparation time. They are really only suitable for customers with the most unusual research needs – or those seeking the most extraordinary images for their initiative.

PAYLOAD QUALIFICATION AND SAFETY

Payloads are tested to be qualified for space flight. The tests must show that the payload can withstand the launch itself, that it can function after launch, that it is safe for the crew and systems on board and that it will function flawlessly throughout its expected lifetime.

The five international partners have established processes for the qualification and evaluation of payload safety. ESA will be happy to perform these processes, which consist of tests, verification and the preparation of standard documentation, for you, or to arrange for a qualified partner to carry them out on your behalf.

DATA SERVICES

Data between your payload and the Station's equipment will be exchanged through a MIL-STD-1553 (two wires) Bus system. Payloads placed on dedicated racks offer local Ethernet connection with speeds up to 100 Mbps. Communication with the ground is charged per minute of satellite link.

Other resources and services

ESA or its Cooperation Agreement Partners offer a variety of additional ground services including training, design, engineering, ground segment operations, mission operations and payload operations management.

ISS BUSINESS GLOSSARY

This glossary contains explanations of the key-terms used in this website. The explanations are not legal or contractually binding definitions.

Active Payload: a payload that needs to interface with the facilities on board the ISS or those related to it and uses the associated consumable resources and services.

Business Plan: the written document that must be attached to the Commercial Proposal if there is a request for ESA Promotion Support. The Business Plan should provide additional information (in particular financial information) about the commercial project.

Commercial Equipment Newly Developed (CEND): commercial instruments and equipment specifically designed, developed and manufactured to work in weightlessness conditions and which meet the specific technical and safety requirements of space use.

Commercial Evaluation Team (CET): an 'ad hoc' team which is established by the CPO to perform the technical, ethical and financial evaluation of a Commercial Proposal in accordance with a set of internal ESA rules.

Commercial Agents Network: a network of ESA-selected Commercial Agents responsible for marketing and selling the use of ESA facilities of the ISS and the related resources and services provided by ESA and/or its Co-operation Agreement Industrial Partners in certain market sectors. The Commercial Agents represent the interface with the customers, offering and concluding arrangements for the end-to-end services provided by ESA and its Co-operation Agreement Industrial Partners.

Commercial Contract: the final binding document with ESA for the execution of the proposed commercial initiative under the terms and conditions agreed by the parties during the contractual negotiation phase which follows the evaluation phase where the Commercial Proposal has gained acceptance by the CET.

Commercial Proposal: the official document submitted for the attention of the ESA Commercial Promotion Office where details and objectives of the proposed commercial project are presented from a technical, ethical and financial standpoint. This document represents the official starting point for doing business with ESA.

Commercial Promotion Office (CPO): the specialised team within ESA that has been set up to co-ordinate ESA's activities in the area of commercialisation. The Commercial Promotion Office is based in the ESA establishment of ESTEC, at Noordwijk (the Netherlands). The CPO has the key role of being the ESA interface towards the Commercial Agents, the Co-operation Agreement Industrial Partners and the External Communication Agency as well as being a valuable point of reference for the customers.

Co-operation Agreement: an agreement between ESA and a number of European space and non-space companies, aimed at preparing and facilitating the development of commercial utilisation of the ISS. The parties have committed resources and services that are, in principle, available at promotional conditions to the customer.

Co-operation Agreement Industrial Partners: the European private companies operating in the space sector, or in any other sector, that have signed the Co-operation Agreement with ESA. By functioning as ISS Service Providers, they provide ISS related services that are required for a particular commercial project (e.g. payload testing and qualification, logistic operations).

Co-operation Agreement Industrial Partners Promotion Support: the term used to specify the Promotion Support requested to, or granted by, the Co-operation Agreement Industrial Partners.

Commercial Off-The-Shelf (COTS): commercial instruments and equipment developed, produced and distributed for ordinary use on Earth and not necessarily meeting the qualification requirements of space use.

Electromagnetic Interference (EMI): EMI covers the influencing of a systems performance due to radiated or conducted electro- magnetic (electric field and magnetic fields) radiation.

End-to-end services: these include all the services that are necessary to make a project technically and commercially feasible. These services may be provided by ESA, its Co-operation Agreement Industrial Partners and any other third party.

European Space Agency (ESA): an inter-governmental organisation established in 1975 to provide for and to promote, for exclusively peaceful purposes, co-operation among European States in space research and technology and their space applications. Today, 15 European Countries are ESA Member States: Austria, Belgium, Denmark, Finland, France, Germany, Ireland, Italy, Netherlands, Norway, Portugal, Spain, Sweden, Switzerland and United Kingdom.

ESA Medical Board: an ESA independent body established to overview the safety, health and well-being of astronauts and other test subjects involved in all pre-flight, in-flight and post-flight activities and to support ground based investigations in medical matters.

ESA Payload Safety Engineer: the primary contact point within ESA for the Safety Assessment of a payload. He/she will coordinate with the ESA Project Manager, the customer and the Payload Safety Review Panel members and will provide technical support throughout the Safety Assessment.

ESA Project Manager: the single ESA point of contact who assists the Customer, Commercial Agent, and Co-operation Agreement Industrial Partners in all implementation activities. He/she is responsible for including the payload and the Project Scenario of the Commercial Contract into the Space Mission ensuring its correct implementation.

ESA Promotion Support: the term used to specify the Promotion Support requested to, or granted by, ESA. This is granted by ESA upon acceptance of a submitted Commercial Proposal, with an attached Business Plan, on the basis of a number of evaluation criteria and in accordance with the restrictions stated in the ESA Promotion Policy.

External Communication Agency: the ESA-selected communication agency responsible for raising the image and public awareness of the ISS through branding. This Communication Agency assists the Commercial Agents in their marketing activities.

Flight Model (FM): model that will be used on board the ISS.

Flight Service Provider: the International Partners' Agency providing the transportation of the payload to the ISS (e.g. NASA Space Shuttle, FSA Progress, ESA ATV).

Flight Transportation Packaging: customised packaging (e.g. a self-manufactured bag), consisting of a container with the stowage material and any interface cabling inside which may be required for shipping the Flight Model to the ISS. This packaging has to comply with all flight requirements (e.g. space qualified foam materials, standard ISS labels, etc.).

General Promotion: the activities undertaken by ESA and/or its Co-operation Agreement Industrial Partners under the framework of the Co-operation Agreement to heighten the image and public awareness of the ISS and its inherent benefits. These activities are mainly general marketing activities including public awareness campaigns; organisation of conferences, symposia and exhibitions; participation in trade fairs.

Ground Support Equipment (GSE): dedicated equipment used to support the Flight Model integration phase. This equipment does not need to have the same overall quality level as the Flight Model but must have the same quality for interfaces.

Ground transportation container: This transportation container must protect the model during transportation on ground and supply all the services necessary for its correct stowage (e.g. cooling system, sensors, power).

Independent Commercial Activity Board (ICAB): an advisory and decision-making body for matters related to the commercial use of the personal image of ESA astronauts and staff.

Inter Governmental Agreement (IGA): the agreement signed in 1998 between the International Partners which establishes a long-term cooperative framework for the design, development, operation and utilisation of the ISS.

Informed Consent: the necessary written consent of the ESA staff member who is requested to act as a test subject of an experiment or whose personal image is requested for use for commercial purposes.

International Partners: the 15 Governments that have signed the inter-governmental agreement which sets forth the rules for the design, development, operation and utilisation of the International Space Station. They are: 11 European Countries, the United States of America, the Russian Federation, Canada and Japan. The European Countries (11 out of 15 ESA Member States) that are International Partners are: Belgium, Denmark, France, Germany, Italy, Netherlands, Norway, Spain, Sweden, Switzerland and United Kingdom.

Intellectual Property Rights (IPR): these include different forms of property protection established by law over intangibles such as ideas, inventions, signs and information. They all assume an act of creation that occurs when an individual exercises his/her mental effort to manipulate the raw material. IPR include registered as well as unregistered intellectual property rights such as patents, utility models, industrial designs, trademarks, service marks, trade names, copyrights, know-how and trade secrets.

International Space Station (ISS): the permanently inhabited space station orbiting the Earth at 400 km altitude for peaceful purposes. Its design, development, operation and utilisation are based on the Inter Governmental Agreement signed in 1998 between the 15 International Partners (see above list in this glossary). The ISS is managed by the following space agencies: ESA (Europe), NASA (USA), FSA (Russia), CSA (Canada) and JAXA (Japan).

ISS Service Providers: ESA and its Co-operation Agreement Industrial Partners as well as any other company or organisation able to provide ISS related services which are required for a particular commercial project.

Marketing rights: those rights that are involved in the act or process of promoting and selling products or services. Marketing rights are mainly rights in the area of copyright and trademark which are typically subject to negotiation in sponsorship and advertising contracts. For instance, should a customer wish to take pictures or videos on board the ISS, marketing rights will be a matter of negotiation. These rights have to be clarified from the beginning as part of the Commercial Proposal.

Memorandum Of Understanding (MOU): a bilateral agreement between NASA and each International Partner's Space Agency which implements the provisions of the IGA by detailing the roles and responsibilities of the space agencies and recording the commitments of those.

Multilateral Commercialisation Group (MCG): an international group which provides a multilateral forum where International Partners can consult and co-ordinate on policies and procedures related to ISS commercialisation development.

Multilateral Coordination Board (MCB): the international body that has to ensure coordination of activities of the International Partners related to the operation and utilization of the ISS.

Open Call for Commercial Proposals: a permanent and non-prescriptive call for business ideas. It is the channel through which all the Commercial Proposals related to the ISS can be addressed to ESA at any time. Commercial Proposals must be sent to the CPO.

Payload (P/L): any equipment carried by a spacecraft. A product becomes a payload once it is intended to fly it on board a spacecraft. A payload can be an active payload or a passive payload.

Passive Payload: a payload that does not need to interface with the facilities on board the ISS or those related to it and only uses its own consumable resources and services.

Payload Safety Review Panel (PSRP): the ESA panel in charge of executing the Safety Review of any European payload which is to fly on board the ISS. The key role of this panel is to ensure that every possible risk to man or spacecraft has been excluded or properly controlled. The PSRP often includes members of the astronaut crew or their deputy engineers.

Promotion Support: this term indicates all resources and services that are, in principle, available to the customer at promotional conditions within the framework of the Co-operation Agreement. Promotion Support includes Promotion Support from ESA (ESA Promotion Support) and from its Co-operation Agreement Industrial Partners. Promotion Support may be in-cash or in-kind. 'In-cash Promotion Support' includes direct funding, deferred payment and price reduction. 'In-kind

Promotion Support' includes, among others, on-ground payload related services, provision of test facilities and expertise.

Qualification Model (QM): also sometimes refer to as the Ground Reference Model. It is the model of the payload that will be used on ground for a number of testing and qualification activities in substitution for the Flight Model which shall be preserved for the flight.

Steering Board of the Co-operation Agreement: the governing body of the Co-operation Agreement composed of representatives of ESA and of the Co-operation Agreement Industrial Partners which is mainly responsible for general commercial strategies and general marketing and promotion activities. With regard to a specific commercial project, the Steering Board is only involved if there is a request for Promotion Support of more than 3 M Euro.

Training Model (TM): the model of the payload that will be used before the flight for the training of the astronaut who will perform the experiment on board the ISS. The Training Model shall have the identical functions and appearance of the Flight Model, but does not have to be qualified for space activities (e.g. materials may be different due to the fact that the TM will never fly in space). Nevertheless, it shall be equally safe to be used by the astronauts during training.

SELECTED SPACE RESEARCH PROGRAMS

Two main classes of research activities and action areas will be undertaken within the 'Space' theme in the 'Cooperation' Specific Programme:

- Space-based applications at the service of the European society

The objective is to develop appropriate satellite-based and in-situ monitoring and early warning systems as unique and globally available data sources, and to consolidate and stimulate the evolution of their operational use. Support will be provided for the development of operational GMES services, which will enable decision-makers to better anticipate or mitigate crisis situations, as well as issues related to the management of the environment and security.

Research activities should mainly contribute to maximise the use of GMES data collected from space-borne sources and to their integration with data from ground-based, ship-borne and airborne observation systems in complex products designed to deliver information and customised services to end-users through an efficient information management. Other satellite technologies (e.g. communication and navigation) will be integrated into the development of GMES services to enhance monitoring techniques and associated instrument technologies, and to improve interoperability of existing ones and enable their use in (pre-)operational services responding to specific types of demand.

In the environmental domain, the demands include the acquisition of knowledge on the state and evolution of sustainable use of renewable resources (such as vegetation and forests), wetlands, desertification, land cover (including snow and ice) and land use, the food supply, agricultural environment and fisheries, carbon sinks and stocks, and atmospheric processes and chemistry.

In the security domain, the demands include improving acquisition, access and exchange of data, and information needed in the context of emergency relief response and management. Support is to be given for risk management and assessment of natural and technological hazards, as well as to humanitarian aid for the purpose of proper need assessment and emergency planning in the context of humanitarian crises (refugees, internally displaced persons, etc.).

Space services play such a key role in the well-being of European society that protection of critical infrastructures in the space sector is a priority. This may need services and capabilities for surveillance of space-based assets, in addition to protection of terrestrial infrastructure. The space surveillance system could provide information concerning the main characteristics of satellites (orbital parameters, activity status) and potentially threatening debris (trajectory, physical parameters), and pertinent information related to space weather and 'Near-earth objects' (NEOs). Feasibility studies and the financing of demonstration projects can be foreseen in this area.

The multifaceted and integrated nature of GMES will be further enhanced and enriched by complementary space techniques. These techniques will support innovative satellite communication applications and services, seamlessly integrated in global electronic communication networks. The overall objective is to provide citizens and enterprises in application sectors encompassing civil protection, e-government, telemedicine and tele-education, tourism and leisure activities, transport including fleet management and personal navigation, agriculture, forestry and meteorology with all the required information in a timely and user-friendly fashion.

- Exploration of space

The objective is to provide R&D support and to maximise scientific added value through synergies with initiatives of ESA or other entities and agencies at European or national level in the field of space exploration. Research activities will be carried out, in particular, through supporting actions, feasibility studies and pre-operational projects. Additional dimensions will be considered to facilitate access to results/data acquired during exploration missions undertaken in the frame of the European Space Programme for the scientific community.

Current space exploration programmes, in Europe and elsewhere, intend to extend human presence in real or virtual way, through mission to the Moon and Mars or through automatic missions to objects of the solar system. Complementary to these, and in close co-operation with respective activities undertaken by ESA and national space agencies, supporting actions and feasibility studies are envisaged as a means to better coordinate efforts for the development of space-borne telescopes and detectors, as well as for data analysis in space sciences.

- 'Research and technological development' (RTD) support for strengthening space foundations

Space sciences not only provide deep insights into the structure of the Universe, improve understanding of planet Earth and the solar system, and a new approach to life and physical sciences, they are also a strong driving force for new technology developments with numerous applications of benefit to society.

The Seventh Framework Programme should complement the ongoing scientific programmes, where gaps are identified, and be in support of scientific activities, including on-board the 'International space station' (ISS). Existing missions produce data sets of potentially immense value for research. Supporting activities aiming at facilitating access to scientific data, including those obtained from previous missions, are envisaged.

In the context of ensuring European access to space, upstream technology research for the next generation of advanced space transportation systems and system studies will take into account the end-user requirements and assess the long-term needs. The objective is to reduce the space transportation costs and increase the competitiveness of the European space technology sector at large.

Implementation: The activities supported under the 'Space' theme which are primarily implemented on the basis of calls for proposals, will be funded through a range of funding schemes:

- Collaborative projects;
- 'Networks of Excellence' (NoEs);
- 'Coordination and Support Actions' (CSAs).

The following activities will be supported through funding by the 'Space' theme, but will not be subject of a call:

- Coordinated provision of space-based observation data for GMES

GMES service development, validation and operational scenario demonstration requires a comprehensive supply of data from space-based observation systems. The objective is to facilitate the provision of data, thereby enabling easy access for relevant research projects to necessary data. The funding should cover provision for a duration of three years (after which a revision of the action will be undertaken in view of further support), and could cover needs of a specific or several service sectors. This work is expected to complement and integrate, in a coherent way, existing data provision agreements, for which FP7 project participants are eligible (for example the ESA Earthnet harmonised access to ESA and non-ESA missions, the Commission Framework contracts for the supply of remote sensing data - established by the Joint Research Centre - and their image portal), avoiding duplication of procurement.

Sustainable operational GMES services will require additional measures, implemented in a step-wise approach and following user requirements analysis addressing all current and planned missions both a European and national level. The objective will be to ensure data access from European assets or through international cooperation.

Overall, approximately 8% of the 'Space' budget could be made available for this pilot action over the period 2007-2013. Based on the specific capacities provide by ESA in this domain, ESA (together with additional national and international organisations to be selected through competitive calls, organised by ESA according to the applicable rules and procedures of FP7) would be the direct beneficiary for this funding, through 'Coordination and support actions' (CSAs).

- Development of GMES-dedicated space infrastructure

FP7 funding is foreseen to provide a significant part to the 'GMES space component (GSC)' programme of ESA, in particular regarding the development of GMES-dedicated space-based infrastructure. The security of space infrastructure (e.g. in terms of encryption of data transmission) and optimised data relay solutions (e.g. inter-satellite and satellite-to ground transmission technologies) should be examined in this context. Overall, approximately 45% of the 'Space' budget could be made available for this specific action over the period 2007-2013.

- 'Risk-sharing finance facility' (RSFF)

The preparation of operational service capacities, as well as the development of GMES space components corresponds to large undertakings and projects, involving long-term investments, with considerable risks for participating industries. It is for such R&D actions that the European Community will improve the access to private sector finance by contributing financially to the RSFF established by the European Investment Bank (EIB). The Community contribution to RSFF will be used by the Bank, in accordance with eligibility criteria set out in the Work Programme 'Cooperation'.

These are regarded to supplement the activities undertaken as a result of the calls for proposals in the 'Space' theme and participants are invited to take benefit of these in their proposals.

-Cross-border co-operation (and European Research Area Networks)

Local and regional authorities form a mainstay of the GMES user communities. For full service implementation, awareness and support are needed by local and regional policy makers are needed. Furthermore, only localised implementation of several services will un-lock the synergy potential for GMES core services and INSPIRE interoperable contents. The main objective is to demonstrate the feasibility of a federated service capacity and its applicability to regional users. Activities developed within the ERA-NET scheme consisting of CSAs networking research programmes carried out at national or regional level, are regarded for the development and implementation of such joint activities.

- International cooperation

Exploitation and exploration of space are, by nature, global ventures. Effective international space cooperation will help raise the European Union's political standing in the world, strengthen its economic competitiveness and enhance its reputation for scientific excellence. Cooperation in the space sector will also support European's Community external policy objectives.

Space has to be considered a privileged sector for developing international activities, in particular with major and emerging space powers, such as Russia, the United States, China, India, Canada, Japan, Ukraine and other countries carrying out space activities. Efforts will be pursued to promote the use of space-based solutions in support of sustainable development and prevention of risks in the context of natural disasters, particularly in Africa.

Proposals will be sought aiming to develop dissemination activities and to implement information products and services derived or customised from 'Global monitoring for environment and security' (GMES) development activities outside the European Union. Priority will be given to proposals to study the potential for current and foreseen GMES services to provide the building blocks for the EU contribution to 'Global earth observation system of systems' (GEOSS). Services and information products should be assessed against the GEOSS requirements in order to identify gaps and barriers, such as restrictive data use and re-use policies and to suggest actions.

A network of 'National Contact Points' is instrumental for providing access to FP7 calls, and to lower the entry barrier for newcomers and raise the average quality of submitted proposals.

General information: In the last 40 years, excellent technological competence has been built up in Europe, nationally and through the European Space Agency (ESA). Sustaining a competitive industry (including manufacturers, service providers and operators) requires research and innovative technologies. The European Community can contribute to:

- the definition of common and policy objectives, based on user requirements;L- the coordination of activities in order to avoid duplications and maximise interoperability;
-the improvement of cost-effectiveness and the definition of standards.

Public authorities and decision-makers represent important potential users; moreover, the European industry will benefit from a well defined European space policy, implemented through a European 'Space Programme'. European level actions are also needed to support Community policy objectives, for example in the fields of agriculture, forestry, fisheries, environment, health, telecommunications, security and transport, as well as to ensure that Europe is a respected partner in regional and international cooperation.

With particular focus on the use of existing capabilities in Europe, the activities set out in the Research Theme 'Space' aim primarily at:

- the efficient exploitation of space assets (in coordination with in-situ assets) for the implementation of applications, in particular GMES (Global Monitoring for Environment and Security), and their contribution to law enforcement in Community policies;
- space exploration, allowing international cooperation opportunities and dramatic technological breakthroughs, as well as cost-effective missions;
- exploitation of space supported through enabling activities guaranteeing the strategic role of the European Union.

Application-oriented activities are expected to be complementary to actions carried out under other research themes in the 'Cooperation' Specific Programme (notably those carried out under 'Environment' in connection with earth observation and the 'Global earth observation system of systems' (GEOSS), and those carried out under 'Information and communication technologies'). Thematic synergies will be developed with related activities in other specific programmes. Complementary actions are envisaged in the 'Competitiveness and Innovation Framework Programme' and in the 'Education and Training Programme'.

Research and technology transfer activities could be particularly appealing for small- and medium-sized enterprises (SMEs) developing innovative technologies, needing familiarisation with new space technology opportunities, or developing applications for their own space technologies. Management of certain parts of the space activities could be entrusted to existing external entities, such as ESA, and other entities and agencies at European or national level. In the case of GMES, research activities could be implemented through a 'Joint Technology Initiative'.

Research activities carried out within this framework should respect fundamental ethical principles, including those which are reflected in the 'Charter of Fundamental Rights of the European Union'.

Please visit the CORDIS site to check the latest calls for proposals and the official work programme under the FP7 'Space' research theme http://cordis.europa.eu/fp7/dc/index.cfm

Please visit the CORDIS site (http://cordis.europa.eu/fp7/find-doc_en.html) to download the following legal documents:
- DECISION No 1982/2006/EC of the European Parliament and the Council of 18 December 2006 concerning the Seventh Framework Programme of the European Community for research, technological development and demonstration activities (2007-2013).
- COUNCIL DECISION of 19 December 2006 concerning the Specific Programme 'Cooperation' implementing the Seventh Framework Programme of the European Community for research, technological development and demonstration activities (2007 to 2013)

Remarks: Please visit the CORDIS site to check the latest calls for proposals and the official work programme under the FP7 'Space' research theme http://cordis.europa.eu/fp7/dc/index.cfm

Contact Persons

Name:FALETIC , Rado
Organization:
Programme Area:
Telephone:+61-2-61257690
Fax:+61-2-61257815

Name:LINK , Mathias
Organization:
Programme Area:
Telephone:+352-43-62631
Fax:+352-43-8120

Name:MOR , Mika
Organization:
Programme Area:
Telephone:+972-3-5118191
Fax:+972-3-5170020

Name:CARVALHO , Fernando
Organization:
Programme Area:
Telephone:+351-21-7828358
Fax:+351-21-7971689

Name:PAPADOPOULOS , Andreas
Organization:
Programme Area:
Telephone:+357-22205056
Fax:+357-22205001
Email:Contact

Name:SILVA , Arturo
Organization:
Programme Area:
Telephone:+598-2-6040210

Name:PATERNOSTRE , Benjamin
Organization:
Programme Area:
Telephone:+32-10-471961
Fax:+32-10-453343

Name:GARGIR , Geneviève
Organization:
Programme Area:
Telephone:+33-5-61282295
Fax:+33-5-61283084

Name:BOUHEY-KLAPISZ , Céline
Organization:
Programme Area:
Telephone:+33-144767987
Fax:+33-144757679

Name:HUSSON , André
Organization:
Programme Area:
Telephone:+33-5-61283464
Fax:+33-5-61283084
Email:Contact

Name:GUERRERO , Héctor
Organization:
Programme Area:
Telephone:+34-91-5202152

Name:TUZIKOV , Alexander
Organization:
Programme Area:
Telephone:+37-5-172842140
Fax:+37-5-172842140

Name:TOBLER , Marion
Organization:
Programme Area:
Telephone:+31-3-806008
Fax:+31-3-806003

Name:SPANO , Barbara
Organization:
Programme Area:
Telephone:+45-3-3955256
Fax:
Email:Contact

Name:TRIMBOUR , Jean
Organization:
Programme Area:
Telephone:+352-43-62631
Fax:+352-43-8120

Name:DEBONO , Carl
Organization:
Programme Area:
Telephone:+356-23402076
Fax:+356-21343577
Email:Contact

Name:ULAMEC , Brigitte
Organization:
Programme Area:
Telephone:+49-228-447331
Fax:+45-228-447386

Name:RUBIO LOPEZ , Monica
Organization:
Programme Area:
Telephone:+56-2-3654409
Fax:+56-2-3654441

Name:LEE , Chang-Jin
Organization:
Programme Area:
Telephone:+82-42-8697780
Fax:+82-42-8697708

Name:KANG , Sang-Hoon
Organization:
Programme Area:

Telephone:+82-42-8697736
Fax:+82-42-8697708

Name:SIPOSOVA , Tatiana
Organization:
Programme Area:
Telephone:+421-2-57204501
Fax:+421-2-57204599

Name:ZAJKOV , Oliver
Organization:
Programme Area:
Telephone:+389-2-3249874
Fax:
Email:Contact

Name:KAHLOUCHE , Salem
Organization:
Programme Area:
Telephone:+213-41-472580
Fax:

Name:SULONEN , Kati
Organization:
Programme Area:
Telephone:+358-9-77488266
Fax:+358-9-77488393

Name:TOSINA , Alejandro Javier
Organization:
Programme Area:
Telephone:+34-91-5815562
Fax:

Name:PONTE , Ana
Organization:
Programme Area:
Telephone:+351-21-7828316
Fax:+351-21-7971689

Name:JONSDOTTIR , Adalheidur
Organization:
Programme Area:
Telephone:+354-515-5800
Fax:+354-552-9814
Email:Contact

Name:MIKSON , Einar
Organization:
Programme Area:
Telephone:+372-7300328
Fax:+372-7300336

Name:KLEIN , Adrian
Organization:
Programme Area:
Telephone:+49-228-447213
Fax:+49-228-447386

Name:LEYGRAAF , Jessica
Organization:
Programme Area:
Telephone:+49-228-447302
Fax:+49-228-447386

Name:LINDBERG , Claudia
Organization:
Programme Area:
Telephone:+49-228-447380
Fax:+49-228-447386

Name:BENZON , Lada
Organization:
Programme Area:
Telephone:+385-1-5494737
Fax:+385-1-5494720

Name:WAHL , Terje
Organization:
Programme Area:
Telephone:+47-22-511815
Fax:
Email:Contact

Name:JOCHEMICH , Marc
Organization:
Programme Area:
Telephone:+49-228-447512
Fax:+49-228-447386

Name:FENNELL , Barry
Organization:
Programme Area:
Telephone:+353-1-7272562

Name:DE RIDDER , Luc
Organization:
Programme Area:
Telephone:+32-2-7881566
Fax:+32-2-2231181

Name:MOTE , Nadège
Organization:
Programme Area:
Telephone:+32-2-4220046
Fax:+32-2-4220043

Name:SWIERCZYNSKI , Piotr

Organization:
Programme Area:
Telephone:+48-22-8287483
Fax:+48-22-8285370

Name:MÍROVSKÝ , Ondrej
Organization:
Programme Area:
Telephone:+420-774-170126

Name:KARNIOURAS , Panagiotis
Organization:
Programme Area:
Telephone:+30-210-3611758; +30-210-3607690
Fax:+30-210-3636109

Name:ARGOUDELIS , Evangelos
Organization:
Programme Area:
Telephone:+30-210-3611934; +30-210-3607690
Fax:+30-210-3636109

Name:STIGELL , Pauli
Organization:
Programme Area:
Telephone:+358-10-6055856
Fax:+358-10-6055901
Email:Contact

Name:PERSSON , Maths
Organization:
Programme Area:
Telephone:+32-2-5455011
Fax:+32-2-5455020

Name:DANNENBERG , Kristine
Organization:
Programme Area:
Telephone:+46-86276498
Fax:+46-86275014

Name:ROHOWETZ , Hans
Organization:
Programme Area:
Telephone:+43-5-7755-4303
Fax:+43-5-7755-94001

Name:VAN DE BURGWAL , Erik
Organization:
Programme Area:
Telephone:+31-70-3735250
Fax:+31-70-3735650

Name:PUKL , Boris
Organization:
Programme Area:
Telephone:+386-1-4773894
Fax:+386-1-4773906

Name:HORVAI , Ferenc
Organization:
Programme Area:
Telephone:+36-1-4613639
Fax:+36-1-3510353

Name:KORU , Aziz
Organization:
Programme Area:
Telephone:+90-312-4272302
Fax:+90-312-4274024
Email:Contact

Name:LAPIENIS , Saulius
Organization:
Programme Area:
Telephone:+370-5-2127434
Fax:+370-5-2312292

Name:KALNINS , Kaspars
Organization:
Programme Area:
Telephone:+371-26-751614
Fax:+371-72-29727

Name:RACHERU , Anca
Organization:
Programme Area:
Telephone:+40-213168722
Fax:+40-213128804

Name:POPESCU , Antoaneta
Organization:
Programme Area:
Telephone:+40-21-3183065
Fax:+40-21-3183065

Name:PETKOV , Doyno
Organization:
Programme Area:
Telephone:+359-2-9793354
Fax:+359-2-8700178

Name:VASSILEV , Vasil
Organization:
Programme Area:
Telephone:+359-2-9812231

Fax:+359-2-9818216

Name:KARDARA , Rosa
Organization:
Programme Area:
Telephone:+30-210-3607690
Fax:+30-210-3636109

Name:RAMUSI , Mothibi
Organization:
Programme Area:
Telephone:+27-82-9929929
Fax:+27-12-8436471

Name:ADUNMO , Keji Alex
Organization:
Programme Area:
Telephone:+39-06-48939993
Fax:+39-06-48902550

Name:TEGAS , Valentina
Organization:
Programme Area:
Telephone:+39-06-48939993
Fax:+39-06-48902550

Name:RICHARDS , Gill
Organization:
Programme Area:
Telephone:44-870-1910118
Fax:+44-1355-272979

Name:VAN GORP , Ruud
Organization:
Programme Area:
Telephone:+31-70-3735250
Fax:+31-70-3735650

Name:RYCERZ , Renata
Organization:
Programme Area:
Telephone:+48-22-8287483
Fax:+48-22-8285370

GALILEO - THE EUROPEAN PROGRAMME FOR GLOBAL NAVIGATION SERVICES

Implementation: The European Commission has pursued the public-private partnership (PPP) approach for the implementation of Galileo, but has re-profiled it through two alternative scenarios with different times at which a private partner will assume the programme's responsibility:

- 'Initial operational capacity' procurement, followed by a private-public partnership

The public sector finances and procures an operational system with limited performances. This core infrastructure is composed of 18 satellites with the associated ground segment. The 'Initial operational capacity' (IOC) procurement allows provision of early Galileo services for a wide range of users and provides confidence on design robustness to the future concessionaire. The remaining 12 satellites are procured by the private sector under the public-private partnership (PPP) concession scheme, which also contains the operations and exploitation activities.

The IOC will be ready by the end of 2011, with users having access only to early services, while full deployment and service availability can be achieved by the end of 2013. The PPP, provided that it is signed in time, will cover the period from 2010 to 2030.

- Full operational capacity procurement, followed by a private-public partnership

In this scenario, the public sector will finance the complete operational system with full performance. This infrastructure is composed of 30 satellites with the associated ground segment. In an intermediate step the infrastructure will reach a constellation of initial operational capability by the end of 2011 and full deployment before 2013. It will allow the provision of all Galileo services for all targeted users and confidence of design robustness to the future concession holder.

General information: Satellite navigation is a technology allowing users worldwide to pinpoint their location at any time. The possible range of applications is wide and spans a large set of domains, from traditional transport to communication, land survey, agriculture, environment protection, scientific research and others. Furthermore, it can ease civil protection operations in harsh environments, speed up rescue operations for people in distress at sea, and provide tools for coastguards and border controls.

Following the European Council conclusions in Nice in December 2000, the launch of the European satellite navigation programme, Galileo, was approved by the Council Resolution of 5 April 2001. The Galileo Joint Undertaking (GJU) was set up in 2002 to complete the development and prepare for the following phases of the Galileo programme and on 4 July 2005, the GJU agreed to the creation of a merged consortium, the European Global Satellite Navigation systems (GNSS). The latter, located in Toulouse and composed of 8 partners (AENA, Alcatel, EADS, Finmeccanica, Hispasat, Inmarsat, Thales and TeleOp) acts as the regulatory authority for the GNSS during the deployment and operational phases of the Galileo programme.

Galileo is based on a constellation of 30 satellites, placed in a medium earth orbit (at an altitude of approximately 24 000 km) providing continuous coverage of the entire surface of the Earth. The selected configuration is optimal as it ensures the presence of a minimum of four satellites above any point of the Earth at any moment and navigation receivers can calculate their position only if they receive the signals of a minimum of four satellites simultaneously.

The system characteristics are the result of approximately ten years of design and technical qualification. Many possible configurations were assessed in an open process which allowed experts and potential users of navigation systems to express their views in order to ultimately determine and agree on the Galileo mission requirements. Design teams both in the European Space Agency (ESA) and in industry, defined the system in an interactive process and tailored the programme in line with these mission and performance requirements.

The first Galileo satellite was launched in December 2005. Since then, close and fruitful cooperation has been developed with the United States of America which has led to a European Union - United States agreement on the full interoperability of Global Positioning System (GPS) and Galileo open signals together with a recent joint decision to improve their characteristics, effectively establishing a global standard for satellite navigation.

Global Satellite Navigation systems (GNSS) are rapidly developing into critical infrastructures for modern society and Galileo has become a flagship project for both its strategic value and its contribution to Community policies. Moreover, Galileo is a pillar of the emerging European Space Policy and signifies Europe's ambitions in space, technology and innovation.

The European Parliament reiterated its support for the Galileo programme, expressed its concerns about the progress made, and called on the European Commission to come forward with appropriate proposals for ensuring its political responsibility and leadership.
Communication from the Commission to the European Parliament and the Council Galileo at a cross-road: the implementation of the European GNSS programmes
Council Regulation (EC) No 876/2002 of 21 May 2002 setting up the Galileo Joint Undertaking.
Council Resolution of 5 April 2001 on Galileo.

IMPORTANT OFFICIAL MATERIALS

FRAMEWORK AGREEMENT BETWEEN THE EUROPEAN COMMUNITY AND THE EUROPEAN SPACE AGENCY THE EUROPEAN COMMUNITY, AND THE EUROPEAN SPACE AGENCY

(hereafter also collectively referred to as "the Parties")

WHEREAS the European Community and the European Space Agency ("ESA") consider that closer cooperation between them will strengthen the peaceful use of space as an important tool to contribute to European cohesion and economic growth and will allow space-related activities to be brought to a wider political, economic, scientific, environmental and social framework more directly at the service of European citizens;

WHEREAS each Party is confident that such cooperation will create added value for the benefit of European citizens;

WHEREAS the Parties recognise that they have specific complementary and mutually reinforcing strengths and are committed to cooperating in an efficient and mutually beneficial manner and to avoiding any unnecessary duplication of effort;

WHEREAS space technology has become a unique and critical technology enabling the Community to address and achieve a large number of the goals of its policies, notably related to information society, transport and environmental protection;

HAVING REGARD TO the various Resolutions adopted by the EU Council [1] and by the ESA Council [2] and to the EU Council Conclusions of 10 December 2001, the said two Councils have encouraged the establishment of a framework for cooperation between the Parties, while maintaining their respective distinct tasks and responsibilities;

WHEREAS Decision No 676/2002 of the European Parliament and of the Council of 7 March 2002 on a regulatory framework for radio spectrum policy in the European Community ("Radio Spectrum Decision") is relevant, given that any space systems or applications will depend on the availability of radio frequencies,

HAVE AGREED AS FOLLOWS:

[1] The EU Council Resolutions of 22 June 1998 (OJ C 224, p. 1), 2 December 1999 (OJ C 375, p. 1), 16 November 2000, (OJ C 371, p. 2).

[2] The ESA resolutions of: 23 June 1998: ESA/C/CXXXVI/Res.1 (Final), 11 May 1999: ESA/C-M/CXLI/Res. 1 (Final); ESA/C(2000)67; ESA/C-M/CXLVIII/Res. 1 (Final), 16.11.2000, referring to the European Strategy for Space; ESA/C-M/CLIV/Res. 1 (Final), 15.11.2001; ESA/C-M/CLXV/Res.3 (Final), 27.5.2003.

ARTICLE 1 PURPOSE OF THE COOPERATION

The aim of this Framework Agreement is to address the following issues:

1. The coherent and progressive development of an overall European Space Policy. Specifically, this policy shall seek to link demand for services and applications using space systems in support

of the Community policies with the supply of space systems and infrastructure necessary to meet that demand.

2. The establishment of a framework providing a common basis and appropriate operational arrangements for an efficient and mutually beneficial cooperation between the Parties with regard to space activities in accordance with their respective tasks and responsibilities and fully respecting their institutional settings and operational frameworks. The cooperation under this Framework Agreement between the Parties aims at:

(a) securing Europe's independent and cost-effective access to space and the development of other fields of strategic interest necessary for the independent use and application of space technologies in Europe;

(b) ensuring that the overall European Space Policy takes into particular account the general policies pursued by the European Community;

(c) supporting Community policies by using space technologies and space infrastructures where appropriate and promoting the use of space systems in support of sustainable development, economic growth and employment;

(d) optimising the use of expertise and available resources and contributing to the consolidation of the close cooperation between the European Community and ESA, thereby linking the demand and supply of space systems within a strategic partnership;

(e) achieving greater coherence and synergy of research and development in order to optimise the use of resources available in Europe, including the network of technical centres.

ARTICLE 2 PRINCIPLES OF COOPERATION

1. The cooperation between the Parties shall be pursued in the light of the common objectives as defined under Article 1, with due regard to their respective tasks and responsibilities and their respective institutional settings and operational frameworks.

2. Each Party shall take the decisions necessary for the implementation of this Agreement, as described in Article 4, in accordance with its own internal procedures.

3. Bearing in mind the nature of space technologies and infrastructures, both Parties, in implementing this Agreement, shall take into account their security dimension.

ARTICLE 3 FIELDS OF COOPERATION

1. The Parties have identified the following specific fields of cooperation:

– science

– technology

– earth observation

– navigation

– communication by satellite

– human space flight and micro-gravity

– launchers

– spectrum policy related to space.

2. The Parties may identify and develop new fields for cooperation.

ARTICLE 4 IMPLEMENTATION

1. For the implementation of this Agreement each Party shall undertake, in compliance with its own prerogatives, legal instruments and procedures, such actions as are required to achieve the purpose of the cooperation provided for in Article 1.

2. Such actions shall aim at fostering the utilisation of space research and development and space applications in the public and private sectors, the promotion of the adoption of legislative, regulatory and standardisation measures in this sector, the funding and carrying out of joint initiatives pursuant to Article 5.

3. Each Party shall refer to the competencies and capabilities of the other, whenever an action is necessary, to pursue the purpose of the cooperation, and shall provide the other Party with expertise and support in its own specific fields of competence.

ARTICLE 5 JOINT INITIATIVES

1. Subject to paragraph 3, the joint initiatives to be carried out by the Parties may take, without being limited to, the following forms:

(a) the management by the ESA of European Community space-related activities in accordance with the rules of the European Community;

(b) the participation by the European Community in an optional programme of the European Space Agency, in accordance with Article V.I.b of the ESA Convention;

(c) the carrying out of activities which are coordinated, implemented and funded by both Parties;

(d) the creation by the Parties of bodies charged with pursuing initiatives complementary to research and development activities, such as the provision of services, the promotion of operators formation and the management of infrastructures;

(e) the carrying out of studies, the organisation of scientific seminars, conferences, symposia and workshops, the training of scientists and technical experts, the exchange or sharing of equipment and materials, the access to facilities, and the support of visits and exchanges of scientists, engineers or other specialists.

2. When the implementation of a joint initiative requires a detailed definition, it shall be provided for in specific arrangements to be entered into between the Parties. Whenever applicable, such specific arrangements should include at least:

(a) the overall mission definition;

(b) a description of the objectives;

(c) a consolidated set of user requirements;

(d) a work plan;

(e) an appropriate management scheme;

(f) the role and financial implications of the Parties;

(g) an industrial policy scheme;

(h) budgetary aspects;

(i) rules of intellectual property rights, rules of ownership including the transfer of ownership, the implementation principles including voting rights, and the participation by third Parties.

Both Parties shall work out guiding principles in addition to these specific arrangements as soon as possible.

3. Any financial contribution made by one Party in accordance with a specific arrangement shall be governed by the financial provisions applicable to that Party. Under no circumstances shall the European Community be bound to apply the rule of "geographical distribution" contained in the ESA Convention and specially in Annex V thereto. Compliance with the rules relating to financial control and auditing of the Party contributing to the joint initiatives, or of both Parties in case of joint contribution, shall apply to any joint activity.

ARTICLE 6 CONSULTATION AND INFORMATION

1. The Parties shall consult each other regularly in order to coordinate their activities to the fullest extent. Each Party shall inform the other of any initiatives within its own decision-making process, in the fields of cooperation under Article 3, which may be of interest to the other Party.

2. The Parties shall exchange all information at their disposal which may be required for the implementation of this Agreement, subject to their respective rules.

3. Except when otherwise provided, the Parties shall not disclose any information exchanged in connection with this Agreement to any persons other than those employed by them or officially entitled to handle such information nor shall they use it for commercial purposes. Such disclosure shall extend only so far as may be necessary for the purpose of this Agreement set out in Article 1 and shall be in strict confidence.

ARTICLE 7 EXTERNAL DIMENSION OF THE COOPERATION

1. Each Party shall inform the other of its activities of an international dimension which may be of interest to the other Party.

2. Whenever appropriate a Party may, in relation to any matters relevant to its international activities, consult the other Party.

3. Once a specific arrangement has been concluded between the parties in accordance with Article 5, the external aspects of this joint activity vis-à-vis third parties shall be pursued jointly by the parties in accordance with that specific arrangement.

ARTICLE 8 COORDINATION AND FACILITATION OF COOPERATIVE ACTIVITIES

1. The coordination and facilitation of cooperative activities under this Agreement shall be accomplished by regular joint and concomitant meetings of the Council of the European Union and of the Council of ESA at ministerial level ("Space Council").

2. The objectives of the joint and concomitant meetings shall include the following:

(a) providing orientations supporting the achievement of the objectives of this Agreement and identifying actions required;

(b) making recommendations, in particular related to the main elements of the specific arrangements;

(c) advising the parties on ways to enhance cooperation consistent with the principles set out in this Agreement;

(d) reviewing the effective and efficient functioning of this Agreement.

3. A Secretariat shall assist the concomitant meetings and shall elaborate the initiatives deriving from the implementation of this Agreement. The Secretariat shall implement the guidelines provided by the concomitant meetings of the two Councils. The Secretariat shall establish its own rules of procedure and be composed of officials of the Commission of the European Communities and of the ESA Executive. The Parties shall undertake, in accordance with their respective rules and procedures, to contribute to the required administrative support.

4. Without prejudice to the Parties' internal decision-making procedures, the Secretariat shall consult on a regular and informal basis high-level representatives of the Member States of the European Community and of the European Space Agency, with the purpose of reaching common understanding on issues related to the implementation of this Agreement.

ARTICLE 9 EXCHANGE OF PERSONNEL

1. The Parties may second members of their staff to each other for specified periods in order to share expertise and develop mutual understanding.

2. Rules for the implementation of this Article shall be established by the Secretariat, as referred to in Article 8, and be agreed to in the form of a specific arrangement under this Framework Agreement.

ARTICLE 10 PUBLIC RELATIONS

1. The Parties undertake to coordinate in advance their public-relations, press and media activities concerning any joint public activities relating to subjects covered by this Agreement.

2. In all relevant media activities, the role of each Party in this Agreement shall be clearly identified and mentioned.

3. The detailed arrangements for implementing public relations activities provided for in this Article shall be adopted jointly.

ARTICLE 11 SETTLEMENT OF DISPUTES

1. Any disputes which may arise between the Parties relating to the interpretation or application of this Agreement shall be submitted for direct negotiations within the Secretariat.

2. If it is not possible to settle the dispute in accordance with paragraph 1, either of the two Parties may notify the other of the appointment of an arbitrator. The other Party shall then appoint its own arbitrator within a period of two months. The arbitrators shall then appoint a third arbitrator within one month.

3. The arbitrators' decisions shall be taken by majority vote.

4. The award of the Arbitration Tribunal shall be final and binding on the Parties.

5. Each Party to the dispute shall take the appropriate steps required to implement the arbitrators' decisions.

ARTICLE 12 ENTRY INTO FORCE, DURATION, AMENDMENTS AND TERMINATION

1. This Agreement shall enter into force on the date of the last written communication by which the Parties notify each other that their respective internal procedures necessary for its entry into force have been completed.

2. This Agreement shall remain in force for four years from the date of its entry into force. It shall be automatically extended for subsequent periods of four years unless either of the Parties notifies the other Party in writing, at least one year before the expiry of any of its periods of duration, of its intention to terminate it.

This Agreement shall terminate upon the expiry of twelve months after the receipt of written notification by one Party sent by the other Party.

3. The termination or expiry of this Agreement shall not affect the validity of the specific arrangements entered into between the Parties in accordance with Article 5, which shall remain in full force and effect until the terms for their execution or termination take place.

4. This Agreement shall be amended only by written agreement between the Parties.

5. This Agreement is not intended to modify or supersede any previous agreements entered into between the Parties, which shall remain in full force and effect in accordance with their own terms and provisions.

ARTICLE 13 SIGNATURE AND AUTHENTICITY

This Agreement shall be drawn up in duplicate in the Danish, Dutch, English, Finnish, French, German, Greek, Italian, Norwegian, Portuguese, Spanish and Swedish languages, each of these texts being equally authentic.

EURPEAN SPACE POLICY

THE INTERNATIONAL DIMENSION

Space activities in the 21st century have become a demanding global venture. With no single country able to absorb the risk of developing new technologies, worldwide co-operation has replaced US-Soviet Cold War competition, and Europe is now leading the way towards a future where common interests and friendly ‘co-opetition’ combine for the betterment of society.

In the space industry, shared investment means shared benefits. As worldwide satellite-based services such as multimedia communication and navigation become part of the daily lives of people around the world, space-based earth observation is helping humanity to deal with global environmental challenges. With space scientists working in virtually every country around the world, space science has become a model for international cooperation.

Russia still a primary player

The mid to late 1980s saw a radical restructuring of the international political landscape, coupled with an explosion of technological capabilities around the world. The Russian Aviation and Space Agency, also known as Rosaviakosmos, has since entered into co-operative space agreements with the national space agencies of the USA, France, Germany, Canada, China, India, Bulgaria, Hungary, Pakistan, Portugal and Israel. Russian co-operation with ESA dates back to the 1970s. More recently, Rosaviakosmos and the Russian Federation have signed agreements with the European Commission.

According to European Research Commissioner Philippe Busquin, co-operation with Russia is a mutually beneficial exercise. Speaking recently, he said, “We would like to achieve a certain level of autonomy in Europe, and for that we need to develop a real European manned space programme with our own launch systems. The Russians remain unsurpassed in this area and this kind of experience can be invaluable to us. At the same time, we in Europe have extensive experience in technology transfer, that is to say taking technologies developed for space and transferring them to non-spacebased industrial and commercial applications.”

“The Russians are obviously very advanced in the area of human space flight,” says Frank De Winne, the ESA astronaut who travelled to the International Space Station in a Russian spacecraft in October 2002. “The experience they have amassed since the time of the Soviet Union is still very relevant. Having been fortunate enough to live and work with them, I can say personally that we have a great deal to learn from the Russians.”

ESA Director General Antonio Rodotà has also spoken in positive terms of Euro-Russian co-operation, saying at the EU-ESA space workshop in Moscow, “We have seen an impressive list of historic co-operative efforts between Europe and Russia in space, resulting in enormous benefits to both sides. The question is how best to use new resources, and that means getting together with our partners and setting our goals and priorities.”

The political context has never been more favourable to broadened co-operation between Europe and the Russian Federation. The ongoing enlargement process is bringing new countries into Europe, including many with strong former ties to Russia, and the EU’s new Sixth Framework Programme has recognised for the first time the strategic importance of space research, allowing for Russian participation as a full and equal partner.

Former Soviet block

Many of the former members and associates of the Soviet Union possess considerable experience in the space sector. For example, a number of the instruments installed on the Interkosmos satellites, providing important information about the earth’s environment, were designed and manufactured by scientists from Bulgaria, then Czechoslovakia, Hungary and Poland. Perhaps ironically, as a new spirit of co-operation takes hold between Europe and Russia, many of these scientists are working with the Russians again, this time as EU accession countries and soon-to-be Member States.

Ukraine I The Ukraine inherited approximately 15% of the space-related capabilities of the Soviet Union. Important research centres have been established since independence, now representing a significant pool of available expertise. Increased co-operation with the EU is a key priority for the Ukranian government. Deputy Director General of the National Space Agency of Ukraine (NSAU), Eduard Kuznetsov, has called for increased collaboration between the Ukraine and Europe in space. Speaking at the first meeting of the ‘EU-Ukraine Joint ad hoc Working Group on Peaceful Use of Outer Space’ in March 2003, Kuznetsov offered to modify the Ukraine’s long-term space programme with the objective of integrating it into the emerging EU space strategy.

The development of space co-operation with the Ukraine was referred to explicitly in the EU-Ukraine Partnership and Co-operation Agreement of March 2000.

Poland I Zbigniew Klos of the Polish Academy of Sciences' Space Research Centre has said, "The development of a common space research strategy is a great challenge for all of the countries of Europe, including for those of us preparing to join the European Union. Poland has come a long way, starting from the days of the Interkosmos programme and now as a full research partner with the EU. This comes as Polish legislators are finally recognising the indispensable nature of space research for all sorts of applications – environmental monitoring, to name just one."

The United States – a long-standing partnership

Europe's relations with the United States with respect to space have been privileged, given the family links of scientific, technological and industrial cultures. Europe and the United States therefore have a long history of co-operative exchange in space on many levels. Europe is a partner of the USA, along with Russia, Canada, and Japan, in the International Space Station (ISS), one of the largest-ever co-operative ventures in science and technology. ESA's primary contribution is the Columbus laboratory.

Europe's impressive long-term efforts in the area of launcher technologies has made it the main competitor of the USA in the commercial launch field, but EU officials do not see the need to class the Americans as competitors in the absolute sense. Co-operation in appropriate areas will continue to be beneficial to all partners, while the stimulus of economic competition can contribute to maintaining the commercial and industrial sectors leading to a healthy sense of 'co-opetition'.

Emerging space players

The USA, Russia and the EU are by no means the world's only space faring communities. More than ever, space exploration is a global adventure and the major space projects of the future are likely to be undertaken by partnerships representing humankind as a whole. Europe is currently forging closer ties with a number of lesser-known but highly motivated and dynamic space players.

Canada I Canadian activities in space are extensive for a country of its small population. Since 1978, a far-reaching co-operation agreement has existed between Canada and ESA. Canada and the Canadian space industry have actively participated in many ESA programmes. Canada participates directly in ESA decision-making and Canadian companies bid for and receive contracts on the same basis as their European counterparts. The EU and Canada have developed close contacts in global satellite navigation. A joint Working Group on Satellite Navigation was set up in 1999 by the EC and Canada. Canada also participated in GALILEO definition phase studies, providing expertise and funding.

Japan I The Japanese Space Agency, NASDA, has been extremely busy over the past few years with a number of successful space programmes. Japanese triumphs include the H2 space launcher.

China I Learning lessons from both the Russians and the Americans, the Chinese have created a credible space enterprise. The Chinese have developed their launch capability into a flourishing commercial enterprise by lowering the prices substantially, cutting into the European and American markets. Several different countries have used Chinese launchers successfully.

India I India comprises some one billion people living within a country with a vast north-to-south expanse and requiring a highly advanced communications system. The country is also heavily reliant on agriculture, which makes remote sensing and meteorological data a vital necessity.

India has wasted no time in establishing an autonomous space capability. Formerly dependent on the USA and the Soviet Union for their space vehicles, India has now developed its own indigenous remote sensing satellite. As Land-sat 4 and 5 become outmoded, the US is likely to have to rely upon India to feed its remote sensing database.

In addition to these, a few developing countries have advanced their status by launching their own rockets and in some cases their own satellites.

To co-operate or not to co-operate?

Given Europe's accomplishments in space, it is clearly capable of taking the initiative, performing on a par with its major partners and playing a key strategic role in major space projects. But what should the criteria be for deciding when to work together and when to go it alone? The Commission's Green Paper on a European Space Policy calls for a review among European stakeholders of just what the proper balance should be.

THE AMBITIONS OF EUROPE IN SPACE

José Manuel Durão Barroso
President of the European Commission
Conference on European Space Policy
Brussels, 15 October 2009

Ladies and gentlemen,
Let me start by welcoming you all to this groundbreaking conference.

Europe now faces some fundamental challenges. Fighting the economic crisis; ensuring the well being of our citizens; tackling climate change; finding ways to unleash our full potential for innovation and job creation, and to bring about a true knowledge society. We also need to reinforce our position in the world scene. All these challenges need the support of enabling tools: and space applications is one of them.

Our citizens' well-being depends increasingly on space-based applications in areas such as environment, security and transport. As demographics change, we will have to turn increasingly to space applications to develop social, medical and mobility services.

Climate change affects the quality of citizens' lives and has enormous economic implications. Space-based Earth observation has substantially contributed to understanding the full scale of climate change, and without space applications we will not be able to tackle it and anticipate its consequences.

Space-based applications are increasingly important to many other EU policy areas as well, such as agriculture, environment and health.

And space activities also play a useful role in invigorating European competitiveness and economic growth. The reason is simple. Space both requires and generates new technologies, knowledge intensive services, new products and new forms of cooperation. All this stimulates innovation and creates new jobs beyond the space industry.

Space can certainly contribute to economic recovery in the short term and to robust industrial development in the medium and long term.

Space is also essential to project the image of the EU as a world player.

And without space research, our knowledge society will simply not come about.

If I have underlined all these aspects it's because sometimes politically we speak about space, people believe that we are speaking about some priority very distant in the future. And I think it is a very important task for all of us that our political and decision making responsibility to underline that when we are speaking about space policy, we are not simply talking about a symbolic, a great project for the future, it is about very concrete applications for the life of our citizens and I think that this is important if we want to keep the political support for this policy.

What has the EU done so far?

Well, the European Space Agency and several EU Member States have an outstanding record of achievements, such as the Arianne launchers or the Columbus laboratory of the International Space Station.

The EU has also taken the lead in two projects of fundamental importance for our future: Galileo and Global Monitoring for Environment and Security.

Galileo will contribute to the safety, efficiency and comfort of private and commercial transport. It will also help us to develop social services for disabled or elderly people or, in the agricultural sector, to enhance farming and livestock management, just to name a few examples.

Our project Global Monitoring for Environment and Security, or GMES, will allow us to monitor phenomena such as floods and fires, helping us improve emergency response services and citizens' safety. It can also gather data on our land and monitor the conditions and composition of the atmosphere or the ocean, which is essential to understand climate change.

The EU is devoting an average of €700 million per year to support space projects over the period 2007-2013.

Ladies and gentlemen,

Since 2007 - following a Commission Communication which, for the first time, outlined the elements of a European space policy - the Council has put space firmly on the political agenda. Four priority areas were identified: climate change, security, innovation and exploration.

The European Parliament has endorsed the European Space Policy and asked the Council and the Commission to make concrete proposals on these four priority areas.

And the Lisbon Treaty now unambiguously enshrines space as a shared responsibility for the EU and its Member States.

So let me ask the obvious follow-up question: does the EU have the ambition to lead in space, or do we leave the leading role to others?

A lot depends on where we go from here. So let me share my views with you today.

First, we must guarantee the success of our flagship projects Galileo and GMES. Galileo implementation is well on course and GMES is now making a critical transition from research to an operational stage. Both represent long-term commitments for the EU.

We must ensure that long-term funding or governance issues do not get in the way of their success. At stake is not just potential economic returns that run into billions of euro, but also our credibility.

Second, we must develop a strong, space-based capacity to deal with climate change. Such capacity will build on GMES and Galileo applications. But we must make adequate use of all space resources available, including those in Member States and bodies like the European Organisation for the Exploitation of Meteorological Satellites (EUMETSAT) and the European Space Agency (ESA).

We must also set up international partnerships. Our objective should be to have at our disposal the necessary space-based instruments, applications, and robust coordination mechanisms to tackle climate change.

Third, we need more security in space and from space. Our space assets and infrastructure are indispensable for our economy and security and we need to protect them. The EU should develop an independent capacity to monitor satellites and debris orbiting the Earth and the space environment, and tackle possible hazards.

We should also exploit the potential of space infrastructure (already available, for example, through GMES) to protect our citizens and our ground infrastructure against natural and man-made hazards and to be at the service of European Security and Defence Policy goals. These capacities should be developed in partnership with Member States.

Ladies and gentlemen,

We need to ask ourselves what role we want the EU to play in space exploration over the next two to three decades. Space exploration is essential to expand human knowledge and to stimulate innovation. By better understanding space and the evolution of other planets we will better understand our own environment.

Human space exploration of the solar system, including Mars and possibly the return of humans to the moon, could be the backbone of such a space exploration strategy.

The 1st EU-ESA international conference on human space exploration, which will take place in Prague on 23 October and is organized by the Commission and the ESA, will bring together representatives of all EU and ESA Member States, as well as our international partners.

The Commission and, I hope, the ESA will argue that space exploration is important to the EU, and that we want to launch discussions about the role of the EU in this international endeavour.

From the Commission viewpoint, important issues will have to be addressed, including:

- how to assure independent access to space;

- the issue of independent human spaceflight capability, in the context of an international partnership; and

- finally, how to support the International Space Station.

We also must reinforce support for bottom-up space research, which is the breeding ground for a growing knowledge society and is indispensable for us to reap the full benefits of space.

Ladies and gentlemen,

Space represents a fantastic political and economic challenge for the EU.

The Commission and the Council have identified the priority areas for EU involvement in space. As the European Parliament has reminded us, we now need to translate those priorities into a consistent strategy.

In the political guidelines I presented to the European Parliament for my reelection for a second term I have mentioned explicitly: space is one of the areas I want to see in the future as progressing at EU level and I believe that with the vote on my nomination, the Parliament has endorsed that as well.

So the question is: will we be up to that challenge?

For the sake of those whose future we build today, I trust we will.

And I hope that we will reinforce and I am sure that you will reinforce a real European space strategy.

Thank you.

CONVENTION FOR THE ESTABLISHMENT OF A EUROPEAN SPACE AGENCY

INTRODUCTORY NOTE

(1) The text of the ESA Convention (Ref.CSE CS(73)19,rev.7) was approved by the Conference of Plenipotentiaries held in Paris on 30 May 1975.
The Convention was signed after this Conference by all Member States of the European Space Research Organisation and of the European Organisation for the Development and Construction of Space Vehicle Launchers and opened for signature by the States which are members of the European Space Conference.

(2) In accordance with Resolution No.1 of the Conference of Plenipotentiaries, the European Space Agency functioned de facto from 31 May 1975. The ESA Convention was signed by Ireland on 31 December 1975, a special agreement being negotiated to cover the period preceding the entry into force of the Convention in Ireland's case. Signed on 29 November 1976, this agreement entered into force on 9 December 1976, with effect from the date of signature, after being approved by Dail Eireann (ESA/ C(76)122, att: ESA/AF(76)53, Annex rev.3).

(3) The European Space Agency functioned de facto from 31 May 1975. The ESA Convention entered into force on 30 October 1980. Date of deposit of instruments of ratification:

Member States of ESA	**Ratification**
Austria	30.12.1986
Belgium	03.10.1978
Denmark	15.09.1977
Finland	01.01.1995
France	30.10.1980
Germany	26.07.1977
Ireland	10.12.1980
Italy	20.02.1978
Netherlands	06.02.1979
Norway	30.12.1986
Spain	07.02.1979
Sweden	06.04.1976
Switzerland	19.11.1976
United Kingdom	28.03.1978

A Cooperative Agreement between ESA and Canada entered into force on 1 January 1989 and will remain in force for 10 years.

ARTICLE I ESTABLISHMENT OF THE AGENCY

1. A European organisation, called the "European Space Agency", hereinafter referred to as "the Agency", is hereby established.

2. The members of the Agency, hereinafter referred to as "Member States", shall be the States which are parties to this Convention in accordance with Articles XX and XXII.

3. All Member States shall participate in the mandatory activities referred to in Article V, 1 *a*, and shall contribute to the fixed common costs of the Agency, referred to in Annex II.

4. The Headquarters of the Agency shall be situated in the Paris area.

ARTICLE II PURPOSE

The purpose of the Agency shall be to provide for and to promote, for exclusively peaceful purposes, cooperation among European States in space research and technology and their space applications, with a view to their being used for scientific purposes and for operational space applications systems :

a. by elaborating and implementing a long-term European space policy, by recommending space objectives to the Member States, and by concerting the policies of the Member States with respect to other national and international organisations and institutions;

b. by elaborating and implementing activities and programmes in the space field;

c. by coordinating the European space programme and national programmes, and by integrating the latter progressively and as completely as possible into the European space programme, in particular as regards the development of applications satellites;

d. by elaborating and implementing the industrial policy appropriate to its programme and by recommending a coherent industrial policy to the Member States.

ARTICLE III INFORMATION AND DATA

1. Member States and the Agency shall facilitate the exchange of scientific and technical information pertaining to the fields of space research and technology and their space applications, provided that a Member State shall not be required to communicate any information obtained outside the Agency if it considers that such communication would be inconsistent with the interests of its own security or its own agreements with third parties, or the conditions under which such information has been obtained.

2. In carrying out its activities under Article V, the Agency shall ensure that any scientific results shall be published or otherwise made widely available after prior use by the scientists responsible for the experiments. The resulting reduced data shall be the property of the Agency.

3. When placing contracts or entering into agreements, the Agency shall, with regard to the resulting inventions and technical data, secure such rights as may be appropriate for the protection of its interests, of those of the Member States participating in the relevant programme, and of those of persons and bodies under their jurisdiction. These rights

shall include in particular the rights of access, of disclosure, and of use. Such inventions and technical data shall be communicated to the participating States.

4. Those inventions and technical data that are the property of the Agency shall be disclosed to the Member States and may be used for their own purposes by these Member States and by persons and bodies under their jurisdiction, free of charge.

5. The detailed rules for the application of the foregoing provisions shall be adopted by the Council, by a two-thirds majority of all Member States.

ARTICLE IV EXCHANGE OF PERSONS

Member States shall facilitate the exchange of persons concerned with work within the competence of the Agency, consistent with the application to any person of their laws and regulations relating to entry into, stay in, or departure from, their territories.

ARTICLE V ACTIVITIES AND PROGRAMMES

1. The activities of the Agency shall include mandatory activities, in which all Member States participate, and optional activities, in which all Member States participate apart from those that formally declare themselves not interested in participating therein.

2.

a. With respect to the mandatory activities, the Agency shall :

i. ensure the execution of basic activities, such as education, documentation, studies of future projects and technological research work;

ii. ensure the elaboration and execution of a scientific programme including satellites and other space systems;

iii. collect relevant information and disseminate it to Member States, draw attention to gaps and duplication, and provide advice and assistance for the harmonisation of international and national programmes;

iv. maintain regular contact with the users of space techniques and keep itself informed of their requirements.

b. With respect to the optional activities, the Agency shall ensure, in accordance with the provisions of Annex III, the execution of programmes which may, in particular, include:

i. the design, development, construction, launching, placing in orbit, and control of satellites and other space systems;

ii. the design, development, construction, and operation of launch facilities and space transport systems.

3. In the area of space applications the Agency may, should the occasion arise, carry out operational activities under conditions to be defined by the Council by a majority of all Member States. When so doing the Agency shall :

a. place at the disposal of the operating agencies concerned such of its own facilities as may be useful to them;

b. ensure as required, on behalf of the operating agencies concerned, the launching, placing in orbit and control of operational application satellites;

c. carry out any other activity requested by users and approved by the Council.The cost of such operational activities shall be borne by the users concerned.

4. With respect to the coordination and integration of programmes referred to in Article II *c*, the Agency shall receive in good time from Member States information on projects relating to new space programmes, facilitate consultations among the Member States, undertake any necessary evaluation and formulate appropriate rules to be adopted by the Council by a unanimous vote of all Member States. The objectives and procedures of the internationalisation of programmes are set out in Annex IV.

ARTICLE VI FACILITIES AND SERVICES

1. For the execution of the programmes entrusted to it, the Agency :

   a. shall maintain the internal capability required for the preparation and supervision of its tasks and, to this end, shall establish and operate such establishments and facilities as are required for its activities;

   b. may enter into special arrangements for the execution of certain parts of its programmes by, or in cooperation with, national institutions of the Member States, or for the management by the Agency itself of certain national facilities.

2. In implementing their programmes, the Member States and the Agency shall endeavour to make the best use of their existing facilities and available services as a first priority, and to rationalise them; accordingly they shall not set up new facilities or services without having first examined the possibility of using the existing means.

ARTICLE VII INDUSTRIAL POLICY

1. The industrial policy which the Agency is to elaborate and apply by virtue of Article II *d* shall be designed in particular to :

a. meet the requirements of the European space programme and the coordinated national space programmes in a cost-effective manner;

b. improve the world-wide competitiveness of European industry by maintaining and developing space technology and by encouraging the rationalisation and development of an industrial structure appropriate to market requirements, making use in the first place of the existing industrial potential of all Member States;

c. ensure that all Member States participate in an equitable manner, having regard to their financial contribution, in implementing the European space programme and in the associated development of space technology; in particular the Agency shall, for the execution of its programmes, grant preference to the fullest extent possible to industry in all Member States, which shall be given the maximum opportunity to participate in the work of technological interest undertaken for the Agency;

d. exploit the advantages of free competitive bidding in all cases, except where this would be incompatible with other defined objectives of industrial policy.
Other objectives may be defined by the Council by a unanimous decision of all Member States. The detailed arrangements for the attainment of these objectives shall be those set out in Annex V and in rules which shall be adopted by the Council by a two-thirds majority of all Member States and reviewed periodically

2. For the execution of its programmes, the Agency shall make the maximum use of external contractors consistent with the maintenance of the internal capability referred to in Article VI, 1.

ARTICLE VIII LAUNCHERS AND OTHER SPACE TRANSPORT SYSTEMS

1. When defining its missions, the Agency shall take into account the launchers or other space transport systems developed within the framework of its programmes, or by a Member State, or with a significant Agency contribution, and shall grant preference to their utilisation for appropriate payloads if this does not present an unreasonable disadvantage compared with other launchers or space transport means available at the envisaged time, in respect of cost, reliability and mission suitability.

2. If activities or programmes under Article V include the use of launchers or other space transport systems, the participating States shall, when the programme in question is submitted for approval or acceptance, inform the Council of the launcher or space transport system envisaged. If during the execution of a programme the participating States wish to use a launcher or space transport system other than the one originally adopted, the Council shall make a decision on this change in accordance with the same rules as those applied in respect of the initial approval or acceptance of the programme.

ARTICLE IX USE OF FACILITIES, ASSISTANCE TO MEMBER STATES, AND SUPPLY OF PRODUCTS

1. Provided that their use for its own activities and programmes is not thereby prejudiced, the Agency shall make its facilities available, at the cost of the State concerned, to any Member State that asks to use them for its own programmes. The Council shall determine, by a two-thirds majority of all Member States, the practical arrangements under which the facilities will be made available.
2. If, outside the activities and programmes referred to in Article V but within the purpose of the Agency, one or more Member States wish to engage in a project, the Council may decide by a two-thirds majority of all Member States to make available the assistance of the Agency. The resulting cost to the Agency shall be met by the Member State or States concerned.
3. *a.* Products developed under a programme of the Agency shall be supplied to any Member State that has taken part in the funding of the programme in question and asks for such products to be supplied for its own purposes

   b. The Council shall determine by a two-thirds majority of all Member States the practical arrangements under which such products will be supplied and in particular the measures to be taken by the Agency in regard to its contractors to enable the requesting Member State to obtain those products.

   c. This Member State may ask the Agency to state whether it considers that the prices proposed by the contractors are fair and reasonable and whether, under similar circumstances, it would consider them acceptable for the purposes of its own requirements.

   d. The fulfilment of the requests referred to in this paragraph shall not involve the Agency in any additional costs, and all costs resulting from such requests shall be borne by the requesting Member State.

ARTICLE X ORGANS

The organs of the Agency shall be the Council, and the Director General assisted by a staff.

ARTICLE XI THE COUNCIL

1. The Council shall be composed of representatives of the Member States.

2. The Council shall meet as and when required, either at delegate level or at ministerial level. The meetings shall be held at the Agency's Headquarters unless the Council decides otherwise.
3. *a.* The Council shall elect for two years a Chairman and vice-chairmen, who may be re-elected once for a further year. The Chairman shall direct the proceedings of the Council and ensure the preparation of its decisions; he shall inform the Member States of proposals for the execution of an optional programme; he shall assist in coordinating the activities of the organs of the Agency. He shall maintain liaison with the Member States, through their delegates to the Council, on general policy matters affecting the Agency and shall endeavour to harmonise their views thereon. In the interval between meetings, he shall advise the Director General and shall obtain from him all necessary information.

   b. The Chairman shall be assisted by a Bureau, the composition of which shall be decided by the Council and which shall be convened by the Chairman. The Bureau shall advise the Chairman in the preparation of Council meetings.
4. When the Council meets at ministerial level it shall elect a chairman for the meeting. The next ministerial meeting shall be convened by him.
5. In addition to the functions set forth elsewhere in this Convention and in accordance with its provisions, the Council shall :

   a. as regards the activities and programme referred to in Article V, 1 a *(i)* and *(ii:)*

      i. approve the activities and programme by a majority of all Members States; decisions to this effect may only be changed by new decisions adopted by a two-thirds majority of all Member States;

      ii. determine, by a unanimous decision of all Member States, the level of resources to be made available to the Agency for the coming five-year period;

      iii. determine, by a unanimous decision of all Member States, towards the end of the third year of each five-year period and after a review of the situation, the level of resources to be made available to the Agency for the new five-year period starting at the end of this third year;

   b. as regards the activities referred to in Article V, 1 a *(iii)* and *(iv)*:

      i. define the policy to be followed by the Agency in pursuit of its purpose;

      ii. adopt, by a two-thirds majority of all Member States, recommendations addressed to Member States;

   c. as regards the optional programmes referred to in Article V, 1 *b* :

      i. accept each programme by a majority of all Member States;

      ii. determine, as appropriate, in the course of their implementation, the order of priority of programmes;

   d. adopt the annual work plans of the Agency;

   e. as regards the budgets as defined in Annex II :

      i. adopt the annual general budget of the Agency by a two-thirds majority of all Member States;

ii. adopt each programme budget by a two-thirds majority of the participating States;

f. adopt, by a two-thirds majority of all Member States, the Financial Regulations and all other financial arrangements of the Agency;

g. keep under review expenditure on the mandatory and optional activities referred to in Article V, 1;

h. approve and publish the audited annual accounts of the Agency;

i. adopt the Staff Regulations by a two-thirds majority of all Member States;

j. adopt, by a two-thirds majority of all Member States, rules under which authorisation will be given, bearing in mind the peaceful purposes of the Agency, for the transfer outside the territories of the Member States of technology and products developed under the activities of the Agency or with its help;

k. decide on the admission of new Member States in accordance with Article XXII;

l. decide on the arrangements to be made in accordance with Article XXIV in the event of a Member State's denouncing this Convention or ceasing to be a member under Article XVIII;

m. take all other measures necessary for the fulfilment of the purpose of the Agency within the framework of this Convention.

6. *a.* Each Member State shall have one vote in the Council. However, a Member State shall not have the right to vote on matters concerning exclusively an accepted programme in which it does not take part.

b. A Member State shall have no vote in the Council if the amount of its arrears of contributions to the Agency in respect of all activities and programmes covered by Article V in which it participates exceeds the assessed amount of its contributions for the current financial year. Moreover, if the amount of a Member State's arrears of contributions to any one of the programmes under Article V, 1 a *(ii)* or V, 1 *b* in which it participates exceeds the assessed amount of its contributions to that programme for the current financial year, then that Member State shall have no vote in the Council on questions relating exclusively to that programme. In any such case, the Member State may nevertheless be authorised to vote in the Council if a two-thirds majority of all Member States considers that the non-payment of contributions is due to circumstances beyond its control.

c. The presence of delegates from a majority of all Member States shall be necessary to constitute a quorum at any meeting of the Council.

d. Except where this Convention provides otherwise, decisions of the Council shall be taken by a simple majority of Member States represented and voting.

e. In determining the unanimity or majorities provided for in this Convention, account shall not be taken of a Member State which has no vote.

7. The Council shall adopt its own rules of procedure.

8. *a.* The Council shall establish a Science Programme Committee, to which it shall refer any matter relating to the mandatory scientific programme under Article V, 1 *a (ii)*. It shall authorise that Committee to take decisions regarding that programme, subject always to the Council's functions of determining the level of resources and adopting the annual budget. The terms of reference of the Science Programme Committee shall be

determined by the Council by a two-thirds majority of all Member States and in accordance with this Article.

b. The Council may establish such other subordinate bodies as may be necessary for the purpose of the Agency. The establishment and terms of reference of such bodies, and the cases in which they have powers of decision, shall be determined by the Council by a two-thirds majority of all Member States.

c. When a subordinate body examines a question relating exclusively to one of the optional programmes referred to in Article V, 1 *b*, non-participating States shall have no vote unless all participating States decide otherwise.

ARTICLE XII DIRECTOR GENERAL AND STAFF

1. *a.* The Council shall, by a two-thirds majority of all Member States, appoint a Director General for a defined period and may, by the same majority, terminate his appointment.

   b. The Director General shall be the chief executive officer of the Agency and its legal representative. He shall take all measures necessary for the management of the Agency, the execution of its programmes, the implementation of its policy and the fulfilment of its purpose, in accordance with the directives issued by the Council. He shall have authority over the establishments of the Agency. He shall, in regard to the financial administration of the Agency, act in accordance with the provisions of Annex II . He shall make an annual report to the Council, and this report shall be published. He may also submit proposals concerning activities and programmes as well as measures designed to ensure the fulfilment of the Agency's purpose. He attends meetings of the Agency without the right to vote.

   c. The Council may postpone the appointment of the Director General for such period as it considers necessary either upon the entry into force of this Convention or in the event of a subsequent vacancy. In this event, it shall appoint a person to act in his place, who shall have such powers and responsibilities as the Council may determine.

2. The Director General shall be assisted by such scientific, technical, administrative and clerical staff as he may consider necessary, within the limits authorised by the Council.

3. *a.* Senior management staff, as defined by the Council, shall be appointed and may be dismissed by the Council on the recommendation of the Director General. Appointments and dismissals made by the Council shall require a two-thirds majority of all Member States.

   b. Other staff members shall be appointed and may be dismissed by the Director General, acting on the authority of the Council.

   c. All staff shall be recruited on the basis of their qualifications, taking into account an adequate distribution of posts among nationals of the Member States. Appointments and their termination shall be in accordance with the Staff Regulations.

   d. Scientists who are not members of the staff and who carry out research in the establishments of the Agency shall be subject to the authority of the Director General and to any general rules adopted by the Council.

4. The responsibilities of the Director General and the staff in regard to the Agency shall be exclusively international in character. In the discharge of their duties they shall not seek or receive instructions from any government or from any authority external to the Agency. Each Member State shall respect the international character of the responsibilities of the Director General and the staff, and shall not seek to influence them in the discharge of their duties.

ARTICLE XIII FINANCIAL CONTRIBUTIONS

1. Each Member State shall contribute to the costs of the activities and programme referred to in Article V, 1 *a* and, in accordance with Annex II, to the common costs of the Agency, in accordance with a scale adopted by the Council, by a two-thirds majority of all Member States, either every three years at the time of the review referred to in Article XI, 5 *a (iii)*, or whenever the Council, by a unanimous vote of all Member States, decides to establish a new scale. The scale of contributions shall be based on the average national income of each Member State for the three latest years for which statistics are available. Nevertheless,
   a. no Member State shall be required to pay contributions in excess of twenty-five percent of the total amount of contributions assessed by the Council to meet these costs;
   b. the Council may, by a two-thirds majority of all Member States, decide in the light of any special circumstances of a Member State to reduce its contribution for a limited period. In particular, when the annual per capita income of a Member State is less than an amount to be decided by the Council by the same majority, this shall be considered as a special circumstance within the meaning of this provision.
2. Each Member State shall contribute to the costs of each optional programme covered by Article V, 1 *(b)*, unless it has formally declared itself not interested in participating therein and is therefore not a participant. Unless all participating States decide otherwise, the scale of contributions to a given programme shall be based on the average national income of each participating State for the three latest years for which statistics are available. This scale shall be revised either every three years or whenever the Council decides to establish a new scale in accordance with paragraph 1. However, no participating State shall, by the operation of this scale, be required to pay contributions in excess of twenty-five percent of the total amount of contributions to the programme concerned. Nevertheless, the percentage contribution to be made by each participating State shall be equivalent to at least twenty-five percent of its percentage contribution established under the provisions of paragraph 1, unless all the participating States decide otherwise when adopting the programme or during the execution of the programme.
3. The statistical systems to be used for establishing the scales of contribution referred to in paragraphs 1 and 2 shall be the same, and shall be determined in the Financial Regulations.
4. *a.* Any State that was not a party to the Convention for the establishment of a European Space Research Organisation or to the Convention for the establishment of a European Organisation for the Development and Construction of Space Vehicle Launchers and which becomes a party to this Convention shall make, in addition to its contributions, a special payment related to the current value of the assets of the Agency. The amount of this special payment shall be fixed by the Council by a two-thirds majority of all Member States.
   b. Payments made in accordance with the provisions of sub-paragraph *a* shall be used to reduce the contributions of the other Member States unless the Council decides otherwise by a two-thirds majority of all Member States.
5. Contributions due under this Article shall be paid in accordance with Annex II.
6. Subject to any directions given by the Council, the Director General may accept gifts or legacies to the Agency provided that they are not subject to any conditions inconsistent with the purpose of the Agency.

ARTICLE XIV COOPERATION

1. The Agency may, upon decisions of the Council taken by unanimous votes of all Member States, cooperate with other international organisations and institutions and with

Governments, organisations and institutions of non-member States, and conclude agreements with them to this effect.

2. Such cooperation may take the form of participation by non-member States or international organisations in one or more of the programmes under Article V, I *a (ii)* and V, I *b*. Subject to the decisions to be taken under paragraph 1, the detailed arrangements for such cooperation shall be defined in each case by the Council by a two-thirds majority of the States participating in the programme in question. These arrangements may provide that a non-member State shall have a vote in the Council when the latter examines matters pertaining exclusively to the programme in which that State participates.

3. Such cooperation may also take the form of according associate membership to non-member States which undertake to contribute at least to the studies of future projects under Article V, 1 *a (i)* . The detailed arrangements for each such associate membership shall be defined by the Council by a two- thirds majority of all Member States.

ARTICLE XV LEGAL STATUS, PRIVILEGES AND IMMUNITIES

1. The Agency shall have legal personality.

2. The Agency, its staff members and experts, and the representatives of its Member States, shall enjoy the legal capacity, privileges and immunities provided for in Annex I.

3. Agreements concerning the Headquarters of the Agency and the establishments set up in accordance with Article VI shall be concluded between the Agency and the Member States on whose territories the Headquarters and establishments are situated.

ARTICLE XVI AMENDMENTS

1. The Council may recommend to Member States amendments to this Convention and to Annex I thereto. Any Member State that wishes to propose an amendment shall notify the Director General thereof. The Director General shall inform the Member States of any amendment so notified at least three months before it is discussed by the Council.

2. Any amendment recommended by the Council shall enter into force thirty days after the Government of France has received notification of acceptance from all Member States. The Government of France shall notify all Member States of the date of entry into force of any such amendment.

3. The Council may, by a unanimous vote of all Member States, amend any of the other Annexes to this Convention, provided that such amendments do not conflict with the Convention. Any such amendment shall enter into force on a date to be decided by the Council by a unanimous vote of all Member States. The Director General shall inform all Member States of any such amendment and of the date on which it will enter into force.

ARTICLE XVII DISPUTES

1. Any dispute between two or more Member States, or between any of them and the Agency, concerning the interpretation or application of this Convention or its Annexes, and likewise any dispute referred to in Article XXVI of Annex I, which is not settled by or through the Council, shall, at the request of any party to the dispute, be submitted to arbitration.

2. Unless the parties to the dispute decide otherwise, the arbitration procedure shall be in accordance with this Article and with additional rules to be adopted by the Council by a two-thirds majority of all Member States.

3. The Arbitration Tribunal shall consist of three members. Each party to the dispute shall nominate one arbitrator; the first two arbitrators shall nominate the third arbitrator, who shall be the chairman of the Arbitration Tribunal. The additional rules referred to in paragraph 2 shall determine the procedure to be followed if the nominations have not taken place within a specified time.

4. Member States or the Agency, not being parties to the dispute, may intervene in the proceedings with the consent of the Arbitration Tribunal if it considers that they have a substantial interest in the decision of the case.

5. The Arbitration Tribunal shall determine its seat and establish its own rules of procedure.

6. The award of the Arbitration Tribunal shall be made by a majority of its members, who may not abstain from voting. This award shall be final and binding on all parties to the dispute and no appeal shall lie against it. The parties shall comply with the award without delay. In the event of a dispute as to its meaning or scope, the Arbitration Tribunal shall interpret it at the request of any party to the dispute.

ARTICLE XVIII NON-FULFILMENT OF OBLIGATIONS

Any Member State which fails to fulfil its obligations under this Convention shall cease to be a member of the Agency on a decision of the Council taken by a two-thirds majority of all Member States. The provisions of Article XXIV shall apply in such a case.

ARTICLE XIX CONTINUITY OF RIGHTS AND OBLIGATIONS

On the date when this Convention enters into force, the Agency shall take over all rights and obligations of the European Space Research Organisation and of the European Organisation for the Development and Construction of Space Vehicle Launchers.

ARTICLE XX SIGNATURE AND RATIFICATION

1. This Convention shall be open until 31 December 1975 for signature by the States which are members of the European Space Conference. The Annexes to this Convention shall form an integral part thereof.

2. This Convention shall be subject to ratification or acceptance. Instruments of ratification or acceptance shall be deposited with the Government of France.

3. After the entry into force of the Convention and pending the deposit of its instrument of ratification or acceptance, a signatory State may take part in the meetings of the Agency, without the right to vote.

ARTICLE XXI ENTRY INTO FORCE

1. This Convention shall enter into force when the following States, being members of the European Space Research Organisation or the European Organisation for the Development and Construction of Space Vehicle Launchers, have signed it and have deposited with the Government of France their instruments of ratification or acceptance: the Kingdom of Belgium, the Kingdom of Denmark, the French Republic, the Federal

Republic of Germany, the Italian Republic, the Kingdom of the Netherlands, Spain, the Kingdom of Sweden, the Swiss Confederation and the United Kingdom of Great Britain and Northern Ireland. For any State ratifying, accepting or acceding to this Convention after its entry into force, the Convention shall become effective on the date of deposit by such State of its instrument of ratification, acceptance or accession.

2. The Convention for the establishment of a European Space Research Organisation and the Convention for the establishment of a European Organisation for the Development and Construction of Space Vehicle Launchers shall terminate on the date of the entry into force of this Convention.

ARTICLE XXII ACCESSION

1. After the entry into force of this Convention, any State may accede thereto following a decision of the Council taken by a unanimous vote of all Member States.
2. A State that wishes to accede to this Convention shall notify the Director General, who shall inform the Member States of this request at least three months before it is submitted to the Council for decision.
3. Instruments of accession shall be deposited with the Government of France.

ARTICLE XXIII NOTIFICATIONS

The Government of France shall notify all signatory and acceding States of:

a. the date of deposit of each instrument of ratification, acceptance or accession;

b. the date of entry into force of this Convention and of amendments covered by Article XVI, 2;

c. the denunciation of the Convention by a Member State.

ARTICLE XXIV DENUNCIATION

1. After this Convention has been in force for six years, any Member State may denounce it by notifying the Government of France, which shall notify the other Member States and the Director General. The denunciation shall take effect at the end of the financial year following that during which it was notified to the Government of France. After the denunciation has taken effect, the State concerned shall remain bound to honour its due share of the payment appropriations corresponding to approved contract authority used both under the budgets to which it was contributing for the year in which the denunciation was notified to the Government of France, and under previous budgets.
2. A Member State denouncing the Convention shall indemnify the Agency for any loss of property on its territory, unless a special agreement can be concluded with the Agency for the continued use of this property by the Agency or the continuation of certain activities of the Agency on the territory of the said State. Any such special agreement shall determine in particular to what extent and on what conditions the provisions of this Convention shall continue to apply, after the denunciation has taken effect, to the continued use of this property and the continuation of these activities.
3. A Member State denouncing the Convention, and the Agency, shall jointly determine any additional obligations to be borne by the said State.

4. The State concerned shall retain the rights it has acquired up to the date on which the denunciation takes effect.

ARTICLE XXV DISSOLUTION

1. The Agency shall be dissolved if the number of Member States becomes less than five. It may be dissolved at any time by agreement between the Member States.

2. In the event of dissolution the Council shall appoint a liquidation authority, which will negotiate with the States on whose territories the Headquarters and establishments of the Agency are situated at the time. The legal personality of the Agency shall subsist for the purposes of the liquidation.

3. Any surplus shall be distributed among those States that are members of the Agency at the time of the dissolution, in proportion to the contributions actually made by them from the dates of their becoming parties to this Convention. In the event of a deficit, this shall be met by the same States in proportion to their contributions as assessed for the financial year then current.

ARTICLE XXVI REGISTRATION

Upon the entry into force of this Convention, the Government of France shall register it with the Secretariat of the United Nations in accordance with Article 102 of the Charter of the United Nations.

EUROPEAN SPACE POLICY: "ESDP AND SPACE"

Following a detailed study of the military needs issued by the Hellenic presidency on 15 March 2003, the importance of space applications and functions was recognised by the Council on 19 May 2003 as well as in the Presidency report on ESDP, endorsed by the European Council at Thessaloniki on 1920 June 2003.

On 25th June 2003, the PSC contributed to the consultation process of the Green Paper on European Space Policy from the Commission and the European Space Agency, (doc 11209/03 RESTREINT), recognising the importance of space applications and functions to support and enhance the EU capabilities to carry out crisis management operations.

On 27 November 03, the Commission made a presentation on the White Paper on "Space: a new European frontier for an expanding Union An Action Plan for Implementing the European Space Policy" (circulated as doc 14886/03 17 Nov 03) to the PMG, which then discussed the matter.

With the aim of furthering the general discussions on the importance of space applications, the Italian Presidency organised a seminar entitled "Space and Security Policy in Europe" in Rome (2 December 2003). A report, drafted together by six European research institutes, was presented to this seminar, and further published by the EU ISS in December 2003 (ISS occasional papers n° 48).

On 09 December 2003, the PSC reiterated its position that further and regular interpillar reflection is needed to ensure that the security and defence aspects of CFSP and ESDP are taken into account during the deliberations on an EU Space Policy and its associated programmes. This interpillar reflection should take into account the work being done in the context of other EU initiatives including the ECAP project groups (such as Space Assets) identified in the Capabilities Conference Declaration, which was endorsed at the GAERC 19 May 2003 and other possible future projects linked to ESDP. In addition, the PSC noted that chapter 3.4 of the Commission White Paper on Space makes recommendations. On this basis, initial work began in Council bodies on possible ESDP aspects of the future EC Space Programme. This work would benefit from clear guidelines.

At the same time, a Group of Personalities (GoP)[1] developed the cornerstones of an EU Security Research Programme and the contribution it could make to address the new security challenges. It recognised the crucial character of Space based assets for a secure Europe. A panel of experts gathered by the European Commission is now working on the possible defence and security aspects of the future EC space programme.

On this background, it was felt useful that the EU Council developed a Space Policy, as a guideline for the coordination of all actions in the field of the use of Space assets for ESDP purposes. The PSC agreed on 16 November on the contents of this document, that is now submitted to COREPER with a view to its approval by the Council.

[1] Cochaired by European Commissioners Busquin and Liikanen, composed of Security Industry Chairmen and Chief Executives, serving Members of the European Parliament, Heads of major Research Institutes, highlevel European Defence Ministry officials, two highlevel political figures (Artisaari / Bildt), Commissioner Patten and the High Representative for the CFSP.

The European Security Strategy endorsed by the European Council in Brussels on 12 December 2003 has clearly stated that the European Union needed to be more active, more coherent and more capable. It has defined the main threats that needed to be addressed, among them:

the terrorist threat, and its linkages with international organised crime;

the proliferation of Weapons of Mass Destruction (WMDs), addressed inter alia through verification of the provisions of the Treaties;

the regional conflicts and their consequences. It also recognised that the first line of defence and security will often be abroad, though interconnected with European home security. This is true for all major threats, which causes, if not the actors, are most often rooted in remote countries.

Being an integral part of the Common Foreign Security Policy (CFSP), the European Security and Defence Policy (ESDP) has, during the last years, developed a number of tools to address these threats. It draws on all those instruments, civilian as well as military, made available to the EU by its Member States to prevent, manage and resolve crises. The necessity for a comprehensive civilian/military approach to address crisis in an effective and lasting way has been made evident by experience, including lessons learnt from United Nations and NATO operations. The considerable variety of the means and resources available from the different institutions composing the EU has led to a more and more coherent approach.

However, the continuous analysis of the European capabilities in the framework of the Headline Goal (HLG) process has identified a number of strategic and operational needs that are not yet fulfilled. EUMC has been requested to update the military requirements for Space assets. Following the findings of the initial phase of the European Capabilities Action Plan (ECAP), an ECAP Project Group on Space assets has been created to propose practical solutions for making space assets available for the planning and conduct of EUled crisis management operations (CMOs), thus contributing to filling some of the main identified capability gaps. Filling these gaps, when necessary by making use of space assets as necessary, is one of the objectives in the

Headline Goal 2010[2], which refers to the development of a space policy by 2006. The work on operational requirements carried out by the Space and Security panel (SPASEC) and its working groups concerning the security aspects of space should also be taken into account.

THE ADDED VALUE OF SPACE FOR CFSP/ESDP

Reliable information is the basis for early warning, which is itself the condition for early action and conflict prevention. In recent years, EU Member states were several times confronted with the difficult task of making decisions related to foreign crises. Unanimity is the rule for making decisions on ESDP matters. Ensured access to reliable information, available to all, minimises uncertainty and increases the chances for timely political decisions.

It is also essential to prevent proliferation and to ensure worldwide verification of treaties: our own experience in Europe shows that security may be reinforced by confidence building measures and armaments control systems. Information on water resources, large scale pollution, proliferation activities, movements of population including illegal immigration, all kinds of trafficking and many other elements which constitute the warning factors of major threats, can be essential for conflict prevention and fight against all less visible threats to European security such as terrorism and organised crime.

But this information is not always easy to collect with due respect to international law and foreign states' sovereignty over their territory and airspace. Spacebased sensors have the advantage of unrestricted access over potential or actual areas of operation and areas that are otherwise difficult to gain access to for political or military reasons. They can provide evidence of illicit activities, therefore contributing to the fight against those who would wish to undertake terrorist actions from foreign territory. Interpretation of satellite imagery by specialists of the EU Satellite Centre (SATCEN) and the Joint Research Centre (JRC/Ispra) can thus provide a valuable source of intelligence for assessments elaborated by the Situation Centre (SITCEN) to support the EU decision making process and planning activities.

The EU also needs to achieve an adequate level of operational capabilities and readiness, to ensure its own security as well as for contributing to the world security, in accordance with the objectives set in the European Security Strategy, in particular in the conduct of Crisis Management Operations (CMOs). Space assets can contribute to many capabilities needed for any civilian and military operation, such as communications, intelligence, positioning and weather forecast. Intelligence gathering at the tactical level can often be met by military means other than space assets, such as drones or reconnaissance aircraft, where that is politically and operationally feasible.

Space imagery can provide very valuable support to the planning and conduct of military, but also civilian aspects of Crisis Management Operations (CMO) precisely assessing the situation on the ground.

Secure and reliable communications are essential for exercising political control and strategic direction of any operation. They are also vital at the operational and tactical level. On external theatres, these capabilities may often depend upon spacebased assets, especially where local infrastructure is deficient.

Space based positioning and time distribution systems have become indispensable to all military forces and civilian units since the fielding of the first generation of satellite radio navigation systems. These are today vital to the conduct of all operations, from the most sophisticated command and control systems down to the individual element. For civilian as well as for military operations, precise and secure knowledge of the position of own troops, that is essential for the conduct of the operation and the safety of our personnel, is heavily dependant upon satellite radio navigation systems (GPS, Galiléo, Glonass) and reliable communications.

Space assets are major enablers for many operational capabilities. But too much reliance on space based assets, including in the economy sector, could induce new vulnerabilities in case these systems are defeated. This should be taken into account when considering European security and appropriate measures envisaged to identify, prevent, or at least to limit, these risks. Such measures could include space surveillance, spacebased detection, monitoring and identification of illicit activities. This could concur to the fight against proliferation of weapons of mass destruction (WMDs).

In providing valuable elements to the early decisionmaking process, to the planning and to the execution of military and civilian tasks, space assets could thus further contribute to making the EU more capable in the field of crisis management. They would at the same time contribute to fighting other recognised threats to the security of the Union.

IMPROVING EU CAPABILITIES

Providing the EU with access to the space assets able to contribute to early detection of crisis, crisis prevention and crisis management at the political, strategic and operational levels is therefore a way to enhance its decision making process and operational capabilities.

Some EU Member States have included space assets in their military priorities. Recently, significant military or multipleuse programmes were undertaken and preserved by several States. Different levels of cooperation exist between these Member States, ranging from full participation to common programmes, to agreements for mutual access to national capabilities.

Military capability will continue to remain within the remit of Member States. This should not prevent Member States to look for achieving the best possible level of capability through extensive cooperation, sharing and pooling of assets and capabilities wherever possible, within the limits acceptable with regard to their national sovereignty and vital interests. This is one of the aspects studied by the ECAP project Group on Space assets. Initiatives have also been taken by the EU SecretaryGeneral / High Representative for CFSP to initiate practical cooperation measures such as the arrangement on access by SATCEN to Hélios 1 products, and other exploratory talks with Member States owning or developing military space systems for EU access to their products. Meanwhile the Military Committee has undertaken, on the basis of ECAP previous work and of the Headline Goal 2010, an initial analysis of military needs for space assets. On the civilian security side, significant steps have been taken by the European Communities to include security objectives in civilian space programmes, as illustrated by the Global Monitoring for Environment and Security (GMES). It must be noted that, although not driven by military needs, almost all space programmes have a multipleuse capacity that could provide solutions to some military needs.

There are several ways for the EU to have when required access to space assets for ESDP purposes, that could be envisaged in the form of a stepbystep process, driven by actual capability requirements as a first step, and considering existing military assets in EU Member States and multipleuse capacities offered by existing civilian programmes. In parallel, ways other than recourse to space systems and use of data provided by these systems to fulfil requirements should also be considered, with a view to costeffectiveness, performances, and actual availability.

As a second step, the EU should be able to make use of already existing assets, belonging to its Member States, but also to commercial companies provided they are able to guarantee integrity and availability of the service offered including in times of crisis; in this regard, it is essential to draw lessons from experience. There are already agreements among EU Member States to share or to exchange capacities. The EU having no system of its own, the Member States political will to share information with the EU in support of a possible collective action is therefore essential. This access might be either based on permanent access to data or on a casebycase optin basis, depending upon the exact operational requirement. Costs eventually incurred would obviously be very different according to the nature of service provided (imagery or communications) and the degree of priority requested by the EU. Financial implications and appropriate financing modalities will have to be discussed, minimising costs as far as possible, and agreed upon before concrete measures are taken.

As a third step, the EU should ensure that it would be able to take advantage of multiple use capabilities inherent to existing civilian programmes planned in the framework of the Community programme. Many requirements issued by the first, second or third pillar, are met by identical technical solutions. Monitoring borders for example would basically draw upon the same instruments wherever in the world, and advantage could thus be taken of portions of the orbit, useless for Communities civilian objectives, to monitor borders for ESDP purposes in crisis areas. Satellite imagery can be used either to monitor a crisis or to assess a humanitarian urgency or an ecological disaster. A communication satellite designed to bridge the "digital divide" could easily[3] support operational traffic, encrypted offline, without any modification. Appropriate provisions as required, such as defined by the ECAP project Group on Space, should be made at an early stage of the programmes to ensure that ESDP requirements are known and that the programme specifications will take them into account to the extent compatible with its own priorities. Multipleuse technologies should be used to the maximum extent in order to avoid additional costs and unnecessary duplications. The process begun in May 2004 with the panel of experts on security called by the European Commission as a followup to the White paper on Space has been a first move towards this aim. It should be developed further in close cooperation between all potential users within the EU.

16. Possible agreements with third parties providing access to their own spacebased assets should also be explored to the extent possible. This should be complemented by appropriate recourse to service providers (such as Meteosat) with a view to avoid duplication wherever security of access is reasonably guaranteed.

A GLOBAL EU SPACE POLICY

Unlike most other space actors, Europe has developed its space capacities as an almost purely civilian endeavour. As a consequence, defence spacebased assets launched by European States are often just an extra load "piggybacking" on civilian platforms. Any comprehensive EU space policy should not attempt to break away from this heritage, but build on it. This is all the more appropriate when considering the dramatic expansion of multipleuse technologies. Therefore, the EU should not attempt at designing a standalone "Defence" space policy, but rather a global space policy, drawing as much as possible on existing and potential synergies. But while civilian space in the EU is already at the leading edge of the world's technology, defence applications have been developed and deployed by individual Member States and the EU as such has no automatic access to these systems.

EU approach to crisis management emphasises the existing and necessary synergy between civilian and military actors, and between ESDP and Community instruments. With due respect to the respective institutional competencies, a global space policy should emphasise the same synergy between civilian and military assets contributing to a coherent EU action, starting from the decisionmaking process down to the requested endstate, through the planning, the conduct and the reconstruction phases.

Galiléo, EGNOS[4], GMES and SATCOM[5], and their potential capacities, is a cornerstone of the European Community Space Programme. They also have the potential to contribute to civilian and/or military crisis management (in the case of GALILEO, such a contribution could be subject to the agreement of the Council). When adding to it existing and planned national military and mixed satellites (Hélios 1 and 2, SARLUPE, Cosmos/Skymed, TerrasarX, XstarEur, Pleïades, Cerise, Syracuse, Skynet, Sicral…), the civilian systems already used in Member States for security and defence purposes (such as Meteosat, SPOT, or maritime information satellites), and the independent launching capability provided by the Ariane family and the Kourou launching pad, it looks like many of the required tools are already in place. European actors would mainly need to consider bringing together civilian and military programmes, ensure interoperability and organise collective access to the subsequent capabilities in a way which allows Member States to profit also nationally from the multiplier effect. It should be noted in this regard that the principle of arrangements allowing the EU to benefit from several nationally developed military programmes has been agreed by Ministers of Defence of interested Member States[6], and that work is already ongoing on their contents.

Based on agreed operational needs, the following actions could be undertaken:

" In the short term, arrangements allowing the EU to have access to some Member states' owned

military assets or data originated by them, as well as to civilian assets with dualuse capabilities,

would constitute a first step towards providing the EU with space capacities to support ESDP.

" In the medium term, Member States should aim at complementing this pool of capacities

through voluntary contributions or other proposals in terms of partnership, exchange of

capacities or sharing of data.

" In the longer term, the requirements for space capabilities needed for security and defence as

well as for other purposes should be developed and agreed upon, and drive future programmes

that may be the subject of multilateral cooperative projects supported or possibly managed by

the EDA on behalf of Member States.

[4] Positioning programme complementing the American GPS system in the European region [5] digital data transmission satellites designed "to bridge the digital divide" [6] Letters by SG/HR to MODs of BE, GE, FR, IT and SP on 10 February 2004 and subsequent answers.

But for the EU to take full benefit of these successive steps, permanent access to a minimum number of assets such as communications terminal units should be considered. EU Member States own rather limited numbers. In case of an EU operation with recourse to NATO common assets and capabilities, access to NATO's owned equipment in the framework of Berlin Plus provides a possibility, but these are scarce assets and are not interoperable with all satellites. An EU data processing capability should also be envisaged, possibly based upon extension of existing EU SATCEN and JRC/Ispra capabilities[7], to make use of the access to space imagery, be it from commercial or military origin. Close cooperation between SATCEN and Community services, in particular JRC/Ispra, should be reinforced to avoid duplication.

The main flaw when trying to bring together several space programmes is actually interoperability. In the absence of any agreed standard, every space system has its own technical specifications. It is therefore almost impossible today to have a common ground segment, able to receive and process data provided by the different available sources. An agreed common standard[8] for future programmes, including civilian and defenceoriented ones, might allow over the long term for a dramatic limitation of the numbers of ground assets needed to receive and process data from all spacebased sources. The need for interoperability and common technical standards, including between civilian and military assets, is underlined in the document on Headline Goal 2010[9]. Promoting the definition and the use of common standards for future Member States' programmes as well as for cooperative programmes between Member States should therefore be a priority task for relevant bodies including the European Defence Agency. A practical step towards rationalisation was the agreement by six EU Member States on a Common Operational Requirement[10]. Extension of this agreement to other EU Member States might improve rationalisation of security and defence capabilities.

[7] capability to integrate information from several sensors could be considered to increase effectiveness [8] see project of Treaty establishing a Constitution for Europe Art III248 §2 [9] paragraphs 8 and 9 [10] "Besoin Opérationnel Commun" (BOC) signed by six European Staffs (B, D,E, F,GR, I)

CONCLUSION AND WAY AHEAD

The current EU Space Strategy[11] developed jointly by the European Commission (EC) and the European Space Agency (ESA) focuses on transport, environment and research. An EU space programme is already under development, namely driven by users' requirements such as satellite positioning, communications and Earth observation. But this Strategy had not taken into account the developments regarding the ESDP, which is now an integral part of the EU policy. The EU should take into account all identified and agreed upon ESDP civilian and military requirements.

To be more active, more coherent and more capable and to become, as proposed by the EU Security Strategy, a worldwide global actor ready to share responsibility for international security, Europe should have access to the best affordable capabilities for autonomous political assessment, sound decisionmaking, and effective conduct of actions. Space assets could provide a significant contribution to this endeavour and should be considered alongside other means. Identified and agreed upon ESDP requirements should therefore be reflected in the global EU Space Policy and its corresponding European Space Programme.

Developing such a global approach to Space Policy certainly requires a strong political will by Member States, based on an improved sense of solidarity and acknowledged sharing of vital interests, within the framework of existing EU principles on the respective roles of the EU and its Member States and institutional competencies. Sharing and pooling resources of the European Community and its Member States, drawing on multiple use technology and common standards, would certainly allow over time for significant costeffective collective achievements.

In order to achieve these objectives, a comprehensive roadmap including the following steps should be developed: " ESDP requirements should be specified on the basis of HLG 2010 and the initial study by the Military Committee.

" Arrangements for EU access to existing and planned military systems or data originated from such systems belonging to Member states should be concluded;

" ESDP requirements should be provided to the Commission and Member States to allow for identification of possible multipleuse capabilities inherent to civilian systems under development;

" In the context of the European Space Programme, a permanent interpillar dialogue should be established to ensure global coherence of all EU needs and requirements, with a view to optimise all programmes since the initial design phase and avoid unnecessary duplications and spending while respecting the institutional framework, competencies and prerogatives;

" A global EU Space policy should be developed and regularly updated, including the agreed ESDP requirements;

" Appropriate contracts of the SATCEN with commercial companies should be updated;

" In the longer term, harmonisation of military requirements for instance through the European Defence Agency should allow for more dedicated cooperation in the conception, design and development of future programmes.

" Once requirements have been defined, financial issues will have to be resolved before next steps are concluded.

" Possible agreements with third parties providing access to their own spacebased assets should also be explored to the extent possible.

THE INTERNATIONAL SPACE STATION AND THE SPACE SHUTTLE[1]

The International Space Station (ISS) program began in 1993, with Russia joining the United States, Europe, Japan, and Canada. Crews have occupied ISS on a 4-6 month rotating basis since November 2000.

The U.S. Space Shuttle, which first flew in April 1981, has been the major vehicle taking crews and cargo back and forth to ISS, but the shuttle system has encountered difficulties since the *Columbia* disaster in 2003. Russian Soyuz spacecraft are also used to take crews to and from ISS, and Russian Progress spacecraft deliver cargo, but cannot return anything to Earth, since they are not designed to survive reentry into the Earth's atmosphere. A Soyuz is always attached to the station as a lifeboat in case of an emergency.

President Bush, prompted in part by the *Columbia* tragedy, made a major space policy address on January 14, 2004, directing NASA to focus its activities on returning humans to the Moon and someday sending them to Mars. Included in this "Vision for Space Exploration" is a plan to retire the space shuttle in 2010. The President said the United States would fulfill its commitments to its space station partners, and the shuttle *Discovery* made the first post-*Columbia* flight to the ISS in July 2006. Shuttle flights have continued and completion of the space station is scheduled before the shuttle is retired in 2010. Meanwhile NASA has begun development of a new crew launch vehicle, named Ares, and a crew exploration vehicle, named Orion.

NASA programs were funded for FY2008 in Division B of the Consolidated Appropriations Act

(P.L. 110-161). The Space Operations program, which includes the space shuttle and the ISS, was funded at $6.734 billion. For FY2009 NASA requested $5.775 billion for these programs, but in the process revised its budgeting to move its overhead costs to a new account called Cross-Agency Support. Under the new system, the FY2008 Space Operations program would have received $5.526 billion, about $250 million less than the FY2009 request. NASA is currently operating under a continuing resolution (Division A of P.L. 110-329), which funded most civilian activities through March 6, 2009. Under the continuing resolution, Space Operations are funded at the $5.526 billion rate appropriated for FY2008.

An FY2009 NASA authorization bill (H.R. 6063) was introduced May 15, 2008. Among the provisions in the one-year authorization bill was a "Sense of the Congress" urging cooperation in the Moon/Mars activities with other nations pursuing human space flight. It also requires that NASA "terminate or suspend any activity of the Agency that, if continued between the date of enactment of this Act and April 30, 2009, would preclude the continued safe and effective flight of the Space Shuttle after fiscal year 2010 if the President inaugurated on January 20, 2009, were to

[1] Carl E. Behrens Specialist in Energy Policy March 18, 2009 Congressional Research Service

make a determination to delay the Space Shuttle's scheduled retirement." Congress passed the bill September 27, and it was signed by the President October 15 (P.L. 110-422).

MOST RECENT DEVELOPMENTS

With the signing of the Omnibus Appropriations Act for FY2009 (H.R. 1105, P.L. 111-5) on March 11, 2009, the National Aeronautics and Space Administration (NASA) was funded at $17.78 billion for the fiscal year. Of that total, $5.76 billion was allocated to Space Operations, which include the Space Shuttle and the International Space Station. For FY2008, NASA had received $5.53 billion for Space Operations.

As NASA continued to fly Space Shuttle missions to the International Space Station, the agency awaited the announcement of a new administrator to replace Michael Griffin, who resigned in January. On March 11 President Obama said he would appoint a new NASA director soon, and that one of biggest tasks of the new director would be "shaping a mission for NASA that is appropriate for the 21st Century."

THE INTERNATIONAL SPACE STATION (ISS)

NASA launched its first space station, Skylab, in 1973. Three crews were sent to live and work there in 1973-1974. It remained in orbit, unoccupied, until it reentered Earth's atmosphere in July 1979, disintegrating over Australia and the Indian Ocean. Skylab was never intended to be permanently occupied, but the goal of a permanently occupied space station with crews rotating on a regular basis, employing a reusable space transportation system (the space shuttle) was high on NASA's list for the post-Apollo years following the moon landings. Budget constraints forced NASA to choose to build the space shuttle first. The first launch of the shuttle was in April 1981. When NASA declared the shuttle "operational" in 1982, it was ready to initiate the space station program.

In his January 25, 1984 State of the Union address, President Reagan directed NASA to develop a permanently occupied space station within a decade, and to invite other countries to join. On July 20, 1989, the 20th anniversary of the first Apollo landing on the Moon, President George H. W. Bush voiced his support for the space station as the cornerstone of a long-range civilian space program eventually leading to bases on the Moon and Mars. That "Moon/Mars" program, the Space Exploration Initiative, was not greeted with enthusiasm in Congress, primarily due to budget concerns, and ended in FY1993, although the space station program continued.

President Clinton dramatically changed the character of the space station program in 1993 by adding Russia as a partner to this already international endeavor. That decision made the space station part of the U.S. foreign policy agenda to encourage Russia to abide by agreements to stop the proliferation of ballistic missile technology, and to support Russia economically and politically as it transitioned from the Soviet era. The Clinton Administration strongly supported the space station within certain budget limits.

The International Space Station program thus began in 1993, with Russia joining the United States, Europe, Japan, and Canada. An Intergovernmental Agreement (IGA) established three phases of space station cooperation. The IGA is a treaty in all the countries except the United States, where it is an Executive Agreement. It is implemented through Memoranda of Understanding (MOUs) between NASA and its counterpart agencies.

During Phase I (1995-1998), seven U.S. astronauts remained on Russia's space station *Mir* for long duration (several month) missions with Russian cosmonauts, Russian cosmonauts flew on the U.S. space shuttle seven times, and nine space shuttle missions docked with *Mir* to exchange crews and deliver supplies. Repeated system failures and two life-threatening emergencies on *Mir* in 1997 raised questions about whether NASA should leave more astronauts on *Mir*, but

NASA decided *Mir* was sufficiently safe to continue the program. (*Mir* was deorbited in 2001.) Phases II and III involve construction of the International Space Station itself, and blend into each other. Phase II began in 1998 and was completed in July 2001; Phase III is underway.

President George W. Bush, prompted in part by the February 2003 space shuttle *Columbia* tragedy, made a major space policy address on January 14, 2004, directing NASA to focus its activities on returning humans to the Moon and eventually sending them to Mars. Included in this "Vision for Space Exploration" was a decision to retire the space shuttle in 2010. The President said the United States would fulfill its commitments to its space station partners.

ISS DESIGN, COST, SCHEDULE, AND LIFETIME

Under the original ISS schedule, assembly of the station would have been completed in 2002, with operations at least through 2012. President Bush restructured the space station program in 2001, and left it unclear when assembly would be completed. NASA briefing charts in March 2003 showed space station operations possibly continuing until 2022. Under President Bush's January 2004 "Vision for Space Exploration," however, NASA plans to complete its utilization of ISS in 2016 (though the other partners may continue to use it after that time).

ISS segments have been and continue to be launched into space on U.S. or Russian launch vehicles and assembled in orbit. The space station is composed of a multitude of modules, solar arrays to generate electricity, remote manipulator systems, and other elements. (Details can be found at http://spaceflight.nasa.gov/home/index.html.)

The U.S. space shuttle has been the major vehicle taking crews and cargo back and forth to ISS, but the shuttle system encountered difficulties after the *Columbia* disaster and did not resume flights until 2006. Russian Soyuz spacecraft are also used to take crews to and from ISS, and Russian Progress spacecraft deliver cargo, but cannot return anything to Earth, since it is not designed to survive reentry into the Earth's atmosphere. A Soyuz is always attached to the station as a lifeboat in case of an emergency.

"Expedition" crews have occupied ISS on a 4-6 month rotating basis since November 2000. Originally the crews had three members (two Russians and one American, or two Americans and one Russian). Crew size was temporarily reduced to two (one American, one Russian) while the U.S. shuttle was grounded in order to reduce resupply requirements. The number of astronauts who can live on the space station is limited in part by how many can be returned to Earth in an emergency by lifeboats docked to the station. Only Russian Soyuz spacecraft are available as lifeboats. Each Soyuz can hold three people, limiting crew size to three if only one Soyuz is attached. The plan is that crew size will grow to six once assembly is completed.

Each Soyuz must be replaced every six months. The replacement missions are called "taxi" flights since the crews bring a new Soyuz up to ISS and bring the old one back to Earth. Therefore, under normal conditions, the long duration Expedition crews are regularly visited by taxi crews, and by the space shuttle bringing up additional ISS segments or exchanging Expedition crews. When the shuttle is unavailable, Expedition crews are taken back and forth on the "taxi" flights.

In order to contract for Soyuz service to the ISS, NASA has needed an exemption from the Iran Nonproliferation Act (INA) (P.L. 106-178), which banned U.S. payments to Russia in connection with the International Space Station (ISS) unless the U.S. President determined that Russia was taking steps to halt proliferation of nuclear weapons and missile technology to Iran. In 2005 Congress amended INA to exempt Soyuz flights to the ISS from the ban through 2011. It also extended the provisions of the INA to Syria and North Korea, and renamed it the Iran, North Korea, and Syria Nonproliferation Act (INKSNA). NASA asked for a legislated extension of this exemption, and waiver authority was extended until July 1, 2016, in the Continuing Appropriations

Act of 2009 (P.L. 110-329). (For details see CRS Report RL34477, *Extending NASA's Exemption from the Iran, North Korea, and Syria Nonproliferation Act*, by Carl E. Behrens and Mary Beth Nikitin.)

SPACE STATION COSTS

From FY1994 to FY2001, the cost estimate for building ISS grew from $17.4 billion to about $25 billion. The $17.4 billion estimate did not include launch costs, operational costs after completion of assembly, civil service costs, or other costs. NASA estimated the program's life-cycle cost (all costs, including funding spent prior to 1993) from FY1985 toFY2012 at $72.3 billion. In 1998, GAO estimated the life-cycle cost at $95.6 billion (GAO/NSIAD-98-147). More recent, comparable, life-cycle estimates are not available from NASA or GAO.

As costs continued to rise, Congress voted to legislate a $25 billion cap on development of the ISS program, plus $17.7 billion for associated shuttle launches, in the FY2000-FY2002 NASA authorization act (P.L. 106-391). In January 2001, however, NASA announced that the cost would be over $30 billion, 72% above the 1993 estimate, and $5 billion above the legislated cap. NASA explained that program managers had underestimated the complexity of building and operating the station. The Bush Administration signaled it supported the legislated cap, would not provide additional funds, and NASA would have to find what it needed from within its Human Space Flight account.

"CORE COMPLETE" CONFIGURATION

In February 2001, the Bush Administration announced it would cancel or defer some ISS hardware to stay within the cap and control space station costs. The decision truncated construction of the space station at a stage the Administration called "core complete." In 2001, the space station program office at Johnson Space Center (JSC) estimated that it would cost $8.3 billion from FY2002 toFY2006 to build the core complete configuration, described at that time as all the U.S. hardware planned for launch through "Node 2," plus the launch of laboratories being built by Europe and Japan. NASA subsequently began distinguishing between "U.S. Core Complete" (the launches through Node 2, which, prior to the *Columbia* tragedy, was scheduled for February 2004) and "International Partner (IP) Core Complete" which included the addition of European and Japanese laboratory modules (then anticipated in 2008).

The new policy was followed by President Bush's January 2004 "Vision for Space Exploration," which directs that U.S. research on ISS be restricted only to that which supports the Vision. A new research plan, incorporating the President's Vision, was issued by NASA in June 2006, as mandated by the 2005 NASA authorization act (P.L. 109-155).[1]

At a January 2005 Heads of Agency meeting, the partners endorsed a final configuration of ISS, but NASA subsequently announced changes to it. The agency now plans to conduct only 16 (instead of 28) shuttle launches to the ISS, all before the end of FY2010 (September 30, 2010), and has dropped plans to launch the centrifuge and its accommodation module, and Russia's Science Power Platform. The agency plans to meet with the other ISS partners to discuss these changes.

The changes to the ISS are largely due to the new direction NASA is taking in response to the Vision for Space Exploration. The Vision calls for development of a Crew Exploration Vehicle, now named Orion, to take astronauts to and from the Moon, and a Crew Launch Vehicle, now named Ares I. Orion also can take them to and from the ISS, and NASA Administrator Griffin stated at a September 19, 2005 press conference that Orion would be used to take crews to and from the ISS, and to serve as a lifeboat for them. If Orion is built as announced, it would fulfill the U.S. commitment to build a crew return capability, and allow the ISS crew size to increase to its originally planned complement of seven. An Earth-orbit capability is planned by 2014 (although

NASA now considers early 2015 more likely) with the ability to take astronauts to and from the Moon following no later than 2020.

Table 1. U.S. Space Station Funding

(in $ millions)

Fiscal Year	Request	Appropriated
1985	150	150
1986	230	205
1987	410	410
1988	767	425
1989	967	900
1990	2,050	1,750
1991	2,430	1,900
1992	2,029	2,029
1993	2,250	2,100
1994	2,106	2,106
1995	2,113	2,113
1996	2,115	2,144
1997	2,149	2,149
1998	2,121	2,441a

[1] The National Aeronautics and Space Administration (NASA).*Research and Utilization Plan for the International Space Station (ISS) A Report to the Committee on Science of the United States House of Representatives and the Committee on Commerce, Science, and Transportation of the United States Senate*. June 2006. http://www.exploration.nasa.gov/documents/reports/NASA_Research_and_Utilization_Plan_for_the_ISS.pdf

Fiscal Year Request Appropriated

1999	2,270	2,270
2000	2,483	2,323
2001	2,115	2,115
2002	2,114	2,093
2003	1,839	1,810
2004b	2,285	2,085
2005	2,412	2,058
2006	1,995	1,972
2007	1,894	NAc
2008	1,894	2,209
2009	2,060d	2,060

Note: These numbers reflect NASA's figures for "the space station program." Over the years, what is included in that definition has changed. In recent years, funding for ISS research has been located in a different account from ISS development funding. The figures here represent the ISS development and ISS research request and appropriations to the maximum extent possible.

a. NASA's FY1999 budget documents showed $2.501 billion in the expectation Congress would approve additional transfer requests, but it did not.

b. Reflects shift to full cost accounting.

c. Space shuttle funding was not specified in P.L. 110-5.

d. Reflects change in budgeting for overhead costs.

THE SPACE SHUTTLE

The Space Transportation System (STS)—the Space Shuttle—is a partially reusable launch vehicle and is the sole U.S. means for launching humans into orbit. It consists of an airplane-like Orbiter, with two Solid Rocket Boosters (SRBs) on each side, and a large, cylindrical External Tank (ET) that carries fuel for the Orbiter's main engines. The Orbiters and SRBs are reused; the ET is not. NASA has three remaining spaceflight-worthy Orbiters: *Discovery*, *Atlantis*, and *Endeavour*.

THE *CHALLENGER* AND *COLUMBIA* TRAGEDIES

More than 100 shuttle launches have taken place since April 1981. Two ended in tragedy, each killing seven astronauts. In 1986, the space shuttle *Challenger* exploded 73 seconds after launch because of the failure of a seal (an O-ring) between two segments of an SRB. In 2003, the space shuttle *Columbia* disintegrated as it returned to Earth after 16 days in orbit (see CRS Report RS21408, *NASA's Space Shuttle Program: The Columbia Tragedy, the Discovery Mission, and the Future of the Shuttle*, by Marcia S. Smith). A hole in *Columbia's* left wing, caused during launch by a piece of foam insulation that detached from the ET, allowed hot gases to enter the wing during reentry, deforming it and causing the shuttle to break up. The *Columbia* Accident Investigation Board (CAIB) found that the tragedy was caused by technical and organizational failures, and made 29 recommendations, 15 of which it said should be completed before the shuttle returned to flight.[2]

Sean O'Keefe, NASA's Administrator from December 2001-February 2005, said NASA would comply with the CAIB recommendations.

RETURN TO FLIGHT (RTF)

NASA launched the space shuttle *Discovery* on the first of two "Return to Flight" (RTF) missions—STS-114—on July 26, 2005, and it successfully landed on August 9. On July 27, however, NASA announced that a piece of foam had detached from STS-114's ET during launch, similar to what happened to *Columbia*. Cameras and other sensors on *Discovery* and on the International Space Station—to which *Discovery* was docked for much of its mission—imaged the Orbiter and determined that it was not damaged, but further shuttle launches were suspended. Meanwhile, the images revealed that two "gapfillers"—ceramic coated fabric placed between thermal protection tiles—were protruding on the belly of the Orbiter that could have affected aerodynamic heating during reentry. One of the *Discovery* astronauts removed them during a space walk. The second RTF mission—STS-121—was scheduled for September 2005, but deferred.

STS-121 launched on July 4, 2006, and returned safely to Earth on July 17. The shuttle *Atlantis* launched September 9 on STS 115, during which construction of the International Space Station was resumed.

Current plans for the shuttle include nine more flights to complete the ISS before the shuttle is permanently grounded in 2010. Also planned is another flight to service the Hubble Space Telescope. Following the Columbia disaster, then-Administrator Sean O'Keefe had cancelled the Hubble servicing mission, partly on the grounds that shuttle astronauts would not be able to reach the ISS as a haven in case the shuttle was unable to return to earth. The decision was put under review by the new Administrator, Michael Griffin, and on October 31, 2006, he announced that the Hubble mission would be undertaken in 2008. The servicing would extend the life of the telescope through 2013. To deal with emergencies, NASA planned to prepare a "launch on need" mission with a second shuttle ready to launch on a rescue mission if the first was found defective during the servicing mission.

The launch was in final stages of preparation when a major data handling unit already in place in the Hubble telescope failed in late September 2008. A backup unit in the telescope was activated, but the service mission was revised to include carrying a second data handling unit, which had been stored on earth, to replace the failed one. NASA determined that assessing and preparing the second unit for installation and service would delay the mission until May or June of 2009.

The Shuttle's Future

NASA attempted unsuccessfully for many years to develop a "second generation" reusable launch vehicle (RLV) to replace the shuttle. In 2002 NASA indicated the shuttle would continue flying

[2] National Aeronautics and Space Administration. *Columbia Accident Investigation Board Report*. August 2003. See CRS Report RS21606, *NASA's Space Shuttle Columbia: Synopsis of the Report of the Columbia Accident Investigation Board*, by Marcia S. Smith.

until at least 2015, and perhaps 2020 or beyond. The *Columbia* tragedy, and President Bush's 2004 Vision for Space Exploration—to return astronauts to the Moon by 2020 and someday send them to Mars—forced NASA to revise that plan.

The President's Vision calls for the shuttle program, which absorbs approximately 25% of NASA's annual budget, to be terminated in 2010. A primary motivation is to make that funding available to implement other aspects of the Vision, although there also is concern about shuttle safety. Congress has been debating the Vision, including its impact on the shuttle and on U.S. human access to space. Some Members wanted to terminate the shuttle earlier than 2010 because they feel it is too risky and/or that the funds should be spent on accelerating the Vision. Others want to retain the shuttle at least until a new spacecraft, the Crew Exploration Vehicle (CEV), is available to take astronauts to and from the ISS. The CEV is now planned for 2015 at the earliest, leaving a multi-year gap during which U.S. astronauts would have to rely on Russia for access to the ISS.

The 2008 NASAAuthorizationAct (P.L. 110-422) included a provision requiring NASA to "terminate or suspend any activity of the Agency that, if continued between the date of enactment of this Act and April 30, 2009, would preclude the continued safe and effective flight of the Space Shuttle after fiscal year 2010 if the President inaugurated on January 20, 2009, were to make a determination to delay the Space Shuttle's scheduled retirement." (Sec. 611d.)

Shuttle Budget

Funding for the shuttle for FY2008 was $3.981 billion. For FY2009, NASA requested $2.982 billion for the shuttle, but that amount reflects NASA's new system for funding program overhead costs, which created a new Cross-Agency Support account. By the new accounting system, the comparable shuttle funding for FY2008 was $3.267 billion. The omnibus appropriations bill (P.L. 111-8) appropriated the requested $2.982 billion. (For details on the NASA budget, see CRS Report RS22818, *National Aeronautics and Space Administration: Overview, FY2009 Budget, and Issues for Congress*, by Daniel Morgan and Carl E. Behrens.)

ISSUES FOR CONGRESS

In passing the 2005 NASA authorization act (P.L. 109-105), Congress basically agreed with the President's plan for directing NASA's attention to a return to the Moon and manned missions to Mars. Included in the Moon-Mars "Vision" is the plan to end flights of the Space Shuttle in 2010, and restriction of U.S. experiments on the ISS mostly to those that forward the goal Moon-Mars goal. A number of critical questions remain, however.

Adequacy of funding is the chief question raised about NASA's activities. In presenting the Moon-Mars vision, the President did not request significantly increased money for NASA, despite chronic indications that the missions it was already charged with were underfunded. NASA has responded to the new mission by cutting back funding for its other activities, primarily in scientific research and aeronautics.

Although *Discovery's* "Return to Flight" mission of July 2006 was a success, the ability of the shuttle fleet to carry out enough flights to complete construction of the ISS by 2010 is still in question. With a history of more than a hundred

successful missions, it might be assumed that another 15 or so would be considered more or less routine, but instead, each launch is still a major and risky event. The great complexity of the vehicle and the extreme environment in which it operates require constant attention to possible accidents and malfunctions, many of which must be addressed on an ad hoc basis.

The future role of the ISS is also unclear. Assuming that enough shuttle flights are made to carry out "core completion" of the station by 2010, it is not clear what will be done with the ISS after that. In particular, there will be a gap of several years between retirement of the shuttle in 2010 and beginning of flight of the Crew Exploration Vehicle, to be designed for the return to the moon but able to serve as a vehicle to reach the ISS.

THE EUROPEAN SPACE POLICY

THE COUNCIL HAVING REGARD to the Framework Agreement between the European Community and the European Space Agency, which entered into force in May 2004, and to the increasing cooperation between the two parties;

RECALLING the orientations of the 'Space Council' meetings of 25 November 2004, 7 June 2005 and 28 November 2005;

EMPHASISING the Resolution of the 'Space Council' on 22 May 2007 which welcomed and supported the European Space Policy and established the policy base for space in Europe;

NOTING that the Resolution invited the European Commission, the ESA Director General and the European Union and ESA Member States, to monitor and evaluate the implementation of the policy within the scope of the Framework Agreement, including the implementation of the key issues defined in the annexes of the Resolution;

NOTING that the Member States, on the basis of the European Space Policy Implementation Plan, have identified as priorities two programmatic areas for action which are the successful implementation of both GALILEO and GMES (Global Monitoring for Environment and Security), as well as a number of horizontal issues;

RECOGNISING the significant progress made in these areas as set out in the joint ESAEC progress report, and WELCOMING the progress made in the settingup of an international relations strategy for space in Europe; REAFFIRMS in this context the importance for Europe to maintain an autonomous access to space, a worldclass scientific programme, its leading satellite applications services in operational meteorology and commercial communications, and a sustained and innovative technology base;

UNDERLINES the importance to strengthen ECESA coordination of space technology development programmes, in particular on critical space technologies for European strategic nondependence;

RECALLS the discussions among European ministers in charge of space at their informal meeting in Kourou, the space port of Europe, on 21 and 22 July 2008.

I A VISION FOR EUROPE IN SPACE

RECOGNISING that the European Space Policy established the vision to strengthen Europe as a worldclass space leader responding to the needs of European policies and objectives, in terms of applications, services and related infrastructures, contributing to its societal, cultural, economic and scientific influence, developing its industrial and scientific potential and assuring its political and technological autonomy in a reasoned, coherent and realistic manner;

RECOGNISING that this policy, based on the EU, ESA and their respective Member States involved in the European Space Programme, should continue to be implemented and further developed, maintaining ambitious goals within the capacities made available for research and operational applications; EMPHASISING that all of Europe's space activities contribute to the goals of, and fully respect the principles set out by, the United Nations' "Outer Space Treaty", in particular:

- the exploration and use of outer space for the benefit and in the interests of all countries and the recognition of outer space as a province of all mankind;
- the use of outer space for exclusively peaceful purposes;
- the promotion of international cooperation in the exploration and use of outer space; and that Europe supports the ongoing efforts of the United Nations' Committee on the Peaceful Uses of Outer Space (COPUOS) on the mitigation and prevention of space debris;

UNDERLINING the importance of reinforcing public support for the development of space technologies, ensuring complementarities of actions and maximising synergies with nonspace developments;

RECOGNISING that the European Union, ESA and their respective Member States are the three key actors of the European Space Policy, and HIGHLIGHTING that the European Union is taking increased responsibilities for space matters, especially related to space applications, consistent with those of a global actor and bringing an addedvalue to ESA and Member States while respecting roles and responsibilities of each of them;

CONSIDERING that, in these conditions and in the framework of the European Space Policy, the European Union, as well as ESA and their respective Member States, are main space actors, and they will develop Europe as a leading space power on the international scene. In this context, IDENTIFIES the following issues to be addressed:

- In line with the international relations strategy, promoting a coherent approach to international cooperation in space programmes in view of their global nature, while recognising that Europe should be able to face global competition. Solar System exploration, Earth environment and sustainable development are the priority domains for implementing international cooperation;

- Ensuring for all the EU and ESA Member States an open and equitable access to the benefits of space activities in terms of public policies, scientific data, technological development, industrial activities and services;

- Strengthening the existing mechanisms to coordinate European expertise and investments in space funded from Community, intergovernmental and national sources as well as settingup the mechanisms to improve synergies between civil and defence space programmes, while respecting the specific requirements of both sectors, including their decision competences and finance schemes;

- Guaranteeing the continuity of autonomous, reliable and costefficient access to space at affordable conditions for the EU, ESA and their respective Member States, based on both the availability of a set of adequate and competitive worldclass launchers and an operational European space port;

- Federating through the EU, based on the policy needs of the EU, and of ESA and EU Member States, their demand for space applications, through a transparent process enabling the EU to identify user requirements, to establish priorities, and to ensure the continuity of services. Maintenance of the necessary tools to provide these services, including their funding, should be executed in partnership with the stakeholders concerned and the operators when appropriate;

- Promoting the development of an appropriate regulatory framework to ease the swift emergence of innovative and competitive downstream services, in particular with the objective of guaranteeing sustained access to spectrum for all spacebased applications;

- Organising the governance of space in line with the Resolution of the 4th Space Council and with the political ambitions of EU, ESA and their respective Member States, in particular the optimisation of the decisionmaking process in the field of space in the Council of the European Union as well as in other EU institutions;

- Developing adequate EU instruments and funding schemes, taking into account the specificities of the space sector, the need to strengthen its overall and its industry's competitiveness and the necessity of a balanced industrial structure; and allowing appropriate longterm Community investment for space related research and for the operation of sustainable spacebased applications for the benefit of Europe and its citizens, in particular by examining all spacerelated policy consequences within the framework of the next financial perspective;

- Strengthening the cooperation with developing countries;

UNDERLINES the added value for EU and ESA Member States' ministers in charge of space to meet as frequently as useful to address the main political issues on the basis of an appropriate roadmap.

II CURRENT PRIORITIES

WELCOMES the following significant advances in the GALILEO and GMES programmes:

- the successful launch and inorbit validation of GIOVEB, allowing to demonstrate critical new technologies needed for the performance of the Galileo system;

- the conclusions of the EU Council in November 2007 and the subsequent adoption by the European Parliament and the Council of the Regulation on the further implementation of the European GNSS programmes, clarifying the public governance of the Galileo deployment phase and the EGNOS operations and the implications of the actions for GALILEO funding;

- the decision by ESA Member States to initiate the GMES Space Component programme; the conclusion of the ECESA agreement providing the Community contribution to this programme; and the provision by EC of initial operational funding through the implementation of a GMES preparatory action in 2008;
- the demonstration at the Lille GMES Forum of preoperational GMES services;
- the launch of the GMES and Africa partnership through the "Lisbon Process on GMES and Africa" with a view to serving the African users;
- the proposal on the fundamental architecture of GMES described in the Munich roadmap;

REAFFIRMS the continuing priority to implement both GALILEO and GMES rapidly.

A. GALILEO

RECOGNISING that Galileo constitutes the first flagship space programme of the EU;

INVITES the Commission to take into consideration and analyse past difficulties in order to reap the full benefits of this experience;

LOOKS FORWARD the creation of the Galileo InterInstitutional Panel;

UNDERLINES the need for increased coordination between the European Commission, ESA and their respective Member States, in relation to R&D for satellite navigation systems, services and applications; HIGHLIGHTS the continued cooperation with international partners on issues of system compatibility and interoperability;

INVITES the Commission to address the legal implications of the European Community becoming the owner of those tangible and intangible assets it has funded related to space applications, such as those of the Galileo and EGNOS programmes, in particular with respect to liability issues.

B. GMES

RECALLING that GMES is a userdriven initiative that should maximise the use of existing space and nonspace Earth Observation centres, capacities and services in Europe, including EUMETSAT, the EU Satellite Centre ...;

STRESSES that the insitu Earth observation infrastructures which Member States support, together with space observation infrastructures, represent a major contribution to the Earth observation capacities and should be made available to GMES on a permanent basis;

HIGHLIGHTS that data and service continuity is indispensable and that such continuity must be guaranteed by the European Union, in particular through longterm funding, based on partnerships for the various GMES components;

REAFFIRMS the role of ESA as development and procurement agency for the dedicated GMES Sentinel missions, and as coordinator for the whole GMES Space Component, including contributions made available by Member States, EUMETSAT and further GMES partners;

INVITES the Commission to define an adequate GMES legal framework, involving the Council General Secretariat where appropriate, and to explore the implications of certification of satellite remote sensed data;

STRESSES that many GMES information services have the nature of a European public good and

must be made available according to a full and open access principle, subject to some constraints such as security;

IDENTIFIES the need to elaborate an action plan leading to the settingup of an EU GMES programme, aiming at securing the continuity of GMES services and of the critical observation data which they require. This action plan should include:

- An approach for the overall GMES governance and all its components, identifying the relevant actors with their role and responsibilities, and based on a series of GMES partnerships, as well as arrangements for appropriate participation of ESA Member States which are not members of the EU;
- A plan for sustainable funding of GMES, based on an assessment of the overall financing needs for GMES and the definition of the budgetary strategy at national and European levels, taking into account the three successive stages: R&D stage to be funded from R&D appropriations, transition stage with mixed R&D and operational funding, operational stage with dedicated funding for operations involving the users;
- The definition of operational service delivery mechanisms for each GMES service, including identification of their operators;
- The definition between the EU and Member States of a process to formalise their commitments to contribute to GMES through existing insitu observation and service infrastructures;
- The identification of the role of the GEO initiative and other intergovernmental or multilateral initiatives, such as CEOS, in accessing the whole range of data available, as well as the contribution of GMES to these international endeavours;
- A process to establish a comprehensive data policy for all data generated by the GMES system, including appropriate labelling and a data security policy which will ensure that all sensitive data is fully protected and kept confidential.

WELCOMES

- the proposal of the European Commission for a new preparatory action in the Preliminary Draft Budget for 2009, paving the way for a future funding of the operational phase of GMES;
- the intention of the Commission to address all of these issues in a Communication to be adopted by the end of October 2008, having consulted with the main stakeholders, in particular agreeing with ESA an overall programmatic approach for the GMES Space Component;
- the intention of the ESA DG, having consulted with ESA Member States and the Commission, to submit a proposal for the GMES Space Component Segment 2 programme for subscription to the ESA Council at Ministerial level in November 2008.

NEW PRIORITIES WITHIN THE EUROPEAN SPACE POLICY

HIGHLIGHTS that the European Council welcomed on 14 March 2008 the joint report from the High Representative and the European Commission on Climate Change and International Security which in particular recalled that the majority of UN emergency appeals for humanitarian aid in 2007 were climate related, and identified the multiplier effect of climate change on security risks;

RECALLS that the European Council asked the Council of the European Union to submit recommendations on appropriate followup action in the field;

IDENTIFIES the following four priority areas in the implementation of the European Space Policy for the coming period.

A. SPACE AnD CLIMATE CHANGE

CONSIDERING that climate challenges facing humanity are of global concern, and that the EU is adapting its policies to address them;

EMPHASISES the objective to improve the qualitative and quantitative understanding of the extent of climate change and of its consequences and the need to continue and expand the European contributions to this understanding and related modelling, in order to provide the evidence base for key decisions to be taken in environment policy;

RECOGNISES the unique contribution of space programmes which, through their global observation capacity and longterm coverage, provide the series of data requested by the scientific community for research into climate change, while complementing other observation and measurement tools;

RECOGNISES the contribution of the ESA Living Planet Programme and the national Earth science space missions, of EUMETSAT operational programmes, and of the GMES Space Component infrastructure to the collection of observations enabling Europe to derive time series of climate parameters and to understand the major climate processes;

CALLS FOR the scientific community, in conjunction with the European Commission, ESA and EUMETSAT, to define how the range of GMES services and European space observation archives can contribute most effectively to the provision of data including Essential Climate Variables for scientific research;

INVITES the Commission to conduct a study to assess the needs for full access to standardised data and for increased computing power, and the means to fulfil them, taking into account existing capacities and networking in Europe; WELCOMES the joint preparation by ESA and EUMETSAT of a programme proposal for Meteosat Third Generation (MTG) to be submitted to the ESA Council at Ministerial level in November 2008 and subsequently to the EUMETSAT Council; its central role being in operational meteorology, MTG will also contribute to GMES, to the monitoring of climate and thus to the detection of global climate change.

B. CONTRIBUTION OF SPACE TO THE LISBON STRATEGY

EMPHASISES that space, as a high tech R&D domain and through the economic exploitation of its results, can contribute to reaching the Lisbon goals so as to fulfil the economic, educational, social and environmental ambitions of the EU and the expectations of its citizens, and so as to achieve the objectives for growth and employment by providing new business opportunities and innovative solutions for various services, throughout Europe, thus contributing to territorial cohesion;

CONSIDERS that, with the adoption by the European Parliament and Council on 18 December 2006 of the Community Seventh Framework Programme for Research, Technological Development and Demonstration and its new thematic chapter Space as part of the Cooperation Specific Programme, space has been recognised by the EU as one of the priorities and key building blocks of the European knowledgebased society;

UNDERLINES that space applications, such as satellite telecommunications, the EGNOS and GALILEO systems and GMES, are expected to create substantial global market opportunities, especially for SMEs, through the development of valueadded downstream services; and that the EU, ESA and their respective Member States must accordingly maximise the value they secure from these space assets. This growth should be promoted to accelerate the emergence of economic opportunities and the development of services seamlessly integrating navigation, observation and communications satellite systems and combining them with terrestrial networks. To achieve this requires appropriate regulatory framework, sustained access to radiospectrum for space applications, and development of standards in relevant areas; TAKES NOTE that space activities could thus be considered for inclusion into the Lead Market Initiative.

C. SPACE AND SECURITY

HIGHLIGHTS the important contribution of space to the CFSP/ESDP including the Petersberg tasks, and thus to the security of European citizens;

RECALLS that space assets have become indispensable for our economy and that their security must thus be ensured; UNDERLINES the need for Europe, in line with its ambition to strengthen its status as worldclass space leader, to develop a European capability for the monitoring and surveillance of its space infrastructure and of space debris, initially based on existing national and European assets, taking benefit of relationships which may be established with other partner nations and their capabilities;

CONSIDERS that, taking into account the international and political nature of this capability, the European Union will take, liaising with ESA and their respective Member States, an active role to set up progressively this capability and an appropriate governance structure;

UNDERLINES the need for Europe to have the ability to detect noncompliance with implementation of international treaties and obligations, being a key instrument to safeguard and promote European values;

WELCOMES, within the decision competences and finance schemes of the existing framework, the setting up of the structured dialogue among European institutional actors in response to the 2007 Space Council Resolution, with the aim of achieving a substantial increase in the coordination of space, security and defence related activities, including the European Commission, the General Secretariat of the Council, the European Defence Agency, ESA and Member States;

RECALLING that GMES relies on some dual use observation capacities and that GALILEO, GMES and satellite communications systems will provide services which may be of interest for some security applications; RECOGNISES that the uses made by any military users of Galileo or GMES must be consistent with the principle that Galileo and GMES are civil systems under civil control, and consequently that any change to this principle would require examination in the framework of the Title V/TEU and in particular Articles 17 and 23 thereof, as well as in the framework of the ESA Convention;

HIGHLIGHTS the need to:

- define the way and means to improve the coordination between civilian and defence space programmes in longterm arrangements;
- develop a capacity to meet European user needs for comprehensive situational awareness of the space environment through a coordinated activity within Europe, and possibly with other partners;
- recognise Europe's dependence on overseas suppliers for selected critical space technologies and components, establish mitigation strategies to ensure guaranteed European access, and take practical steps to pursue reduction of Europe's dependence;

UNDERLINES the benefits of drawing on existing capacities and infrastructures at national as well as European level;

TAKES NOTE of the intention of the ESA DG to submit a proposal for a programme on space situational awareness, for subscription at the ESA Council at Ministerial level in November 2008, setting the basis for the operational capability and respecting the roles of the European Defence Agency and of the EU and ESA Member States.

D. SPACE EXPLORATIOn

WELCOMES the successful launch of the ESA Columbus laboratory and the successful demonstrations of the Automated Transfer Vehicle "Jules Verne" as truly European technology development projects and crucial elements for ensuring European access to the International Space Station ISS and its sustained utilisation;

AFFIRMS that space exploration is a political and global endeavour and that Europe should undertake its action within a worldwide programme, without any monopoly or appropriation by one country; the different actors taking part with their own capacities and priorities;

HIGHLIGHTS the need for Europe to develop a common vision and longterm strategic planning for exploration, ensuring key positions for Europe, therefore based on its domains of excellence; thus the necessary political dialogue with the other states involved in the worldwide exploration programme has to be further developed and promoted on the international scene by the European Union, ESA and their respective Member States, each one in its own role, and in close coordination among each other;

WELCOMES the proposal by the Commission to organise a high level political conference on a long term global vision for space exploration, opening a public debate on the European role in this global endeavour, and based on appropriate preparatory studies coordinated by ESA to assess the European domains of excellence, and elaborate different scenarios for a European contribution with associated costs and planning;

TAKES NOTE of the Global Exploration Strategy outlining the global coordination of the major powers' plans for human and robotic exploration, including the possibility, at a later stage, of a human expedition to Mars; AFFIRMS that Europe, building on its successful track record in exploration over a number of decades, in which science has been the key driver, is committed to playing a significant role in the international enterprise to explore the Solar system and to develop a deep understanding of the conditions for life to function beyond our planet and ACKNOWLEDGES the fact that establishing Europe as a fundamental pillar of these activities will be achieved only through sustained investment;

REALISES that the technologies to be developed must be assessed carefully with a perspective of taking key decisions, and HIGHLIGHTS that these may have a lasting impact on the perception of Europe's scientific and technological capabilities in the world and the selfperception of European citizens;

UNDERLINES the value of space exploration for inspiring young Europeans to choose a career in science and technology and to strengthen these capabilities in Europe.

EUROPEAN SPACE PROGRAM - PRELIMINARY ELEMENTS

1. INTRODUCTION: RATIONALE OF THE EUROPEAN SPACE PROGRAMME

The European Space Programme constitutes a common, inclusive and flexible programmatic base , on which Europe performs its space activities by utilising the available resources most efficiently at all levels. The Programme shall be in compliance with the objectives and guidelines set out in the European Space Policy and provide programmatic objectives per space domain in support of its implementation. It will allow major actors involved to monitor progress achieved and support their efforts towards increasing transparency, reducing unnecessary duplication and enhancing complementarity among all space-related programmes. It will thereby help to achieve in due course a coordinated joint European space effort, responding to European and national user needs and requirements.

The European actors taking part in the Programme are

- The European Space Agency (ESA) : Key instruments for delivery will be the Agency's mandatory and optional programmes within an ESA long-term strategy taking into account other intergovernmental, EU and national capacities and activities so as to effectively organise synergies and integrated approaches between them.

- The European Union (EU): Key instruments for delivery will be in particular the 7th Framework Programme for Research and Technological Development (FP7) and the Trans-European Network programmes and resources coming from non R&D sources.

- Member States: Initiated and executed at Member State level in line with national rules and funding instruments, national space programmes are responding to national needs while also aiming at supporting wider objectives pursued by the European Space Policy. Bi- and multilateral activities also contribute.

- Other intergovernmental organisations operating at European level , in particular agencies operating and exploiting European space assets such as the European Organisation for the Exploitation of Meteorological Satellites (EUMETSAT).

Activities performed in European industry and by operators and service providers need to be duly taken into account and close cooperation ensured on technology R&D as well as mission development and operations. Public-private partnership (PPP) schemes for applications and service provision need to be further developed.

The preliminary elements of the European Space Programme in the fields of Applications and Foundations represent a non-binding collection of activities that are currently on-going and envisaged for the short to medium term. They correspond to inputs provided by the respective stakeholders, and aiming to increase transparency of existing space activities in Europe. In the applications field, particular focus is given to joint European programmes such as GMES and GALILEO.

The activities decided prior to the establishment of the European Space Policy are grouped by objectives derived from the European Space Policy - an exercise that will gain in coherence as the Programme is successively updated. Further activities at a lower level of detail such as the development of specific payloads, instruments or experiments, are not brought out in this document, yet actively contribute to the overall European space effort.

The Programme's content and the methodology of its use will be reviewed and updated regularly in close coordination with users and all stakeholders to reflect or adapt it to overall policy objectives. Future activities shall be included gradually so as to build a coordinated and common strategic framework , displaying the complementarity of space activities across Europe. After further discussion within the High-Level Space Policy Group on the future scope and specific design of the European Space Programme, a first revision of the document will be prepared during 2007 and 2008 by the ESA/EC Joint Secretariat. The revision will take account of the preparation of ESA's Ministerial Council and the further evolution of EC programmes and national plans. A revised European Space Programme will be presented to the Fifth meeting of the Space Council to endorse it through its formal adoption by the Competitive Council and by the ESA Council at Ministerial level.

Member States are therefore invited to inform the Joint ESA/EC Secretariat on planned new programmes as well as on updates to existing programmes; the information should show how such programmes fit with applicable ESP objectives and guidelines.

Indicative budget information for the time period 2007-2013 is provided for major European-level activities. Similar detailed national budget information by space domain needs to be collected during the revision phase of the European Space Programme. The current document provides an indication on the overall weight of national programmes within the overall European space effort by indicating their share in percentage, taking 2006 as a reference year. The inclusion of an activity in the European Space Programme framework does not imply any exchange of funds or transfer of responsibility amongst the stakeholders.

2. DRAFT PROGRAMMATIC OBJECTIVES

In support of overall policy objectives outlined in the Strategic mission statement of the European Space Policy, the European Space Programmes identifies programmatic objectives by space domain based on provisions within the European Space Policy document, the ESA Long-Term Plan 2007-2016 and the 7th Framework Programmes for Research and Technological Development (FP7). Implementation should build on ongoing and short to medium term activities as outlined in chapter 3.

Overall Space Policy Objectives | Draft Programme Objectives |

APPLICATIONS To take account of the evolution of user needs, integrated space systems shall be developed and the integration of space and terrestrial systems shall be promoted, to provide effective and cost-efficient services. |

SATELLITE NAVIGATION |

Foster innovation, competitiveness and economic growth. Meet Europe's security needs. Secure unrestricted access to new and critical technologies, systems and capabilities. | Secure European independence regarding state-of-the-art satellite navigation technology and develop services offered by navigation systems increasing the quality, quantity and variety of data offered and contributing to the competitiveness of the European industry, by: Proceeding with the full-fledged development of the GNSS infrastructure Preparing future GNSS infrastructures and launching the technology demonstration of a 2nd generation PNT System Promoting the use of PNT systems within integrated applications Ensuring implementation of international partnerships on GNSS |

EARTH OBSERVATION |

Foster innovation, competitiveness and economic growth. Meet Europe's security needs. Secure unrestricted access to new and critical technologies, systems and capabilities. Serve Europe's public interest in sustainable policy making in the field of Environment and Climate Change | Develop a full-fledged European Earth Observation Infrastructure and associated operational services for Environment and Security, taking into account dual-use assets, by: Proceeding with GMES space component development based on national and ESA developed assets. Reinforcing the dialogue with user communities and fostering the development and validation of new services and applications, exploring data policies, mechanisms for data provision and management (space and in-situ), focusing in the first place on a set of GMES fast-track services by 2008. Reinforcing the dialogue within appropriate international bodies; identifying the role of GMES within GEOSS Ensuring continuity of European capacities in operational meteorology |

SATELLITE COMMUNICATIONS |

Foster innovation, competitiveness and economic growth and be the market leader in commercial space. Meet Europe's security needs. Secure unrestricted access to new and critical technologies, systems and capabilities. | Contribute to the competitiveness of the European space industry and to the development of the information society in Europe, by: Developing advanced satellite communication technologies in cooperation with industry and operators leading to new demonstration missions, taking due account of dual-use requirements Increasing integration with terrestrial systems in support of European and global communication infrastructures and linking to other application domains Developing end-user services offered by satellite communications increasing the quality, quantity and variety of data, and developing multimedia satellite systems (merging mobile, broadband and broadcast). |

SECURITY AND DEFENCE Future national and European-level developments. |

Meet Europe's security and defence needs. Secure unrestricted access to new and critical technologies, systems and capabilities. | Future national and European developments |

FOUNDATIONS |

SCIENCE and TECHNOLOGY |

Foster innovation, competitiveness and economic growth Enhance the contribution of space research to the knowledge-based society Meet Europe's security needs Secure unrestricted access to new and critical technologies, systems and capabilities Serve Europe's public interest in sustainable policy making in the field of Environment and Climate Change | SPACE SCIENCE |

In the context of the Lisbon Agenda and ESA's actions in support of competitiveness and discovery, develop global scientific leadership and expand the knowledge base, by: focusing on specific priority issues: Life and Planetary formation, Solar System, Fundamental laws of the Universe, Origins and evolution of the Universe Supporting synergies of space science activities with other science activities and technology feed-off to applications Increasing international cooperation activities |

EARTH SCIENCE |

Extend Earth Science activities aimed in support of global change assessment and environmental policies, by: Developing new missions in support of core topics: Ocean/Hydrosphere, Air/Atmosphere, Ice/Cryosphere, Land Surface/Biosphere, Solid Earth/Geosphere Ensuring effective exploitation of science data in conjunction with EO applications within GMES Increasing international cooperation activities |

TECHNOLOGY |

Contribute to innovation and competitiveness, by: Maximising synergies between civil and defence, space and non-space technology developments Identifying critical technologies and perform associated technology demonstration missions Harmonising technology developments |

INTERNATIONAL SPACE STATION AND EXPLORATION OF THE SOLAR SYSTEM |

Enhance the contribution of space research to the knowledge-based society Secure unrestricted access to new and critical technologies, systems and capabilities | Reap the scientific and technological benefits of investments made in the ISS project and prepare future exploration activities to become a key player within the international exploration architecture, by: Ensuring maximum scientific return especially in Life and Physical Sciences on investment and optimum utilisation of the ISS Strengthening life and physical sciences activities in support of non-space applications and exploration-related activities. Preparing and demonstrating core capabilities (enabling technologies and infrastructures) for next step in exploration, notably robotic Mars exploration and possible activities linked to Lunar Exploration. Cooperation with international partners on human space transportation according to scenarios to be decided by Member States. |

ACCESS TO SPACE |

Secure unrestricted access to new and critical technologies, systems and capabilities. Foster innovation, competitiveness and economic growth | Maintain independent access to space, by: Maintaining Europe's space port (Guiana Space Centre)under operational conditions Consolidating the European family of launchers: Ariane 5, Vega, Soyuz at CSG Preparing and safeguarding technological and industrial capabilities for the development of next generation launchers Exploring possible long-term options for cooperation with strategic partners |

3. EUROPEAN-LEVEL AND NATIONAL ACTIVITIES SUPPORTING THE DRAFT OBJECTIVES OF THE EUROPEAN SPACE PROGRAMME

The following tables provide an overview by space domain about activities that are currently on-going and envisaged for the short to medium term by the actors taking part in the European Space Programme and that are disposed to support the draft programmatic objectives outlined in chapter 2.

3.1. Satellite Navigation

Programmatic Objectives | Activities |

Proceeding with the full-fledged development of the GNSS infrastructure | I. European-level : Galileo IOV and EGNOS/GNSS support programme (funded by EC and ESA and technically managed by ESA) Galileo FOC deployment and Galileo EGNOS operations managed by the Galileo Supervisory Authority (GSA) and the Galileo Operating Company (GOC) under a concession contract. Giove-A (2005), Giove-B (2007), IOV 1-2-3-4, FOC |

Preparation of future GNSS infrastructures: Launch of technology demonstration of 2nd generation PNT System | I. European level : FP7 Programme (GSA) GNSS Evolution Programme (under preparation by ESA) |

II. National level : National PNT-related technology development |

Promoting the use of PNT systems within integrated applications | I. European-level : GSA: FP7 SESAR (air traffic management) Proposed ESA Integrated Applications Programme |

II. National level : Diverse National applications development activities [e.g. GATE (Galileo test environment for hardware, applications and services) (D), Galileo Test Range project (I), Navigation Project (F)] National PNT-related technology developments [e.g. Argos 3/Sarsat 3 (F), GATE (D), HIGAPS, INDOOR, GALTEC, SEAGATE (D)] |

Ensuring implementation of international partnerships on GNSS | I. European level : EC activities with technical support from GSA: cooperation with the United States (Galileo/GPS-Agreement of July 2004), Russia (GLONASS, negotiations ongoing) and other countries relating to interoperability and compatibility of Galileo with existing and coming GNSS Systems. ESA activities relating to Galileo and EGNOS |

3.2. Earth Observation

Programmatic Objectives | Activities |

Proceed with GMES space component development based on national and ESA developed assets | I. European level : GMES Space Component Programme (ESA) Planned : GMES Sentinel 1a (2011) and 2a (2012), Sentinel-3a (2012), Sentinel-1b and 2b (2013), Sentinel-3b (2014) FP7-Space Theme: Contribution to the GMES Space Component (EC) Coordination of national or bilateral/multilateral EO mission developments |

II. National level : National technology development programmes/Preliminary activities and precursor missions, e.g. PASO studies (F), SAFARI (D), METIMAGE (D) Development of national or bilateral/multilateral EO missions Under operation: TerraSAR-X (2006/D), DMC/Disaster monitoring constellation (UK2002/2005), Spot-4/5, Jason-1 (2001/F) Planned: Rapid-Eye (2007/D), TanDEM (2009/D), TerraSAR-X 2nd gen. (2012), Venus (2009/F), SARAL (2009/F) En MAP (2010/D), Bissat (2010/I) Future Spanish EO satellite, Future Norwegian Sea monitoring satellite; Pleiades (2008/F), Cosmo-SkymMed (2007/08/09/I) Cosmo-Skymed 2nd gen. (2012/2013/I), Pleiades (2009/2010/F-B), SVEA: Swedish national surveillance mission, HYPSEO (I), Microsat (I), Nanoform (I) |

Reinforce dialogue with user communities and foster the development + validation of new services and applications, also by exploring mechanisms for data provision and management (space and in-situ), focusing in the first place on a set of GMES fast-track services in the field of: Emergency Management Land Monitoring Maritime Services Atmospheric services (in preparation) | I. European level : FP7-Space Theme (e.g. grant agreement or other mechanisms for space and non-space data provision). Additional activities foreseen in other FP7 themes (e.g. ICT, environment), in JRC direct actions, and in other EU sectoral policies (e.g. agriculture, fisheries, development, ...) (EC) GMES Service element transfer activities (ESA) EUSC activities in support of EU Security Policies |

II. National level : Availability of national or regional data Other service and product development activities: [e.g. SIASGE (Italian-Argentinian cooperation on emergency EO satellites/Cosmo-Skymed); Disaster Management Pilot project (I); MOSAIC (Microsatellites Applications in collaboration(UK); Stereo programme (B); Project on development of application products and Cosmo-SkyMed Ground segment (I); SatHav (maritime applications) and SatNat (land applications) (N); National Earth observation Users' Platform (NL); Ether, Mercator, Postel, Aviso, Icare (F); EO centres of excellence (UK) DeCover, DeSecure, DeMarine, Enviland(D)] |

Reinforce dialogue within appropriate international bodies in view of embedding GMES into the GEOSS infrastructure | I. European level : a) EC: FP7-Environment Theme (additional activities foreseen in other FP7 themes (e.g. ICT, Space) and in JRC direct action) b) ESA: Availability of Earth observation data (e.g. Webportal, Data Clearinghouse) c) EUMETSAT: Continuation of Satellite Application Facilities, Geonetcast |

II. National level : National contributions |

Ensure continuity of European capacities in operational meteorology: developing and operating state-of the-art meteorology missions developing and operating innovative meteorological services and applications | I. European level : Development of meteorological satellites, also contributing to GMES (ESA/EUMETSAT) Under operation: Meteosat 5/6/7/8/9 (1991/93/97/02/05), Metop-A (2006) Planned:MSG-3 (2009), METOP-B (2010), MSG-4 (2012), MTG (2015) METOP-C (2015); Post-Eumetsat Polar System (EPS) satellite generation studies Development of associated services and applications (EUMETSAT) EUMETSAT Satellite Application Facilities (SAFs) within the Applications ground segment: Ocean + Sea Ice, Ozone Monitoring, Climate Monitoring, Numerical Weather prediction, Land surface analysis. High precision weather forecast for 4D-aircraft trajectory prediction (SESAR). |

II. National level activities, e.g. Jason-2 (2008/F), METIMAGE (D). |

3.3. Satellite Communications

Programmatic Objectives | Activities |

Development of advanced satellite communication technologies in cooperation with industry and operators leading to new demonstration missions, also by taking into account dual-use requirements | I. European level : EC: In FP7 and TEN-T, general (i.e. non-proprietary space) technologies development in research programmes in TREN, ENTR, RTD and INFSO. ESA: Preparatory mission, system and general configuration studies, technology for satellite based telecom and multimedia, development of payloads and ground segments, in-orbit validation,

Alphabus/Alphasat, Small GEO platform (Artes-11 programme) ; Preliminary System and architecture studies (Proposed contribution to European Integrated Secured Communication network) Hylas, Alphasat (2010), Small GEO satellite |

II. National level : National telecom-related technology R+D activities: payload development (e.g. Programme Stentor (F);COMED NG/Santana/LCT (D); National in-kind contributions (Alphasat), telecom-related technology activities (I), parallel platform development programme (D) Spainsat/Xtar (E), Athena-Fidus (2010/F/I) |

Increasing integration with terrestrial systems in support of European and global communication infrastructures with other application domains | I. European level : EC: FP7: ICT Challenge, Pervasive and trusted network and service infrastructures ESA: Telecom application demonstration (e.g. Artes). Possible future Data-Transmission System (DTS) including a data relay component in support of Earth observation missions (proposed DTS architecture and technology study within TRP/GSTP) |

II. National activities : Integration of space/terrestrial infrastructures (e.g. 'Village communicant'/F), Institutional Communication for security and emergency (I) |

Develop end-user services increasing quality, quantity and variety of data by developing a multimedia satellite system (merging mobile, broadband and broadcast) | I. European level : EC: FP7, TEN-T, Space Theme: Space-based end-user application developments (e.g. GMES, Galileo), Telemedicine; SESAR Joint Undertaking (air traffic management); ICT Pervasive and trusted network and service infrastructures ESA: Proposed contribution to SESAR as well as telemedicine applications |

II. National activities : TANGO: Telecom advanced networks for GMES operations (F); Activities in support of the integration of telecom and navigation services (e.g. D), Tele-Education/Tele-Medicine project (I) |

Provision of a harmon-ised regulatory environ-ment on a pan-European scale (e.g. concerning spectrum availability, service licensing). | I. European level : EC: Revised eCommunications and TV without frontiers regulation directives.Harmonised spectrum and standardisation activities (EC with ESA support). |

II. National activities: Harmonised spectrum and standardisation activities. |

3.4. Science and Technology

3.4.1. Space Science

Programmatic Objectives | Activities |

Focusing on specific priority issues: Life and planetary formation Solar System Fundamental laws of the Universe Origins and evolution of the Universe | I. European-level : ESA Scientific Programme: Cosmic Vision 2025 EC: FP7 activities for the optimal preparation of scientific payloads and for the effective scientific exploitation of their data. Under operation: HST (1990/US), SOHO (1995), Newton (1999/US), Cluster2 (2000), Integral (2002), Mars Express (2003), SMART-1 (2003), Rosetta(2004), Double Star (2003/04/China), Venus Express (2005), AKARI/Astro-F (2006/Japan), Solar B (2006/Japan) Planned: Chandrayaan1 (2007/India), Herschel-Planck (2008), Lisa PF (2009), Lisa, Gaia(2011), Bepi- Colombo (2013), MIRI/ JWST (2013/US) , Solar Orbiter (2015) |

II. National activities : National in-kind contributions to ESA missions by ESA Member States and European Cooperating States National science programmes: Development of instruments/platforms relying notably on national technical centres for R+T for orbital systems (e.g. Platform for mini-satellites Myriade and Proteus(F)), Balloon operation centre (F), Long-duration stratospheric balloons: SnowCake/ Boomerang (I) Under operation: Corot (2006/F) Planned: Picard (2008/F), T2L2 (2008/F), Pharao/ACES (F, CH), Microscope(2009/F), Taranis (F), Smese (F), Agile (I), New hard x-ray mission (2010/I), eRosita (2011+/D) |

Supporting synergies of space science activities with other science activities and towards applications | Diverse national data exploitation activities (e.g. CNES, DLR, ASI Science Data Center) [Scientific data treatment, archiving, processing capabilities, including data valorisation for ESA and national missions] Link between Space Science and Exploration activities (e.g. Exomars) |

Increasing international cooperation activities | Activities performed by ESA, its Member States and Cooperating states |

3.4.2. Earth Science

Programmatic Objectives | Activities |

Developing new missions in support of core topics: Ocean/Hydrosphere Air/Atmosphere Ice/Cryosphere LandSurface/ Biosphere Solid Earth/ Geosphere | I. European level : Earth Observation Envelope programme/Earth Explorer missions (ESA) FP7 Space work programme/actions area strengthening of the foundations of space sciences and technology (EC) Under operation: ERS-2 (1995), ENVISAT (2002) Planned: GOCE (2007), SMOS (2007), ADM-Aeolus (2008), Cryosat-2 (2009), SWARM (2010), EarthCare (2012) |

II. National level : Development of instruments/platforms relying notably on national technical centres and of full-fledged national missions. National in-kind contributions to ESA missions by ESA Member States and European Cooperating States Under operation: Champ (2001/D), Jason-1 (2001/F), Odin (2001/S), GRACE (2002/D), Parasol (2004/F), Demeter (2004/F), Calipso (2006/F), Spot 4/5 (F), Rosa (I) Planned: Jason-2 (2008/F), MeghaTropiques (2009/F), Venus (2009/F), SARAL (2009/F) |

Ensuring effective exploitation of science data in conjunction with EO applications within GMES | ESA and national data treatment capabilities (e.g. CADTS Centre Archivage et Traitement Données SMOS/ F, NL-SCIA-DC Sciamachy Data Center, Matera Space Geodesy Center (I)) National data valorisation activities/R+D for pilot applications/product development (e.g. Ether, Mercator, Aviso, Icare, Postel/F); German Remote Sensing Center DFD/D) |

Increasing international cooperation activities | Activities performed by ESA, its Member States and Cooperating States |

3.4.3. Technology

Programmatic objectives | Activities |

Maximising synergies between civil and defence, space and non-space technology developments Identifying critical technologies and perform associated technology demonstration missions | I. European level : Basic Technology Research programme/TRP (ESA) General Support Technology Programme/GSTP (ESA) European Component Initiative Technology Transfer Programme/TTP (ESA) ESA proposed NEWPro (technologies focusing on non-dependence, spin-in, security) Proposed in orbit demonstration for technologies and techniques (ESA) FP7 Space Work Programme/actions area strengthening of the foundations of space sciences and technology (EC) Planned: Proba-2, Proba-3, Expert. Proposed: Further Proba elements for technology demonstrators and precursors |

II. National level : National transversal technology R+D programmes Planned: Prisma (S), Simbol-X (F), Tandem-X (D), TET108/210 (D), Future national micro-satellite missions |

Harmonising technology developments | Technology harmonisation (ESA and EC) European Space technology Platform, European Space Technology Master Plan |

3.5. International Space Station and Exploration of the solar system

Programmatic objectives | Activities |

Ensuring maximum scientific return on investment and optimum utilisation of the ISS Strengthening life and physical sciences activities in support of non-space applications and exploration-related activities | I. European level : ISS Exploitation Programme (ESA) Planned: Node-2 (2007), ATV-1 (2007), Columbus (2007), ERA (2009) ATV-2(2009), ATV-3(2011), ATV-4(2012), ATV-5(2013) ISS utilisation programme/ELIPS (ESA) II. National level : Nationally funded experiments within the ELIPS programme National contributions to the ISS: [e.g. Declic facility/F; Multiuser facilities for Columbus/D; Pharao ACES (F, CH)] National activities promoting the commercial use of ISS. National infrastructure/activities: e.g. Cardiolab (D/F), Neurolab (D); Cardiomed (F); DCMC (I), OSMA (I), MOMA/Biotech applications (I), GPM and CAB (I) User Support Operational Centre USOC's: e.g. CADMOS (F), MUSC (D), Immulab (D), BEC-Lab (D) |

Preparing and demonstrating core capabilities (enabling technologies and infrastructures) for next step in exploration, notably for robotic Mars exploration and possible activities linked to moon exploration and cooperation with international partners on human space transportation according to scenario to be decided by Member States | I. European level : Proposed Aurora Core Programme (MSR, MSR precursor mission, Lunar exploration/Moon Orbit infrastructure) Preliminary studies Crew Space Transportation System) (ESA) FP7 Space work programme/actions area strengthening the foundations of space science and technology (EC) Planned:ExoMars mission (2013) |

II. National technology development in support of exploration : e.g.: MSL-Mars Surface laboratory (F) Network of geophysical stations on Mars (2011/F) Moon exploration (I, D) Inflatable structures-FLECS (I) |

3.6. Access to space

Programmatic Objectives | Activities |

Maintaining Europe's space port (Guiana Space Centre) under operation-al conditions/launch infrastructure | I. European level: CSG Kourou (ESA) Ariane 5 Infrastructure (ESA) VEGA (ESA) Soyuz at CSG (ESA), partly supported by Soyuz in Kourou/FP7 (EC) |

[II. National launch infrastucture] CNES-CSG Kourou (F) Esrange rocket range (S) Andoya rocket range (N), Other national rockets ranges: e.g. Broglio Space Center (I), Broglio launch base Trapani (I), Mobile rocket base (MORABA/D), Propulsion Test Center Lampoldshausen (D), Malindi (I) |

Consolidating the European family of launchers: Ariane 5, Vega, Soyuz at CSG | I. European level: Ariane (ACEP, ARTA, EVOLUTION, PLUS, EGAS, ...) (ESA) VEGA(VERTA) (ESA) Soyuz at CSG (ESA), partly supported by Soyuz in Kourou/FP7 (EC) |

II. National technical support to Ariane, Vega. CNES/F as prime contractor for Soyuz at CSG. Exploration of potential upgrades for Ariane and Vega/Evolution of the family of Launchers e.g. Ariane (F) and VEGA surveillance (I) |

Preparing technological and industrial capabilities for the development of next generation launchers | I. European level: FLPP 1, FLPP 2 (ESA) Re-entry technology: Expert (ESA) FP7 programme on the Strengthening of space foundations (EC) |

II. National R+T for future launchers R+T launchers and phases 0/A (F) Launcher development activities: [Tekin 2010, Tehora 3, Astra, Phoenix 1, TETRA, Tanks and structures (D); Future launchers/LYRA (I) Re-entry technology: [SHEFEX(D); Pre-X(F), Compere(D/F)] |

Exploring possible long-term options for cooperation with strategic partners | Agreement between ESA and the Russian Federal Space Agency on long-term cooperation and partnership in the field of development, implementation and use of launchers First Implementing Arrangement between ESA and the Russian Federal Space Agency on cooperation in research and technology development for future launchers France-Russia long-term cooperation/OURAL EU-Russia Dialogue on Space Cooperation (EC, ESA) |

4. INDICATIVE BUDGETS FOR MAJOR SPACE PROGRAMMES ON EUROPEAN LEVEL

ORIGIN | NAME OF PROGRAMMATIC ACTIVITY | TIMEFRAME | BUDGET/EXPENDITURE (in bn€) |

European-level activities |

ESA | Indicative figures (current e.c.) provided for ESA represent overall expenditure as indicated in ESA's Long Term Plan 2007-2016. They do not represent binding commitments for ESA Member States and include proposed future activities not yet approved. |

Navigation and Telecommunication | 2007-2013 | 3.4 |

Earth Observation | 2007-2013 | 4.5 |

Integrated Applications | 2007-2013 | 0.5 |

Basic Activities | 2007-2013 | 1.4 |

Science Programme and Science Support (Prodex) | 2007-2013 | 3.4 |

Technology | 2007-2013 | 0.8 |

Human Space Flight, Microgravity and Exploration | 2007-2013 | 4.2 |

Launchers | 2007-2013 | 5.0 |

EC | FP7 Space WP | 2007-2013 | 1.4 (of which 85% for GMES) |

FP7 Transport WP | 2007-2013 | 0.45 (incl. SESAR) |

FP7 Environment, ICT | 2007-2013 | Not determined (annual commitments) |

Galileo budget line | 2007 onward | 1,0 (under review) |

Activities other than Research or Galileo (e.g. AGRI, FISH, DEV, REGIO, ...) | 2007 onward | Not determined (annual commitments) |

EUMETSAT | MSG | 1992-2018 | 2,1 incl. ESA contribution of 400 M€ |

EPS | 1994-2019 | 2,4 (estimates), incl. ESA contribution of 550 M€ |

Post-EPS | 2012-2034 | 2,4 (estimates) |

MTG | 2015-2034 | 2,5 (estimates), incl. ESA contribution |

National-level activities |

Taking 2006 as a reference year, national programmes, including civil and defence-dedicated activities account for approximately 40 % of the overall European space effort. |

In line with figures provided by EUROCONSULT.

EUROPEAN PARLIAMENT RESOLUTION OF 10 JULY 2008 ON SPACE AND SECURITY

he European Parliament,

– having regard to the European Security Strategy entitled "A secure Europe in a better world", adopted by the European Council on 12 December 2003,

– having regard to the EU Strategy against proliferation of Weapons of Mass Destruction, likewise adopted by the European Council on 12 December 2003,

– having regard to Council resolution of 21 May 2007 on the European Space Policy(1)

– having regard to the Treaty on the Functioning of the European Union (TFEU) and the Treaty on European Union (TEU), as amended by the Treaty of Lisbon, and their relevant provisions on

European space policy (Article 189 of the TFEU), permanent structured cooperation on security and defence matters (Articles 42(6) and 46 of the TEU and Protocol 10) and enhanced cooperation in the civilian area (Part Six, Title III of the TFEU), as well as the solidarity clause (Article 222 of the TFEU) and mutual assistance provisions in the event of armed aggression against a Member State or States (Article 42(7) of the TEU),

– having regard to its resolution of 29 January 2004 on the action plan for implementing the European space policy(2) ,

– having regard to its resolution of 14 April 2005 on the European Security Strategy(3) ,

– having regard to the 1967 Treaty on Principles Governing the Activities of States in the Exploration and Use of Outer Space, including the Moon and Other Celestial Bodies ("the Outer Space Treaty"),

– having regard to the EU-Russia cooperation on space policy, which in 2006 created the Tripartite Space Dialogue between the European Commission, the European Space Agency (ESA) and Roscosmos (the Russian Federal Space Agency),

– having regard to Rule 45 of its Rules of Procedure,

– having regard to the report of the Committee on Foreign Affairs and the opinion of the Committee on Industry, Research and Energy (A6-0250/2008),

A. whereas freedom from space-based threats and secure sustainable access to, and use of, space must be the guiding principles of the European Space Policy,

B. whereas the various political and security challenges which the European Union is increasingly facing make an autonomous European Space Policy a strategic necessity,

C. whereas the lack of a common approach to space policy between EU Member States results in overly costly programmes,

D. whereas the crisis management operations within the framework of the European Security and Defence Policy (ESDP) suffer from a lack of interoperability between space assets operated by EU Member States,

E. whereas the European Union is lacking a comprehensive European space-based architecture for security and defence purposes,

F. whereas the development of a new generation of launchers takes approximately 15 years and the present generation of launchers will need replacing in the next 20 years,

G. whereas development of space assets by the USA, Russia, Japan and other emerging space-faring states, most notably China, India, South Korea, Taiwan, Brazil, Israel, Iran, Malaysia, Pakistan, South Africa and Turkey, is rapidly advancing,

H. whereas the French Presidency of the European Union during the second semester of 2008 sets out an advancement of the European Space Policy as one of its priorities,

I. whereas one of the most cost-effective elements of a space architecture and of achieving a sustainable fleet of space assets is on-orbit servicing, using in-situ means,

General considerations

1. Notes the importance of the space dimension to the security of the European Union and the need for a common approach necessary for defending European interests in space;

2. Underlines the need for space assets in order that the political and diplomatic activities of the European Union may be based on independent, reliable and complete information in support of its policies for conflict prevention, crisis management operations and global security, especially the monitoring of proliferation of weapons of mass destruction and their means of transportation and verification of international treaties, the transnational smuggling of light weapons and small arms, the protection of critical infrastructure and of the European Union's borders, and civil protection in the event of natural and man-made disasters and crises;

3. Welcomes the endorsement of the European Space Policy by the "Space Council" as proposed by a joint communication presented by the Commission and the European Space Agency (COM(2007)0212), especially the chapter on security and defence, while regretting the absence of any reference to the threat of weaponisation of space within the "key issues to be considered in the development of a strategy for international relations" (as mentioned in Annex 3 to the above-mentioned Council Resolution of 21 May 2007); recommends, therefore, that the revised European Security Strategy should take this policy appropriately into account, and is of the view that space matters should be reflected in the possible White Paper on Security and Defence Policy;

4. Notes the inclusion of a legal basis for the European Space Policy in the Treaty of Lisbon; welcomes the opportunity given to it and to the Council to lay down, under the ordinary legislative procedure, the measures needed to shape a European Space Programme; calls on the Commission to submit to it and to the Council an appropriate proposal for such measures, together with a Communication relating to the establishment of appropriate relations with the European Space Agency; also welcomes the possibilities of permanent structured cooperation in security and defence matters and enhanced cooperation in the civilian area;

5. Encourages the Member States of the European Union , the European Space Agency and the various stakeholders to make greater and better use of the existing national and multinational space systems and to foster their complementarity; notes in this respect that common capabilities are needed for ESDP in at least the following areas: telecommunications, information management, observation and navigation; recommends the sharing and exchange of these data in line with the EU concept for Network Centric Operations Architecture;

6. Applauds the efforts of the International Academy of Astronautics and the International Association for the Advancement of Space Safety to promote remediation, understanding and measures in respect of space debris;

Autonomous threat assessment

7. Calls on the EU Member States to pool and exchange the geospatial intelligence necessary for autonomous EU threat assessment;

Earth observation and reconnaissance

8. Urges that the European Union Satellite Centre (EUSC) be fully developed to make full use of its potential; moreover, recommends the urgent conclusion of agreements between the European Union Satellite Centre and the EU Member States to provide imagery available to ESDP operation and force commanders while ensuring complementarity with Global Monitoring for Environment and Security (GMES) observation capacities and derived security-related information; in this regard, welcomes the Tactical Imagery Exploitation Station project, run jointly by the European Defence Agency (EDA) and the European Union Satellite Centre;

9. Recommends that the EU develop a common concept for geospatial intelligence, creating conditions for involvement of the EUSC in the planning for each ESDP operation requiring space-based observation and space-based intelligence; recommends that the EUSC establish a secure communication link in support of ESDP operations not only with the Operations Headquarters (OHQ) based in the EU but also with the Force Headquarters (FHQ) in the deployment region; furthermore, suggests that the EU explore the possibility of a financial contribution to the EUSC from the EU budget in order to provide sufficient funds to meet the increasing needs of ESDP operations;

10. Urges the EU Member States having access to the various types of radar, optical and weather observation satellites and reconnaissance systems (Helios, SAR-Lupe, TerraSAR-X, Rapid Eye, Cosmo-Skymed, Pleiades) to make them compatible; welcomes the bilateral and multilateral agreements between the leading EU countries (e.g. SPOT, ORFEO, the Helios cooperative framework, the Schwerin agreement and the future MUSIS); recommends that the MUSIS system be brought within a European framework and financed from the EU budget;

11. Emphasises the importance of GMES for foreign as well as security and defence policies of the European Union; urges the creation of an operational budget line to ensure the sustainability of GMES services in response to users" needs;

Navigation – positioning – timing

12. Underlines the necessity of Galileo for autonomous ESDP operations, for the Common Foreign and Security Policy, for Europe's own security and for the Union's strategic autonomy; notes that, in particular, its public-regulated service will be vital in the field of navigation, positioning and timing, not least in order to avoid unnecessary risks;

13. Notes the first-reading agreement between Parliament and the Council on the proposal for a regulation on the further implementation of the European satellite radionavigation programmes (EGNOS and Galileo), which establishes that the Community is the owner of the system and that its deployment phase is fully financed by the Community budget;

14. Draws attention to its position adopted on 23 April 2008 on the European satellite radionavigation programmes (EGNOS and Galileo)(4) , in particular, to the fact that the EGNOS and Galileo programmes should be considered as one of the major pillars of the future European Space Programme, and to the governance of these programmes, together with the Galileo Interinstitutional Panel, which may serve as a model in the development of a European Space Policy;

Telecommunications

15. Underlines the need for secure satellite-supported communication for ESDP operations (EU Military Staff, EU Headquarters, deployable headquarters) and EU Member States' deployments under UN, NATO and other similar organisations;

16. Requests that the current and future satellite telecommunication systems at the disposal of the EU Member States (e.g. Skynet, Syracuse, Sicral, SATCOM Bw, Spainsat) be interoperable in order to provide for cost reduction;

17. Supports the cooperative development of a Software-Defined Radio (SDR) by the Commission and the European Defence Agency; notes that SDR will contribute to better interoperability of the ground segment of telecommunications systems;

18. Recommends that savings be achieved by shared use of the ground infrastructure supporting different national telecommunications systems;

19. Supports the possibility of funding future European satellite telecommunications systems supporting ESDP operations from the EU budget;

Space surveillance

20. Supports the creation of a European space surveillance system leading to space situational awareness (including, for example, GRAVES and TIRA) to monitor the space infrastructure, space debris and, possibly, other threats;

21. Supports the possibility of funding the future European space situational awareness system from the EU budget;

Satellite-based early warning against ballistic missiles

22. Deplores the fact that EU Member States do not have access to instant data on ballistic missile launches around the world; expresses support, therefore, for projects leading towards satellite-based early warning against ballistic missile launches (such as the French "Spirale"); furthermore, calls for information acquired through these future systems to be available to all EU Member States in order to protect their population and to support possible countermeasures, as well as to serve in the verification of compliance with the Nuclear Non-Proliferation Treaty, and for the purposes of ESDP operations and safeguarding Europe's security interests;

Signal intelligence

23. Supports the exchange of signal intelligence (electronic intelligence such as the French "Essaim" and communications intelligence) at European level;

Autonomous access to space and international environment

24. Supports secure, independent and sustainable access to space for the European Union as one of the preconditions of its autonomous action;

25. Recommends that the European non-commercial satellites be carried into orbit by European launchers, preferably from the territory of the European Union, bearing in mind the aspects of security of supply and protection of the European Defence Technological and Industrial Base;

26. Points out that it is necessary to increase the development effort in order for an enhanced Ariane 5 to be available before 2015;

27. Recommends that strategic long-term investment in new European launchers be initiated as soon as possible, in order to keep up with the rising global competition; demands a greater degree of discipline for this project, in budgetary and time-frame terms;

28. Recommends that on-orbit servicing be established as a means of support to enhance the endurance, persistence, availability and operational efficiency of operational space assets and, at the same time, to reduce asset deployment and maintenance costs;

Governance

29. Encourages strong inter-pillar cooperation for space and security, involving all the relevant actors (i.e. the Commission, the Council, the European Defence Agency and the European Union Satellite Centre), in order to safeguard the security policy and data security linked with the ESDP;

30. Strongly recommends the promotion of equal access for all EU Member States to operational data gathered using space assets under a reinforced ESDP framework;

31. Recommends that administrative and financial capacities for the management of space-related activities be developed by the European Defence Agency;

Financing

32. Points out that the EU budget commits expenditure amounting to approximately EUR 5 250 million in the years 2007-2013 on common European space activities, resulting in an average expenditure of EUR 750 million per year over that period;

33. Calls on the European Union to set up an operational budget for space assets that serve to support the ESDP and European security interests;

34. Is alarmed by the fact that the lack of coordination among Member States results in a scarcity of resources due to unnecessary duplication of activities; therefore supports the idea of the launching of joint programmes by the Member States, which will provide costs savings in the longer term;

35. Furthermore, notes that the cost of the absence of a common European approach to the procurement, maintenance and functioning of space assets is estimated to amount to hundreds of millions of euros;

36. Points out that, as experience has shown, large-scale common projects cannot be properly managed when 27 different national budget authorities applying the principle of "fair return" are involved; therefore strongly recommends that these projects and programmes be financed from the EU budget;

37. Notes that the estimates of available expertise suggest that the level of investment needed to address the European security and defence needs in terms of satellite telecommunications, and the appropriate expenditure of the European Union on Earth observation and intelligence gathering, including signal intelligence, should be substantially increased in order to provide for the needs and ambitions of a comprehensive space policy;

38. Takes the view that the European Union, the European Space Agency, the European Defence Agency and their Member States should provide for reliable and adequate funding for the space activities envisaged and the research connected therewith; attaches great importance to the financing from the budget of the EU, such as on the Galileo project;

Protection of space infrastructure

39. Underscores the vulnerability of strategic space assets as well as the infrastructure allowing access to space, e.g. launchers and space ports; therefore stresses the need for them to be adequately protected by ground-based theatre missile defence, planes and space surveillance systems; furthermore supports the sharing of data with international partners in the event that satellites are rendered inoperable by enemy action;

40. Calls for the vulnerability of future European satellite systems to be reduced through anti-jamming, shielding, on-orbit servicing, high-orbit and multi-orbital constellation architectures;

41. Emphasises that the protective measures must be fully compliant with international standards regarding peaceful uses of outer space and commonly agreed transparency and confidence-building measures (TCBMs); asks EU Member States to explore the possibility of developing legally or politically binding "rules of the road" for space operators, together with a space traffic management regime;

42. Stresses that, as a result of this vulnerability, advanced communication should never be made fully dependent on space-based technologies;

International legal regime for uses of space

43. Reiterates the importance of the principle of the use of space for peaceful purposes expressed in the above-mentioned 1967 Outer Space Treaty; is therefore concerned by the possible future weaponisation of space;

44. Urges that under no circumstances should European space policy contribute to the overall militarisation and weaponisation of space;

45. Calls for the international legal regime to be strengthened so as to regulate and protect non-aggressive space uses and for the strengthening of TCBMs, within the framework of the drafting by the UN Committee on the Peaceful Uses of Outer Space (COPUOS) of space debris mitigation guidelines consistent with those of the Inter-Agency Debris Coordination Committee as well as the development by the UN Conference on Disarmament of a multilateral agreement on the prevention of an Arms Race in Outer Space; furthermore, asks the EU Presidency to represent the EU proactively in COPUOS; calls on the EU institutions to promote a conference to review the Outer Space Treaty, with the aim of strengthening it and expanding its scope to prohibit all weapons in space;

46. Calls on all international actors to refrain from using offensive equipment in space; expresses its particular concern about the use of destructive force against satellites, such as the Chinese anti-satellite system tested in January 2007, and the consequences of the massive increase in debris for space security; recommends, therefore, the adoption of legally binding international instruments focusing on banning the use of weapons against space assets and the stationing of weapons in space;

47. Calls on all space users to register their satellites, including military satellites, by way of a space security confidence-building measure promoting transparency; supports the Council's pursuit of a comprehensive EU Code of Conduct on Space Objects; demands that this Code be transformed into a legally binding instrument;

48. Urges the United Nations and the European Union to engage in the active diminution of, and protection from, space debris harmful to satellites;

Transatlantic cooperation on space policy and missile defence

49. Urges the European Union and the North Atlantic Treaty Organization to launch a strategic dialogue on space policy and missile defence, while bearing in mind the legal imperative of avoiding any action that might be incompatible with the principle of the peaceful use of space, especially on the complementarity and interoperability of systems for satellite communications, space surveillance, and early warning of ballistic missiles, as well as protection of European forces by a theatre missile defence system;

50. Calls on the European Union and the United States of America to engage in a strategic dialogue on the use of space assets and to take the global lead within and outside the UN to make sure that outer space is preserved for peaceful policies only;

Other international cooperation

51. Welcomes the strengthened cooperation between the European Union and the Russian Federation within the framework of the above-mentioned Tripartite Space Dialogue set up in 2006 between the European Commission, the European Space Agency and Roscosmos, including space applications (satellite navigation, Earth observation

COMPETITIVENESS (Internal Market, Industry and Research) Council meeting Brussels, 22 May 2007

The fourth meeting of the "Space Council"[1] was held between the Council of the EU and the Council of the European Space Agency (ESA).

It was jointly chaired by Peter Hintze, Secretary of State to the German Federal Ministry of Economics and Technology and presidentinoffice of the EU Council, and by Maria Van Der Hoeven, Minister for Economic Affairs of the Netherlands and current chair of the ESA Council. Günther Verheugen, vicepresident of the European Commission and JeanJacques Dordain, ESA director general, also attended the meeting[2].

After an exchange of views and its endorsement by the Space Council, the following resolution[3] was adopted:

[1] An agreement between the EU and the ESA in force since 2004 provides a common basis for developing a European space policy. The agreement establishes regular joint and concomitant meetings of the EU and the ESA at ministerial level within a "Space Council", for coordinating and facilitating cooperative activities.

2 The Commission and the director general of the ESA presented on 26 April a joint document on European space policy (9052/07).

3 The resolution was endorsed by the Space Council and formally adopted by both organisations according to their respective internal rules.

"THE COUNCIL

HAVING REGARD to the Framework Agreement between the European Community and the European Space Agency, entered into force in May 2004 and the increasing cooperation between the two parties,

RECALLING the orientations of the "Space Council" meetings of 25 November 2004, 7 June 2005 and 28 November 2005,

RECALLING the decisions of the ESA Council at Ministerial level in 2005 and the adoption of the European Community's Seventh Framework Programme in 2006, implying a longterm commitment to support the development of the GMES space component and for GMES data access,

HAVING REGARD to the United Nations Outer Space Treaty framework,

I VISION FOR EUROPE AND GENERAL STRATEGY

HIGHLIGHTING that the space sector is a strategic asset contributing to the independence, security and prosperity of Europe and its role in the world and RECOGNISING the actual and potential contributions from space activities towards the Lisbon strategy for growth and employment by providing enabling technologies and services for the emerging European knowledge society and contributing to European cohesion,

EMPHASISING the unique contributions spacebased systems can provide to the overall research effort and to applications responding to European policies and objectives, RECOGNISING that the exploration of space contributes to answer farreaching questions on the origin and evolution of life in the Universe as well as on the fundamental laws of physics,

UNDERLINING that space represents a significant element of Europe's Sustainable Development Strategy and is relevant to the Common Foreign and Security Policy, supporting their goals by providing vital information on critical global issues such as on Climate Change[4] and humanitarian aid,

With reference to the recent report of the United Nations' Intergovernmental Panel on Climate Change and the significant contribution spacebased information systems can provide in this context for the future of our planet.

RECOGNISING that for these reasons Europe cannot afford to lose out securing the benefits of space for its citizens and its policies and that Europe's space policy will allow Europe to continue to develop and make the best use of world class space infrastructures and applications, in order to stay a major player, solve global problems and improve the quality of life,

EMPHASISING that all of Europe's space activities contribute to the goals and fully respect the principles set out by the United Nations' "Outer Space Treaty", in particular:

- the exploration and use of outer space for the benefit and in the interests of all countries and the recognition of outer space as a province of all mankind,
- the use of outer space for exclusively peaceful purposes,
- the promotion of international cooperation in the exploration and use of outer space,

and that Europe supports the ongoing efforts of the United Nations' Committee on the Peaceful Uses of Outer Space (COPUOS) on the mitigation and prevention of space debris,

RECOGNISING the inspirational ability of space activities in attracting young people into science and engineering,

HIGHLIGHTING the rapid growth of the markets for satellitebased navigation and telecommunication applications,

EMPHASISING that Europe is among the leading spacefaring actors in the world and remains committed to maintaining its position both via strengthened intraEuropean and international cooperation,

1. WELCOMES AND SUPPORTS the document on the European Space Policy, presented as a proposal of the ESA Director General and as a Communication of the European Commission, as a next step in establishing a coordinated and effective European space effort at the service of the European citizens,
2. TAKES NOTE OF the "Preliminary elements" of the European Space Programme associated with the ESP as a strategic planning tool, comprising all major space activities in Europe thereby supporting the optimization of public resources and skills when deciding and implementing the space policy,
3. INVITES the Member States to continue to support European objectives and Europeanlevel programmes including, where appropriate, with their national programmes and activities, thereby ensuring effectiveness and complementarity as to the European effort,

4. INVITES the European Commission, the ESA Director General and Member States, within the scope of the Framework Agreement, to monitor and evaluate the implementation of the European Space Policy,

II FURTHER STEPS – PROGRAMMES AND IMPLEMENTATION

A. APPLICATIONS

1. WELCOMES the combined efforts of ESA and the European Union to implement large useroriented initiatives such as GMES and GALILEO as well as the beginning efforts for increased development and exploitation of space related integrated applications, including in particular satellite communication services,

2. WELCOMES the European Commission's activities to further federate userdriven institutional demand in Europe, stemming from the policies of the European Union, CALLS FOR the introduction of regular independent quality and costefficiency assessments of large useroriented spacebased initiatives, involving users and Member States, with the objective of validating quality, relevance and costefficient performance of the overall systems and their services in the operational phase in order to further strengthen the user oriented approach,

3. RECOGNIZES the strategic value of sustainability for GMES and REAFFIRMS the objective for an operational and autonomous capability for GMES before the end of 2008 and EMPHASISES that the European Commission needs to propose for GMES in due time and after full consultation with Member States and ESA, arrangements for:

    1. financing, including facilitation of funding by the users

    2. operational infrastructures, and

(iii) effective management to become fully operational and to ensure sustainable services responding to identified user needs,

WELCOMES the initiatives under the Austrian and German EU Presidencies towards the European Earth Observation Services GMES (i.e. the Graz Dialogue and the Munich Roadmap),

WELCOMES the approach to set up a preparatory action of the European Commission for the operational phase of GMES,

REAFFIRMS that GMES will use to the maximum extent possible existing capacities on European and national level, complementing each other.

7. SUPPORTS the joint efforts of the European institutions, ESA and the European industry to establish in the coming years a commercially sustainable global civil navigation satellite system under European civil control,

B. SECURITY AND DEFENCE

8. RECOGNIZES that space technologies are often common between civilian and defence applications and that Europe can, in a userdriven approach, improve coordination between defence and civilian space programmes, pursuing in particular the synergies in the domain of security, whilst respecting the specific requirements of both sectors and the independent decision competences and financing schemes,

AFFIRMS the need to set up a structured dialogue with the competent bodies of the Member States and within the EU Second and Third Pillars and the European Defence Agency for optimizing synergies between all aspects of the European Space Policy within the framework of the existing attribution of competences,

RECOGNISES that the uses made by any military users of GALILEO or GMES must be consistent with the principle that GALILEO and GMES are civil systems under civil control, and consequently that any change to this principle would require examination in the framework of Title V/TEU and in particular Articles 17 and 23 thereof, as well as in the framework of the ESA Convention".

C. ACCESS TO SPACE

9. EMPHASISES the vital importance for Europe to maintain an independent, reliable and costeffective access to space at affordable conditions, as underlined in the ECESA Framework Agreement and in the Resolution on the evolution of the European launcher sector adopted during the ESA Council at Ministerial level in 2005, bearing in mind that a critical mass of launcher activities is a precondition for the viability of this sector,

RECOGNIZES the need for Europe to take advantage in a coherent way of the launcher assets under its control,

INVITES the ESA Director General to ensure continued development and coordination of European technological capabilities in order to pursue the longterm competitiveness of the European launcher sector with the objective to maintain and increase the presence in the commercial market,

D. INTERNATIONAL SPACE STATION AND EXPLORATION

10. EMPHASISES the political and scientific importance of the International Space Station (ISS) and of exploration, and REAFFIRMS the continued strong and unified European commitment regarding its ISS contributions undertaken by ESA and its Member States,

CALLS on the international partners to the ISS to continue their support to ensure that the objectives of ISS partnership are maintained in their entirety, and STRESSES that the continuity of such partnership is a asset for future exploration endeavours,

ENCOURAGES the utilization of the ISS for research and development in the European Community's research framework programme,

EMPHASISES the importance of a proactive ESA participation in the preparation of future international exploration programmes, with the objective of ensuring a significant targeted and coordinated European role in this endeavour,

E. SCIENCE AND TECHNOLOGY

11. STRESSES the goal of maintaining world class scientific programmes and a clear European leading role in selected areas contributing to the buildup of the European Research Area,

RECOGNISES that the existing combined European skills and efforts, in particular in the frame of ESA, allow Europe to succeed in the most challenging enterprises and to reach a level of excellence for discovery and innovation in the global context,

CALLS on the European Commission, ESA and Member States to stimulate educational programmes in Europe,

EMPHASISES the importance of innovation and technological development also for the competitiveness of industry and the commercial success of its products and services,

STRESSES the need for a targeted approach for the development of strategic components, concentrating on selected critical components, for which dependency of European industry on international suppliers should be avoided, in order to achieve the optimum balance between technological independence, strategic cooperation with international partners and reliance on market forces,

F. GOVERNANCE

12. APPRECIATES that ESA has, for more than 30 years, provided an efficient structure for European cooperation on joint space projects, which could require though further flexibility and some evolution, and NOTES that the independence and reliability of ESA, thanks to the growing support of its Member States, contributes to the increasing role of Europe through the successful development of the European space sector and to the strong position of European space industry on world markets,

REAFFIRMS the roles and responsibilities of the European Union, ESA and Member States, as identified in the Orientations of the second meeting of the "Space Council". On the basis of such roles and in order to draw advantage of ESA experience and institutional setting, CALLS on the European Commission to draw on the management and technical expertise of

ESA for managing the European Communityfunded R&D space infrastructure programmes with ESA coordinating the relevant agencies and entities in Europe,

Such ESA role should also include:

supporting the European Commission as technical expert in the elaboration of European Community initiatives involving spacerelated activities and relevant work programmes, and in the selection and monitoring of relevant work contractors,

the management by ESA of European Community spacerelated activities in accordance with the rules of the European Community,

INVITES Member States under the coordination of ESA and in the case of significant European Community activities, in close cooperation with the European Commission:

to provide the best expertise for European space programmes (such as GMESSpace Component, exploration programmes and future launcher programmes),

to increase synergy between national, ESA and EC contributions to these programmes leading progressively to an integrated programmatic approach while respecting national sovereignty,

SUPPORTS the continuation of the Framework Agreement beyond May 2008 as the basis for the cooperation between the European Community and ESA, in the understanding that the Framework Agreement and its implementation will be periodically assessed and improved, if necessary, and RECALLING the invitation expressed in the orientations of the second meeting of the Space Council for a wideranging appraisal of possible costefficient scenarios for optimizing the organization of space activities in Europe, INVITES Member States, the European Commission and the ESA Director General to look for possible improvements of this cooperation, in order to further develop the orientations of the second meeting of the Space Council into more operational and practical arrangements, notably with regard to the issues listed in Annex 1,

13. RECOGNIZES the valuable contribution to the European Space Programme made by EUMETSAT, and INVITES EUMETSAT to keep participating in future meetings of the Space Council as an observer,

G. INDUSTRIAL POLICY

14. RECOGNIZES that ESA has a flexible and effective industrial policy based on costefficiency, competitiveness, fair distribution of activities and competitive bidding, which secures adequate industrial capacities, global competitiveness and a high degree of innerEuropean competition for efficient European cooperation on joint space projects, thus providing the basis for the successful development of space in Europe,

EMPHASISES in this context in particular the political and economic dimension of ESA's "fair return" principle; and the importance to assess and improve, when necessary, the implementation of the "fair return" principle in view of the future challenges for industry to remain competitive in a changing environment worldwide while maintaining, and possibly increasing, Member States' motivation to invest in space,

1. EMPHASISES the crucial role of SMEs and the supplier industry for innovation and the exploration of new market opportunities,

2. INVITES the European Commission to develop adequate instruments and funding schemes for Community actions in the space domain, addressing notably the issues listed in Annex 2, taking into account the specificities of the space sector, the need to strengthen its overall and its industry's competitiveness and the necessity of a balanced industrial structure,

H. INTERNATIONAL RELATIONS

17. INVITES the European Commission, the ESA Director General and the Member States to develop and pursue a joint strategy and establish a coordination mechanism on international relations. This strategy should be consistent with Member State activities and is aimed at strengthening Europe's role in the global space field and at benefiting from international cooperation, notably with respect to the issues listed in Annex 3,

I. IMPLEMENTATION

18. INVITES the European Commission and the ESA Director General to propose an implementation plan for the European Space Policy in order to establish a process of regular monitoring and priority setting, taking also into account the issues listed in the Annexes.

Annex 1

1. Key issues for further developing the orientations of the second meeting of the Space Council into more operational and practical arrangements:

- Developing financial instruments suitable for an efficient implementation of space projects,
- Identifying final users of GMES services and their needs; develop an integrated and customized offer, including also the regional and local level,

- Defining the conditions under which satellites belonging to Member States and their data and services will be made available to GMES; the treatment of the contributions of national programmes to EUinitiatives, here in particular GMES.

Annex 2

2. Key issues to be considered in the implementation of instruments and funding schemes for Community actions:

- Developing a coherent data policy including data access and pricing conducive to the rapid development of the space services sector,
- Encouraging new financing schemes such as Public/Private Partnerships in the market for space applications and services, including through public support for R&D,
- Provision of suitable measures in support of technological innovation, involving leadmarket initiatives, public procurement and support for suppliers and small and mediumsized companies and industries,

Annex 3

3. Key issues to be considered in the development of a strategy for international relations:

- Improving access to third markets for European space products and services,
- Reducing the cost of acquiring space systems by the targeted use of international cooperation,
- Enabling Europe to participate in ambitious programmes the cost of which is too great for any one space power,
- Attracting international partners to European conceived programmes, like in the case of Galileo and reinforcing the contribution of Europe to global initiatives, like in the case of GMES,
- Making full use of the potential of space systems for sustainable development, namely in support of developing countries, in particular in Africa."

"SPACE COUNCIL" ORIENTATIONS/ COUNCIL RESOLUTION

THE 'SPACE COUNCIL'

EMPHASISING the orientations and resolutions adopted at past meetings of the 'Space Council', in particular the Resolution on the European Space Policy of 22 May 2007[1] establishing a political framework for space in Europe and the Resolution "Taking forward the European Space Policy" of 26 September 2008[2] setting out new priority areas for the further implementation and development of the European Space Policy, the results of the ESA Council at ministerial level of 2526 November 2008 and the EU Competitiveness Council Conclusions "Towards a GMES Programme" of 2 December 2008[3];

RECOGNISING the progress made in the implementation of these Resolutions, in particular in the framework of the Structured Dialogue the increased coordination of space, security and defence related activities between key actors of the European Space Policy, including the identification of critical space technologies for European nondependence; the acceptance of the Multinational Spacebased Imaging System (MUSIS) as a new European Defence Agency (EDA) ad hoc category B programme; and, on Space Situational Awareness (SSA), the adoption of the ESA Preparatory Programme, while recalling that the EU will take, in liaison with ESA and their respective Member States, an active role to setup progressively a European capability for SSA and an appropriate governance structure;

[1] Doc. 10037/07 [2] Doc. 13569/08 [3] Doc. 16722/08

EMPHASISING the potential of space to impact on innovation in the economy, as well as on

economic recovery, and the need for further orientations to the Commission and ESA in particular on the short and longterm progress of the Global Monitoring for Environment and Security (GMES) initiative:

I) On the contribution of space to innovation and competitiveness in the context of the European Plan for Innovation and the European Economic Recovery Plan

EMPHASISES the Conclusions on the European Council of 1112 December 2008, notably its support to the European Economic Recovery Plan (EERP) and its call for the launching of a European Plan for Innovation, which should also include space technology and services derived from it, as one of the main technologies of the future[4];

CONSIDERS that, in view of the acknowledged contribution of space to the overall competitiveness and innovation potential of the European economy, space activities and their applications should receive full consideration in the use of funds allocated to economic recovery;

EMPHASISES the need to mobilise existing innovation support mechanisms at European, national and regional level, and consider new support instruments to ensure crossfertilisation of knowledge, innovation and ideas between space and nonspace sectors, and between space industry and leading research organisations and universities;

EMPHASISES the need to:

- identify innovationboosting measures for the space sector in the framework of the European Plan for Innovation and in coordination, as appropriate, with national plans;
- encourage more prominent presence of the European space industry in transsectoral innovation clusters and networks;

Doc. 17271/08 point 18, page 8

  - define adequate conditions for the development of downstream services based on EGNOS,
  - Galileo and GMES, taking full benefit of an integrated approach that combines satellite navigation, communications and Earth observation technologies with groundbased assets;
- consider including space applications among any further selection of new lead markets under the Commission's Lead Market Initiative, in the light of the review of that initiative[5]; and
- analyse and measure the innovative impact of space technologies on other economic sectors in an effort to provide solid analytical input to the preparation of future European programmes;

Further UNDERLINES the potential of space to develop enabling technologies and promote future economic growth in Europe. In particular:

• HIGHLIGHTS the potential of satellite communications technologies to bring broadband to European citizens and enterprises, ensuring a better access to modern ICT particularly in rural and remote areas[6], in the context of the European broadband strategy called for by the European Council of 1920 March; CALLS on the Commission, ESA and the EU and ESA Member States to consider integrating satellite technologies in future broadband projects with a view to support the implementation of the EERP, while respecting the principles of open competition, technology neutrality, and open and neutral internet architecture; and further RECOGNISES the need to explore innovative approaches and architectures for the provision of global satellite communications services in response to institutional demand in support of European programmes and policies, including transport, energy[7] and security;

[5] Doc. 5121/08 [6] Doc. 7201/09 [7] Doc. 7566/09

• STRESSES that space can provide a significant contribution to the 'Factories of the Future'[8] initiative, as well to other strategic priorities of the EERP.

II) On GMES Initial Operations

REAFFIRMS the importance of the rapid implementation of GMES services and TAKES NOTE of the Commission's proposal for a Regulation of the European Parliament and of the Council on the European Earth observation programme (GMES) and its initial operations (20112013)[9], which aims at achieving a significant step towards a GMES Programme ensuring the sustainable longterm operation of GMES services, meeting the requirements of national and European users, while pursuing the development of a detailed data access and dissemination policy for these services[10];

STRESSES the need, in this context, to give funding priority to the operations of the GMES Space Component;

UNDERLINES the need to ensure that GMES services are supplied on a competitive basis, when relevant, and that appropriate SME involvement is ensured in their provision;

STRESSES the need for a coherent and complementary approach for funding schemes of GMES services and the observation data and infrastructure implemented through the Space Theme of the Seventh Framework Programme for research, technological development and demonstration activities[11], the proposed Regulation on a GMES Initial Operations Programme,[12] the ESA GMES Space Component Programme and activities implemented at Member State level.

[8] Designed to enable European industry to adapt to global competitive pressures by improving the technological base of EU manufacturing across a broad range of sectors (http://ec.europa.eu/research/press/2009/pdf/pppfactsheet_en.pdf)

[9] Doc. 10285/09 [10] As detailed in the Council conclusions on Global Monitoring for Environment and Security (GMES): "Towards a GMES Programme" (Doc. 16722/08)

[11] 2006/971/EC:"Council Decision of 19 December 2006 concerning the Specific Programme Cooperation implementing the Seventh Framework Programme of the European Community for research, technological development and demonstration activities (2007 to 2013)", OJ L 400/86 30.12.2006

[12] Doc. 10285/09

III) On the longterm arrangements for the GMES Space Component (GSC)

RECALLS the need to define, at national and European levels, a sustainable funding approach for the GMES Space Component based on an assessment of the overall financing needs for this infrastructure, taking into account the three successive stages: R&D stage to be funded from R&D appropriations, transition stage with mixed R&D and operational funding, and an operational stage with dedicated funding for operations involving the users; EMPHASISES that some GMES Space Component elements are entering into the operational stage and WELCOMES that, with the adoption of a Regulation on the GMES Initial Operations Programme, operational funding would be introduced into GMES;

RECOGNISES the need to identify and ensure funding for the remaining elements of the initial GSC buildup and INVITES the Commission and ESA to elaborate in consultation with the EU and ESA Member States a funding strategy for these elements, without prejudging the next EU Multiannual Financial Framework;

Concerning observations related to operational oceanography and atmospheric composition monitoring, respecting the overall coordination role of ESA for the GMES Space Component, INVITES the Commission and ESA to lead a dialogue with EU and ESA Member States and with EUMETSAT and its Member States to explore options for the role of EUMETSAT to coordinate the user requirements for space observations;

Concerning observations related to land monitoring, emergency response and security, INVITES the Commission and ESA to explore options for the longterm operation of relevant missions including procurement of data, by starting dialogues, based on terms of reference to be determined following close consultation of EU and ESA Member States, with those Member States which own infrastructure, in order to discuss programmatic, governance and financial aspects; UNDERLINES the importance of the Commission and ESA defining the data policy for, and the ownership of, the Sentinel missions consistent with the INSPIRE directive[13] and the provisions of the ESA GMES Space Component Programme Declaration approved at the ESA Ministerial Council 2008;

TAKES NOTE of the preliminary analysis carried out by ESA, notably the GMES Space Component Longterm Scenario[14], as a basis for the estimations of the GMES Space Component evolution and costs, INVITES ESA to consolidate this analysis through further consultation with EUMETSAT and Member States owning infrastructure by the end of 2009, and REAFFIRMS the need for the EU to establish swiftly a longterm budget strategy, within the framework of the definition of the next EU Multiannual Financial Framework.

IV) On space exploration

REAFFIRMS the need to assess the possibilities offered by European Union policies to embed space exploration in a wider political perspective and, recognising that space exploration has the potential to provide a major impact on innovation, LOOKS FORWARD to the Commission's proposed HighLevel Political Conference on Space Exploration, on the basis previously agreed in the Space Council, as a first step towards the elaboration in due time of a fullyfledged political vision on "Europe and Exploration" encompassing a longterm strategy/roadmap and an international cooperation scheme.

[13] Directive 2007/2/EC of the European Parliament and of the Council of 14 March 2007 establishing an Infrastructure for Spatial Information in the European Community (INSPIRE) [14] ESA/C(2009)36

V) On adequate instruments and funding schemes

RECALLS the need to develop adequate EU instruments and funding schemes taking into account the specificities of the space sector (in particular, the relatively small size of its market and its dependence on public funding/programmes), the need to strengthen the space industry's competitiveness and the necessity of a balanced involvement of capacities in Europe, and examining the modalities for the full association of all ESA Member States;

WELCOMES in this context the Commission's initiative to conduct indepth studies on these issues, on which it is consulting ESA and the results of which will provide much needed input to accelerate work in this domain, within the framework of the definition of the next EU Multiannual Financial Framework and NOTES the invitation of the ESA Council at Ministerial level[15] to its Director General to start reflections with the European Commission and Member States, with a view to making a common analysis of the current rules for joint ESAEU programmes.

EUROPEAN SPACE POLICY PROGRESS

1. INTRODUCTION

Following the adoption of the Space Council Resolution in May 2007, this Report provides an overview on the main progress achieved in the first year of the implementation of the European Space Policy (ESP), as elaborated jointly by the European Commission and the Director General of the European Space Agency (COM(2007)212). The need to establish a European Space Policy has also been endorsed by EU Heads of State and Government. The Member States of the EU and ESA highlighted that the further implementation of the GALILEO and GMES programmes, the development of a Strategy on International Relations in Space and the need to develop adequate instruments and funding schemes for Community actions in the space domain should be first priorities, followed by improved coordination and synergies between defence and civilian space programmes and technologies, in a user-driven approach. This report describes both the important steps forward made since May 2007 and the further actions which are priorities in the coming period.

2. SPACE APPLICATIONS

2.1. SATELLITE RADIO NAVIGATION PROGRAMMES: GALILEO / EGNOS

GALILEO and EGNOS[1] are European investments in essential European infrastructure for crucial applications such as border control, transport management and logistics, financial operations and the surveillance of critical energy and communications infrastructures. In late 2007, the Council of the EU reached conclusions on the re-profiling and on the future development of the European satellite radio navigation programmes, including governance and procurement aspects, based on a full public, EU funding of the deployment phase.

Governance

Public governance of the programmes shall be based on the principle of a strict division of responsibilities between the European Commission, the European GNSS Supervisory Authority (GSA) and ESA. The European Commission will be responsible for the overall management of the programmes as the European GNSS Programme Manager. ESA will act as procurement agent for the GALILEO Full Operational Capability (FOC), and as design agent for the programmes. The GSA, in accordance with guidelines issued by the Commission, will accomplish specific tasks related to the programmes. Furthermore, a new GALILEO Interinstitutional Panel (GIP) with representatives of the Council, the European Parliament and the Commission will be set up to follow the programmes.

Programme implementation

Important technical progress has been achieved in the development and in-orbit validation phase of the GALILEO programme. GIOVE-B, the second GALILEO experimental satellite, has been successfully launched on 27 April 2008. It will work in conjunction with the first GALILEO experimental satellite, GIOVE-A, carrying critical new technologies to be tested in

1

European Geostationary Navigation Overlay Service

EN EN

space and needed for the performances of the GALILEO systems, notably the most accurate atomic clock ever put into orbit.

The additional Community funds[2] allocated to the implementation of the GALILEO and EGNOS programmes are 3405 M€ for the period from 1 January 2007 to 31 December 2013. The first four operational GALILEO satellites will be launched in 2010, by which time the related ground control infrastructure will also be established.

In line with the revised European GNSS Regulation[3], the Commission and ESA launched the tender for the procurement of the remaining 26 satellites and ground control infrastructure on 1 July 2008. The full operational capability of GALILEO (30 satellites + ground stations) is targeted for 2013.

At the same time, the EGNOS infrastructure is progressively being phased into operation. EGNOS is monitoring and correcting signals emitted from existing global satellite navigation systems to make them suitable for safety critical navigation applications. The transfer of EGNOS assets from ESA to the European Community is due to take place in early 2009.

International cooperation

The European Commission and ESA have established international cooperation to ensure proper access to resources (frequencies, technologies, hosting of ground stations) necessary to the building up of EGNOS and GALILEO infrastructures.

Key issues ahead:

- Completion of the in-orbit validation phase through the preparation and launch of the first four operational GALILEO satellites in 2010;
- Implementation of the 2007 Council conclusions on the GALILEO re-profiling, including the governance arrangements and the relevant agreements with ESA;
- Completion of the tender for the procurement of the remaining 26 GALILEO operational satellites and associated ground control infrastructure;
- Accompanying regulatory and policy measures in view of factors such as third party liability and export control, Public Regulated Service access, and the handling of the programme exploitation phase.
- Continue to promote applications that take full advantage of EGNOS and, in the future, of GALILEO services including in intelligent transport systems. Commission to propose a relevant Action Plan and European Radio Navigation Plan, following the publication in December 2006 of the Green Paper on satellite navigation applications.

2.2. Earth Observation: GMES

GMES - the European initiative for Global Monitoring for Environment and Security - is being built up in a phased approach, aiming at targeted Earth observation services to cover the

2

Financing arrangements for the development and IOV phases are in place from TEN-T funding.

3

683/2008; OJ L196 of 24 July 2008

EN EN

needs of European citizens in the areas of environment, security, emergency response and climate change.

Services

GMES requires the integration of data from space-based and in-situ Earth observation capacities into operational European application services. Three user-based GMES services in the areas of *Emergency Response, Land and Marine Monitoring* will be pre-operational by the end of 2008. Work was also launched on identifying user requirements for *security services*, on the development of an additional *Atmosphere Pilot Service,* as well as on the potential contribution of GMES to addressing *climate change*.

Tackling climate change and other environmental challenges depends on further research into understanding these phenomena and on the assessment of reliable data from a variety of sources, notably satellites. The continuous and sustained provision and analysis of high-quality satellite data on essential climate variables (ECVs) is supported by relevant programmes of EUMETSAT and ESA. An ESA Climate Change Initiative is under preparation, in view of the November 2008 ESA Ministerial Council, targeting a consolidation and preservation of its archives of 30 years of Earth observation data to support the re-analysis processes by climate research centres.

During the GMES pre-operational phase 2008-2010, the coordinated data provision for GMES services in this period has been guaranteed through a 48 M€ EC grant to ESA. EUMETSAT has also decided that all data and products from its operational satellites and archives shall be made freely available to GMES services during this period.

Overall, for the setting-up of GMES services, from 2002 to 2009, 100 M€ have been dedicated to the ESA GMES Service Element (GSE). The FP7 Space theme has devoted 35 M€ in 2007 and 70 M€ in 2008 for the further development and consolidation of GMES services.

Programmatic and institutional framework

The May 2007 Space Council recognised that, after ten years of R&D financing, GMES now needs to move firmly towards an operational basis in order to ensure its long-term availability.

The sustainability of GMES requires an adequate management and institutional framework. GMES is based on several interlinked components (service component, space component, in-situ component) which produce data and information for users and for the further processing by the downstream service sector. The Commission plans to propose appropriate governance and financial schemes in a Communication to the EU Council and European Parliament in autumn 2008.

The GMES in-situ infrastructure is an asset of Member States and of their local or regional authorities. Commitments will therefore be sought from these authorities to continue data availability. An In-Situ Observation Working Group composed of Member State representatives, and supported by the European Environment Agency (EEA), has been set up to address issues related to European infrastructure coordination and harmonisation of data exchange.

Progress on the space component

EN EN

ESA is responsible for the coordination of all European contributions to the GMES Space Component (GSC), in line with user needs. It will implement the development of a set of satellites (the Sentinels) and their related ground segment through the ESA GSC Programme.

The Community contribution to the ESA GSC Programme is implemented through an ECESA agreement starting with 419 M€ for the 1320 M€ GSC 'Segment 1'. An amendment to the Agreement is expected to be concluded to cover the envisaged Community contribution of another 205 M€ for GSC 'Segment 2', which will be submitted for approval to the November ESA Ministerial Council.

International cooperation

The meteorological field has already shown that, to ensure access to a wide range of data at global level, Europe needs to find the right balance between an autonomous Earth observation capacity and engaging in cooperation with third countries, in particular on the coordination of Earth observation infrastructure and the exchange of data. At multilateral level, Europe is already strongly engaged in the GEOSS process[4], and GMES is defined as the main European contribution to this international endeavour.

In December 2007, the "Lisbon Process on GMES and Africa" was launched, responding to African Union requests to integrate African user requirements in the GMES services.

Key issues ahead:

- Maintain a firm link between establishing user requirements and securing the further development of services and infrastructure, in a cost-efficient manner;
- Strengthen coordination and the joint commitment by all stakeholders, especially that of Member States to the in-situ infrastructure;
- Obtain the commitment of ESA Member States and European Community to the funding of the GSC 'Segment 2';
- Further develop the future programmatic, financial and institutional framework (governance) for GMES as a whole and for its services, space and in-situ components. This framework will provide a basis for its operational sustainability.

2.3. Security and Defence

European space capacities have become critical information tools in addressing a diversity of environmental, economic and security challenges of a global or regional scale. Autonomous access to information derived from space is thus a strategic EU asset. The EU will need to further strengthen its ability to respond to these challenges, including in the security and defence domains, both through improved coordination and through the development of own capacities.

The importance of European space capacities as strategic assets has been highlighted by the 2008 report from the High Representative and the European Commission on the impact of

4

Global Earth Observation System of Systems

EN EN 6

climate change on international security. At the same time, space programmes like GMES and GALILEO have a multiple-use capacity and may, along with their civil security capabilities, also have military users.

Within the framework of existing EU principles and institutional competencies, the European Commission and the EU Council General Secretariat are currently working on the identification of relevant user requirements for *GMES security services*, involving potential users and policy makers, as well as providers and developers of data. Following a workshop organised by the Institute for Security Studies in June 2007 in Paris, the following key areas have been identified as worthwhile to be explored: *Border Surveillance*[5], *Maritime Surveillance*, and *Support to EU External Action*. A horizontal action on *Security of Information* is being pursued in order to prepare the implementation plan for data exchange in the security domain.

In order to address the complex capacities and skills required for the provision of security related data and services a number of test and pilot projects have already been implemented or launched under Community Research Programmes and the ESA GSE, with participation of the EU Satellite Centre. An example is the LIMES Maritime Surveillance project[6], which also responds to EU Maritime Policy requirements.

In view of an improved coordination between civil, security and defence related space activities, the services of the European Commission and the EU Council General Secretariat have set-up a structured dialogue, involving also the European Defence Agency (EDA) and the EU Satellite Centre. The objective is to exchange information and optimise the synergies between the various actors' activities and programmes, in the context of ESDP and other EU Policies.

KEY ISSUES AHEAD:

- Pursue the structured dialogue between relevant EU services and agencies in view of creating synergies between the various actors' activities and programmes;
- Continue identification of user requirements for GMES security services, involving potential users, policy makers, providers of data and system developers, accompanied by further test and pilot projects under the relevant programmes.

3. SPACE FOUNDATIONS

3.1. SCIENCE AND TECHNOLOGY

The EU, ESA and their Member States recognised the need to continue to invest strongly to maintain leadership in space-related S&T. This is reflected in the relevant ESA programmes as well as in the EU's research programme (FP7).

5 Responding also to the creation of a European Border Surveillance System (EUROSUR)

6 Land and Sea Integrated Monitoring for Environment and Security

Strengthening the foundations of space science and technology has been specifically included in the EU's FP7. Coordination between the EU's FP7 and ESA's technology programme has been substantially strengthened during the past year.

Europe continues to be ambitious in terms of innovation, identifying critical technologies and guaranteeing their funding, while closely monitoring technology transfers, both for security and commercial reasons. The European Commission, ESA and EDA are closely cooperating in this endeavour. A joint event to raise political awareness for the definition of a harmonised Europe-wide approach on Critical Technology for European Non-Dependence in space is scheduled for 9 September 2008. ESA will propose to its Ministerial Council in November 2008 a programme element related to critical space technologies, European strategic non-dependence and industrial competitiveness.

The ESA mandatory Science Programme will complete its first 20 year Long-Term Plan, started in 1984 under the name "Horizon 2000", with the dual launch in early 2009 of the "Herschel" Space Observatory and the "Planck" spacecraft by an Ariane-5 launcher. A wealth of scientific satellites and space telescopes has been launched under the Plan, such as NEWTON and INTEGRAL[7].

Key issues ahead:

- Maintain commitment and investment in space-related science and technology;
- Define a harmonised Europe-wide approach on Critical Technology for European non-dependence in space technology. ESA is to submit a related programme proposal to its 2008 Ministerial Council.

3.2. Access to Space

An independent, reliable and cost-effective access to space is of vital importance for the implementation of the ESP.

Progressively, a flexible range of launchers will be made available through a single operator from the Guiana Space Centre, with the ESA-developed Vega launcher and the Russian Soyuz launcher joining Ariane 5. In addition, several medium-size European satellites are launched on Russian launchers from the space port of Baikonour.

In 2006-2007, Arianespace placed a total of 22 telecommunication satellites in orbit through eleven successful Ariane 5 launches, carrying 80% of all commercial satellites in 2007. Seven launches are planned for 2008.

Key issues ahead:

• For Ariane to remain the reference commercial launch service on the market against the current unfavourable US Dollar/Euro exchange rates is a major challenge for Europe. This must be addressed during 2008;

7

Aimed in particular at collecting evidence of the objects responsible for producing the antimatter and the first detection of the long sought 'cosmic web'

EN EN 8

• ESA is to prepare scenarios for the next generation of launchers.

3.3. Exploration of the Solar System, International Space Station and Human Space Flight

ESA and a number of Member States have been playing a key role in the definition of an international Global Space Exploration Strategy and in preparing the framework for international coordination of space faring nations through the International Space Exploration Coordination Group (ISECG). A number of important European missions have been launched or are being prepared.

ESA's ExoMars mission has significantly evolved to a high performance Mars exploration mission[8]. Cooperation agreements have been established between ESA and NASA in order to enhance the mission's robustness and its scientific value. In parallel, an agreement has also been concluded with the Russian Federal Space Agency for cooperation with the Russian sample return mission from Phobos, a moon of Mars.

The International Space Station (ISS) Programme is proceeding towards the 'Assembly Complete' stage by 2010, with a 6-person crew planned for May 2009. The facility offers unique opportunities for fundamental and applied research. European participation with the successful launch of Node2[9] in October 2007, the Columbus laboratory in February 2008, the Automated Transfer Vehicle (ATV-1) "Jules Verne" in March 2008, as well as the presence of European crew, secures a visible European role in this endeavour. These successes have confirmed Europe's ability to make significant contributions to global space exploration, and indeed to expand its role beyond its level of 8 per cent participation in the ISS. Time has now come for reaping the benefits of long-term investments for scientific progress and for preparing exploration of the Solar System. However, space exploration requires very substantial resources and therefore has to be an international endeavour.

Key issues ahead:

- The important resources necessary for space exploration call for a strong commitment from Europe to define its contribution and pool its resources to offer a coherent and efficient European contribution to this global initiative;
- The European Commission intends to conduct a political debate to assess the potential EU contribution to this endeavour.

4. A COMPETITIVE EUROPEAN SPACE INDUSTRY

The **commercial space market** has created a significant value chain in derived services, but also produced socio-economic and indirect benefits. **Public commitments** are however required to create a critical mass stimulating further public and private investment. The European **GALILEO and GMES** initiatives **will create significant opportunities** for user 1st mission in ESA's Aurora Exploration Programme.

It provided the interconnection point between the US Destiny, ESA Columbus and Japanese Kibo laboratories and has hence been named 'Harmony' **driven applications and services and contribute to the emergence of new European downstream markets.**

The evolution of European user needs requires the development of integrated space systems, seamlessly linking satellite and terrestrial telecommunications, positioning and monitoring in areas of strategic, economic and/or societal value. The development of GMES and GALILEO services as well as their integration with satellite communications has been supported under the EC framework programmes for RTD. ESA is developing a proposal for an Integrated Applications Promotion (IAP) programme, designed to systematically foster the use of integrated space technologies, in a wide range of operational services.

The ESP underlined the need for an industrial policy taking into account the specificities of the space sector. The regulatory framework is a crucial element of any industrial policy. The European Commission has initiated a consultation process with industry to identify its needs for regulatory and/or deregulatory action in the space domain. In addition, it has mandated the European Committee for Standardization (CEN) to conduct an assessment of future standardisation needs of the space sector and to establish a standardisation programme proposal for space. As a start, a feasibility study, presented in June 2008, identified those specific sectors for which a detailed needs analysis will be performed.

Given the established track record of the satellite communications sector, ESA is increasingly successful in introducing public-private partnerships into its development programmes, including tenders for relevant mission payloads from interested private Satellite Operators.

KEY ISSUES AHEAD:

- **Promote the further integration of satellite-based as well as terrestrial observation, navigation and communication services to strengthen European downstream markets for applications and services;**
- **Further develop an industrial policy taking into account the specificities of the space sector and stimulating innovation and competition while supporting industry to manage highly cyclical variations in demand, to invest in technology and to ensure the maintenance of critical technologies.**
- **Complete ongoing needs analysis for regulatory and/or deregulatory action in the space domain, as well as future standardisation requirements. Prepare a standardisation programme.**

5. GOVERNANCE

5.1. INSTITUTIONAL AND FINANCIAL FRAMEWORK

The Framework Agreement between the European Community and ESA entered into force in 2004 and has been extended in 2008 for a further four years until 2012. Its effectiveness will be kept under review.

This institutional framework for space should continue to encompass activities in which Member States would participate optionally under intergovernmental arrangements, while, in addition, drawing on resources from research and, as appropriate, operational Community budgets.

The European Commission launched a call for tender for an expert study to analyse the framework conditions affecting the European space sector. This analysis will in particular focus on financing instruments and schemes required for long-term space activities in Europe and key regulatory issues affecting the European space sector.

Key issues ahead:

- **EU and ESA to pursue closer and more efficient cooperation, based on the Framework Agreement, while exploring the need and mechanisms for future adaptations;**
- **Address the future programmatic, financial and institutional framework (governance) for European space activities;**
- **Tackle the need to ensure sustainable services through operational Community funding for space applications.**

5.2. European Space Programme

First elements of a European Space Programme, that should encompass all important European and national programmatic activities, were submitted by the European Commission and ESA in association with the ESP in April 2007.

The European Space Programme is the practical implementation of the ESP whose success relies on a European coordinated approach to space activities. The European Space Programme will be further developed in 2009, through the High Level Space Policy Group, based on recommendations from a dedicated *ad hoc* working group composed of Member State representatives.

5.3. International Relations

With the main initial objective to improve transparency and coordination among ESP stakeholders, the EC-ESA Joint Secretariat, in collaboration with Member States and EUMETSAT, has developed *'Elements for a European Strategy for International Relations in Space'* (annexed).

This document emphasises the need and desire of European stakeholders involved in space to speak with one voice on the international scene. It aims to set common principles while providing a tool to enable ESP stakeholders to share and exchange information on their activities and relevant priorities and coordinate their actions. The document stipulates that international cooperation in space must be coherent with the EU's external policy priorities, e.g. through using the potential of space systems for sustainable development, in particular in Africa. International cooperation must furthermore contribute to the practical implementation of European space programmes.

Key issues ahead:

- Further develop transparency, information exchange and coordination on the space related International cooperation activities of EU, ESA, their Member States and EUMETSAT, in line with the 'Elements for an International Relations Strategy';
- Continue work on the future elaboration of a fully fledged ESP International Relations Strategy, including specific strategies for GMES and GALILEO.

- Further strengthen coherence between ESP, international cooperation in space and EU external policies.

6. EMERGING ISSUES

6.1. UN CODE OF CONDUCT ON OUTER-SPACE ACTIVITIES

In view of the global nature of space activities and in the interest of sustainability of space activities and infrastructure, the EU has been preparing a draft code of conduct / guidelines on outer-space activities for the consideration of the relevant UN bodies, based on the principles of free access to space for its peaceful exploration and use; preservation of security and integrity of satellites in orbit and the right to legitimate self defence by states.

Key issues ahead:

• Pursue EU efforts to strengthen the basis for sustainability of space activities and objects within the UN.

6.2. SECURITY OF SPACE INFRASTRUCTURE AND SPACE SITUATIONAL AWARENESS

Any disruption in the availability and functioning of space-based systems could today have significant consequences on security, safety and economic activities. It is thus crucial to understand and to monitor the population of space objects, the environment of space itself, and the potential of existing threats and risks to space systems, known collectively as Space Situational Awareness (SSA). Up to now Europe does not have its own independent capacity and is partly dependent on US data to monitor the population of space objects.

As a result, ESA is currently preparing a programme proposal with a view to creating a European SSA capacity. Guidance on the needs and requirements for such a system has been provided by a user group representing user communities (civil, military, operators, insurance companies, scientific community, and other institutions). The EDA has created a project team tasked to define ESDP-related SSA requirements by 2009.

The current ESA proposal provides for such a system to be based on the federation of existing European ground assets and cooperation of available space segments, supplemented by new ground infrastructure deployment, data centres and space-based precursor services. ESA is discussing with its Member States the results of a study on 'SSA Governance and data policy'. The EU Council General Secretariat, the European Commission and EU Member States will be involved in this discussion, including international implications, in view of finding a commonly acceptable solution.

KEY ISSUES AHEAD:

• ESA and the European Commission will continue to identify potential threats to the functioning of space-based-systems and the way to monitor these, leading potentially **to the creation of a European Space Situational Awareness capacity, based on an ESA programme proposal.**

ELEMENTS FOR A EUROPEAN STRATEGY FOR INTERNATIONAL RELATIONS IN SPACE

I. BACKGROUND

Europe must remain a leader in space systems and an indispensable international partner providing first class contributions to global initiatives and exerting leadership in selected domains in accordance with European interests and values.

The European Space Policy has identified that, in order for Europe to respond to global challenges and to play a global role, the strategic mission of space activities in Europe must be to seek:

– to develop and exploit space applications serving Europe's public policy objectives and the needs of European enterprises and citizens, including in the field of environment, development and global climate change;
– to meet Europe's security and defence needs as regards space;
– to ensure a strong and competitive space industry which fosters innovation, growth and the development and delivery of sustainable, high quality, cost-effective services;
– to contribute to the knowledge-based society by investing strongly in space-based science, and playing a significant role in the international exploration endeavour; and
– to secure unrestricted access to new and critical technologies, systems and capabilities in order to ensure independent European space applications.

The impact assessment done by the European Commission [10] for the European Space Policy concluded that cooperation with key international partners is indispensable to the delivery of many of these objectives. Further refinement of the International Strategy will make use of the analyses performed annually by ESA on the global space sector and on the European space sector in the global context.

Optimal results in such cooperation can be achieved through an improved coordination of international cooperation activities across Europe and the sharing of resources in the best way.

International cooperation, embedded in the EU's external relations, can also serve as a market-opener for the promotion of European technology and services in the space field and in this way reinforce this strategic industrial sector. In addition, it can support the promotion of the values as they have developed for Europe through projects focused on environmental protection, climate change, sustainable development, education, access to knowledge/data for support of the infrastructure of developing countries, and humanitarian actions.

The May 2007 Space Council Resolution on the European Space Policy, invited *'...the European Commission, the ESA Director General and the Member States to develop and* SEC (2007) 506 / supported by an external expert study.

pursue a joint strategy and establish a coordination mechanism on international relations. This strategy should be consistent with Member State activities and is aimed at strengthening Europe's role in the global space field and at benefiting from international cooperation, notably with respect to issues listed in Annex 3 [to the Resolution].'

The present European Strategy for International Relations in Space shall provide for a tool to enable stakeholders under the European Space Policy to coordinate actions and share information and resources and to define their relevant priorities in terms of actions and international partners and their respective roles.

II. PRINCIPLES

- International cooperation on space is not a goal in itself. The fundamental principle underlying cooperation is that it must serve the interests of Europe while enabling it to contribute to global initiatives. It must contribute to the implementation of European Policy objectives, for example in the areas of environment, transport and agriculture, in coherence with European values.

- It must equally contribute to the practical implementation of European space programmes, through the optimisation of the available technical and financial resources.

- It needs to be coherent with and support the implementation of the EU external and trade policy priorities through greater systematic integration of space based applications and services into European foreign policies, whether at EU level, or nationally in coordination.

- It must seek to enhance the European space industry competitiveness in order to give the EU autonomous and independent decision making and policy implementation capabilities. Depending on the specific objective, and given the availability of European resources and capacities, a right balance has to be found in each case between cooperation and the sharing of resources among international partners, on the one side, and the creation and enhancement of autonomous European capacities, on the other side, through the development of European space based and space related assets and infrastructure, including technologies.

- Europe can cooperate in a substantial way with a limited number of parties. While dialogue and exchange of information could involve all partners with a substantial interest in space, practical international cooperation at a European level has to follow priorities set on the basis of the principle of mutual benefit and driven by political, programmatic and budgetary considerations.

- In pursuing international cooperation objectives and activities, European stakeholders are committed to fully comply with UN Treaties and Conventions, specifically those designed to address activities in outer space.

III. OBJECTIVES

The priority objectives of the European Strategy for International Relations in Space are to:

- Create synergies and complementarities between European services (notably GMES and GALILEO), their international dimension, and key strategic policy objectives and demands of the European Union. Ensure EU autonomous capacity as well as interoperability, cooperation and exchange with global, regional and national services run by relevant international partners.

- Reinforce the contribution of Europe to global initiatives, such as through the development of GMES as European contribution to worldwide efforts in establishing a Global Earth Observation System of Systems (GEOSS), as well as through the Global Exploration Strategy (GES) Group. Make full use of the potential of European space systems for the relevant EU policies on addressing Global challenges, notably sustainable development, humanitarian aid and climate change.

- Define a coherent European data policy in view of cooperation with international partners on the use of space based applications and services and relevant data exchange, to maximise the public interest.

- Contribute to innovation through international cooperation in space science, space related research, space based applications and space exploration, including enabling Europe to participate in ambitious programmes the cost of which is too great for any one space power. Seek to create synergies and coherence between different technology and research programs.

IV. METHODOLOGY

Coordination mechanism

- The European Commission, ESA, EUMETSAT and Member States will exchange information and consult each other on ongoing and planned major international cooperation activities related to space. The High-level Space Policy Group (HSPG) is to give general guidance on the coordination of international relations.

- The EC-ESA Joint Secretariat will provide for the necessary practical coordination, annual update, and access to the provided information, including through the setting-up of an e-information-network for international relations[11]. All stakeholders will inform partners through the Joint Secretariat / e-network about their major cooperation activities (e.g. conclusion or revision of important cooperation agreements or projects). Member States will receive regular progress reports at HSPG or Space Policy Expert Group meetings.

- In full coherence with the general targets set by this strategy, the European Commission and ESA will undertake a regular analysis in order to define their

Consisting of a network of e-mail contact points coordinated by the Joint Secretariat.

individual programmatic needs for concrete international cooperation actions, based also on relevant existing and planned specific strategy and programme documents.

- **The coordination mechanism will rely on the existing structures for international relations within EU and ESA, notably the relevant geographical or thematic EU Council groups and the ESA International Relations Committee (IRC) with their established responsibilities. Established competencies of the EU Council and Presidency in representing and coordinating EU positions in international relations in general, together with the European Commission, will be fully respected.**

- **Europe will be in a better position to achieve its jointly formulated objectives when coordinating actions and speaking with one voice on the international scene. The coordination of dialogue and cooperation on space with international partners will be based on an agreed set of priorities in terms of partners and activities, and the respective roles. The EU will take the lead in the overall representation of applications programmes for its policies (in particular GALILEO / EGNOS, GMES and joint EU-Africa Partnership on Science, Information Society and Space[12]), while the European Space Agency will take the lead in the overall representation of Europe on programmes in the areas of science, exploration, launchers, technology and human spaceflight, each in consultation with the other and with Member States and, as appropriate, other relevant European partners such as EUMETSAT.**

Coordination in a multilateral context

• EU and ESA Member States will increase their coordination in the framework of **international organisations** and **multilateral space cooperation**, including the relevant **UN** bodies. Together with the ESA Executive and the European Commission, they aim at an improved and consistent coordination of their positions prior to international meetings. The ESA Executive and the European Commission will propose those topics for which a common European position could be envisaged. Key thematic areas for such coordination could include:

– The peaceful use of outer space.
– The mitigation of space debris, the protection of space infrastructure and potential hazards from space.
– nuclear power sources
– disaster management
– GNSS

– International space law

Prior to United Nations Committee on the Peaceful Uses of Outer Space (UNCOPUOS) meetings, ESA and the European Commission will organise a coordination session with participating ESA and EU Member States to decide on such common positions.

• Where appropriate, the European Commission and the EU Council Secretariat will consult ESA on EU initiatives on space related issues within the UN framework, notably the **General Assembly and its First Committee** (Disarmament and International Security).

Coordinated Space Dialogue with international partners

- The European Commission and the European Space Agency will **jointly represent** Europe in a **structured space dialogue and cooperation** with the **strategic partners, U.S.** and **Russia**. They will ensure a shared co-leadership on the different topics, in line with their political, programmatic and financial responsibilities. They will be accompanied by EUMETSAT where appropriate. Dialogues with other international partners could be envisaged, following a proper assessment of needs and benefits, notably in terms of the development of a mutually beneficial cooperation, and the identification of other potential strategic partners.

- The European Commission and ESA will **coordinate** their **dialogue and cooperation** activities on space **with other established and emerging space powers**, and provide regular information to each other, and to the HSPG. Particular attention should be paid to countries covered by the European Neighbourhood Policy.

- The implementation of the **joint EU-Africa Partnership on Science, Information Society and Space** will require the establishment of a Space Applications Working Group to be set up by the EC and the African Union Commission, with ESA and EUMETSAT participation. Priority actions and projects will be based on requirements laid down by African stakeholders, through the African Union Commission. The first such priority identified in the Lisbon Declaration of December 2007 is the preparation of an **Action Plan on GMES and Africa.** EU and ESA Member states will be invited to play an active role, including through their national policy instruments.

REPORT OF THE PANEL OF EXPERTS ON SPACE AND SECURITY

Improving the security of human beings is one of the most important contributions which space technologies and services can offer. Space, a strategic and multiple-use technology by nature, is a key instrument for a comprehensive approach to security.

An enlarged Europe takes an increasingly important role on the world stage. However, as a Union of 25 states with over 450 million people producing a quarter of the world's Gross Domestic Product (GDP), Europe must now accept a higher level of responsibility. These considerations, along with the clarification of EU competences in the areas of space and security in the Constitutional Treaty, demonstrate why the input of the Space and Security Pane of experts is valuable to the work of the Commission.

The magnitude 9 earthquake and subsequent tsunami disaster that ravaged Indonesia, Sri Lanka, India, Thailand, the Maldives, and as far west as Somalia has been recognised by the United Nations as "the worst natural disaster in recent history". Satellite technologies have played a key role in assessing tsunami damage as well as boosting relief and aid efforts. However, integrated monitoring and communications systems, combining satellite and terrestrial technologies on an operational basis, have the potential to reduce loss of life, assets, and natural resources arising from future such events. The European initiative Global Monitoring for Environment and Security (GMES) will make a major contribution to the establishment of such systems.

The General Affairs Council (7th January 2005) tasked the European Commission to evaluate the advantages of establishing a European voluntary humanitarian aid corps. I shall invite my colleagues to take this Report into account and to identify the role space based assets can play to support this potential force.

I would like sincerely to thank all the members of the Panel of Experts who participated in this exercise. The diversity of the experts gathered in this unique group allowed the identification of collective needs of different users in the fields of border monitoring, anti-fraud, transport, air control, civil protection, justice, defence.

The Panel, whose primary mission was to deliver a Report on Space and Security issues, has made a preliminary assessment of European security needs from space. Even though further work is necessary to detail the identified needs and to translate them into requirements, this Report is a significant step forward in planning for information independence and raising awareness regarding the current capability gap.

The Report formulates concrete recommendations which represent significant inputs for the elaboration of the future European Space Programme to be presented to the European Space Council.

It offers a meaningful basis for Europe to move forward into the new era of support for the enhanced security by effective usage of the space based capability developed over the last 30 years.

The Global Monitoring for Environment and Security (GMES) and GALILEO navigation satellite programmes are good examples of initiatives that will help Europe to build a coherent, efficient and strong space policy in support of many other EU policies and objectives, in particular the Common Foreign Security Policy (CFSP) and European Security Defence Policy (ESDP). Space technologies must play a key role in assisting the police, emergency response services, armed forces and agencies supporting humanitarian relief efforts to respond, for example, more effectively to natural disasters, especially those which occur rapidly, or terrorist attacks.

As Europe moves into a new era of responsibility concerning space activities, it is clear that security is a central issue for policy makers. This report reinforces the importance of space in achieving long-term European objectives in this critical area.

It is time for the European Union to play a much greater role in international security. Space is a unique tool to help achieve this strategic goal and this report points the way to ensure that it makes that contribution.

Günter Verheugen

1. THE SPASEC PANEL OF EXPERTS

In June 2004 the Space and Security Panel of Experts (SPASEC) was convened by the EC with participation from:

- EU member states

- European Commission Directorate General and Services (European Anti-Fraud Office, Energy and Transport, Enterprise, Environment, Information Society, Joint Research Centre, Justice, Freedom and Security, Research, Humanitarian Aid Office, External Relations)
- European Space Agency (ESA)
- National space agencies: Agenzia Spaziale Italiana (ASI), British National Space Centre (BNSC), Centro para el Desarrollo Tecnologico Industrial (CDTI), Centre National d'Etudes Spatiales (CNES), Deutsches Zentrum für Luft- und Raumfahrt (DLR).
- Eumetsat
- EU Satellite Centre
- Eurocontrol
- OCCAR (Organization for Joint Armament Co-operation)
- Global Monitoring for Environment and Security (GMES) advisory council
- European Capability Action Plan (ECAP) Space Assets Group
- Common European Priority Area (CEPA 9: Satellite Surveillance & Military Space Technology)
- Eurospace
- NAVOBS (network of SME's)
- European Satellite Operators Association (ESOA)
- Secretariat General of the Council (Observers))
- European Defence Agency (Obervers)

The primary mission of the Panel of Experts was to provide the Commission with a Report on the security issues raised in the White Paper on European Space Policy. This technical work would, in particular, appraise capabilities identified by operational groups and users, define synergies, and make proposals for inclusion in the European Space Programme. This report covers the preliminary assessment of those issues as a contribution to the future European space programme to be established early in 2005.

The panel considered issues relating to both civil and military security, response to terrorism, natural disasters, especially those which occur rapidly such as earthquakes and tsunamis, industrial accidents and shared threats to be within scope of its work. A number of user needs were identified together with a set of requirements to meet them. Existing systems were then considered to identify the gaps between perceived requirements and current capability. The identified needs and requirements form a comprehensive list of possible needs and requirements in this field. Ground based alternatives have not been systematically explored and no priorities have been determined or agreed among experts. Further discussion and decision-making among member states is needed to determine which actually qualify as agreed needs or requirements.

The terms of reference for the panel are included in appendix D.

2. THE NEW SECURITY ENVIRONMENT

The global security environment has undergone dramatic, fundamental and profound change in recent years. The threats of today have a completely different shape, direction and pace when compared to those of the cold war era. Europe, along with the rest of the world, faces threats with greater diversity, unseen command structures and business-like financing mechanisms.

The ready availability of technology to well financed groups who are willing to use unlimited violence to inflict massive casualties means that the technological edge that gave many developed countries a feeling of security has been significantly eroded. This means that Europe must re-evaluate how it protects its citizens with today's assets and also how it develops both the assets and operating procedures in order to keep pace with the ever changing threat. In this environment no single country is able to tackle such complex problems on its own.

Many member states are actively pursuing "Homeland Security" programmes but even these need to be considered in a collective way. Without multilateral co-operation, terrorists have the advantage in the battle for internal security of the Union. For scenarios which meet a common need, EU member States should plan collaborative efforts in order to share the costs of space-based assets. This can only be achieved if common needs and requirements are clearly identified.

It has long been the case security authorities of all types have acknowledged that information is key to defeating the enemy. The new environment has created not just a greater need for information but more importantly, a greater need to share that information with effective controls over access. This is the single biggest challenge facing the security authorities of Europe today.

Paradoxically, this means that control and reliability of information can only be achieved by collaborative operations across multiple agencies and boundaries which have previously acted like firewalls. These issues create a need to change the dynamic for policing and cross border control aspects of security. They are mirrored by the same need for radical rethink of information management for the joint and combined operations which are now the key characteristic of the expeditionary actions which European forces may undertake.

3. SOURCES OF THREAT

The European Security Strategy[1] identifies the key sources of threat for us to consider. These are:

- **Terrorism:** groups are well resourced, network enabled and willing to use unlimited violence for maximum casualties. Europe is both target and base for such terrorists. Concerted European action is indispensable.
- **Proliferation of weapons of mass destruction:** potentially the greatest threat to our security. The spread of missile technology (with evidence of collaborative efforts across several states) adds a further element of instability and could pose increasing risk.
- **Regional conflicts:** can pose both direct and indirect threats to European interests and lead to extremism, terrorism and state failure. Tackling new threats is often achieved by dealing with older problems.
- **State failure:** bad governance and civil conflict corrode states from within. Collapse of states can be associated with obvious threats such as organised crime or terrorism which impacts both global governance and regional stability.
- **Organised crime:** Europe is a prime target for organised crime. This threat to internal security has important external dimensions with cross border trafficking in drugs, women, illegal immigrants and weapons.

Terrorism and organised crime are also identified in The Hague Programme[2] as important issues and an action plan will soon be finalised presenting concrete measures on how to achieve the goals of The Hague Programme.

In its wider definition, security refers to combating all threats that might affect our population, our institutions, our environment, our economic infrastructure and socio-economic interests. Many threats are man-made as listed above, but the impact of major natural catastrophes should not be underestimated. The terrible example of the Asian Tsunami of 26.12.2004 showed that it the developments of early warning and crisis management tools for natural disasters are also crucial.

At the heart of the European Security Strategy is the need to think globally and act locally. This philosophy is inherent in the three strategic objectives identified in the paper:

- **Addressing the objectives:** distant threats are as much a concern as those near at hand since the first line of defence will often be abroad. The new threats are dynamic which implies the need for readiness to act before a crisis occurs. Since none of these threats are purely military they cannot be handled by military means alone.

• **Building security in our neighbourhood:** Our borders must be well governed. Europe should consolidate our achievements in the Balkans and promote a ring of democratic and stable countries to the East of the European Union and on the borders of the Mediterranean.

• **International order based on effective multilateralism:** security and prosperity depend upon an effective multilateralism. Strengthening the UN is a priority and the transatlantic relationship is one of the core elements of the international system with NATO as an important expression of this relationship.

– [1] European Security Strategy, J. Solana, Dec. 2003, "A Secure Europe in a Better World".

– [2] The Hague Programme strengthening Freedom, Security and Justice in the European Union, Presidency conclusions of the European Council of 4/5 November 2004, 14292/1/04, REV 1 annex I.

The policy implications of this strategic thinking are that Europe needs to be:

More active in pursuing strategic objectives: this applies to the full spectrum of instruments for crisis management and conflict prevention. Active policies are needed to counter dynamic threats with the capability for preventative engagement to avoid serious incidents.

More capable: transformation of our militaries into more flexible, mobile forces focussed on the new threats with more effective use of resources. Systematic use of pooled and shared assets would avoid duplication and increase capabilities. Post crisis situations require greater capacity to bring civilian resources to bear. Common threat assessments are the best basis for common action.

More coherent: the major challenge is to bring greater coherence amongst our various instruments and capabilities including the external activities of member states. Problems are rarely solved on a single country basis.

Working with partners: the common threats that we now face are shared by all of our closest partners so international cooperation is a necessity. The European aim should be to establish an effective and balanced partnership with the USA and seek closer relations with Russia as well as strategic partnerships with those who share our goals and values.

4. DIVERSE COMMUNITIES, COMMON OBJECTIVES

The events of September 11th, 2001 and in Madrid on March 11th, 2004 highlighted the fact that the public is at risk in all areas of human activity. Protecting against the type of asymmetric threats which we all now face requires vigilance from an extremely diverse number of communities of interest each with their own particular priorities and objectives. The same groups who would threaten transport services can equally well turn their attention to core infrastructure, energy supplies or financial institutions.

With a common threat facing security agencies across such a wide range of communities of interest there is much to be gained by increased co-operation or collaborative action. However, collaborative action across multiple agencies each with their own operational procedures and processes is notoriously difficult even if it is of such vital importance in the current environment.

The organisations responsible for civil protection in Germany or France have a completely different structure from those in the Netherlands or Spain. Policing or information gathering organisations in larger member states will often have a completely different structure from those in the smaller member states. There is, therefore, a high degree of fragmentation across the large number of organisations and agencies that are responsible for our security across Europe.

More broadly, the global nature of this threat means that Europe must protect its interests both inside and outside our borders. In a recent study report[3] for DG Energy and Transport, the strategic importance to Europe of monitoring the security of our energy supply was highlighted together with the need for a dynamic external trade and foreign and security policy towards certain regions of the world.

With the current commitments to crisis management (Petersberg tasks) and the Headline Goal 2010[4], the overlap between both military and civil security operations becomes ever more important. The advance warning which enables action before a crisis occurs will often be triggered by indicators or information gathered from civil sources just as often as from military ones. Therefore, increased interaction between the activities of both civil and military agencies will be needed in the future. The final resolution for the 6th European Interparliamentary Space Conference underlined that: "...an integrated approach to the development of space applications that use multiple use technology and common (civil and security) standards, is the best guarantee for significant cost-effective collective achievements in the European Space field"[5].

This issue is further complicated by the diversity of structures and procedures amongst security organisations in the new member states. The process of practical integration will derive tremendous benefit from collective action amongst all 25 member states in areas where the satellite community can play an effective part.

Despite the current fragmentation and limited co-ordination between the various agencies responsible for European security they are each tackling the same basic requirements with the same common objectives. Pooling resources and sharing access to core support services which can be established at a pan European level will not only bring cost savings but also efficiency improvements. Targeting those "common" needs and requirements across Europe and providing mechanisms for collective action from the space community is the focus of the SPASEC panel of experts.

4.1 Civil and military interrelationship

Consider the story of change leading to revised balance of effort. The changing shape of the geopolitical landscape brings with it increasing threats from such new forces as international terrorism, organised crime, and the potential for regional conflicts in both civil and military spheres of interest. The protection of Europe's borders could easily become a single focus for our efforts in security. Europe must establish a new balance between the civil and military uses of space[6]. There is little point in concentrating on purely civil applications and ignoring the military requirements or vice versa. Striking this balance effectively will require continued effort as international events unfold.

- [3] Study on Energy Supply Security and Geopolitics Issued in January 2004 by the Clingendael International Energy Programme (CIEP), Institute for International Relations 'Clingendael', The Hague, The Neterlands.
- [4] The *Headline Goal 2010 provides a new framework for the conduct of European military operations and refers to "the development of an EU Space policy by 2006".*
- [5] Final resolution for the 6th European Interparliamentary Space Conference (EISC); Madrid, 10/11 November 2004.
- [6] The need to change the relationship of military-civil capabilities is underlined in the *Human Security Doctrine* presented to Solana the 15 September 2004.

The major space endeavours in Europe over the last thirty years have been primarily focussed on civil and commercial applications. Consequently, the space community does not have a long track record of engagement with the communities of interest serving the security sector (with the noticeable exception of several large Member States where industry has provided synergy between civil and military space activities).

Greater emphasis should therefore be placed on supporting the security authorities of the Union.

Thanks to the past investments of members states through ESA or through their national programmes in civil, military or multiple use systems, the European space industry has reached a significant level of excellence and knowledge which enables it to offer a complete range of capabilities, including a family of launchers, satellites and payloads for all kind of applications, end to end systems, space vehicles and manufacturing, testing and maintenance facilities. As a result, industrial capacity currently exists in European Member States to meet the perceived needs of the European Union for space systems for security missions. Furthermore, due to their inherent large-scale investment, and their common interest, security and defence programmes in particular represent a unique way to foster greater efficiencies at European level and a well developed programme for space and security can help achieve this goal.

4.2 Communities of interest

The communities of interest (COI) active in the security area considered by the panel that could benefit from a range of satellite services are shown in Table 1 below

COMMUNITIES OF INTEREST		MAJOR SECURITY ISSUES
COI1: Law enforcement services	• Customs • Policing • Justice	Cross border control and border surveillance Fight against illegal immigration, Fight against humans/drugs Trafficking Fight against organised crime and fraud Schengen Information System (SIS) Fight against illicit trafficking of small arms and light weapons and proliferation sensitive goods (e.g. WMD) Anti-terrorism, Surveillance of criminals on parole or probation.
COI2: Civil crisis management operators & search and rescue teams	• Medical services • Fire services • Humanitarian aid teams • Civil protection and other emergency teams	Management of natural, technological or epidemiological risks, in a predictive, preventive or response mode. Authorities exist at local/national/regional level and includes a growing community of decision makers at the European level. Examples of benefits to be brought by space capabilities : • Mapping with information on the disasters, health structures, access routes, travels plans; critical infra-structures, epidemiological mapping; tracking and tracing of

		refugees flows • Low cost and easily deployable telecommunication services for exchange and capitalisation of data • Navigation services for redefining geography of disaster struck areas • Telemedicine applications
COI3: Services operators	COI3A: Services operators already make extensive use of space capabilities: • Transport operators and associated agencies for traffic control (road, rail, aviation, maritime) • Telecommunications • Environmental information systems (environmental observatories; weather forecast; including space systems themselves) COI3B: Service operators with potential benefits from use of space based capabilities: • Energy production and distribution • Water supply • Food Safety • Health Agencies • Economic networks (Banks, Insurance)	The major issue is to ensure the security and availability of critical infrastructures and services, with the objective to make them less vulnerable and more efficient. This concerns all structures or organisations which are very critical to society life cohesion, including (but not only) those for which SPACE is already a core component of their process. A few examples of benefits to be brought by space capabilities • Ensuring the security of all modes of transport with security related specification for access to GNSS information • Undertaking a review of Pan European assets tracking for road, rail, air • Monitoring status of critical industrial infrastructures • Anticipating major meteorological events • Tracking and tracing of food safety • Use of observation space based systems to survey ground energy supply infrastructure • Providing with weather and sea state data for energy consumption and production prevision; • Using GNSS timing capabilities to implement a more reliable management of telecoms or power networks over continental areas. GALILEO will provide additional performance in this respect.
COI4: Political and Military users	• Decision making authorities (national and EU bodies) • Intelligence community • Headquarters (including civil and	Covering the overlap with military needs where the synergy between both civil and military activities may be provided. This includes crisis management teams

	military planners) • Forces (including Rapid Reaction Battlegroups) • Other international organisations such as UN or NATO

Table 1 Communities of Interest (COI)

4.3 New approaches, new partnerships

As an example of the new approaches and new partnerships which are evolving in response to the current shifts in threat, EUROCONTROL together with EU, the European Civil Aviation Conference (ECAC), EUROPOL, several national police and security authorities, national governments and NATO have been acting in concert to enhance the security of civil aviation and air traffic management (ATM) in Europe. In close co-ordination with NATO and the aviation industry, EUROCONTROL has developed four strategic security initiatives that concern:

- Sharing of civil and military ATM related information
- Creating a focal point for essential civil ATM information
- Improving communications with aircraft including the need for encrypted data
- Reviewing air traffic procedures and training concerning unlawful interference with aircraft

One of these initiatives has resulted in the development and concept validation of the European Regional Renegade Information Dissemination System (ERRIDS). This system is designed to distribute potentially confidential information via encrypted links to member states, the appropriate military community, airlines and other ATM and non ATM authorised users. It uses NATO accredited security communication ground components. A system wide EUROCONTROL accreditation process may be introduced for implementation. A first live cross border pilot demonstration and evaluation is planned and it is expected to have between 40 and 50 terminals installed across Europe in support of the follow on concept validation.

One of the key issues to be recognised is that the major challenge for ERRIDS is not the technology but harmonisation of different international and national legislation, operating concepts and procedures. ERRIDS creates a “minimum common language” that brings together, in a safe and secure way, the different cultures of organisations and state-specific elements.

Aviation security is primarily a civil issue which needs inputs from all sources and sometimes requires responses from both civil and military communities. The priority is for appropriate means of access control to services with suitable interface standards. Some tasks lend themselves to civil leadership whilst others create the requirement for military leadership. This naturally creates the need for a pragmatic mix of services rather than a single network or set of facilities that are completely integrated at every level.

Satellite technology is being used in EUROCONTROL programmes where it is operationally and economically advantageous. Such programmes could become a useful model for future developments to support CFSP/ESDP initiatives.

Another recent initiative is the European Mobile Wideband Global Link System (MOWGLY) research and development project. The objective is to study the implementation of new appropriate standards for provision of broadband access to users on aircraft, trains and ships.

These initiatives illustrate what is possible given an appropriate degree of cooperation between interested parties in a particular area. Substantial work needs to be done in many other areas to reach the same level of insight.

5. TRENDS AND TACTICS

In today's environment forces must be rapidly deployable and flexible enough to undertake peacekeeping, humanitarian or military missions with limited infrastructure or local support. Typically these missions will focus on joint and combined operations with multiple partners. In the same way that the military groups must evolve in both their thinking and their concepts of operation so too must the civil security communities.

5.1 The need for radical change

Experience from the Balkans showed that Europe needs to improve its overall capability if it is to meet its objectives for Common Foreign Security Policy (CFSP). Space has a unique role to play not only because of the ability to quickly install essential infrastructure but also because of the ability to configure common systems which protect the assets of partners. Many governments have recognised this and introduced "transformation" programmes to reshape the strategic approach taken all the way from procurement to prosecution of security operations. It is therefore a time for the broader space community to better understand the trends and tactics being employed by both the traditional agencies (and also the new emerging ones) in order to ensure that we make our best contribution to the next phase of development for security in Europe.

During this period of radical change it is the responsibility of the space community to engage with a sufficiently broad range of agencies in defining their new doctrines, operational requirements and programme plans if we wish to make the best of our potential contributions. This includes the need for the EU to have assured access to reliable information and services, available to the authorities in all member states.

.

5.2 Security drivers

Issues which currently drive thinking in the security domain include:

Pace of change; The most vivid image of the new security environment must surely be the picture of the twin towers in New York. This image touched the world and has left its indelible mark on the start of the twenty first century. As a direct result, the level of common threat to the worldwide aviation community changed the style and spirit of cooperation and improved operational procedures for air travel overnight. Getting "inside the decision cycle" of the opposition is the critical issue for all military planners. This increase in pace creates a real need for focused efforts in shortening the time between gathering information and acting upon it. The fact that the opposition is grouped not by geography or nationality but by association of objective means we cannot organise security in "silos". The cross over between policing, intelligence, humanitarian aid, peacekeeping and military action is increasingly blurred. Managing our response to that characteristic lies at the heart of an effective response.

Need to share data; Such objectives will require major shifts of culture and operating procedures. Therefore the major challenge is how to marshal our resources in a way which enables secure handling of sensitive data across many agencies. This aspect of the new requirement is something which no single country has yet conquered. Regional police forces in many countries are trying to overcome such problems now as are the intelligence services.

Part of the challenge facing Europe today is the task of aggregation of demand for a diverse range of distinct user communities each of whom derives a benefit from the systems or procedures that the threat demands. If the groups active in the civil protection area are to benefit from information, services or investment available to the crisis management community then the European space community needs to establish a new management organisation in which public sector bodies can aggregate demand so that private sector bodies can aggregate supply. This requires a fresh approach to the co-ordination of requirements and capabilities in the space and security area. The recent tsunami disaster identified the urgent need for a management structure to coordinate demand for satellite imagery and the supply and distribution of derived products.

Precision; The importance of precision location has been highlighted in all recent operations. This is best ensured by making use of secure space positioning systems. Such systems are central to network enabled operations. In particular, continuous and precise knowledge of the position of our own personnel (blue force tracking) is essential, e.g. to ensure extraction of monitors in unsafe areas.

Mobility; The fact that areas of conflict are much less predictable means that we must now focus on mobile forces able to provide rapid response virtually anywhere in the world (including civil protection, fire brigade and humanitarian aid). This has changed the dynamic and increased the requirement for well managed and up-to-date geospatial data. Not only is it important to have improved access to the latest map and information but the fusion of data, including imagery, from a number of sources is also becoming a critical issue. Again, this was identified in the recent tsunami disaster, which showed that only the fusion of data from different sensors would allow a partial assessment of the extent and degree of the disaster, which would have been a boost to rescue and relief efforts.

Standards; This increased requirement for a diverse range of data needs a fresh approach to the tasks of acquisition, processing, storage and dissemination of such data. Unfortunately, since many of the relevant systems are based on programmes from individual member states, there is insufficient progress being made with regard to interoperability, standards, data formats. Harmonised standards and operating procedures are critical to cost effective ground segments.

Technology of opposition; The trend is not only for our own systems to become ever more performant but it is also for the ready availability of technology to our opposition. Consequently, the implementation of suitable controls over export and design information is essential.

Protection of critical infrastructure; One of the issues highlighted by the ability of hostile forces to understand and deploy space technology against our forces in recent conflicts is the fundamental need to protect our own space assets and services. This is a very broad ranging issue and includes the need for protection of our basic commercial satellite systems as well as those aimed specifically at the security and defence sector. For example, if the systems such as INMARSAT, EUTELSAT or GALILEO were hit by terrorists then not only would the defence related traffic have problems but there would be serious implications for our commercial and economic well being.

Europe therefore needs to consider the range of protection measures needed to ensure successful operation of both civil and military satellite systems (including defensive anti jam countermeasures). Part of the requirement for protection of assets includes the ability to monitor what is happening in space in order to ensure that we understand whence might originate sources of potential threat.

5.3 The importance of interoperability

In terms of military procurement strategies there is a very clear shift away from the procurement of large platforms towards network enabled capabilities. These are increasingly focussed on the needs of joint and combined forces in which interoperability lies at the heart of the requirement.

Such programmes are also moving away from systems aimed at support for a single service and more towards systems which cut across the traditional boundaries of an army, a navy and an air force. Even where operations are not necessarily “combined” they are increasingly “joint”.

Many of these trends are mirrored in the civil protection, policing and fraud prevention communities. Historically, regional police forces operated with high degree of autonomy but increasingly the types of threats considered by the panel of experts has created a real need for police services to be better "joined up" than is traditionally the case (eg project Airwave[7] in UK provides full interconnectivity between all police forces with consideration being given to it's use by fire, ambulance and others).

The on-going INSPIRE (INfrastructure for SPatial InfoRmation in Europe) initiative aims at establishing interoperability between geographic datasets of EU Member States[8]. In several Member States, crisis centres are already connected to national geodata portals federated under INSPIRE for integrated data exchange. Another similar initiative – RESPOND - is an alliance of European and International organisations working with the humanitarian community to improve access to maps, satellite imagery and geographic information.

– [7] Project Airwave is a TETRA based radio system used by Police Forces in UK.

- [8] Draft directive (COM[2004]516 final).presently under co-decision procedure.

Concepts of operation (Conops) and standard procedures paired with education and training exercises must be a basic foundation for achieving required capability. This of course brings us back to the most difficult questions of all. How do multiple agencies control and manage sensitive data sets across their respective interfaces. The ability to securely update and access data in different "Joint Situation Centres" is a particular challenge for the intelligence community for all types of data.

5.4 Concepts of Operation

The range of mission types of scenarios that must be undertaken by all types of security authorities has increased dramatically because of the diversity of location, opposition, source of threat and appropriate response. Therefore our security authorities need to be able to rapidly adapt their style of operation in both civil and military domains.

Traditionally, the defence community have made significant investments in facilities for war gaming where the chain of command can act out given scenarios to demonstrate operational effectiveness. This thinking evolved into more complex synthetic environments where the precision or levels of simulation facilities took advantage of the rapid evolution of processing capability. Increasingly, civil protection, policing and crisis management teams all need to evolve their concepts of operation to participate in the multi-agency environment of today's security environment.

The ability to use high speed links to connect remote environments offered another dimension to the ability to check through concepts of operation with a mix of service personnel at different sites or even countries. Such capability provides an excellent starting point for harmonising operations across Europe. For the enlargement agenda, there is real merit in using satellite services to provide underpinning infrastructure as part of a demonstration and training capability so that security authorities in both new and existing member states become more familiar with each others concepts of operation or training regimes. Over and above the wargaming, simulation or training considerations, it is important for the space community to understand and anticipate how the concepts of operation for all types of security missions will evolve.

The pace at which these concepts of operation will evolve for the Rapid Reaction Battlegroups will be different from that for cross border control, policing or tracking organised crime.

One of the direct consequences of the networked enabled approach to the "system of systems" thinking is that any asset whether it is a satellite, an unmanned airborne vehicle (UAV) or a more traditional platform are each part of an increasingly integrated system. Therefore, the concepts of operation for satellite based systems must be entirely complementary with those of other parts of the security and defence community.

6. USER NEEDS

The SPASEC panel of experts considered a large number of different types of organisations when evaluating their operational needs and requirements. The panel differentiated between the **"needs"** of user groups or communities of interest and the **"requirements"** for systems or services that would be necessary to fulfil those needs.

It is clear that some organisations have clearly defined interests and understand well what role satellite services can play in helping them to achieve their objectives. It is also clear that detailed operational assessments are needed for many of the user communities before operational needs and requirements can be precisely defined. However, this section identifies those needs or requirements which, in the opinion of some panel members, require action today. It was also acknowledged by the panel that the process of developing both needs and requirements is continuously ongoing. The conclusions of this report therefore need to be adapted as time goes by.

6.1 Sources of need

Operational needs and requirements for security authorities come from a wide range of organisations around Europe. Some of these organisations are engaged in **military activities** which are well understood and organised. There is a very clear dividing line between those activities which are undertaken by member states and those which are carried out at European level. The Headline Goal Task Force and the ECAP Project Groups have identified needs and requirements which are still evolving but nevertheless have focussed activities with a high degree of cohesion.

The operational needs and requirements involving the **civil aspects of security** come from a much wider range of organisations. There is a greater diversity and fragmentation in these communities with much less cohesion or cooperative programmes. Within the scope of the SPASEC panel of experts there is, therefore, a limit to how precise we can be about such needs and requirements.

However, the panel established an initial grouping as a working model which includes the following communities of activities:

- **Services:** this includes security aspects of Transport (road, rail, aviation, maritime, inland navigation) inter alia facilitating affordable real time communication on position information and securing the navigation and positioning systems themselves, Energy (surveillance of production and distribution of energy), Environment (including natural disasters and industrial accidents, terrorist attacks e.g. dirty bomb) and Telecommunications (all forms of critical infrastructure).
- **Civil protection and search and rescue operations:** including tasks within the borders or territorial waters of Europe for management of natural and technological risks and disasters.
- **Policing and intelligence:** the shifting pattern of co-operation between agencies both in internal and external related tasks creates new needs and requirements for which space services can provide added value, including early warning, situation awareness, and critical event monitoring.
- **Cross border control and border surveillance:** illegal immigration, organised crime, trafficking of humans/drugs , illicit trafficking of small arms and light weapons as well as goods of proliferation concern (e.g. WMD), and other things have created a real need for greater multi-agency cooperation and efficient use of technology to combat today's set of threats.
- **Crisis management teams:** civilian, military and mixed crisis management operations, both during the crisis prevention phase together with the planning and conduct of crisis management phases, including early warning, preparedness, and response.

• **Humanitarian aid and international co-operation:** covering both civil and military involvement in specific operations.

6.2 Management of needs

One of the primary difficulties addressed by the panel was the difficulty of **aggregation of needs** for the diverse range of organisations covered by this diverse set of communities.

The communities of interest covered by the stakeholders for the SPASEC panel of experts have a tremendous range of different needs. No single agency spans the complete set of needs, situational awareness or competence. Therefore it is important to establish an effective mechanism for assessment of a multilevel approach to operational needs. This approach must extend to the management or support of implementation programmes which may be established under a common European project team, by multilateral action by groups of member states or alternatively by individual member states in areas where visible activity is made known. A good example of such an approach exists within the GMES programme which has produced much relevant work under the auspices of the GMES Working Group on Security.

The panel of experts discussed potential mechanisms by which a structured approach to this problem could be established. This approach centred on the definition of mission types that would highlight the needs of different groupings of user communities and that for each mission type there would be a number of scenarios each generating their own set of needs. Before such missions and scenarios can be constructed a series of operational effectiveness evaluations need to be carried out for each of the primary communities of interest.

6.3 Information gathering, processing and dissemination

Fundamental to all forms of security operation is the requirement for information gathering, processing and dissemination. In these tasks satellite services have a unique and indispensable role to play in support of each community of interest for situational awareness, support to decision making and undertaking direct operations. Much of this data is in the form of geospatial information as described in a user needs technical note from DG External Relations[9]. Satellite services that provide risk free access to information in denied or hostile areas are required for many phases of operation including:

• **before the occurrence of a crisis**, continuous information derived from different sources, notably from space assets, supports the situational assessment, conflict prevention and decision-making, helps authorities to prepare the adequate measures, it leads to the availability of documented information, ready for use during a possible intervention (police, anti-fraud, civil protection, military, and others)
• **during the crisis management phase**, information gathering from space in a timely manner is a highly valuable tool for:
• the planning of Crisis Management Operations
• assessment of adverse activities within the Area of Responsibility (AOR), including rear zones and lines of communication
• the assessment and evolution of the extent and impact of natural disasters,
• preparation, deployment and conduct of own intervention resources
• humanitarian relief operations, search and rescue operations, including combat rescue
• damage assessment, and situational awareness/assessment
• dynamic evaluation of the success of the intervention
• tracking the movements and emplacements of refugees and vulnerable sectors of the population
• in the framework of **post-crisis operations**, information gathering allows the monitoring of:
• the implementation and/or the respect of peace/cease-fire agreements,
• demobilization and disarmament operations,
• the monitoring of the resettlement of displaced populations
• implementation of recovery and reconstruction operations

- satellite based information gathering is of great value ensuring **ongoing compliance** with international treaties (proliferation, disarmament)

– [9] Geospatial Information Needs of DG RELEX, Michalis Ketselidis, March 2004.

Requirements for satellite based information gathering encompass different aspects such as:

- geographical environment including border surveillance, types of deployments, locations of and activities at sensitive infrastructures, possible support and/or constraints linked to the populations, local resources
- the capacities of hostile forces, including doctrine, combat structures, procedures and performance of their fighting assets
- the actual forces volumes, combat structures and capabilities including regular military forces, police forces, militia, terrorists, populations/refugees,
- the situation linked to humanitarian and rescue tasks,
- the overall or specific situation to support EU and Third Countries in combating terrorism
- Geographical data (mapping) on relevant theatres.

At the pre-operational and operational stages for Civil Protection, space-based early-warning systems are required for both natural and technological hazards such as volcanic, seismic, and tsunami events, pollutant activities and so on. The architecture of the data network is based on the idea of data sharing and exchange in real time among the hosts as well as the recovery and organisation of all the dataset available in order to support the decisions of the civil protection authorities.

Further, the improvement of technologies and infrastructures for communication and data exchange at different levels and detail should increase the capability of the early-warning system as well as the better integration of ground data and remote data. A relevant issue, involves the availability of the high-resolution satellite data in real-time of damaged areas, pre and post natural or technological event, as "quick" decision support in order to define intervention strategies and rescue resources allocation for civil protection activities. For the particular case of tsunamis, a disaster prevention system could be set up in the Euro-Mediterranean region.

6.4 Primary user needs in support of security policies

The primary user needs identified by the panel[10] in support of security policies are:

N1: **Improved performance** data acquisition with:

- world-wide coverage
- high image quality, including high to very high (one meter or better) spatial resolution electro-optical and radar imagery where appropriate
- all weather night and day observations
- adequate acquisition and frequent revisit times

N2: Improved collection of critical data:

- population (location of people, health statistics, poverty index)
- infrastructure (road, rail, hospitals)
- resources (oil, water, food)
- geography (maps)

N3: Improved production of information and response to user' needs:

- integration of data from different sources, images combined with GIS-generated background data
- rapid data interpretation and integration, as well as visualisation of the information
- off-the-shelf applications to meet users' priority needs
- further analysis of users' needs

N4: Improved access to critical data:

- better interface between users and data providers
- improved access to existing database

N5: Improved dissemination of critical and security information services to diverse user communities:

- Secure communications networks
- More data exchange programmes

N6: Improved interoperability of systems used by various organisations and rescue services in different countries and adequate communication tools.

6.5 Operational needs

The nature and scale of satellite investments frequently make it impossible for individual user groups to cover the full costs themselves. However, when a number of services are combined over a single system, it becomes clear that space can make a major contribution in achieving the effectiveness, efficiencies and synergies called for in the financial perspectives communication[11]. The panel considered the primary needs identified in section 6.4 and identified a set of system and services to satisfy those needs. These are mapped without any prioritisation in Table 2:

– [10] Taking into account earlier work of the GMES working group on security.
– [11] COM (2004) 487; Communication from the Commission to the Council and European Parliament, Final perspectives 2007-2013.

	N1	N2	N3	N4	N5	N6
S1Satellite communications services		x	x	x	x	X
S2Space based Earth observation services	x	x	x	x		x
S3Space based SIGNAL Intelligence		x	x	x		
S4Space based early warning systems		x			x	x
S5Space based Positioning, Navigation and Timing services		x	x		x	x
S6Space Surveillance systems				x	x	
S7 Harmonisation of operational standards and procedures	x	x	x	x	x	x

Table 2 Needs and servicesmapping

The following sections describe these services/systems and indicate some of the priority issues but further analysis and quantification will be required once a full appraisal of user needs has been conducted.

6.5.1 Satellite communications

Secure communications services are needed for a range of applications. These services are required to support the evolving "network enabled capability" that some member states are developing as well as the more general institutional communications networks required by the transport, policing and information gathering communities. In order to meet these requirements, these systems must ensure:

- a very high level of secure connectivity, an appropriate number of highly responsive and reconfigurable links, connecting headquarters (crisis management centres, police HQ,

ISTAR & C2), sensors and the forces deployed in operational areas anywhere in the world (including maritime areas) and ad-hoc operations management centres in Europe
• interoperability with member states, user communities and defence NATO systems
• high data rate communications (bi-directional and multidirectional including videoconferencing) and datacast, between fixed users (decision and operations management centres, headquarters, harbours, airfields, information systems, logistics)
• high to very high data rate interconnections between space-based, aerial, maritime and terrestrial sensors, platforms and assets and monitoring "existing communication" networks and instrumentation, including information systems and early warning systems; apt and robust communications to relay information from early warning centre to population at risk is also critical
• low to medium data rate communications between mobile terminals (handheld, ground vehicle mounted, aerial platforms) and between mobile and fixed terminals
• Wide band air to ground communications for which it is clear that operational users need such services on a highly reliable basis but with real cost effective solutions that are affordable to a wide range of user categories. The user ground segment must ensure high reliability and availability with terrestrial telecommunication infrastructure.

6.5.2 Space-based Earth observation

Earth observation systems are needed to support geographic information for strategic applications. They must provide accurate weather and sea state data in particular in areas of interest. After image analysis either by interpreters or using automatic processes, space-based Earth observation systems must provide:

• detection and characterisation of any related civilian, industrial, natural or military activity
• analysis of the evolution of a crisis situation, specific environment or infrastructure
• a contribution to dossiers for analysis at political, strategic, operative or tactical levels in order to support the decision making process and any kind of related operations
• geospatial-products (topographic maps, digital elevation data)
• weather and sea state forecast (e.g. to be able to improve natural hazard forecasts).

The Earth observation space segment must:

• include the appropriate sensors
• provide worldwide coverage
• be as flexible and robust as possible in order to provide timely information on dedicated areas of interest
• be protected against jamming and deception actions
• ensure the availability, the security and the integrity of the imagery data

Taking into account that the effectiveness of Earth observation systems is strongly dependent on the architectural design, user ground segments must be designed to:

• maximise the information gathering capacity through the timely co-ordinated use of all existing types of sensors
• integrate any new space asset without excessive modification
• ensure the availability, the security and the integrity of the imagery data

In the absence of an agreed ESDP surveillance requirement, the SPASEC panel has not made a comprehensive review of the common European surveillance requirements although this step is seen as a priority action. Work on these ESDP requirements is ongoing in the framework of the ECAP project group on space assets. However, much good work has already been done in the framework of the GMES and BOC initiatives identified in section 8.

6.5.3 Space-based signal intelligence

Some members of the panel felt that there is a need for an autonomous worldwide Signal Intelligence capability. Signal Intelligence systems make use of an adversary's electromagnetic broadcasts to obtain intelligence and are required to provide:

- the characterisation and the location of telecommunications and radar systems [12]
- access to the content of the communications to obtain information on documentation/content, situation and action[13]

As a key element for information gathering multiple space-based systems are required for:

- the monitoring of potentially hostile activities
- the detection and characterisation of related human activity
- the support of counter-terrorism operations
- the detection of emitters with a high degree of accuracy

6.5.4 Space-based early warning systems

Some members of the panel felt there is a need for an early warning space capability which would provide worldwide, timely detection of missile firings from assets placed in highly-elliptical or geostationary orbits. Early warning satellites are mainly used for the launch detection of ballistic strategic (intercontinental) and medium range missiles.

During crisis operations, space-based early warning systems are required to:

- alert the forces and national authorities of an incoming threat, providing impact prediction information (time and location) of the strike to enable passive defence and the use of protection measures
- cue counterforce actions against the incoming missiles and counterforce actions against hostile launch capabilities;
- locate the launch site with a sufficient precision to allow the identification of the aggressor and provide evidence to high level decision makers.

In a pre-crisis situation, these systems are required to:

– [12] more specific for military applications.
– [13] dual use nature, especially in law enforcement activities as fight against terrorism or organised crime (e.g. monitoring telephonic conversation)

- monitor the activities of potentially proliferating countries (missile development activities, frequency of test firings)
- measure the performance and characteristics of the missiles being tested
- determine the signature of these missiles
- monitor and detect hostile launches even when EU countries are not involved.

6.5.5 Space-based Positioning-Navigation-Timing

GALILEO is a civil navigation satellite programme under civil control, in comparison with other Global Navigation Satellite Systems (GNSS) which have been designed in the late sixties for military applications. It will provide positioning, navigation and timing signals on a global scale.

Out of its five different services, the GALILEO public regulated service (PRS), encrypted and resistant to jamming and interference, is reserved principally for the public authorities responsible for civil protection, national security and law enforcement which demand a high level of continuity. It enables secured applications to be developed in the European Union.

Security aspects of GALILEO will be managed by the European GNSS Supervisory Authority[14] on the establishment of structures for the management of the European satellite radio-navigation programmes.

A Council Joint Action has also been approved in July 2004 on aspects of the operation of the European satellite radio-navigation system affecting the security of the European Union[15].

It is noted that the European Commission, with the help of the GALILEO Supervisory Authority, will propose to Council a policy of access to PRS in 2005. The financing of the deployment and commercial operating phase should include a financial contribution of the European Union for the period 2007 to 2013 to be defined in the context of the financial perspectives.

GPS system is the current base of development of European applications and services on the field of Navigation and Timing. However the availability of EGNOS[16], which increases the quality of GPS services fosters the development of new applications. EU has launched numerous pilot projects to emulate those new markets..

The location information, that GPS/EGNOS and GALILEO provide, needs to be completed. It is necessary to couple it with a data base (cartography, logistic, control and command, emergency). The combination of the most recent Information Communication Technologies (ICT) with the navigation satellites signals will be the key of the success of Security applications. Mastering the combination of ICT and SatNav is an asset for Europe.

– [14] as per COUNCIL REGULATION (EC) No 1321/2004 of 12 July 2004
– [15] Reference: 2004/552/CFSP, 12/07/2004
– [16] European Geostationary Navigation Overlay Service

6.5.6 Space surveillance system

The growing importance of space to every facet of life in Europe means that protection of our space asset is a fundamental need. Therefore, there is a need for a sufficiently independent European space surveillance system to:

- acquire and maintain a sufficient knowledge of the environment in space in order to safeguard the functional capabilities of any European satellite assets
- monitor European satellites in order to detect any damaging risk due to either aggression or collision with debris
- characterise any threat to these satellites
- observe and possibly forecast space weather[17] in order to protect own space-based assets
- verify the application of international treaties in outer space
- participate in the strategic evaluation of technological and operational capabilities of other countries/organisations;
- provide decision makers with pertinent information regarding the situation in space within the decision process or the planning/conducting of operations

The space surveillance system could provide information concerning:

- the main characteristics of satellites (e.g. orbital parameters, activity status)
- the main characteristics of potentially threatening debris (e.g. trajectory, physical parameters)
- pertinent information related to space weather and Near Earth Objects (NEO).

Quasi-real time responsiveness is required for all operations related to atmospheric re-entry of satellites or debris.

ESA is currently examining options for providing a space surveillance capability.

6.5.7 Harmonisation of standards and operating procedures

One of the overriding needs of the user communities is the easy integration of satellite services into their existing activities without the need to re-design interfaces for each proprietary system. Interoperability is critical for efficient systems for European security and defence applications.

The tradition of using systems developed under member states programmes as a contribution to pan-European efforts has created a number of interoperability issues in the past. Therefore, there is an urgent need to take stock of the security related projects which will be undertaken in the coming years and ensure that an appropriate set of standards, procedures and concepts of operation are built into the programme development stages at the outset.

– [17] E.g. solar activities.

This initiative will have a large impact on the development and operation of ground segments but will also impact space segment designs as well.

The interoperability or standardisation must be achieved at the level of ordering and product formatting for Earth observation data as well as at the level of information management (e.g. cross calibration between similar sensors and similar satellites to make data fusion possible). The highly successful CCSDS (Consultative Committee on Space Data Standards) initiative could be a suitable model for future efforts. The standards were based on civil developments but were later adapted for security applications.

A table “Space Systems Needs and Scenarios Matrix” is given in Appendix A.

7. CROSS CUTTING ISSUES

There are several cross cutting issues which must be addressed if Europe is to make effective use of its capability in the security and defence field. There is a clear need both to establish new structures and also to better harmonise existing ones if we are to maximise our effectiveness. The following points cover some of the key issues considered by the SPASEC panel of experts.

Security and Defence Doctrine; the expected nature of engagement is based on collective action in some form of joint and coalition activities. This applies to operations at all levels of crisis management in both civil and military spheres. A recent study on European Defence by the European Institute for Security Studies spells out the need for a "doctrine centre" and for developing a real culture, to the point of suggesting the birth of a European Defence College.

Even if this is a long way off, then at least a body of practical knowledge and of accepted procedures should be established. The evolution of new and existing institutional structures will take time. However, the cornerstone of our thinking is that Europe should establish a clear security and defence doctrine based on the perceived needs of Europe.

Interoperability; this is not just a buzz word, it is the word. Interoperability between communities of interest within Europe is seen to be essential. This increasingly means interoperability of command structures as well as network protocols. Europe should evolve its own view of network enabled capability and ensure that researchers, development teams and the operational users are all clear about the vision that this embodies.

Standards; Europe has an outstanding track record of cooperation based upon common standards. The success of the GSM standard is the most outstanding demonstration of that. Many member states actively employ European standards such as CCSDS, DVB or NATO STANAGS which in themselves are evolving. Standards are the cornerstone upon which equipment manufacturers are able to provide cost effective solutions.

Operational Requirements Management; with such a diversity of user communities in an environment of continuous institutional change the task of identifying common operational needs and then managing the operational requirements to meet those needs is one of the most challenging aspects to the implementation of security policies (including CFSP/ESDP). However, the aggregation of demand by public sector agencies coupled with coordinated supply from the private sector is the essence of success in an environment with limited resource.

The range of mission types with the natural groupings of communities of interest mean that no single organisation is likely to tackle this in the coming decade. Therefore, a special action of cooperation in space between agencies that are credible for individual groupings of requirement should be at the heart of the management process.

Regulatory, Spectrum management and frequency coordination; the various forms of security service in Europe are equipped with an extremely wide range of assets that make use of the electromagnetic spectrum. Adequate access to the radio spectrum by these services is therefore key to fully exploiting operational capabilities. Radio communications systems, radar and weapons control devices, radio navigation aids and identification systems operate on land, at sea and in the air.

Many of these systems have conflicting requirements for the allocation of radio spectrum. Cooperation with activities such as NATO standardisation and coordination of common frequency allocations is essential to ensure interoperability among multinational forces in peacekeeping missions or humanitarian aid. International cooperation in this area is not a nicety it is an absolute necessity.

The Commission is seeking to support and to balance the radio spectrum requirements of all Community policies. Tackling the fragmentation of the radio spectrum in Europe improves the interoperability of all sectors using wireless equipment, including in the security domain. The legal basis for the harmonisation of frequencies in the European Union is the Radio Spectrum Decision, 676/2002/EC.

Legal issues; there are a large number of legal issues to be addressed in each of the areas of security operation. These range from the conditions for communications interception through to special investigative methods in administration or criminal investigations. These are areas with which the traditional space community has generally not had to concern itself. However, there is a real need for interaction between the space community and the public sector agencies responsible for management of the operational requirements and those charged with implementation of the resultant programmes.

Export controls/design control; the EU like USA belongs to the same export control regimes which define items for which export controls apply and has adopted binding regulation on export controls of dual use technologies. EU is very vigilant that export controls are efficient and proportionate.

Data policy issues; EO satellites will provide data with high spatial resolution to commercial markets, to the scientific community, and to users. Data distribution has to follow a reliable and transparent policy. The earth observation data policy will be applicable to all data providers exploiting advanced satellite remote sensing technologies with specific performance characteristics and consists of two major elements:

- an up-stream auditing/classification in which a governmental authority will determine in an individual assessment whether the satellite has the potential of generating data or data products with exceptionally high information content.
- in the case where a satellite is classified as being of specific "high-quality"(meaning that it could generate data products with a specifically high information content), individual transactions for application, transfer, distribution, sale or marketing always require predefined procedures to check the permissibility of individual transactions.

The "sensitivity" of an individual transaction will be defined by technical parameters of the specific data set at hand as well as by the target area, data take location, the distribution chains, and the intended end user. In the above mentioned technical parameters, the spatial resolution of the data obviously is of major importance. However, there are also other parameters such as spectral resolution, spectral coverage, or number of spectral channels.

Access to space: Europe has repeatedly stated the need for a guaranteed and affordable access to space including – if appropriate – international cooperation[18]. The ability to launch satellites is beneficial to maintain a space-based capacity for security**.** This should include rapid capabilities, not only to ensure adequate coverage but also to ensure availability in orbit and/or recovery of specific tools in times of crisis. In the context of the White Paper, the need for an assured access to space is reflected in all considerations supporting the setting up of a European Space Programme.

Research for security: A key element for improving the European Union's ability to ensure a better security for its citizens is to develop a coherent security equipment policy at European level.

As a first step in addressing the need for Community action and preparing the basis for a fully-fledged "European Security Research Program" (ESRP) from 2007, the Commission has launched a 3-year long Preparatory Action[19] to support mission-oriented projects. It addresses 5 main areas: (i) improving situation awareness, (ii) optimising security and protection of networked systems, (iii) protecting against terrorism, (iv), enhancing crisis management, (v) and achieving interoperability and integrated systems for information and communication.

For the period to come, the main objectives for the Commission are to capitalize on the positive momentum it has created by consolidating its position with respect to other stakeholders and finalising the definition of the ESRP.

This full fledge programme will be propose in 2005, on the content, multi-annual financial plan and institutional framework as part of the next Framework Programme. Its aim will be to conduct multi-disciplinary mission oriented or capability-driven research for security applications and activities to support the coherent development of Community policies that contribute to protecting the EU citizen and strengthen the technological and industrial base of European industry.

8. CAPABILITIES AND CAPABILITY GAPS

Europe has both existing industrial capability and infrastructure for most types of satellite services. This capability is currently applied in a variety of ways. However, fragmentation of the various user groups and lack of coordinated requirements capture and procurement strategies have created varying degrees of effectiveness. The following sections identify some of those existing capabilities as a starting point for evaluating both the current and future gaps.

One of the systematic issues which occurs in all service areas is the lack of a concerted needs assessment mechanism for aggregation of needs and requirements across the multiple agencies active in the security communities of interest. A second systematic issue is the lack of interoperability which stems from different organisational structures and concepts of operation for the same service in each member state. Some panel members felt the solution to this problem was to establish a common agreed security architecture which would provide both civil and military communities of interest common interfaces and standards.

– [18] EU Council Resolution on European Strategy for Space, 16 November 2000; ESA Council Resolution on European Strategy in the launcher sector ESA/C(2000)36; ESA Council Resolution on European Strategy for Space, 16 November 2000.
– [19] See COM (2004) 72, adopted on 3 February 2004 and Commission Decision 2004/213/EC published in OJ L67 from 5.3.2004. This preparatory action is carried out in cooperation between DG RTD and DG INFSO.

Space systems contribute significantly to quality of life and the European economy. So the continued security and protection of these systems becomes increasingly important (including the monitoring of space debris which could threaten space based assets). While Europe is able to detect and catalogue some space debris using facilities implemented by Member States, most of the data are still provided by the United States of America. The lack of a European Space Surveillance Capability is potentially a serious capability gap.

8.1 Satellite Communication Services

There is a range of both civil and military satcom services available for security applications. Table 3 provides an overview of the most well known ones.

Name	*Owner*	*Characteristics*	*Remarks*
SKYNET IV	UK,	5 Satellites, UHF SHF X-Band, Paradigm took over operations in 2004	Military/Operational
SKYNET V	Paradigm Secure Communication	2 Satellites, UHF, SHF X-Band, EHF	Military/Private Financed Initiative Launch 2006/2007
SICRAL	Italy	1 Satellite, S-Band, UHF, SHF X-Band, EHF	Military/Operational
SYRACUSE III	France	1 Satellite, SHF X-Band SHF, EHF	Military Launch 2005
SYRACUSE II	France	1 Satellite, SHF X-Band	Military/Operational
SPAINSAT	Spain	1Satellite SHF X-Band, Ka Band	Military Launch 2005/2006
XTAR-EUR	US/Spain	1 Satellite SHF X-Band	Military Launch 2005
SATCOMBw Stufe 2	Germany	2 Satellites, UHF, SHF X-Band, C-Band, Ku-or Ka-Band	Military Launch 2008
NATO IV	NATO	2 Satellites UHF, SHF X-Band	Military/Operational
NATO SATCOM Post 2000	NATO	UHF, SHF X-Band, EHF UHF, SHF X-Band Service Provider: FR, IT, UK EHF Service Provider: TBD	Military SHF X-Band, UHF Operational: 2005 EHF operational: 2008
HELLAS SAT	Greece	Ku-Band	Commercial/Operational

ARTEMIS	ESA	1 Satellite, S-and Ka-Band, optical data relay, navigation and L-Band mobile	Operational
SeSat	EUTELSAT	2 Satellites, Ku-Band	Commercial/Operational
e-bird	EUTELSAT	1 Satellite, Ku-Band	Commercial/Operational
W-Series	EUTELSAT	6 Satellites, Ku-Band	Commercial/Operational
HOTBIRD	EUTELSAT	6 Satellites, Ku- and some Ka-Band	Commercial/Operational
EUROBIRD	EUTELSAT	2 Satellites, Ku-Band	Commercial/Operational
ATLANTICBIRD	EUTELSAT	3 Satellites, Ku- and some C-Band	Commercial/Operational
ASTRA	SES GLOBAL	36 Satellites, mix of C-, Ku, and C/Ku-Band Satellites	Commercial/Operational
I-2, I-3, I-4	INMARSAT	10 Satellites, C- and L-Band	Commercial/Operational

Table 3 Milsatcom capability

Four European nations currently possess some form of military satellite communications (milsatcom): France, Italy, Spain and UK. This capability is used for normal military, antiterrorism and humanitarian relief operations involving defence and government personnel. In addition, Germany is planning the SATCOMBw Stufe 2 system for launch in 2008.

France: France joined the milsatcom community in 1984 when it launched its Telecom 1 satellites. These satellites were what are termed hybrid satellites where a military (SHF) payload (Syracuse 1) was added to an existing commercial communications satellite. This hybrid pattern was continued with the launch of the follow-on Telecom 2 satellites which carried a Syracuse 2 (also SHF) payload, in 1991. The Telecom 2 satellites are now nearing the end of their useful life.

The next generation of French milsatcom capability will be the first provided on dedicated military satellites, under the Syracuse 3 programme fully owned and operated by the French MOD. The first of the Syracuse 3 satellites is due for launch late in 2004. The Syracuse 3 satellites will be fully military hardened and have steerable spot beams and an anti-jamming capability as part of their SHF and EHF capability.

Germany: SATCOMBw Stufe 2 is a military satellite communication project by the German Armed Forces. It consists of a space segment of at least 2 satellites at 37 degree west and 63 degree east, 2 anchor stations and different types of user terminals for tactical and strategic communications and an improved control segment. is planned in 2005 with a duration of 10 years.

Italy: The most recent addition to the European milsatcom club is Italy, which joined in 2001 with the launch of SICRAL 1 in February of that year. SICRAL 1 is a dedicated military communications satellite which operates in the SHF, EHF and UHF bands. Italy plans to follow up on SICRAL 1 with the launch of SICRAL 1 bis scheduled for 2005/6, which will also have UHF, SHF and EHF and an even more capable SICRAL 2 satellite around 2009.

Spain: Spain joined the European milsatcom club in 1992 with the launch of HISPASAT 1A, which again, was a hybrid with a Military (SHF) payload on a Direct Broadcast TV satellite. Spain has contracted its next capability to HISDESAT which will operate the Spanish MOD capability from one of two satellites (SPAINSAT and XTAR/EUR) owned by HISDESAT. They will also offer SHF capability on these satellites to other customers on a commercial basis.

UK: The UK MOD first initiated a dedicated military communications satellite some 40 years ago. Skynets 1 & 2 operated at SHF only but the later Skynet 4 stage 1 and stage 2 systems use military SHF and UHF frequencies. These later satellites are also designed with full military hardening and anti-jamming capability.

Skynet 5, the next generation milsatcom capability for the UK MOD, will be provided under a service provision contract on a commercial basis using fully militarised satellites. Skynet 5 satellites and the associated ground system will be owned and operated by Paradigm, a UK commercial company, under a Private Finance Initiative. This will allow Paradigm to provide milsatcom services to other nations with the consent of the UK MOD. The first Skynet 5 satellite is due for launch late in 2006 and will have powerful and sophisticated SHF and UHF payloads with steerable spot beams and an ultramodern anti-jamming capability. This service provision, which will run for 15 years, has commenced with the contractor Paradigm Secure Communications taking over the Skynet 4 satellites.

NATO: NATO has also been a user of milsatcom since 1970 when it acquired its NATO I satellites. Its latest and most technologically advanced NATO IV satellites were provided by the UK in 1991 and are a version of the Skynet 4 stage 1 satellite produced specially for NATO. These satellites provide a SHF and UHF capability. NATO is looking to replace these satellites, which are now both well past their designed life, and has recently selected a European Service Provision capability from the MODs of UK, France and Italy, using the Skynet, Syracuse and SICRAL satellites, to meet its requirements.

8.2 Earth Observation services

The majority of Europe's Earth Observation services have been established in the civil sector. This trend is now shifting with several member states making progress with plans for both national and multilateral surveillance systems (including military systems).

The EU Satellite Centre operates in the military domain but uses predominately civil imagery. Table 4 provides an overview of the main services available today.

Name	*Owner*	*Characteristics*	*Remarks*
HELIOS I	France Italy Spain	2 optical satellites .	Next upgrade is Helios II
HELIOS II	France Belgium Spain	2 optical satellites and IR,	Operational 2005
PLEIADES	France	2 optical (res 70cm)	Operational after 2008
SAR LUPE	Germany	5 satellites SAR X-band, res.<1m	Operational after 2006
COSMO-SkyMed	Italy	4 sat. SAR X-band	Operational after 2006

ENVISAT	ESA	ASAR and MERIS	Operational
Topex-POSEIDON	France/US	Oceans monitoring	Operational
CRYOSAT	ESA	3 SAR Radar altimeter	Launch 2005
JASON 1	France/US	Oceans monitoring/Forecast	Operational
JASON 2	France/US	Oceans monitoring/Forecast	Launch 2008
ERS-2	ESA	SAR	Operational
SPAINISH EO System	Spain	optical/radar satellite	In definition
SPOT 5	France	Panchromatics/multispectral	EoL 2007
PROBA	ESA	High Resolution Imaging Spectrometer /Hyperspectral	Operational
MSG-1	EUMETSAT	Visible and Infrared/ Search and Rescue transponder	Operational
METOP	EUMETSAT	Advanced Very High Resolution Radiometer and Advanced Scatterometer	Launch 2005
TerraSAR-X	Germany	1 sat. SAR X-band, res. from 16 m to 1 m	Launch 2006 Public Private Partnership
Rapid Eye	Germany	5 optical satellites, res. 6,5 m	Launch 2007 Public Private Partnership
Disaster Monitoring Constellation (DMC)	Algeria, Nigeria, Turkey, Thailand, UK	optical satellites , 32m multispectral + 12m pan (Trukey)	Launched 2003/4
DMC Phase 2	China, Vietnam	satellites, 32m M/S, 4m pan	Launch 2005

Table 4 Earth observation capability

Europe has established an extremely strong capability in Earth observing systems over the last twenty years. With the Meteosat system, the MSG system and the Metop system, the role of Eumetsat in the international community is a real success story. With long track records of success in oceanography from ERS-1, ERS-2 and Envisat, combined with the well established skill base in processing Altimeter, SAR, ASAR and Meris data Europe can rightly be proud of its achievements to date. However, most of these activities have been centred in the civil domain.

Apart from progress in one or two member states, and the successful EU Satellite Centre at Torrejon, there has been limited activity in the military domain.

Europe has yet to establish its own strategic surveillance system. There are two major on-going initiatives in this domain: GMES (Global Monitoring for Environment and Security) and the BOC (Besoins Opérationnels Communs).

GMES has already concretely contributed to aggregate areas of demand from a wide variety of user communities. This programme has a strong security element and will be able to offer several of the services identified under the operational needs and requirements section. GMES has been the primary focus for civil security activities in space to date. It covers a number of policy areas including Foreign and Security Policy (CFSP), European Security and Defence Policy (ESDP), policies related to the objectives of Justice, Freedom and Security and Cross Border Control. The GMES initiative has already acknowledged the added-value of aggregating needs and sharing infrastructure wherever possible.

Besoins Opérationnels Communs (BOC); Initiated outside the EU policy by a group of member States, the joint document on the "Common Operational Requirements for a European Global Earth Observation System by Satellites", commonly known by its French acronym BOC[20] was conceived as the first step towards an eventual autonomous European capacity in strategic imagery "aimed at supporting all the information requirements necessary to undertake the 'Petersberg Tasks'". The set of common operational requirements developed by the signatories of BOC is intended for a military satellite observation system. The BOC brings together contributions from a number of member states to form a collaborative programme that builds on the individual elements of SAR-Lupe, Cosmo-SkyMed, Pleiades/Helios.

Building on some of the ongoing initiatives such as the GMES activities for civil security, the work of the ECAP space assets working group and the BOC, there is an opportunity for Europe to enhance the contribution which earth observation programmes make to security policy. Several members of the panel acknowledged the potential for a more strategic approach to the surveillance area.

Earth observation systems currently in use or development have mostly been conceived as stand alone systems with specific user ground segments that are not interoperable. Customers who want to have access to the raw data and want to process these raw data must buy a dedicated user ground segment that is not interoperable with other existing ground segments. This situation creates significant additional costs and time consuming procedures that do not permit efficient operation.

Some current examples highlight this issue:

- The Italian Ministry of Defence will need to install different user ground segments for COSMO-SKYMED system and for the HELIOS II
- The German Ministry of Defence will need to install independent user ground segments for SAR Lupe and for HELIOS II
- The French Ministry of Defence will need to install different user ground segments for each of the HELIOS II, COSMO-SKYMED, SAR Lupe and the PLEIADES systems
- ESA has dedicated user ground segment for each systems (ERS, ENVISAT and others).

This situation is slowing the use of space based earth observation systems in many areas in which their capabilities would be particularly valuable. Tackling this fundamental issue by launching a concerted initiative in this field based on a common agreed architecture and set of interface standards is important. The availability of this standardised architecture will help to reduce duplication, lower the cost of the access to the EO satellite systems and improve responsiveness.

During the GMES Advisory Council of 8 December 2004, Member States operating or developing high resolution satellites asked the GMES Programme Office to address the issue of co-ordinating the various contributions of national missions in support of GMES. This could be done by implementing a suitable discussion forum involving the agencies in charge of the development and operation of these missions.

– [20] Besoins Opérationnels Communs

8.3 Position, Navigation and Timing Services by satellite

Most current applications of positioning, Navigation and Timing services in Europe are based on the existing GPS system. The ready availability of the EGNOS system for applications across the transport sector has prompted pilot projects in a range of areas.

Aiming to reach operational status after 2008, the GALILEO system is planned to offer positioning, navigation and timing (PNT) services worldwide. It will join the ranks of the current GPS and GLONASS systems allowing users to pinpoint their exact locations.

The GALILEO signals will meet security needs during natural disasters or crisis situations to manage actions under the responsibility of civil security and emergency services. It can also be used for a range of operations whose boundaries are often difficult to determine and for which satellite navigation system is a mission critical feature capable of significantly improving their efficiency, as well as their logistic support. GALILEO service may also be useful for redrawing maps in the aftermath of devasting natural disasters such as the recent Asian tsunami which drastically changes the geography of the affected areas.

With a growing number of users dependent on precise positioning services to carry out their daily functions, economic security would be adversely affected should there be an intentional or accidental service shutdown. Thus, besides protecting the system from unauthorised use, it will be important to safeguard the system to ensure signal continuity at all times.

All necessary actions and structures are already being implemented in order to address potential vulnerabilities of GNSS.

8.4 Non European Systems

In addition to its own current systems European organisations also have access to a wide range of other systems as shown in Table 5:

Name	*Owner*	*Mission*	*Characteristics*	*Remarks*
NAVSTAR GPS	USA	NAVIGATION	24 satellites (+3) Cep <10m	On-going upgrade
GLONASS	Russia	NAVIGATION	Foreseen 24, activ. 11 <60m	On-going refurbishment
QUICKBIRD	USA	OBSERVATION	Res : 0.6 m panchromatic	Commercial provider
IKONOS	USA	OBSERVATION	Res : 1m panchromatic	Commercial provider
Orbview	USA	OBSERVATION	Res : 1m panchromatic	Commercial provider
RADARSAT	Canada	OBSERVATION	Radar	Commercial provider
GLOBALSTAR	USA	COMMUNICATION	constellation	Commercial provider

IRIDIUM	USA	COMMUNICATION	constellation	Commercial provider
THURAYA	UAE	COMMUNICATION	Operational + 1 sat to be deployed	Commercial provider

Table 5 Non European systems

8.5 Capability Gaps

8.5.1 Transversal gaps

After a first glance at the needs and capabilities in Europe, the SPASEC panel of experts concluded that the gaps that exist today include the lack of:

G1: common operational effectiveness assessments or development of common multi-user needs and requirements to which space community may contribute

G2: **a mechanism to manage operational requirements** for space systems in the multi-user security sector

G3: common concepts of operation across multi-user groups in both civil and military security domains using satellite services

G4: sufficient interoperability of a wide range of both civil and military systems and between national assets

G5: common databases for current and planned IERs for a variety of systems

G6: testbeds or reference facilities to support the civil security communities

G7: focussed demonstration programmes to demonstrate potential of space to users

G8: simulation, planning & training facilities for multi-agency satellite programmes

G9: operational systems that would be of benefit to user communities of interest such as surveillance, satcom and application of location based services

8.5.2 Capabilities Gaps

The common understandings of the members of the SPASEC group permit to identify three capabilities gaps common to the non-security related communities and security/defence communities:

- lack of common agreed architecture and interfaces standards for the user ground segment of the Earth Observation Space based systems;
- lack of European space surveillance capabilities;
- lack of very high data / high data rate mobile telecommunications.

8.5.2.1 Earth Observation User Ground Segment

The earth observation systems, currently in use or development have been conceived as stand alone systems with specific not interoperable user ground segments. The customer who wants to have access to an earth observation space system to buy a dedicated user ground segment that is not interoperable with its existing user ground segments. This situation induced significant additional costs (more people necessary to make use of the ground segment, infrastructure, logistic, maintenance) and time consuming procedures that don't permit to fulfil the reactivity requirements.

This situation is slowing the use of space based earth observation systems in many areas in which their capabilities would be particularly valuable.

Tackling this issue is fundamental by launching an aggressive initiative in this field by a concerted elaboration of a common agreed architecture and interfaces standards for user ground segment. The availability of this standardised architecture will permit to eliminate duplication, to lower the cost of the access to the EO satellite systems and must contribute to more reactivity. By elaborating such standards, European Union must contribute to the birth of an international standard but also be a better position to impose its EO satellite systems.

8.5.2.2 Space surveillance capabilities

Space systems constitute items which contribute significantly to the life of European population but also became invaluable for many areas of the European economy. So the security of these systems become a true challenge taking into account the increasing security issue of the space debris proliferation.

While Europe is able to detect and catalogue some Space debris using European facilities implemented by some European Union Member States, most of the data are still provided for free by the United States of America. This situation could change in the near future and the data already provided are not exhaustive or not be made available at the needed time.

The lack of a European Space Surveillance Capability is identified as a serious capability gap that must be one of the priority of the future European Space Program. Beyond the security of the European space assets, this system must contribute to the control of the application of the International Space Treaties and to the evaluation of the activities of the space faring nations or organisations.

8.5.2.3 Very high data / high data rate mobile telecommunications

All the systems (ground-based, maritime, airborne, space based) contributing to the elaboration of the most comprehensive awareness situation for crisis management or disaster relief operations need to be programmed and to be able to transmit their data in the shortest time. Up to now, the efficiency of all these systems, in particular the current Earth Observation satellite systems, is limited by the lack of worldwide available very high data rate mobile communications systems. The satellites in geostationnary orbit or highly elliptical orbits with very high data rate telecommunications capabilities with geomobile (ground-based, maritime, airborne) and low earth orbit satellites must overcome this capability gap. These satellites, known as data relay satellite system, are needed but development and commissioning of such system is too costly to be borne by each single user. This is an enabling infrastructure capability to support security/defence related activities, in particular in the fields of transportation security, crisis management and disaster relief operations but also to ease the birth of new services (entertainment services aboard aircrafts ...).

9. PROGRAMME OPTIONS

The scope of the programme possibilities that may be derived from the needs assessment or the identified capability gaps are wide ranging. They cover policy issues which run throughout the whole spectrum of current European affairs. Some of these policy issues require unanimous decisions whilst others may be carried forward by groups of member states acting together.

In several areas there is strong evidence of synergy between various communities of interest in the civil security sector even if the mechanisms for achieving those synergies are not foreseen. There is also very clear evidence of overlapping interest between the civil and military security domains even if this is not the case for all aspects of the work covered by the panel. There are three basic options for using space based assets to support our objectives in areas of freedom, security and justice:

- **Option 1:** Rely on non-European systems
- **Option 2:** Rely on assets of individual Member States

• **Option 3:** Augment declared national capabilities with additional operational systems needed to fill identified priority capability gaps

In the static environment of the Cold War, option 1 made the most sense as Europe largely relied on NATO for its collective security and had no foreseen need for an expeditionary capability. Today, the situation has changed and, with the collapse of the Soviet Empire, Europe no longer faces the same threats. However, few would argue that new dangers and challenges have filled the vacuum and European nations have to develop new doctrines and capabilities to face these new issues. Similarly, there is a growing awareness of the environmental threats to European security and the need for an independent monitoring and validation capability.

Europe and the member states are increasing their capabilities to operate outside our own borders in expeditionary forces, with multinational military, civil security and police formations. It is also increasingly working across its internal borders to counter fraud, organized crime and terrorism. However, Europe is still relying mainly on option 1 to support these activities, although there is increasing co-operation under option 2. This is entirely logical given the cost, complexity and high risk of developing Space-based capabilities. However, recent events suggest that this may not be enough. This was particularly obvious during the recent tsunami disaster in the Indian Ocean, whereby in-depth and useful damage assessments undertaken by European and international entities were based primarily on Ikonos and Quickbird; SPOTS 5 (2.5m PAN fused with MS) and other lower resolution systems were shown to lack the necessary spatial resolution for urban damage assessment and delineating the tsunami impact line. On the other hand, low resolution systems such as DMC are well able to provide regular, broad area, coverage for the purposes of monitoring disasters.

Europe can no longer assume a fortuitous coincidence of interest with the USA. Nor, unfortunately, can it guarantee unanimous agreement between the 25 Member States, and that is the weakness of option 2. Even though the risk may be small, Europe cannot guarantee access to Member State assets in support of possible or actual deployments of European multinational units or coalition forces under all circumstances. Europe possesses much expertise in space research and technology, but it is not harmonized. Instead, with the exception of ESA programmes, it is still largely national-based, and that limits its capabilities as economies of scale are not applied effectively.

The cost of doing nothing to redress this imbalance will be high. The importance of space based assets in all fields of security is increasing at a significant pace. If Europe does not capitalize on its investments in capability over the last thirty years, the cost to future generations of recreating that capability in times of crisis will be extremely high. Maximizing cost effective capability by co-operation, sharing and pooling of assets will go some way to minimizing the long term cost of security in Europe.

The utilization of space activities for supporting the CFSP and/or ESDP needs to be thoroughly discussed within the member states at EU level which may lead to new approaches for implementation in the medium and long term. Furthermore, arms control must be considered.

9.1 Mapping of needs, services/systems and gaps

Programme proposals for future satellite systems to support European space and security initiatives must take account of the need for effective links between member states and communities of interest. This is necessary to achieve the effectiveness, efficiency and synergy required to provide greater cohesion and value for money of investments across 25 member states.

Central to achieving this will be a clear mapping between user needs, system requirements and capability gaps.

A starting point for this is shown in table 6:

Needs	Services and systems	Gaps
N1: Improved performance of EO data acquisition	**S1:** Satellite communications services	**G1:** Common operational effectiveness assessments
N2: Improved collection of critical data	**S2:** Space based Earth observation services	**G2**: Mechanisms to manage operational requirements
N3: Improved production of information and response to user' needs	**S3:** Space based Signal Intelligence	**G3:** Common concepts of operation
N4: Improved access to critical data	**S4:** Space based early warning systems	**G4:** Sufficient interoperability
N5: Improved dissemination of critical information	**S5:** Space based Positioning, Navigation and Timing services	**G5:** Common databases
N6: Improved systems interoperability	**S6:** Space Surveillance systems	**G6:** Testbeds or reference facilities
	S7: Harmonisation of operational standards and procedures	**G7:** Focussed demonstration programmes
		G8: Simulation, planning & training

Table 6 Summary of needs, services/systems and gaps

There are four primary categories of tasks that must be undertaken if the current capability gaps are to be overcome. These are:

Operational analysis tasks: including the assessment of common operational effectiveness for space related security initiatives within any given community of interest; the development, management and maintenance of the information exchange requirements for specific operational activities; development of efficient concepts of operation for the overlapping activities in both civil and military areas; life cycle cost modelling and planning facilities for space related services.

Technology developments: including the development and maintenance of testbeds and reference facilities for the demonstration of security applications for space services; specific technological and research activities to ensure European capability in critical areas; effective use of synthetic environments for product proving exercises.

Pre-operational facilities: simulation, planning and exercise infrastructure to support rehearsal and training exercises for pre-operational trials of user equipment and services; interoperability trials and facilities for confirmation of the operational effectiveness of joint procedures or related equipment; facilities of developing and proving common operational procedures; programme tasks to cover Collaborative Coalition Interoperability Projects, (CCIPs).

Operational systems: facilities and programme activities for the development and roll out of operational systems together with key user groups and communities of interest [eg support to transport sector in the effective roll out of low cost operational satcom or asset tracking systems to support road/rail applications, support to the European Agency for the Management of Operational Cooperation at the External Borders of the Member States of the European Union for roll out of surveillance systems to overlap with UAV systems[21].

It will be essential to complete the Operational Analysis Tasks first so as to allow the more detailed technical tasks to be properly scoped and costed before embarking on them.

– [21] A Workshop held in Ljubljana the 18/20 October 2004 on "Research and Technological Challenges in the field of Border Control in the EU-25" stated that "all types of seal technologies are needed for tracking containers including electronic-seal technologies, sensors, and satellite tracking systems…".

9.2 Assessment related tasks

The scope of the proposed assessment related tasks is shown in table 7:

	Proposed tasks
WPOA1	Strategic reviews of each of the needs, requirements and gaps identified in table 5 (N1-N8, S1-S7, G1-G9)
WPOA2	Operational effectiveness assessments of satellite services for communities of interest in logical groupings (e.g. all transport together, Policing and information gathering grouped with cross border control, humanitarian aid and international cooperation grouped with crisis management teams, military taken separately for those items of overlap with the civil security sector)
WPOA3	Information exchange requirements evaluations for each user community of interest
WPOA4	Capability catalogue covering the civil security sector separate from the military sector
WPOA5	Reviews of evolving operational requirements and concepts of operation for each community of interest
WPOA6	Cost modeling and benefits assessments to evaluate those areas where satellite services offer increased value for money
WP0A7	Review of secure communications requirements
WP0A8	Review of common European surveillance requirements
WPOA9	Review of the case for pan European space based signal intelligence and early warning systems

Table 7 Assessment related tasks

Based on the inputs of the four Working Groups, the panel also produced a list of tasks in the technology, interoperability and operational systems areas. These detailed proposals were not sufficiently linked to needs and requirements for them to be agreed but, for illustrative purposes only, they have been enclosed in Appendix B.

10. FINANCIAL PLANNING

Europe has been spending approx 950 M EUR per annum on related activities in the space and security area. The dramatic change in the security environment means that this level of expenditure is considered to be insufficient to meet the user needs or requirements for the future[22].

For the mid and long term, (post 2007) an attached chart (Appendix C) provided to the Panel by industry shows budgetary estimates for the cost of developing a contribution to support European security needs. There is a progression from a current budget of just under 1B€ in 2004 to around 2B€ from 2012 onwards[23].

- [22] Initial assessments of the leader of the Financial planning Working group have lead to the following annual estimations: generic ground segment (10-12 Mio €); interoperability and standards (40-50 Mio €); Earth observation (actual spending around 350 Mio € , it should reach a level of 600 Mio €); Satellite Communication (actual spending: 600 Mio €); Signal intelligence (200 Mio €); Early Warning (200 Mio €); Space Surveillance (100 Mio €); Technology research (250 Mio €); New applications (200 Mio €).
- [23] These figures will have to be confirmed by in-depth assessment of the capability gaps and the options for filling them

11. CONCLUSIONS AND RECOMMENDATIONS

The Members of the Panel:

acknowledged the valuable role that space assets play in the security domain for both the civil and military communities at local, national, regional and global levels.

underlined the fragmentation and lack of coherence across 25 Member States for space applications in support of security authorities. This hampers the sharing of information and effectiveness of operation when joint and combined activities are needed. One consequence of this is that there is no systematic process for aggregation of security needs at the European level. However, the Panel **confirmed** that space can play a valuable role in this respect since satellite services are intrinsically regional or global in nature.

discussed potential mechanisms by which a structured approach to achieving this could be established. This approach is centred on the definition of mission types that would highlight the needs of different groupings of user communities. For each mission type, there would be a number of scenarios generating their own set of requirements.

strongly recommended that the security applications of space should be given a high relevance in the forthcoming European Space Programme (ESP). This programme should be fully harmonised with other national and commercial programmes so as to obtain maximum synergy and affordability offering an enhanced capability for all aspects of security.

welcomed the document on European Space Policy "ESDP and Space", approved by the Council in November 2004. This document contains a comprehensive roadmap proposing in particular to provide to the Commission ESDP requirements to allow for identification of possible multiple-use capabilities inherent to civilian systems under development, and to establish, "in the context of the European Space Programme, a permanent inter-pillar dialogue (...) to ensure global coherence of all EU needs and requirements".

Made the following recommendations:

1. **The need to establish urgently in 2005 a platform or forum** for consolidating the security related user needs (short, long and medium term) for space in a structured way.
2. **The main tasks** of this platform/forum will consist of:
a. **Establishing a network** between the users;
b. **Giving the opportunity to users** to express their needs in a dedicated forum;
c. **Determining how existing capabilities** could be considered in multiple-use systems to fulfil these needs;
d. **Refining** of capability gaps

e. **Translating** the user needs into requirements

f. **Assessing** how space capabilities can match the requirements including definition of scenarios

g. **Examining** how optimum benefit could be gained by combining space based data with existing geospatial datasets[24]

h. **Defining** actor's roles and responsibilities including financial issues

i. **Proposing** inputs to the European Space Programme.

3. **A comprehensive study** of the costs of a contribution by the space sector to the EU security needs is required.
4. The Commission **should ensure** an effective and efficient liaison between the activities of the forum and the European Defense Agency in accordance with the activities of the 2005 EDA Work Programme as far as space is concerned.
5. Amongst the most important areas of convergence and overlapping between the operational needs of the different multiple-users communities existing in Europe, the Panel **identified the need for raise awareness on capabilities**.

No single user community in Europe is sufficiently structured or ready to support autonomously large efforts to fulfill needs in this area in a cooperative way; space, in some cases, could offer an interesting solutions to many user groups.

6. The Panel of Experts also **concluded that it would be unrealistic** at this stage to propose a common approach to provide Europe with a complete system for global situation awareness and recognizes the continued importance of the national support for space activities. Nevertheless, the Panel **recommends setting up a coherent European framework initiative** aimed at contributing to the space elements of such a global situation awareness system. This framework shall be able to implement the above described process and to propose top-down dedicated projects complementing the national and intergovernmental actions and in support of Member States. Some projects need to be initiated immediately in order to be available for the next generation of space systems, for instance standardized architectures, common components to increase response time and cost effectiveness.
7. In order to support the exchange of information, the Commission **should support and develop** a process to ensure interoperability between current space systems in Europe in the fields of earth observation and communication. GMES could be seen as a first step along the road to achieving this. Work has to be coordinated with second pillar (EDA and concerned member states) in order to take in account confidentiality, security, adaptability and availability specific issues.
8. The EU and ESA have been aware for some time of the relevance of telecommunications for security and risk management, and some projects have been financed in order to establish better co-ordination among national initiatives in different emergencies.

It seems therefore appropriate at this point that **a similar initiative should originate in the field of institutional and emergency telecommunications.** Co-ordination among national initiatives in this area appears urgent.

Attention should be focused on:

– [24] Taking into account harmonisation developments through the INSPIRE Directive
- Network and service interoperability
- End-to-end satellite telecommunications systems
- Convergence and integration of satellite telecommunications with other space applications domains.

9. Space services now play such a key role in the well-being of European society that **protection of critical infrastructure in the space sector is a priority**. This may need services and capabilities for surveillance of space based assets as well as protection for terrestrial infrastructure.
10. The Panel **confirmed the relevance** of using earth observation systems and data relay satellites in support of EU borders surveillance, in particular maritime borders, in order to fight against illegal activities (i.e. human trafficking, drug smuggling…) and to monitor transport activities in and around Europe.
11. A large number of members of the Panel **recommended implementing some focussed projects**, especially in terms of demonstrators as a first step, in order to maintain the level of European industry at a competitive state of the art. Short term needs should be covered with existing financial instruments[25], while long-term activities would benefit from Financial Perspectives instruments.
12. The Panel **confirmed the need** to guarantee affordable access to space, including – if appropriate – international cooperation. It is an essential infrastructure to support security policies and objectives.
13. Considering its transversal usefulness and its relevance to many security challenges, the Panel **considers that space applications are an integral part of security capabilities** in the frame of subsequent calls for the Preparatory Action for Security Research and in the future European Security Research Programme.
14. **Co-ordination of activities should be ensured** between the user organisations on one hand and between the procurement and programming organisations on the other hand (ESA, EDA, OCCAR …).

Action Plan: *Short term* :

Launch actions (in an organisational and technical framework to be determined) in order to:

• **establish a user platform** or forum to:

- consolidate common security needs;

- fill horizontal gaps;

• **establish a financial working group** to

- estimate and allocate costs;

- take into account any additional specific MS requirements to be financed by concerned countries;

• **integrate** in the European Space Programme the necessary projects to fill the identified capability gaps (lack of common agreed architecture and interface standards for the user ground segment of Earth Observation Space based systems; lack of European space surveillance capabilities; lack of very high data / high data rate mobile telecommunications) .

– [25] Possible short term priorities could be: networking of monitoring capabilities, position reporting and space surveillance.

For the medium/long terms :

Continue interpillar coordination processes such as the SPASEC in order to support the European Space Programme and launch appropriate programmes for long term operational adequate capabilities.

Acronyms

ASI: Agenzia Spaziale Italiana

BOC: Besoins Opérationnels Communs

BNSC: British National Space Centre

CCIP: Common collaborative interoperability projects

CDTI: Centro para el Desarrollo Tecnologico Industrial

CEPA: Common European Priority Area

CFSP: Common Foreign Security Policy

CNES: Centre National d'Etudes Spatiales

COI: Community of Interest

CONOPS: Concepts of operation

DLR: Deutsches Zentrum für Luft- und Raumfahrt

EC: European Commission

ECAC: European Civil Aviation Conference

ECAP: European Capability Action Plan

EDA: European Defence Agency

EGNOS: European Geostationary Navigation Overlay Service

EO: Earth Observation

ERRIDS: European Regional Renegade Information Dissemination System

ESA: European Space Agency

ESDP: European Security and Defence Policy

ESOA: European Satellite Operators Association

EU: European Union

GMES: Global Monitoring for Environment and Security

GNSS: Global Navigation Satellite Systems

HGTF: Headline Goal Task Force

ICT: Information Communication Technologies

INSPIRE: INfrastructure for SPatial InfoRmation in Europe

MOWGLY European Mobile Wideband Global Link System

NEO: Near Earth Objects

OCCAR: Organization for Joint Armament Co-operation

PASR: Preparatory Action Plan for Security Research

PNT: Positioning Navigation Timing

PRS: Public Regulated ServicesSIS: Schengen Information System SPASEC: Panel of Experts on Space and Security

UAV: Unmanned Airborne Vehicle

APPENDIX A: SPACE SYSTEM NEEDS AND SCENARIOS MATRIX

Area of operations	Missions	Applications	Organisation grouping concern	Space system needs
				Telecom
External Security of EU	Crisis management operations to solve regional conflicts [27]	- Specific military issues	- Military	Worldwide cover Secure connectivity High rate data com. Interoperability Multimedia services Traditional services[28]
	Prevention of an attack involving WMD in the field of CRBN	- Ballistic Missile[34] launches detection and initial tracking - Impact area prevision - Alert diffusion - Intervention units facilities[35]	- Civil protection - Military	Worldwide cover Secure connectivity High rate data com. Interoperability Multimedia services Traditional services
	Peace Support Operations abroad	- High data rate communication net quick deployment - Identification and surveillance of rogue human grouping - Intervention units facilities □	- Law enforcement - Military	Worldwide cover Secure connectivity High rate data com. Interoperability Multimedia services Traditional services
	Anti-terrorism	- Moving and activity tracking of terrorist groups - Interception of terrorist communications 10 - Intervention units facilities	- Civil protection - Law enforcement - Military	Worldwide cover Secure connectivity High rate data com. Interoperability Multimedia services Traditional services

	Control of Mass destruction weapons proliferation	- Identification of WMD sites - Knowledge of WMD fabrication and testing sites activity - Localisation and tracking of sensitive equipment	- Law enforcement - Military	Worldwide cover Secure connectivity High rate data com. Interoperability Multimedia services Traditional services
	Control of international treaty enforcement	- Detection, identification and tracking of military concentrations and flows - Border surveillance - Knowledge of weapons fabrication and testing sites activity - Detection and localisation of polluting emissions - Illegal fishing detection, identification and tracking - Production of juridical direct evidence supports	- Law enforcement - Military	Worldwide cover Secure connectivity High rate data com. Interoperability Multimedia services Traditional services
	EU citizens and interests protection in foreign countries	- Detection, localisation and record of alert messages from EU citizens in foreign countries - Surveillance of sensitive sites (industrial, strategic, ... ones) - Prevision, detection, identification and tracking of refugee concentrations and flows - Cartography and knowledge of access conditions in order to prepare evacuation operations - Intervention units facilities □	- Law enforcement - Military	Worldwide cover Secure connectivity High rate data com. Interoperability Multimedia services Traditional services
Internal Security of EU	Control of borders and territorial waters	- Ship detection and identification in territorial waters - Detection and tracking of human concentrations in frontier vicinity - Hydrocarbon pollution origin detection and alert diffusion Intervention units facilities □	- Law enforcement - Military	Worldwide cover Secure connectivity High rate data com. Interoperability Multimedia services Traditional services
	Fight against organised crimes	- Moving and activity tracking of criminal groups, ships, vehicules - Interception of communications 10 - Intervention units facilities	- Law enforcement	High rate data com. Interoperability Multimedia services Traditional services
	Surveillance of criminals on parole or probation	Permanent localisation of criminals on parole or probation	- Law enforcement	

	Ensuring Security of all modes of transport	- Strengthening mobile tracking in order to prevent collisions - Sea drifting dangerous objects localisation - Distress signal detection and localisation with information exchanges - Meteorology prevision, diffusion and alert - Dangerous cargo tracking - Intervention units facilities □	- Civil protection - Law enforcement - Operator services	Worldwide cover High rate data com. Multimedia services Traditional services
	Ensuring the security and availability of critical infrastructures and services	- Critical sites surveillance (detection and tracking of suspect movements or behaviours in vicinity) - Detection and identification of physical vulnerabilities - Meteorology prevision, diffusion and alert 10 - Intervention units facilities	- Civil protection - Law enforcement - Military - Operator services	Worldwide cover Secure connectivity High rate data com. Interoperability Multimedia services Traditional services
Crosscutting areas	Management of natural, technological or epidemiological crisis	- Detection, identification and moving prevision of radioactive / chemical pollution (clouds, slick), forest fire, flood, ... - Identification of areas propitious to natural disasters (flooding, earthquake, fire, storms, ...) - Cartography of natural disaster areas and damage assessment - Meteorology prevision, diffusion and alert 10 - Intervention units facilities	- Civil protection - Law enforcement - Military	Worldwide cover High rate data com. Interoperability Multimedia services Traditional services
	Stabilisation and reconstruction of thirdcountries, sometimes in a non permissive environment	- Prevision, detection, identification and tracking of human concentrations and flows - Damage assessment - Energy, water and food resources status knowledge - Cartography and knowledge of access conditions - Intervention units facilities □	- Civil protection - Law enforcement - Military	Worldwide cover High rate data com. Interoperability Multimedia services Traditional services
	Humanitarian aid	- Prevision, detection, identification and tracking of refugee concentrations and flows - Water and food resources status knowledge in designed areas - Knowledge of access conditions to designed areas - Marking and tracking of package 10 - Intervention units facilities	- Civil protection - Law enforcement - Military	Worldwide cover Interoperability Multimedia services Traditional services

Observation (Imagery)	Signal related Information	PNT	Space surveillance	Early Warning[26]	Meteo
EHR[29] Geo-products Data base	ELINT[30] COMINT[31] E-M activity Data base	Worldwide cover Secure service[32] High precision High availability Integrity issues	Detection Identification Reconnaissance Characterisation	- Worldwide timely detection, location and impact prevision of missile[33] firings - Potentially proliferating countries monitoring - Characterisation of missiles under testing	Weather forecast Sea-state forecast Oceano altimetry
EHR Geo-products Data base	ELINT COMINT E-M activity Data base			- Worldwide timely detection, location and impact prevision of missile[36] firings - Potentially proliferating countries monitoring - Characterisation of missiles under testing	Weather forecast Sea-state forecast
EHR Geo-products Data base	ELINT COMINT E-M activity Data base	Worldwide cover Secure service High precision High availability Integrity issues		- Worldwide timely detection, location and impact prevision of missile (8) firings - Potentially proliferating countries monitoring - Characterisation of missiles under testing	Weather forecast Sea-state forecast Oceano altimetry
HR Geo-products Data base	COMINT E-M activity Data base	Worldwide cover Secure service High precision High availability Integrity issues		- Worldwide timely detection, location and impact prevision of missile(8) firings - Potentially proliferating countries monitoring - Characterisation of missiles under testing	Weather forecast Sea-state forecast

EHR Geo- products Data base	ELINT COMINT E-M activity Data base			- Worldwide timely detection, location and impact prevision of missile(11) firings - Potentially proliferating countries monitoring - Characterisation of missiles under testing	
EHR Geo- products Data base	ELINT COMINT E-M activity Data base		Detection Identification Reconnaissance Characterisation	- Worldwide timely detection, location and impact prevision of missile(11) firings - Potentially proliferating countries monitoring - Characterisation of missiles under testing	
EHR Geo- products Data base	ELINT COMINT E-M activity Data base	Worldwide cover Secure service High precision High availability Integrity issues			
HR[37] Geo- products Data base	COMINT E-M activity Data base	Worldwide cover Secure service High precision High availability Integrity issues			Weather forecast Sea-state forecast
HR Geo- products Data base	COMINT E-M activity Data base	Worldwide cover High precision High availability Integrity issues			Weather forecast Sea-state forecast
	E-M activity	Worldwide cover High precision High availability			
HR Geo- products Data base		Worldwidecover High precision High availability Integrity issues			Weather forecast Sea-state forecast

HR Geo- products Data base			Detection Identification	- Worldwide timely detection, location and impact prevision of missile(11) firings - Potentially proliferating countries monitoring - Characterisation of missiles under testing	Weather forecast Sea-state forecast
HR Geo- products Data base		Worldwidecover High precision High availability Integrity issues			Weatherforecast Sea-state forecast
HR Geo- products Data base		Worldwidecover High precision High availability Integrity issues			Weatherforecast Sea-state forecast
HR Geo- products Data base		Worldwidecover High precision High availability			Weatherforecast Sea-state forecast

- 26 Early warning : purely 2ond pillar capability ; mentioned here for information
- 27 Specific military needs are mentioned here for information because being taking in account with Council (military committee) issues
- 28 Telecom. Traditional services : fax, telephony, ...
- 29 Extreme High Resolution => Identification, Reconnaissance, Characterisation
- 30 ELINT : Characterisation and location of radar systems
- 31 COMINT : Characterisation, location & access to content of communications
- 32 PNT secure service : ciphered & against jamming robust information ; guarantee of access
- 33 medium-range missiles
- 34 Ballistic Missile : including ICBM (Inter continental), IRBM (Intermediate Range), MRBM (Medium Range) and SRBM (Short Range)
- 35 Intervention units facilities : localisation (PNT) and status / Secured communications / MS interoperability
- 36 ballistic and medium-range missiles
- 37 HR : High resolution : Detection (and reconnaissance, under conditions)

APPENDIX B: SCOPE OF TECHNOLOGY, INTEROPERABILITY AND OPERATIONAL SYSTEMS TASKS

The list of tasks below are included for illustrative purposes only.

Assessments related tasks

	Proposed tasks
WPOA1	Strategic reviews for needs, requirements, gaps
WPOA2	Operational effectiveness assessments
WPOA3	Information exchange requirements

WPOA4	Capability catalogue
WPOA5	Operational requirements and concepts of operation
WPOA6	Cost modelling and benefits assessments
WP0A7	Strategic review of secure communications
WP0A8	Strategic review of common European surveillance
WPOA9	Strategic review of case for space based signal intelligence and early warning systems

Technology related tasks

Proposed tasks

WPOT1 Strategic review of the state of the art in satellite technology for the security domain

WPOT2 Technology development programmes which include:

- observation from high orbits
- enhanced components for on-board imagery chains
- actuators and attitude control systems for better agility
- multispectral and hyperspectral sensors and their linked
- exploitation tools
- radar interferometry capabilities
- bi-static, space based radar techniques
- advanced cryptographic devices for very high data rates
- optical and radar image analysis tools and services
- data fusion techniques
- enhanced components in terms of sensitivity and accuracy
- development of data mining and signal characterisation algorithms for on-board or ground signal processing
- actuators for better agility
- active antennae
- large deployable antennae

WPOT3 Testbed and reference facilities which can be made available both to the user communities of interest and also to industry

WPOT4 Technology demonstrator programmes which target specific groupings of communities of interest

Interoperability related tasks

Proposed tasks

WPOI1 Common collaborative interoperability projects (CCIPs) for specific communities of interest (eg Transport, policing, cross border control)

WPOI2 Cross community CCIPs which could group for example, civil protection, policing and intelligence, cross border control and transport together (using facilities or services developed for individual communities)

WPOI3 Simulation and training facilities and exercises organised with appropriate groupings of communities of interest (including new member states).

Operational system related tasks

Proposed tasks

WPOO1 Short term capacity leasing programme to support replicated database systems for use with any community of interest (e.g. multicast network to update all airports in Europe with latest suspect information)

WPOO2 Programme definition tasks to establish specific initiatives for:

- Secure communications programme
- Common European surveillance system (of the Earth)
- Space surveillance system (of space)
- Harmonised ground segments, standards and procedures

APPENDIX C: COSTS ESTIMATES OF EUROPEAN SPACE SYSTEM FOR ESDP

The chart provided by EUROSPACE shows that a progression from a current budget of just under 1B€ in 2004 to around 2B€ which appears to be necessary from 2012 onwards.

The 2004 costs contain the programmes financed by the different national Ministries of Defence for governmental applications:

- **Satcoms: Skynet, Syracuse, Sicral**
- **Observation : Helios, SAR Lupe, Cosmo-Skymed**
- **R&D Studies/Demonstrators ; EHF, Essaim (Comint), Spirale (Early warning), Lola (laser link), Grave (space surveillance).**

The estimated 2012 costs are a projection to maintain and increase the actual capacities towards a coherent European space system for ESDP:

- **Satcoms: secure systems/services including EHF and data relay capacity**
- **Observation: new generation of optical and radar observation systems including Extremely High Resolution (EHR), Very High Resolution/wide view, Infra-Red and hyperspectral capacity**
- **Signal Intelligence: European Sigint system including Elint and Comint)**
- **Early Warning: First step of a European system**
- **Space Surveillance: space component of a global system (radar and optical)**
- **R&D Studies: studies and technology R&D necessary for the above programmes together with new advanced applications studies Eg. Geostationary observation and sigint, high resolution micro-sats etc.**
- **New Applications: provision for new applications using existing technology Eg. Geo-mobile, mobile receiving stations, space MTI.**

Remarks :

1. These estimates concern only the programmes mentioned above and include launch costs, ground segments and operations.
2. Europe has attained the technical capability to develop such programmes due to efforts at national or European level developing programmes such as SPOT, ERS, Artemis, Silex, Envisat, Jason and Launcher developments (Ariane, Véga). In the future, similar civil oriented efforts in terms of R&D and demonstration will be necessary to sustain the fundamental technical capability.
3. Other civil space applications that will be also used for security and defence (mulitple use) – such as GMES, meteorology or oceanography systems - shall still need to be financed through separate civil budgets that could be allocated at national or European level (not included in the above chart).

4. According to EUROSPACE, an independent access to space is essential for a European space system for ESDP and must continue to be maintained through ESA budgets.
5. Special attention should be paid to ground segments taking into account the necessary level of federation of sensors and fusion of data.
6. The approximate doubling of the budget on space systems for ESDP is consistent with other forecasts for a doubling of the overall space budget in the same timescale yet] will leave the expenditure in Europe on space systems for security and defence at one tenth of that in the US.

Appendix D: Panel of experts in the field of space and Security: Terms of Reference[38]

Context:

The consultation process for the Green paper[39], and the following White paper on European Space Policy[40], identified the strategic importance of space in implementing the Common Foreign and Security Policy (CFSP), including the European Security and Defence Policy (ESDP) and the policy in the area of freedom, security and justice (JHA).

The enlargement of the EU makes this ever more important since space services have a major part to play in enhancement of security of the citizen within Europe. This is largely due to opportunities for better enforcement of border control and surveillance (ie more effective controls on illegal immigration and smuggling), conflict prevention, identification of humanitarian crises at early stages, prevention of and fight against crime and criminal organisations throughout the Union.

Following on from the report by the Group of Personalities, the European Commission has now agreed to establish a Panel of Experts in the field of space and security to which these terms of reference apply.

1. The primary mission of the Panel of Experts is to provide the European Commission with a Report on the current EU needs for multiple-use capabilities needs in accordance with the White Paper on European Space Policy. This technical work would in particular appraise capabilities identified by operational groups and users (referred to in Annex A), define synergies and make proposals for inclusion in the European Space Programme.
2. The Panel of experts will also acknowledge the role of space and the available capabilities for both civil and military use with a focus on the synergies between them.
3. EU Member States have been invited to nominate experts to participate in the work of the panel. The panel will be composed of competent services from the European Commission, National Space Agencies, European Space Agency, relevant working groups, Industries (including SMEs) and other user organisations (see Annex A). Members of the General Secretariat of the Council of the EU will be invited to attend as observers. Exchange of classified information will be restricted to the appropriate subset of participants. Concerning EU classified information, the basic principles and minimum standards contained in the Commission Decision[41] will apply.
4. The Panel of experts will be supported by an appointed "Rapporteur", who will be in charge of drafting the report and ensuring support to the coordination with additional groups when required.
5. The activities of the Panel of Experts will :
• Review the role of space in meeting the objectives of the CFSP/ESDP and of Justice and Home Affairs (civil protection, fight against terrorism, border monitoring...)
• Consider the management options for identifying, maintaining and updating the operational requirements for pan-European space and security capabilities
• Identify, take input from the main groups actively looking at operational requirements at the European level and provide feedback to the appropriate research programmes

• Assess the currently available information (from sources such as ECAP42, and the Preparatory Action on Security Research) on the capability gap that exists in Europe today for space based security services
• Identify priority areas of interest and options for a preparatory action plan to bridge between current capabilities and future anticipated requirements
• Assess the potential funding scenarios necessary to ensure that the appropriate level of resource is available to deliver the primary programme options
6. The panel will call upon ad-hoc expertise as necessary, including expertise in:
a. The content and capabilities of existing civilian space programmes,
b. The process of translating operational requirements into technical requests.
It is foreseen that the panel may benefit as well from the possible input of the EUMC43 regarding an analysis on operational requirements for space assets, taking into account the paper on the Headline Goal 2010.
7. Groups will be created attending to the needs of the Panel of experts. The role of these groups will be to ensure the proper development of the recommendations elaborated by the Panel of experts, to whom they will report. Group leaders participate systematically to the Panel meetings to ensure an appropriate follow-up.
8. The Panel of Experts will meet at least four times and will report its conclusions before the end of 2004.
– [38] Endorsed during the second Panel meeting (19 July)
– [39] COM 2003/17 final
– [40] COM 2003/673
– [41] Commission Decision 2001/844/EC, ECSC, Euratom of 29 November 2001

ANNEX : Composition of the Panel of experts

• Experts of the EU Member States
• European Commission Services
• European Space Agency (ESA)
• National Space Agencies (CNES, DLR, BNSC, ASI, CDTI)
• EUMETSAT
• EUROCONTROL
• OCCAR
• Representatives from relevant existing working groups: European Capability Action Plan Space Group, GALILEO Security Board, GMES Advisory Council, Research Working Group, CEPA 9, External Borders Practitioners' Common Unit Composition and the related Centres (Land Border Centre, Air Border Centre, Western Sea Borders Centre, Eastern Sea Borders Centre, Risk Analysis Centre, Border Training Centre).
• Representatives from Industry
– [42] European Capability Action Plan
– [43] European Union Military Committee

Members from the General Secretariat of the Council of the European Union will be invited as observers.

Appendix E: BACKGROUND DOCUMENTS

- European Commission, *Towards a European Space Policy*, Communication from the Commission to the Council and the European Parliament, Brussels, 7 December 2001

- *Star21*, Strategic Aerospace Research for the 21st Century, July 2002

- European Commission, *Green Paper: European Space Policy*, COM(2003) 17 final, 21 January 2003

- European Commission, White Paper, *Space: a new European frontier for an expanding Union An action plan for implementing the European Space policy*, COM(2003)673

- European Commission, *A Coherent Framework for Aerospace – a Response to the STAR 21 Report*, COM (2003) 600 final, 13/10/2003

- European Commission, *Research for a Secure Europe*, Report of the Group of Personalities in the field of Security Research, Group of Personalities Report, 15/03/2004

- European Commission, *Global Monitoring for Environment and Security (GMES): Establishing a GMES capacity by 2008- (Action Plan 2004-2008)*, COM(2004) 65 final, 3/2/2004

- European Commission, "Space: a new European frontier for an expanding Union" November 2003.

- European Commission, Geospatial Information Needs of DG RELEX, Michalis Ketselidis, March 2004.

- European Commission, Communication from the Commission to the Council and European Parliament, Final perspectives 2007-2013, COM (2004) 487

- Assembly of the WEU, *Developing a European space observation capability to meet Europe's security requirements,* A/1789, 5 June 2002

- Assembly of the WEU, *A joint European space strategy: security and defence aspects,* A/1738, 20 June 2001

- Assembly of the WEU, La dimension spatiale de la PESD, Draft Report, 26 Octobre 2004

- European Commission Staff Working Paper *European Security Strategy, Fight against terrorism*, SEC(2004) 332, 19/3/2004

- *Common Operational Requirements for a Global Satellite Observation System for Security and Defence Purposes* (BOC), signed by six European Staff

- Council of the European Union, *Space Systems Needs for Military Operations*, 19 May 2003

- *Food for thought Paper, ESDP and Space,* Hellenic National Defence General Staff, Alexander Kolovos, March 2003

- Carl Bildt, Jean Peyrelevade and Lothar Spath, *Towards a Space Agency for the European Union*, Report for the Director General of the European Space Agency, November 2001.

- European Security Strategy, J. Solana, *A Secure Europe in a Better World*, December 2003

- Study on Energy Supply Security and Geopolitics, Clingendael International Energy Programme (CIEP), Institute for International Relations, January 2004, The Hague, The Netherlands.

- Council of the European Union, *Headline Goal 2010*, 6309/6/04

- Council of the European Union, *ESDP and Space*, 11616/3/04, 16 November 2004

- Council of the European Union, *Draft ESDP Presidency Report*, December 2004

- Institute for Security Studies, *Space and security policy in Europe*, Occasional Papers n°48, December 2003

- Institute for Security Studies, *The GALILEO satellite system and its security implications*, Occasional Papers n°44, April 2003

- Proceedings, Workshop on "Research and Technological Challenges in the field of Border Control in the EU-25", Ljubljana, 18/20 October 2004

- CNES, *NAUPLIOS, GALILEO Pilot Project*, Final Report, 20/07/04

- The George Washington University, *Bridging the Gap, European C4ISR Capabilities and Transatlantic Interoperability*, October 2004

- International Space University, *Civil, Commercial and Security Space: What will drive the next decade?*, 9th ISU Annual International Symposium, 30/11-3/12 2004, Strasbourg, France

- Final Resolution for the 6th European Interparliamentary Space Conference (EISC), November 10th and 11th 2004, Madrid

- *A Human Security Doctrine for Europe, The Barcelona Report of the Study Group on Europe's Security Capabilities*, Presented to the EU High Representative ofr CFSP Javier Solana, 15 September 2004

- The Hague Programme strengthening Freedom, Security and Justice in the European Union, Presidency conclusions of the European Council of 4/5 November 2004, 14292/1/04, REV 1 annex I.

- European Commission, *Proposal for a DIRECTIVE OF THE EUROPEAN PARLIAMENT AND OF THE COUNCIL establishing an infrastructure for spatial information in the Community (INSPIRE)*, COM(2004) 516 final, 23.7.2004

- The Eisenhower Institute, Space Security 2003, 2004

IMPORTANT PROGRAMS AND PROJECTS

AEROFAST

The discoveries of pioneers such as Columbus, da Gama, and Cook led to transportation across oceans and this paved the way for large scale human settlements on new continents. Similar to the trans-Atlantic boats of the past, ***advanced space transportation systems*** *will take today's pioneer missions into space further and allow for enhanced mobility of humans and cargo between Earth and space. The project AEROFAST supports these developments, refining aerocapture technology.*

"But Man is not a tree – he has no roots; he has feet, he walks", states Spanish author Juan Goytisolo, writing about today's globalised world where **enhanced mobility reshapes reality at high speed. In the future such mobility is taken into a much vaster sphere, as advanced space transportation systems herald enhanced mobility between Earth and space.**

In the decades ahead, aerocapture technology is predicted to become one of the core capabilities needed for **inter-planetary transportation**. The technology allows for the production of vehicles that are mass effective, using atmospheric drag to slow them. Such technology holds the potential to make lunar and Martian missions more affordable and more feasible, assuming high launch rates.

Aerocapture allows for up to 30 percent of mass to be saved when a spacecraft is launched. The technology is fully adapted to large weight missions carrying both cargo and humans.

With current propulsion technology, a spacecraft which would enter into a Mars orbit would only arrive with 41% of its initial mass. With refined aerocapture technology, this number would be doubled.

AEROFAST's main goal is to improve aerocapture transportation technology. Today the technology readiness level (TRL) of an aerocapture mission is roughly 2 to 3 in Europe. AEROFAST's goal is to prepare for a flight demonstration on a planet with atmosphere - the Earth or Mars

- and to reach a TRL level of 3 to 4. The project is an important step towards the development of advanced transportation systems that will allow for **human expansion into the solar system, mov**ing humans and cargo more easily between Earth and space, and also returning humans from the Moon or from Mars. Indeed, looking ahead, today's globalised world might seem small, when future generations live in a time of high speed interplanetary mobility.

QUESTIONS & ANSWERS

What do you want to achieve with this project?

AEROFAST s main goal is to invest and improve the AEROCAPTURE transportation mean. AEROFAST s goal is to prepare for a flight demonstration and to reach TRL 3 - 4 in the frame of this FP7 first call.

Why is this project important for Europe?

An important step for human expansion into the solar system is to develop advanced transportation systems to move humans and cargo between geostationary and Low Earth orbits or return from Moon or Mars. Improving this technology allows Europe to be a valuable partner within the international cooperation.

Human expansion in the solar system is part of our dreams: using the aero capture technology to slow space ve hicles is regarded as one of the largest contributors to making both lunar and Martian missions affordable.

SPACE RESEARCH AND DEVELOPMENT

GMES Space Component Best Practice Invitations to Tenders published by ESA

GMES (Global Monitoring for Environment and Security) is a European initiative for the implementation of information services dealing with environment and security. Under the Seventh Framework Research Programme (FP7) the European Space Agency (ESA) manages the development of GMES space component. The Commission manages the development of GMES services through FP7 and assures optimal integration of data from in-situ monitoring.

As a consequence, a part of the GMES space component related activities will be procured by ESA with FP7 budget in line with the EU procurement rules. The concerned Invitation to Tenders (ITT) will be open also to the 27 EU Member States and the associated FP7 countries[1]. Exceptionally, legal entities from these non-ESA member states will be able to ask for access to the ESA tender information system EMITS (http://emits.esa.int). However, this registration process may take a few weeks and a specific server (https://gmesfp7emits.esa.int) has been put in place as a second means to distribute the information. Both, EMITS and the specific server are described in more detail on the next page.

In addition to the existing process using EMITS, the Commission is publishing the list of these Invitations to Tenders (ITT) on the CORDIS Space site (http://cordis.europa.eu/fp7/cooperation/space_en.html) to ensure that the FP7 participating states who are not ESA Member States are fully aware of the intended procurements. Although we undertake significant efforts to ensure that this list is correct we advise you to consult the individual Invitation Letter published as part of each ITT to confirm that entities from your country are eligible.

Further information on GMES can be found at: www.gmes.info and www.esa.int/esaLP/LPgmes.html .

ESA Tender Information System (EMITS):

An ITT is initially advertised on the ESA tender information system (EMITS) with a status "intended" in parallel to the ESA administrative procedures. On the day it is

In February 2008 legal entities established in Switzerland, Israel, Norway, Iceland, Liechtenstein, Turkey, Croatia, the Former Yugoslav Republic of Macedonia, and Serbia, respectively, are able to receive Community contributions for contracts/grant agreements signed after 1 January 2007. Legal entities established in Albania and Montenegro are able to receive Community contributions for contracts/grant agreements signed after 1 January 2008.

Commission européenne, B-1049 Bruxelles / Europese Commissie, B-1049 Brussel - Belgium. Telephone: (32-2) 299 11 11..

officially opened, its status changes from "intended" to "open". Besides the abstract, the maximum funding, the contact person(s), the deadline, and some other administrative information an open ITT will comprise detailed information (Invitation Letter, Statement of Work, Draft Contract, and Special Conditions of Tender as a minimum).

Specifically for this programme, ESA has opened the possibility to register with EMITS to all FP7 Participating States, which is a prerequisite to respond to an ITT and to access the detailed information. It is mandatory that the interested industry register with EMITS in order to be authorised to submit an offer.

Once the ITT is open (usually for a period of at least six weeks) all the information may be subject to change or to amendments. Change of abstract, extension of deadline, publication of clarifications in response to some received question happen quite frequently. It is advisable for bidders to have their addresses included in the EMITS mailing list, and/or to register with the issuing entity. A template for a registration fax (often referred to as "Acknowledgement of Receipt") is part of the Special Conditions of Tender.

To find the ITTs in EMITS please go to http://emits.esa.int and use the button labelled "ENTITIES" to open a drop-down list with the industrial entities issuing ITTs on EMITS (Note that for some industry with several subsidies there may be a second level list). Select from the list the issuing entity given in the ITT table and confirm the dialog box. Open the folder "Open Invitations to Tenders (ESA Programmes)" or "Intended Invitations to Tenders (ESA Programmes)" respectively and select "Global List". In the main window you will be presented with all ITTs related to this entity, where you can look-up specific information available. It should be noted, that you will see all ITTs (even from other programmes) but only some of them are open to the FP7 Participating States.

ESA GMES FP7 FTP server:

As the registering process at EMITS may be somewhat lengthy, an additional service has been set up on (https://gmesfp7emits.esa.int) to make the tender information available to potential applicants from the FP7 Participating Countries immediately. On the main page of this service the applicants will have to ask for an individual login user ID and a password, which will be sent to them through e-mail. This site provides an electronic archive file comprising the detailed information on the open ITT (as described above). It is

not possible to bid through this service but it is mandatory that the interested industries register with EMITS as stated above.

GEOLAND

With climate change an increasing threat, pressure on na*ture is growing, reducing biodiversity and deteriorating our own living conditions. To mitigate these threats by effective countermeasures and adaptation strategies, monitoring the condition of our natural environment and its changes over time is essential. The project geoland2 constitutes a major step forward towards the implementation of the* ***GMES/Kopernikus Land Services****, operationally providing reliable and affordable geo-information products on the basis of satellite Earth observation data.*

To respond effectively to the effects of climate change, decision makers need to be informed about the current conditions of our natural environment and predictable trends. The GMES/Kopernikus Land Services provide such area-extended, geo-located and cross-boarder harmonized geo-information at global, European, and regional scales. The project geoland2 aims to prepare the operational application capabilities of these GMES/ Kopernikus Land Services, consisting of Core Mapping Services (CMS) and Core Information Services (CIS), to support decision makers with the most accurate and up to date information available.

The Core Mapping Services produce basic **geo-information on land cover and land use and its annual and sea**sonal changes as well as a variety of additional biophysical parameters describing the continental vegetation state, the radiation budget at the surface and the water cycle on the basis of satellite Earth observation data. They cover local to global scales with updating frequencies from one day to several years.

The CMS mapping products are of broad generic use: besides being a valuable information source in its basic form, they are the basis for more elaborated geoinformation services. These focused Core Information Services (CIS) address a wide variety of thematic fields of application, like water quality, forest managing, spatial planning, agri-environmental issues, the carbon cycle, and food security.

These Core Information Services offer **specific information for European Environmental Policies and international treaties and strategies on climate change, food security and the sustainable devel**opment of Africa. Thereby they effectively support responsible public authorities and decision makers on the regional to continental level in the implementation of European policies and international conventions. The goal of geoland2 is to prepare, validate and demonstrate pre-operational production capabilities of the GMES/ Kopernikus Land Services. geoland2 deliverables consist of the organisation of a qualified production network, the building of operational processing lines, demonstration of these services and products on large scales, and the setting up of a product quality assurance process driven by the users, to guarantee that the products meet the real user's needs.

The project's efforts will build up on the achievements of previous or ongoing projects funded under the Sixth Framework Programme, such as geoland and BOSS4GMES, as well as the

GMES Service Elements (GSE) funded by the European Space Agency (ESA) in the field of "Land" and "Forest Monitoring".

KEEPING PEOPLE SAFE IN SPACE

Outside of the Earth's atmosphere, space radiation could become dangerous to humans, depending on space flight location, duration and the Sun's activity. Future interplanetary human space missions need to be able to estimate the risks such as radiation which may harm astronauts. With the HAMLET project, Europe reinforces its worldwide leadership in this important health field of space dosimetry.

Space is a dangerous place for humans. **Astronauts face a high radiation exposure** both inside the International Space Station (ISS), and when undertaking space walks outside its realms.

The European Space Agency's (ESA) facility MATROSHKA (MTR) lead by the German Aerospace Center (DLR) is dedicated **to determining the radiation loads that astronauts face both in and outside the ISS. Launched in January 2004, the project is currently in its fourth experi**mental phase.

Aiming at optimal scientific exploitation, the project HAMLET will bring together a European expert-committee, consisting exclusively of members of the MTR consortium, to process and compile the MTR data.

The MTR project uses over 6,000 radiation detectors that determine the depth and organ dose distribution of radiation in the body. It is the largest international research initiative performed in the field of **space dosimetry**, combining the expertise of leading research institutions all over the world. Consequently it generates a huge pool of data of immense value, which the HAMLET project further exploits.

The aim is to build a three-dimensional model of the radiation dose distribution in an astronaut's body, based on the experimental input obtained in the MTR project, as well as on radiation transport calculations. In this respect, the project goes beyond essential data analysis and incorporates a modelling approach to guide new experimental measurements and strengthen the predictive capacity of such models.

The scientific achievements springing from this research contribute to **radiation risk estimations for future interplanetary human space missions. The synthesis of the data, which is foreseen to considerably extend previous knowledge, con**stitutes a major accomplishment by which Europe can reinforce worldwide leadership in this special branch of space radiation research.

QUESTIONS & ANSWERS

What do you want to achieve with this project?

Bringing together leading European experts in the field of space dosimetry, HAMLET aims at the effective scientific exploitation of experimental data on the radiation dose distribution inside a human phantom as part of the ESA MATROSHKA facility exposed onboard the ISS.

Why is this project important for Europe?

In view of future human space exploration, HAMLET ensures European excellence in evaluating the effects of space radiation on humans and thereby assessing their radiation risk. Focusing European expertise will enable future generations to travel where nobody has gone before.

Experimental assessment of this complex radiation environment will increase the knowledge of organ dose distribution, support the benchmarking of radiation transport codes and the development of radiation detectors, with a direct spin-off for heavy-ion cancer therapy in Europe.

MYOCEAN

Analyzing the ocean enables us to better understand the Earth. For example, in Europe, our climate depends on the state of the oceans and seas. Changes in ocean currents and temperatures have a direct impact on our weather. Helping Europe obtain essential data from a better understanding of the seas, the project MyOcean aims at setting up infrastructures and services in preparation for the ***GMES/Kopernikus Marine Services****.*

Public authorities and ships need to know when an oil spill threatens the marine environment. At the same time, information about the present and future impact of rising sea levels on coastal areas is of critical importance. And the range of applications keeps growing.

In this context, observing, monitoring and forecasting

temperature, salinity, currents and other parameters in oceans and seas provide important insights. Today such information might enable vessels to choose faster shipping routes riding on currents, thereby saving fuel, reducing CO2 emissions and lowering costs.

Amongst possible applications, in the case of an oil spill, complex computer simulation models are used to reverse ocean currents. Comparing this data with shipping routes will enable public authorities to identify the origin of the spill and track down the perpetrators.

In the future, when dealing with climate change, **higher sea temperatures may impact currents such as those found in the Gulf Stream**, with profound impacts on European weather. Detecting higher temperatures requires monitoring and forecasting of the ocean as well as the availability of reference descriptions such as log time series of ocean data.

MyOcean will develop upgraded European capabilities for reference marine information and provide a wide range of key ocean indicators. Hence the project provides the major building blocks that are needed to allow the operational deployment of a full GMES/Kopernikus Marine Service.

In cooperation with national metrological services, the European Environment Agency and the European Maritime Safety Agency (EMSA) amongst others, MyOcean will undertake the pre-operational validation of GMES/Kopernikus Marine Services, and formally commission them. The project will establish a governance structure, which is intended to be adopted by the GMES/ Kopernikus Service.

MyOcean is composed of a consortium of 60 partners from across Europe and is struc-

Programme for Research.

Implementing the European Marine Core Service is one of the top-three priorities of the GMES/Kopernikus program. It will strengthen the eco nomic development of downstream activities and reinforce Europe s voice in terms of environmental policy.

The supported applications are maritime security, oil spill prevention, water quality, marine resources management, coastal activities, seasonal forecasting, climate change and ice sheet surveys. MyOcean products will be open and free, directly accessible by European citizens.

ProVisg

For a probe on another planet, **time is of the essence** since its operational life is often short. The harsh environment, extreme temperatures and pressures, dust and radiation threaten to damage the hardware and compromise the mission at any moment. Given the difficulty and cost of getting to other planets, obtaining **a high return on investment is crucial**. Accelerating the processing and improving the representation of visual data from such missions, the project PRoVisG aims at giving mission operators and scientists a better three-dimensional (3D) understanding of these new worlds, and showing all of us what it looks like to be there.

In order to maximize the use of a robotic probe during its limited lifetime, scientists immediately have to be provided the best achievable visual quality of 3D data products, and mission controllers need to minimize the time spent for planning the next activities. PRoVisG will facilitate this, developing technology for the **rapid processing and effective representation of visual data** by improving Planetary Robotic Vision Ground Processing facilities. Its ambition is to collect a tool set and integrate a versatile and flexible processing chain which can be easily adapted to the various tasks. Thereby, mission controllers and scientists on the ground profit from **improved situational awareness**, enabling them to identify targets of interest and send the next commands with minimum delay.

PRoVisG brings together major EU and US research institutions and stakeholders involved in space robotic vision and navigation to develop a unified approach for robotic vision ground processing. One main result will be a **web-based Geographic Information System (GIS)**, facilitating the comprehensive processing of visual data and the visualization of the context, history, vision data and products of robotic planetary missions. Prototypes of rovers and airborne probes will be used in terrestrial field test campaigns to demonstrate visual processing ability going beyond that currently available with the Mars Exploration Rovers and currently envisaged ESA missions.

As a further benefit, the effective representation of planetary surface imagery will be useful for scientific research, education, and also for increased public awareness regarding space science and exploration.

SPACE WEATHER FORECAST

In space, like on Earth, we need to adapt to changing weather conditions. Yet our knowledge about space weather is still limited. In order to better protect human beings and human assets in space and on Earth, the project SOTERIA aims at improving our understanding of space weather phenomena.

Space weather is the concept of changing environmental conditions in space. It is distinct from the concept of weather within our own atmosphere. Our space weather is a consequence of the behavior of the Sun and the nature of Earth's magnetic field and it can affect the Earth significantly.

Yet we know much less about space weather than we know about weather on Earth. Whilst the International Space Station (ISS), satellites and spacecraft mostly experience calm space weather conditions, at times **solar eruptions and variations in the Earth's magnetic field lead to deteriorating conditions** that represent real risks to astronauts and satellites in space, and may even disturb power supply and telecommunications on Earth.

Studying such events in the fields of solar, space and geophysics is increasingly important. Today more than ever before, space assets such as satellites controlling telecommunication and power lines impact our life on Earth. Hence if they are affected by space weather, we feel the impact instantly.

SOTERIA aims at facilitating a more reliable space weather forecast, based on a space monitoring system. Analysing data from more than 20 satellites - some five of which are ESA missions - this project mobilizes more than 50 experts and resources from across Europe. New methods will be explored to analyse data on space weather not only from satellites but also from outposts on the ground.

This endeavour will lead to the establishment of **new databases on space weather**, the quality of which go beyond the present stateof-the-art in this field. Moreover, the results springing from SOTERIA will be made available online to the scientific community at large, also **facilitating access to open data from relevant satellite missions**.

The goal is to provide new and ex isting data from ground based and spaceborne observations and models crucial for space weather forecasting. The fundamental approach is to make the information from diverse sources readily available to the user in a ho mogeneous format.

Why is this project important for Europe?

Europe has a key interest in the good design and operation of its space technical and human operations and of its large scale infrastructure (power lines, pipelines). Soteria will produce tools to better understand space weather events that pose a serious and even lethal threat to such activities.

Soteria will benefit society by providing tools for the European capability of predicting space weather events that have a key adverse impact on space activities, on human health in space and on large scale infrastuctures and on the ground (power lines, pipelines) .

GMES/KOPERNIKUS

GMES/Kopernikus geo-information services are grouped into six interacting themes: land, atmosphere, climate change, emergency, ocean and security. © Fotolia

Global Monitoring for Environment and Security (GMES/ Kopernikus) provides for improved evidence based policy making. Yet to succeed, such insights need to be effectively disseminated. The support action SWIFT helps raise aware*ness about GMES/Kopernikus, promoting its results.*

GMES/Kopernikus is building European capabilities to **monitor the state of our planet from space**, thereby assessing the probability of future environmental changes. The programme generates knowledge, which can help to keep the Earth healthy and save lives when disasters strike. Space-born data create a better basis for decisions to be taken in an increasingly challenging global environment.

In Europe, major high-level policy fields such as Sustainable Development, the Common Foreign and Security Policy (CFSP) and the long-term competitiveness of European industry are also influenced by successful space activities. Yet information is much more valuable when it is effectively shared.

The **SWIFT** coordination and support action addresses this challenge, as it helps **raise awareness about the GMES/Kopernikus programme**.

SWIFT supports information activities and dissemination efforts of the three GMES/Kopernikus Fast Track Services, which are being implemented by the projects SAFER (Emergency Response), geoland2

(Land) and MyOcean (Ocean), as well as the GMES/Kopernikus Pilot Projects MACC (Atmosphere) and G-MOSAIC (Security). It has two major objectives: the first objective is to maximise and add value to these projects' dissemination activities. The second objective is to support efforts promoting the GMES/Kopernikus initiative as a whole. Hence as GMES/Kopernikus takes form on the ground, and its Fast Track services deliver results for the benefit of citizens, SWIFT helps enhance visibility for such progress, keeping citizens informed about the wide ranging benefits springing from this important European space initiative.

The nature and number of communication and dissemination actions undertaken by SWIFT will include a wide range of means such as video presentations, exhibition booths, articles, website, link to online scientific and educative fora, posters and flyers.

POWER AMPLIFICATION IN A SPACECRAFT

Reducing size and, in parallel, increasing power capabilities of electronic devices in a spacecraft is of immense importance for the overall performance of any satellite. Recent developments have brought Gallium Nitride devices to maturity. As the power density increases it is of critical importance to have packaging technologies available which can transport the generated heat to the surrounding environment and keep the temperature of the device within its specified limits.

For power packages, it is compulsory to provide at the same time minimized thermal resistance and high protection to all devices and circuits with respect to contaminations, mechanical aggressions, radiations and electromagnetic perturbations.

Gallium Arsenide (GaAs) technologies have been introduced in the 80's and are currently operated at about 0.5 W/mm including space application de-rating rules. Gallium Nitride (GaN) has emerged as **the technology of choice for the next generation high power electronics**. Its ability to handling high power also makes it the perfect technology candidate for highly survivable receiver components.

With power transistors providing 5W/mm the GaN devices can be decreased in size, allowing a power density increase of about 10 times compared to existing Galium Arsenide technologies.

According to recent assessments, GaN will lead to a revolution in space-borne electronics.

The project **AGAPAC stands for "Advanced GaN Packaging".**

The ultimate goal of the project is to have a space compliant power micropackage able to dissipate up to **100 W of power with a maximum junction temperature of 200°C**. This new micropackage technology based on innovative high thermal conductivity diamond or nano-composites will be available as an industrial supply chain for European space industry by 2010. It will cover the need for GaN based High Power Amplifiers (HPA) for space applications but also with different designs for other sectors such as base stations.

One of the missions of AGAPAC is to put together actors and industry from material science (in Spain and Austria), thermal and mechanical analysis (UK and France), with the packaging industry (France), and GaN device manufacturing (Germany) around the needs of major space actors in Europe.

The expected impact is to progress towards the sustainable provision of packaging technologies suitable for GaN technologies needed by the European space community to become independent from non-EU manufacturers.

COSMOS

FP7 APPLICANTS

The National Contact Points (NCP) for Space from 32 countries now work together in the project COSMOS. The support action aims at making it easier for applicants to the EU's Seventh Framework Programme for Research (FP7) to find international partners and to exchange good practices.

Cosmos means an orderly or harmonious system. It originates from the Greek meaning "order, orderly arrangement, ornaments", and is the antithetical concept of chaos. Yet cosmos also defines the idea underlying the COSMOS support action, which is to bring about an orderly arrangement for the service of NCPs including **dissemination of information about the FP7 Space theme in a varied context comprising some 32 countries across Europe and the Near East.**

COSMOS - Cooperation Of Space NCPs as a Means to Optimise Services - aims at building a network of Space NCPs.

With the introduction of space as an independent topic in EU Framework Programmes for Research, which contribute to the implementation of the European Space Policy (ESP), NCPs for Space have been set up in almost all EU Member States and Associated Countries, as well as in certain Third Countries. Whilst some countries have a long history and proud legacies in space activities, others are discovering new opportunities dealing with Space in FP7.

Against this backdrop, **NCPs participating in COSMOS will identify and exchange good practices**, elaborate and conduct training courses for staff, and gather and provide up-to-date information on space and space relevant topics for the benefit of citizens.

Moreover, **COSMOS will contribute to improving project partner search, making it easier for FP7 applicants to find international part**ners. The aim is to ensure a more balanced and high quality NCP service for the benefit of new as well as experienced FP7 applicants, whilst raising awareness of the op-

By helping to improve the quality of FP7 proposals the COSMOS network supports the development of the Eu ropean Research Area (ERA). Via the partner network it is further on ensured that all FP7 participating States get their chance to become part of and contribute to the ERA.

Supporting European researchers means ensuring a sustainable de velopment and innovation of space based services like weather forecasting and telecommunication. This is basis for a competitive European industry depending on a leading position in leading-edge technology.

G-MOSAIC

*Being a global actor, the EU has a responsibility to pioneer solutions to today's complex security challenges. Enhancing Europe's ability to attain a peaceful global society, the project G-MOSAIC helps in **supporting EU External Relations policies.***

Reaction to a crisis often proves to be too late. Effective intervention should ideally take place before a situation deteriorates, to minimise damage. This is why **intelligence information is of paramount importance to help keep Europe safe** from threats arising, from the proliferation of Weapons of Mass Destruction (WMD), or the violence of ethnic conflict, state failure and regional crisies.

The project G-MOSAIC will provide intelligence to the EU and its Member States before, during and after a crisis occurs.

In particular, G-MOSAIC **Situation Awareness and Intelligence applications provide information on major Threat Warning Factors. Such factors include monitor**ing of critical assets as part of efforts to combat WMD proliferation. They also consist of extended routes' surveillance, and assessment of structural crisis indicators, such as population density and agricultural production, and monitoring of illegal activities such as illegal mining or logging that contribute to a better understanding of where regional crises - state failure, ethnic conflicts, or government instability - might occur.

Moreover, G-MOSAIC **Crisis Management Operations** provide intelligence once a conflict has erupted, aimed at **supporting EU intervention activities** in the form of preparedness, crisis management, damage assessment, reconstruction and resilience.

G-MOSAIC's activities will be devoted to developing and exploiting GMES/Kopernikus services as assets supporting security-related activities on external regional crisies situations, whilst contributing to identifying the Core and Downstream geospatial intelligence services in the framework of the current status of the GMES/Kopernikus Initiative.

European Commission services such as the External Relations, Development and Environment Directorates-General, and the Office for Humanitarian Aid

Why is this GMES/Kopernikus service important for Europe?

G-MOSAIC services will contribute to understanding where outside Europe, Regional Crises such as state failure, ethnic conflicts, have high probability to occur thus supporting institutions in the prevention of those crises that on the long term may negatively affect Europe.

G-MOSAIC services will support EU intervention in External Regional Crisis, which can be regarded as an indirect threat to Europe as they can likely scale up to a global dimension and as a direct emergency for European citizens living, working or visiting the involved nations.

MACC

Viewed from space, the atmosphere takes the form of a thin layer, a protective and sustaining mantle without which life on our planet would not be possible. Both essential to life and vulnerable to mankind's influence, the atmosphere is at the heart of climatic change. Helping Europe to understand and respond better to the consequences of an evolving climate, MACC is designed to be the pilot project for the future **composition of the Earth's atmosphere** and **predict regional air quality. From 2009 to 2011, MACC will estab**lish the pilot GMES/Kopernikus Atmospheric Service.

MACC will monitor the distributions and long-range transport of greenhouse gases such as carbon dioxide and methane, aerosols that result from both natural processes and human activities, and reactive gases such as tropospheric ozone and nitrogen dioxide.

MACC's products and services will provide information that will support development and implementation of European environmental policy and wider international programmes. They will provide data that are critical to the understanding of climate and to the improvement and validation of the computer models that are used to predict climate change. They will provide information important for the protection of health and for the efficient exploitation of sources of renewable energy. They will provide data that can be used in future downstream services that provide information targeted locally and at specific sectors of the user community. Development and operation of these services will provide opportunities and benefits to both public institutions and private companies.

MACC has been prepared by the consortia of the FP6 integrated project GEMS and the GSE project PROMOTE, whose services will provide its starting point. MACC will maintain and further develop the scientific quality of its products, expand the range of products, and ensure an effective linkage to users at European, national and local levels.

SAFER

Every year in the world, fires, floods, earthquakes and volcanic eruptions, landslides and other humanitarian crises claim the lives of thousands of citizens. With climate change, such emergencies may increase in frequency. The project SAFER is implementing and validating a preoperational version of the ***GMES/Kopernikus Emergency Response Core Service (ERCS)****, reinforcing the European capacity to respond to such disasters.*

European Civil Protection Authorities as well as humanitarian relief organizations such as United Nations agencies or NGOs need **fast and accurate information** when responding to an emergency situation. Such information often takes the form of detailed maps of an area that is affected by an emergency.

Implementing a pre-operational version of the GMES/Kopernikus Emergency Response Core Service, SAFER's main goal is to provide a **rapid mapping capacity** in response to disastrous events. Such information is based on satellite images of the affected area and on reference maps, which SAFER prepares in advance for areas faced with an elevated risk of emergencies.

Such risk areas may be mountain valleys with a history of flooding or landslides, dry lands vulnerable to forest fires or the neighbourhood of a volcano.

From 2008, SAFER delivers services at full scale in response to real events as well as during specific exercises. **The project's main performance criterion is the response time**: with SAFER, reference mapping will be made available to users within just six hours after an emergency situation arises. **Assessment maps of the disaster area will be available within 24 hours**.

Moreover, SAFER aims at extending the use of its products to before the crisis situation (for early warning) and after the crisis situation (for reconstruction). The project seeks to further develop the foundation for the future GMES/Kopernikus Emergency Service through provision of specific thematic products, in particular in the areas of meteorological and geophysical risks.

The SAFER consortium includes European users such as civil protection authorities as well as non-European users such as UN agencies and is built around a core team of European industry and re-

The global climate change increases the need for a better European emergency response capacity. SAFER will guarantee in the long term that Europe can provide adequate information capabilities to support early warning, relief operations and reconstruction activities.

How does your work benefit European citizens?

Natural and man-made disasters take a very high toll in economic and human terms. In the long term, ERCS will provide tangible benefits for all citizens, in Europe and worldwide, in terms of a better quality of life, better health, and increased safety.

STAVE

UNITING EUROPE IN SPACE

Even when Europe was divided by the Berlin wall, Europeans shared a common passion for space. Today a united Europe reaches for new horizons, which is why the need to benefit from the space skills which exist in Central and Eastern European countries is imminent. The project STAVE facilitates such an exchange of knowledge, as it undertakes a comprehensive mapping of the human and technological resources that New EU Member States possess in the area of Space Transportation.

Some thirty years ago the son of a Czech mother and a Slovak father, **Vladimír Remek, became the first European Astronaut from outside the superpowers. For more than seven days he circled the Earth onboard the Soyuz 28 spacecraft.**

Space exploration is strongly rooted all across Europe, and as European space endeavours move forward, harvesting knowledge and potential in Central and Eastern European countries is key to success.

Focussing on the area of Space Transportation, which is essential for future European missions to the Moon and Mars, **the STAVE support action aims at identifying, evaluating and valorising space skills in the New Member States, taking a closer look at research labora**tories, universities, research institutions as well as SMEs and industry that may add value to joint European undertakings. A qualified mapping of technical skills applicable to Space Transportation will be carried out.

In particular, the mapping will include **a focus on novel techniques and methodologies that are poten**tially applicable to heliothermic propulsion, and new generations of solid, electric and cryogenic propulsion.

Hence STAVE contributes to achieving the overall European Space Policy objective of **maintaining an independent European access to space, whilst also facili**tating European efforts in the area of technologies for European strategic non-dependence.

The consortium behind STAVE is composed of partners from France, Germany and Italy that represent 90 percent of European efforts in the Space Transportation domain. In accordance with existing national and European Space Agency roadmaps, this team will **outline scientific and technological needs** that might be filled by Central and Eastern European expertise in the Space Transportation area.

Why is this project important for Europe?

Space Transportation is a European Strategic priority and highlighting the stakes enables strategic decisions for participation in large develop ments of the future. Europe must benefit from the diversity of its technological culture, enhancing the capacity of innovation.

How does your work benefit European citizens?

This project aims at enhancing research and industry in the Space Transportation domain, favouring innovation and technological development through more integration of all potential actors, enhancing knowledge, integration, worldwide competitivity and therefore also the economy.

ULISSE

SPACE STATION

Since 1998, the International Space Station (ISS) provides for a permanent human presence in space. A prime example of successful international cooperation, ISS serves as mankind's outpost laboratory for space experimentation. The project ULISSE provides ground support for the optimum exploitation of ISS experiments.

Some 400 km above Earth, travelling orbits at a speed of 27,700 km/h, the ISS is home to a permanent crew of 3-6 astronauts from Europe, Russia, USA, Canada and Japan. Here at the junction between Earth and outer space, the **ISS' tough environment provides an ideal setting for scientific experiments** that pave the way for future space travel to the Moon and Mars.

ULISSE provides specific services and tools for their exploitation through a software platform. These experiments include **Space Medicine research, biotechnology**, and the life science area of **exobiology**. Further knowledge in these diverse domains offers new insights on how human beings may be able to sustain living in space over extensive time periods, which is essential for the success of future interplanetary space missions. Also, we learn more about how cells are affected by long periods of weightlessness and radiation, and - in the area of exobiology - we aim at learning more about the most extreme conditions any form of life may survive in the universe.

The ULISSE project is conceived by a large number of partners already operative in **space experimentation**. The project links these existing User Support and Operation Centres (USOC) from across Europe and is adding value by facilitating further exploitation of competences and resources, and is complementing ISS activities with new initiatives aimed at increasing the return of scientific space activities.

For this purpose, ULISSE intends to pursue the **valorisation and exploitation of ISS scientific data and of the already available data from pre**vious space experiments as well as data from other space platforms.

The aim of the project is **increased involvement of European researchers in scientific research on the ISS, and enhanced aware**ness among Europeans of the

ULISSE will contribute to further capitalize on the investments made by the European society in space re search. ULISSE also increases the citizens awareness of the contribution of space research to human knowledge and its daily life application.

SUPPLEMENTS

SPACE AGENCIES

SPACE AGENCIES WITH LAUNCH CAPABILITY

Space agency		Country	Founded	Capabilities of the space agency			
Name	Acronym			Launch capable	Multiple Satellites Launch capable	Operates Extraterrestrial Probe	Recoverable Satellites capable
China National Space Administration	CNSA	People's Republic of China	22 April 1993	Yes	Yes	Yes	Yes
European Space Agency	ESA ASE EWO	Austria Belgium Czech Republic Denmark Finland France Germany Greece Ireland Italy Luxembourg Netherlands Norway Portugal Poland Romania Spain Sweden Switzerland United Kingdom	31 May 1975	Yes	Yes	Yes	No
Iranian Space Agency	ISA ISA	Iran	2003	Yes	No	No	No
Israeli Space Agency	ISA סל"ה	Israel	April 1983	Yes	No	No	No
Korea Aerospace Research Institute	KCST	North Korea	1980s	Yes	No	No	No
Korea Aerospace Research Institute	KARI	South Korea	October 1989	Yes	No	No	No
Indian Space Research Organization	ISRO	India	15 August 1969	Yes	Yes	Yes	Yes
Japan Aerospace Exploration Agency)	JAXA	Japan	1 October 2003	Yes	Yes	Yes	Yes
National Aeronautics and Space Administration	NASA	United States	1 October 1958	Yes	Yes	Yes	Yes
French: Centre National d'Études Spatiales (National Center of Space Research)	CNES	France	19 December 1961	Yes	Yes	No	No

National Space Agency of Ukraine	**НКАУ NSAU**	**Ukraine**	**2 March 1992**	**Yes**	**Yes**	**No**	**No**
(Russian Federal Space Agency (Roscosmos))	**ROSCOSMOS RFSA**	**Russia**	**ca. 1992**	**Yes**	**Yes**	**Yes**	**Yes**

SPACE AGENCIES WITH MANNED SPACEFLIGHT CAPABILITY

Space agency		**Country**	**Founded**	**Accomplished tasks by the Space Agency**				
Name	**Acronym**			**Manned Space flight capable**	**Manned Space launch capable**	Space walk capable	**Space Rendez vous and Docking capable**	**Operates Space Station**
China National Space Administration (Chinese: 中华人民共和国国家航天局)	**CNSA**	**People's Republic of China**	**22 April 1993**	**Yes**	**Yes**	**Yes**	**Yes**	**Yes**
European Space Agency	**20** countries		**1975**	**No**	**No**	**Yes**	**Yes**	**Yes**
National Aeronautics and Space Administration	**NASA**	**United States**	**1 October 1958**	**Yes**	**No (since 2011)**	**Yes**	**Yes**	**Yes**
Russian: Федеральное космическое агентство (Russian Federal Space Agency)	**ROSCOS MOS RFSA**	**Russia**	**ca. 1992**	**Yes**	**Yes**	**Yes**	**Yes**	**Yes**
Russian: (Soviet space program)		**Soviet Union**	**ca. 1955**	**Yes**	**Yes**	**Yes**	**Yes**	**Yes**

ACHIEVEMENTS OF SPACE AGENCIES WITH LUNAR LANDING CAPABILITY

Space agency		Country	Founded	Accomplished tasks by the Space Agency				
Name	Acronym			Circumlunar Manned Spaceflight	Unmanned Moon Soft Landing	Unmanned (automated) lunar rover operation	Automated Lunar sample return mission	Manned Moon Landing and sample return
China National Space Administration (Chinese: 中华人民共和国国家航天局)	CNSA	People's Republic of China	22 April 1993	No	Yes	Yes	No	No
National Aeronautics and Space Administration	NASA	United States	1 October 1958	Yes	Yes	No	No	Yes
Russian: Советская космическая программа (Soviet space program)	CCCP	Soviet Union	ca. 1955	No	Yes	Yes	Yes	No

EXPECTED FUTURE SPACE AGENCIES

Space agency	Country	Possible	Current status

Name	Acronym		expected date of foundation	
Pan-Arab Space Agency	PASA	Arab League	—	At proposal stage
African Space Agency	AfriSpace	African Union	—	At proposal stage
Philippine Space Agency	PSA	Philippines		At proposal stage
Sri Lanka Aeronautics and Space Agency	SLASA	Sri Lanka		Immediate goal is to construct and launch two satellites. Sri Lankan Telecommunications Regulatory Commission has signed an agreement with Surrey Satellite Technology Ltd to get relevant help and resources.

BUDGETS

The annual budgets listed are the official budgets for national space agencies available in public domain. The budgets are not normalized to the expenses of space research in different countries, i.e. higher budget does not necessarily mean more activity or better performance in space exploration. Note also that budget could be used for different projects: e.g. positioning system GPS is maintained from US defence budget, while ESA's money is used for developing European Galileo positioning system. The data for authoritarian countries are unreliable. For European contributors to ESA, the national budgets shown are separate from their contributions to ESA.

BUDGETS OF DIFFERENT SPACE AGENCIES.

Agency (country/region)	Budget (in millions of US $)
NASA (USA)	17,700
Roscosmos (Russia)	5,600
ESA (Europe)	5,380
CNES (France)	2,822
JAXA (Japan)	2,460
DLR (Germany)	2,000
ISRO (India)	1,320
CNSA (China)	1,300
ASI (Italy)	1,000
ISA (Iran)	500
CSA (Canada)	488.7
UKSA (UK)	414
AEB (Brazil)	343
KARI (South Korea)	300
NSAU (Ukraine)	250

CONAE (Argentina)	180
BELSPO (Belgium)	170
INTA (Spain)	135
NSO (Netherlands)	110
SNSB (Sweden)	100
SUPARCO (Pakistan)	82
SSO (Switzerland)	10
AEM (Mexico)	8.34

BUDGETS BY COUNTRY

Country	Agency	Budget (USD)
United States	NASA (National Aeronautics and Space Administration)	$17,700 million
Russia	Roscosmos (Russian Federal Space Agency)	$5,600 million
	ESA (European Space Agency)	$5,380 million
France	CNES (French Space Agency)	$2,822 million
Japan	JAXA (Japan Aerospace Exploration Agency)	$2,460 million
Germany	DLR (German Aerospace Center)	$2,000 million
India	ISRO (Indian Space Research Organization)	$1,320 million
China	CNSA (China National Space Administration)	$1,300 million
Italy	ASI (Italian Space Agency)	$1,000 million
Iran	ISA (Iranian Space Agency)	$500 million
Canada	CSA (Canadian Space Agency)	$488.7 million
United Kingdom	UKSA (UK Space Agency)	$414 million
Brazil	AEB (Brazilian Space Agency)	$343 million
South Korea	KARI (Korea Aerospace Research Institute)	$300 million
Ukraine	NSAU (National Space Agency of Ukraine)	$250 million
Argentina	CONAE (Comisión Nacional de Actividades Espaciales)	$180 million
Belgium	BELSPO (Belgian Federal Office for Science Policy)	$170 million
Spain	INTA (Instituto Nacional de Técnica Aeroespacial)	$135 million
Netherlands	NSO (Netherlands Space Office)	$110 million
Sweden	SNSB (Swedish National Space Board)	$100 million
Pakistan	SUPARCO (Space and Upper Atmosphere Research Commission)	$82 million
Switzerland	SSO (Swiss Space Office)	$10 million
Mexico	AEM (Mexican Space Agency)	$8.34 million
World	All space agencies (Total of listed budgets)	$40,618.34 million

FUNDED RESEARCH PROJECTS - SPACE

Copernicus (previously known as GMES)	Strengthening Space Foundation (SSF)	Cross-cutting Activities

2013 - PROJECTS UNDER NEGOTIATION

Advanced_SAR APhoRISM AQUA-USERS DECUMANUS ERA-CLIM2 ERMES EUCLEIA FAST FLOODIS GMES-C	HIGHROC INFORM North State PHAROS Polar Ice QA4ECV RASOR SWARP UERRA	CROSS DRIVE EuroVenus EXTraS F-CHROMA GANSAT GENIUS HELP HIPPO LONGESST MacSpace	MERLIN MISW MOONWALK m-PRS PHASER RemoveDEBRIS SLOGAN SPACESTORM VIALACTEA	BEACON DIFFERENT LEOSWEEP MarcoPolo PANDA SAFI SEAM SpaceNav

2012

CHARME CORE-CLIMAX E-AIMS GLASS G-NEXT GMES-PURE * G-SEXTANT ICOS-INWIRE IGAS IMAGINES	INCREO LAMPRE LOBOS LOTUS PREFER SAGRES SENSUM SENSYF	ABLAMOD ARCHES ASTRODEEP BRITESPACE ETAEARTH FISICA GAIA PEASSS PROVIDE PULCHER QI2S	SHEE SOLID SPACE TRIPS SPACEINN SPACEKIDS SR2S STORM THOR STRONGGRAVITY	ASTROMAP GAMALINK MEGAHIT MERMIG MISSION NANOSAT PBSA SME-SAT SPACEPLAN 2020 STAMAS STEP

* under EC - DG Enterprise and Industry responsibility

2011

BRIDGES MACC II MYOCEAN2 MYWAVE	NORS OPEC OSS2015 SANGOMA	μFCU AERSUS DEPLOYTECH DESICOS DISCANALYSIS EHEROES ELSA EUCARBON EUROCIS FASTER	HYDRA L-μPPT MAARBLE NEOSHIELD PLANHAB PRECISE QB50 SHOCK SINPLEX VHISSI	BRAGMA COFSEP COSMOS+ DIPOP ODYSSEUS

2010

ASIMUTH BIO_SOS CoBiOS CryoLand DOLPHIN DORIS_Net ENDORSE EUFODOS FreshMon GLOWASIS GRAAL HELM ISAC	MS.MONINA MyWater NEREIDS OPERR PanGeo ReCover REDDAF SeaU SIDARUS SIMTISYS SIRIUS	: E-SQUID ACCORD AFFECTS ATMOP BETs CESAR CLEANSPACE COMESEP DEORBIT SAIL DSPACE ECLAT ESAIL ESPACE EU-UNAWE EURISGIC FOSTERNAV HarmLES HESPE HISP	IMPEx MAGDRIVE MicroThrust P2-ROTECT PLASMON POPDAT ReVuS ROV-E SEPServer SIDER SKYFLASH SMARTEES SOC2 SPA SPACECAST SPACE-DATA ROUTERS SPARTAN SWIFF	BIOSMHARS LIROC* MAIRES MALAREO MEDEO MOCCCASIN PRE- EARTHQUAKES REDD-FLAME REDDINESS RITD SACOMAR SEMEP SpWRT TransHyBeriAN WatPLAN ZAPÁS

2009

AQUAMAR CARBONES DORIS EAMNET EURO4M EVOSS FIELD_AC	GARNET-E GEO-PICTURES MONARCH-A PASODOBLE SAGA-EO SUBCOAST	AL-IN-WON COMETS EUSIC MIDAS NEWA NORDICBALTSAT	PHYS4ENTRY PROVISCOUT RASTAS SPEAR SATURNE TERACOMP THESEUS	C-SPACE SP4ESP
2007 - brochure				
GEOLAND2 G-MOSAIC MACC	MYOCEAN SAFER SWIFT	AEROFAST AGAPAC GRASP HAMLET HIPER HPH.com	ISP-1 ORPHEE PROVISG SOTERIA STAVE ULISSE	COSMOS

BASIC TITLES ON EUROPEAN UNION (EU)

IMPORTANT!
All publications are updated annually!
Please contact IBP, Inc. at ibpusa3@gmail.com for the latest ISBNs and additional information

TITLE
EU (European Union) Trade and Investment Agreements Handbook - Strategic Information and Basic Agreements
EU Anti Terrorism Activities, Cooperation an d Strategy Handbook
EU Anti Terrorism Activities, Cooperation an d Strategy Handbook
EU Anti Terrorism Activities, Cooperation and Strategy Handbook
EU Anti Terrorism Activities, Cooperation and Strategy Handbook
EU Arms Export Policy and Control Procedures Handbook
EU Arms Export Policy and Control Procedures Handbook
EU Arms Export Policy and Control Procedures Handbook
EU Arms Export Policy and Control Procedures Handbook
EU Aviation and Aerospace Industry Handbook
EU Aviation and Aerospace Industry Handbook
EU Aviation Training and Psychology Handbook
EU Clothing & Textile Industry Handbook
EU Counter Terrorism Strategy and Plans Handbook
EU Customs and Trade Regulations Guide
EU Customs and Trade Regulations Guide
EU Defense Agency Handbook
EU Defense Agency Handbook
EU Defense and Military Cooperation Handbook
EU Defense and Military Cooperation Handbook
EU Defense Export Services Organization Handbook
EU Defense Export Services Organization Handbook
EU Defense Strategy and Armed Forces Handbook
EU Defense Strategy and Armed Forces Handbook
EU Emission Trading Laws, Regulations and Programs Handbook
EU Healthcare Sector Organization, Management and Payment Systems Handbook - Strategic Information, Programs and Regulations
EU Intelligence and Security Policy and Cooperation Handbook
EU Intelligence and Security Policy and Cooperation Handbook
EU Mediterranean Partnership Handbook
EU Military and Special Forces Handbook
EU Military and Special Forces Handbook
EU Monetary Financial Institutions Handbook
EU Money Laundering Prevention Regulations Handbook
EU National Cyber Security Strategy and Programs Handbook - Strategic Information and Developments
EU Nuclear Energy Policy Handbook
EU Pacific Region Countries Economic and Political Cooperation Handbook
EU Pacific Region Countries Economic and Political Cooperation Handbook
EU Pharmaceutical Legislation Handbook. Vol. 1. Legislation on Medicinal Products for Human Use
EU Pharmaceutical Legislation Handbook. Vol. 1. Legislation on Medicinal Products for Human Use
EU Pharmaceutical Legislation Handbook. Vol. 3 Legislation on Gene and Cell Therapy: see in particular Part IV of Annex I (Advanced therapy medicinal products)

TITLE
EU Pharmaceutical Legislation Handbook. Vol. 3 Legislation on Gene and Cell Therapy: see in particular Part IV of Annex I (Advanced therapy medicinal products)
EU Pharmaceutical Legislation Handbook. Vol. 4 Legislation on Medical Devices
EU Pharmaceutical Legislation Handbook. Vol. 4 Legislation on Medical Devices
EU Pharmaceutical Legislation Handbook. Vol. 5 Legislation on the Quality and Safety of human tissues and cells
EU Pharmaceutical Legislation Handbook. Vol. 5 Legislation on the Quality and Safety of human tissues and cells
EU Postal Service Handbook
EU Postal Service Handbook
EU Privatization Yearbook: Major Programs and Projects
EU Security Strategy and Cooperation Handbook
EU Security Strategy and Cooperation Handbook
EU Shipbuilding Industry Handbook
EU Shipbuilding Industry Handbook
EU Shipbuilding Industry Investment and Business Guide - Strategic and Practical Information
EU Shipbuilding Industry Investment and Business Guide - Strategic and Practical Information
EU Shipbuilding Industry Law and Regulations Handbook
EU Shipbuilding Industry Law and Regulations Handbook
EU Terrorism Prevention Regulations Handbook
EU Western European Armaments Organization Handbook
EU Western European Armaments Organization Handbook
EU-China Political and Economic Relations Handbook
EU-China Political and Economic Relations Handbook
EU-Mexico Political and Economic Relations Handbook
Eurasian Economic Union Trade and Investment Agreements Handbook - Strategic Information and Basic Agreements
Euro-Mediterranean Free Trade Area Business Opportunities Handbook
Europe E-commerce Business Handbook
Europe E-commerce Business Handbook
Europe Financial and Economic Development Handbook
Europe Financial and Economic Development Handbook
European Airlines Handbook
European Airlines Handbook
European Association For Aviation Psychology (EAAP) Handbook
European Aviation Safety Agency (EASA) Handbook
European Aviation Safety Handbook
European Bank for Reconstruction and Development (EBRD) Handbook
European Bank for Reconstruction and Development (EBRD) Handbook
European Banking System Handbook Vol. 1 History and Functions
European Banking System Handbook Vol. 2 Banking, Financial System and Regulations
European Countries Antiterrorism Programs and Operations Handbook
European Countries Antiterrorism Programs and Operations Handbook
European Defense Agency Handbook: Strategy, Activities Contacts
European Defense Agency Handbook: Strategy, Activities Contacts
European Defense Policy Handbook: Strategy & Cooperation
European Defense Policy Handbook: Strategy & Cooperation
European Flight Regulations Handbook: System and Procedures
European Flight Regulations Handbook: System and Procedures

TITLE
European Free Trade Association (EFTA) Handbook
European Free Trade Association (EFTA) Handbook
European Investment Bank (EIB) Handbook
European Investment Bank (EIB) Handbook
European Investment Fund (EIF) Handbook
European Investment Fund (EIF) Handbook
European Police Office - EUROPOL Handbook
European Police Office-EUROPOL Handbook
European Police System Organization Handbook
European Publishers Directory
European Publishers Directory
European Space Agency Handbook - Strategic Information, Programs, Contacts
European Space Agency Handbook - International Agreements and Regulations
European Space Policy and Programs Handbook
European Space Policy and Programs Handbook
European System for Security and Cooperation Handbook
European System for Security and Cooperation Handbook
European Union (EU) Government and Business Contacts Handbook
European Union (EU) Government and Business Contacts Handbook
European Union Airport Handbook
European Union Airports Handbook
European Union at the United Nations Handbook
European Union at the United Nations Handbook
European Union Aviation & Aerospace Industry Handbook
European Union Aviation & Aerospace Industry Handbook
European Union Banking & Financial Market Handbook
European Union Banking & Financial Market Handbook
European Union Business Law Handbook - Strategic Information and Basic Laws
European Union Business Law Handbook - Strategic Information and Basic Laws
European Union Company Laws and Regulations Handbook - Strategic Information and Basic Laws
European Union Cosmetics Industry Handbook
European Union Cosmetics Industry Handbook
European Union HANDBOOK Volume 1 Strategic and Practical Information
European Union Insolvency (Bankruptcy) Laws and Regulations Handbook - Strategic Information and Basic Laws
European Union Investment and Business Guide - Strategic and Practical Information
European Union Investment and Business Guide - Strategic and Practical Information
European Union Pharmaceutical Industry Handbook
European Union Pharmaceutical Industry Handbook
European Union Pharmaceutical Legislation Handbook
European Union Pharmaceutical Legislation Handbook
European Union Privatization Programs and Regulations Handbook
European Union Privatization Programs and Regulations Handbook
European Union, The (EC) Handbook
EUROPOL û European Police Office Handbook
EU-Russia Political and Economic Relations Handbook
EU-Russia Political and Economic Relations Handbook

GLOBAL
WORLD INTERNATIONAL ORGANIZATIONS BUSINESS AND DEVELOPMENT LIBRARY

PRICE - $149.95 EACH

1. Abu Dhabi Fund for Development Handbook
2. African Development Bank Group(AfDB) Handbook
3. African Development Fund (AfDF) Handbook
4. Nigeria Trust Fund (NTF) Handbook
5. African Export-Import Bank (AFREXIMBANK) Handbook
6. Andean Community General Secretariat Handbook
7. Andean Development Corporation (CAF) Handbook
8. Arab Authority for Agricultural Investment and Development (AAAID) Handbook
9. Arab Bank for Economic Development in Africa (BADEA) Handbook
10. Arab Fund for Economic and Social Development (AFESD) Handbook
11. Arab Gulf Programme for United Nations Development Organizations (AGFUND) Handbook
12. Arab Maghreb Union (AMU) Handbook
13. Arab Monetary Fund (AMF) Handbook
14. Arab Organization for Agricultural Development (AOAD) Handbook
15. Arab Planning Institute - Kuwait Handbook
16. Arab Trade Financing Program (ATFP) Handbook
17. Asia-Pacific Economic Cooperation (APEC) Handbook
18. Asian and Pacific Coconut Community (APCC) Handbook
19. Asian Clearing Union (ACU) Handbook
20. Asian Development Bank (AsDB) Handbook
21. Association of Natural Rubber Producing Countries (ANRPC) Handbook
22. Association of South East Asian Nations (ASEAN) Handbook
23. Baltic Council of Ministers Handbook
24. Bank for International Settlements (BIS) Handbook
25. Bank of Central African States (BEAC) Handbook
26. Black Sea Trade and Development Bank (BSTDB) Handbook
27. Caribbean Centre for Monetary Studies (CCMS) Handbook
28. Caribbean Community (CARICOM) Handbook
29. Caribbean Development Bank (CDB) Handbook
30. Caribbean Regional Technical Assistance Centre (CARTAC) Handbook
31. Center for Latin American Monetary Studies (CEMLA) Handbook
32. Center for Marketing Information and Advisory Services for Fishery Products in Latin America and the Caribbean (INFOPESCA) Handbook
33. Central American Bank for Economic Integration (CABEI) Handbook
34. Central American Monetary Council (CAMC) Handbook
35. Central Bank of West African States (BCEAO) Handbook
36. Colombo Plan for Co-operative Economic and Social Development in Asia and the Pacific Handbook
37. Colombo Plan Staff College for Technician Education Handbook

38. Common Fund for Commodities Handbook
39. Common Market for Eastern and Southern Africa (COMESA) Handbook
40. Cooperation Council for the Arab States of the Gulf (GCC) Handbook
41. Council of the Baltic Sea States (CBSS) Handbook
42. Council of Europe Development Bank (CEB) Handbook
43. East African Development Bank (EADB) Handbook
44. Eastern Caribbean Central Bank (ECCB) Handbook
45. Economic Community of West African States (ECOWAS) Handbook
46. Economic Cooperation Organization (ECO) Handbook
47. European Bank for Reconstruction and Development (EBRD) Handbook
48. European Central Bank (ECB) Handbook
49. European Free Trade Association (EFTA) Handbook
50. European Investment Bank (EIB) Handbook
51. European Investment Fund (EIF) Handbook
52. European Union, The (EC) Handbook
53. Financial Fund for the Development of the River Plate Basin (FONPLATA) Handbook
54. Food and Agriculture Organization of the United Nations (FAO) Handbook
55. Fund for Co-operation, Compensation and Development (ECOWAS Fund) Handbook
56. Inter-American Development Bank (IDB) Handbook
57. Inter-American Institute for Cooperation on Agriculture (IICA) Handbook
58. Inter-Arab Investment Guarantee Corporation (IAIGC) Handbook
59. International Atomic Energy Regulations Handbook
60. International Civil Aviation Regulations Handbook
61. International Cocoa Production and Trade Regulations Handbook
62. International Coffee Production and Trade Regulations Handbook
63. International Confederation of Free Trade Unions (ICFTU) Handbook
64. International Cotton Advisory Committee (ICAC) Handbook
65. International Fund for Agricultural Development (IFAD) Handbook
66. International Grains Council Handbook
67. International Labour Organization (ILO) Handbook
68. International Lead and Zinc Study Group Handbook
69. International Monetary Fund (IMF) Handbook
70. International Olive Oil Council (IOOC) Handbook
71. International Rubber Study Group Handbook
72. International Sugar Organization (ISO) Handbook
73. International Telecommunications Union (ITU) Handbook
74. International Tropical Timber Organization (ITTO) Handbook
75. Islamic Development Bank Group (IsDB) Handbook
76. Islamic Research and Training Institute (IRTI) Handbook
77. Joint Vienna Institute (JVI) Handbook
78. Kuwait Fund for Arab Economic Development Handbook
79. Lake Chad Basin Commission (LCBC) Handbook
80. Latin American Association of Development Financing Institutions (ALIDE) Handbook
81. Latin American Economic System (SELA) Handbook
82. Latin American Energy Organization (OLADE) Handbook
83. Latin American Export Bank (BLADEX) Handbook
84. Latin American Integration Association (ALADI) Handbook
85. Latin American Reserve Fund (LARF) Handbook
86. League of Arab States Handbook
87. Mekong River Commission (MRC) Handbook
88. Nordic Development Fund (NDF) Handbook

89. Nordic Investment Bank (NIB) Handbook
90. OPEC Fund for International Development Handbook
91. Organisation for Economic Co-operation and Development (OECD) Handbook
92. Organisation of Eastern Caribbean States (OECS) Handbook
93. Organization of American States (OAS) Handbook
94. Organization of Arab Petroleum Exporting Countries (OAPEC) Handbook
95. Organization of the Petroleum Exporting Countries (OPEC) Handbook
96. Pacific Financial Technical Assistance Centre Handbook
97. Pacific Islands Forum Secretariat Handbook
98. Pan American Health Organization (PAHO) Handbook
99. Regional Association of Oil and Natural Gas Companies in Latin America and the Caribbean (ARPEL) Handbook
100. Regional Electrical Integration Commission (CIER) Handbook
101. Saudi Fund for Development (SFD) Handbook
102. Secretariat for Central American Economic Integration (SIECA) Handbook
103. Secretariat of the Pacific Community Handbook
104. Sectorial Commission for the Common Market of the South (MERCOSUR) - Uruguay Handbook
105. South Asian Association for Regional Cooperation (SAARC) Handbook
106. South-East Asian Central Banks (SEACEN) Research and Training Centre Handbook
107. Training Centre for Regional Integration (CEFIR) Handbook
108. United Nations African Institute for Economic Development and Planning (IDEP) Handbook
109. United Nations Conference on Trade and Development (UNCTAD) Handbook
110. United Nations Development Program (UNDP) Handbook
111. United Nations Economic and Social Commission for Asia and the Pacific (ESCAP) Handbook
112. Asian and Pacific Centre for Transfer of Technology (APCTT) Handbook
113. Regional Coordination Centre for Research and Development of Coarse Grains, Pulses, Roots and Tuber Crops in the Humid Tropics of Asia and the Pacific (ESCAP CGPRT Centre) Handbook
114. Statistical Institute for Asia and the Pacific (SIAP) Handbook
115. United Nations Economic and Social Commission for Western Asia (ESCWA) Handbook
116. United Nations Economic Commission for Africa (UNECA) Handbook
117. United Nations Economic Commission for Europe (UN/ECE) Handbook
118. United Nations Economic Commission for Latin America and the Caribbean (ECLAC) Handbook
119. United Nations Educational, Scientific and Cultural Organization (UNESCO) Handbook
120. United Nations Industrial Development Organization (UNIDO) Handbook
121. United Nations Latin American and Caribbean Institute for Economic and Social Planning (ILPES) Handbook
122. World Postal Service Handbook: Volume 1 Strategic information and basic regulations
123. West African Development Bank (BOAD) Handbook
124. West Africa Economic and Monetary Union Handbook
125. World Bank Group Handbook
126. World Food Program (WFP) Handbook
127. World Health Organization (WHO) Handbook
128. World Trade Organization (WTO) Handbook

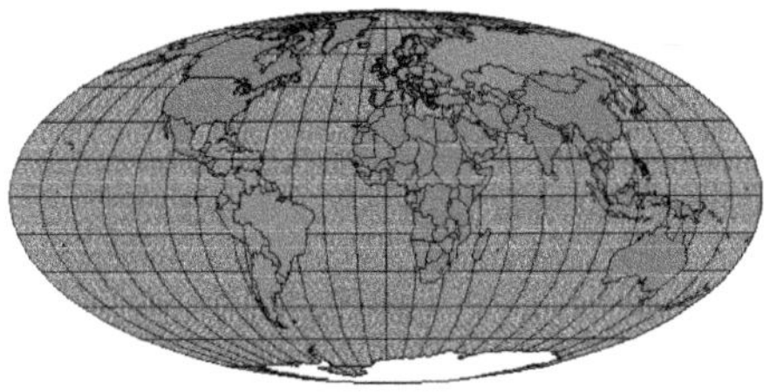

WORLS AEROSPACE, SPACE AND AIR FORCE LIBRARY

Price: $149.95 Each

TITLE
1. Asia/Pacific Space Organisations and Programs Handbook
2. Australia Air Force Handbook
3. Australia Space Agency and Programs Handbook
4. Austria Space Agency and Programs Handbook
5. Canada Space Agency and Programs Handbook
6. China Air Force Handbook
7. EU Defence Export Services Organisation Handbook
8. EU Western European Armaments Organisation Handbook
9. European Defese Policy Handbook
10. European Space Agency Handbook
11. European Space Policy and Programs Handbook
12. Finland Space Agency and Programs Handbook
13. France Space Agency and Programs Handbook
14. Germany Space Agency and Programs Handbook
15. Global Satellite Communications Organization Handbook
16. Global Space Organizations Directory
17. Global Space Programs and Organizations Handbook
18. India Air Force Handbook
19. Israel Aerospace Industries Handbook
20. Israel Air Force Handbook
21. Italy Space Agency and Programs Handbook
22. Japan Air Force Handbook
23. Japan Space Agency and Programs Handbook
24. Korea South Air Force Handbook
25. Norway Space Agency and Programs Handbook
26. Norway Space Agency and Programs Handbook
27. Russia Air Force Handbook
28. Russia Space Agency and Programs Handbook
29. Space Organizations in the Americas Handbook
30. Taiwan Space Agency and Programs Handbook
31. UK Air Force Handbook
32. UK Defence Industry Handbook
33. UK Ministry of Defence Handbook
34. UK Space Programs and Organizations Handbook
35. US Air Force Handbook

For additional analytical, business and investment opportunities information, please contact Global Investment & Business Center, USA at (202) 546-2103. Fax: (202) 546-3275. E-mail: rusric@erols.com

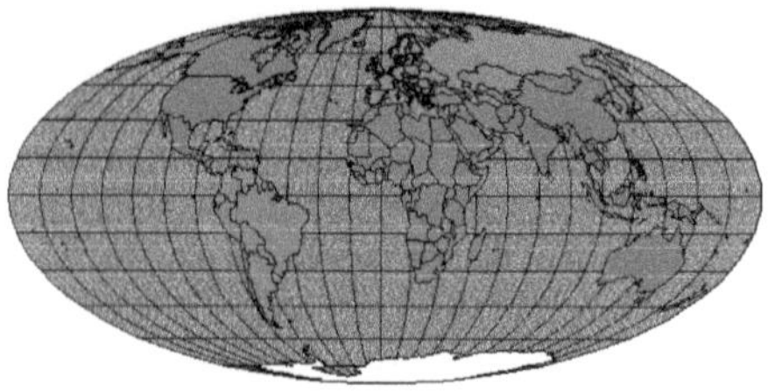

WORLS AEROSPACE, SPACE AND AIR FORCE LIBRARY

Price: $149.95 Each

TITLE
1. Asia/Pacific Space Organisations and Programs Handbook
2. Australia Air Force Handbook
3. Australia Space Agency and Programs Handbook
4. Austria Space Agency and Programs Handbook
5. Canada Space Agency and Programs Handbook
6. China Air Force Handbook
7. EU Defence Export Services Organisation Handbook
8. EU Western European Armaments Organisation Handbook
9. European Defese Policy Handbook
10. European Space Agency Handbook
11. European Space Policy and Programs Handbook
12. Finland Space Agency and Programs Handbook
13. France Space Agency and Programs Handbook
14. Germany Space Agency and Programs Handbook
15. Global Satellite Communications Organization Handbook
16. Global Space Organizations Directory
17. Global Space Programs and Organizations Handbook
18. India Air Force Handbook
19. Israel Aerospace Industries Handbook
20. Israel Air Force Handbook
21. Italy Space Agency and Programs Handbook
22. Japan Air Force Handbook
23. Japan Space Agency and Programs Handbook
24. Korea South Air Force Handbook
25. Norway Space Agency and Programs Handbook
26. Norway Space Agency and Programs Handbook
27. Russia Air Force Handbook
28. Russia Space Agency and Programs Handbook
29. Space Organizations in the Americas Handbook
30. Taiwan Space Agency and Programs Handbook
31. UK Air Force Handbook
32. UK Defence Industry Handbook
33. UK Ministry of Defence Handbook
34. UK Space Programs and Organizations Handbook
35. US Air Force Handbook

www.ingramcontent.com/pod-product-compliance
Ingram Content Group UK Ltd.
Pitfield, Milton Keynes, MK11 3LW, UK
UKHW051458290926
15471UKWH00008B/1282